Nineteenth-Century Britain

Palgrave Foundations

A series of introductory texts across a wide range of subject areas to meet the needs of today's lecturers and students

Foundations texts provide complete yet concise coverage of core topics and skills based on detailed research of course requirements suitable for both independent study and class use – *the firm foundations for future study.*

Published

A History of English Literature (second edition)
Biology
British Politics
Chemistry (third edition)
Communication Studies
Contemporary Europe (second edition)
Economics
Economics for Business
Foundations of Marketing
Modern British History
Nineteenth-Century Britain
Philosophy
Physics (third edition)
Politics (third edition)
Theatre Studies

Further titles are in preparation

Nineteenth-Century Britain

JEREMY BLACK AND
DONALD M. MacRAILD

palgrave
macmillan

First published 2003 by
PALGRAVE MACMILLAN

Palgrave Macmillan in the UK is an imprint of Macmillan Publishers Limited, registered in England, company number 785998, of Houndmills, Basingstoke, Hampshire RG21 6XS.

Palgrave Macmillan in the US is a division of St Martin's Press LLC, 175 Fifth Avenue, New York, NY 10010.

Palgrave Macmillan is the global academic imprint of the above companies and has companies and representatives throughout the world.

Palgrave® and Macmillan® are registered trademarks in the United States, the United Kingdom, Europe and other countries.

ISBN 978-0-333-72559-7 hardback
ISBN 978-0-333-72560-3 paperback

This book is printed on paper suitable for recycling and made from fully managed and sustained forest sources. Logging, pulping and manufacturing processes are expected to conform to the environmental regulations of the country of origin.

A catalogue record for this book is available from the British Library.

Library of Congress Cataloguing-in-Publication Data
Black, Jeremy.
    Nineteenth-century Britain/Jeremy Black and Donald M. MacRaild
        p. cm. — (Palgrave foundations)
    Includes bibliographical references and index.
    ISBN 0–333–72559–X—ISBN 0–333–72560–3 (pbk.)
        1. Great Britain–History–19th century. 2. Great Britain–Civilization–19th century.
    I. MacRaild, Donald M. II. Title. III. Series
DA530 .B54 2002
941.081–dc21   2002022485

Printed in Great Britain by the MPG Books Group, Bodmin and King's Lynn

To George Boyce and
Margaret MacRaild

Contents

List of Tables, Portraits, Figures and Illustrations

Illustrations

Preface

THIS book seeks to provide a comprehensive and up-to-date introduction to nineteenth-century Britain. It is designed to be of use to students taking courses on the subject and to general readers concerned about the recent past and the past of our present. Such a book necessarily involves choices of what to include. There is no point pretending some Olympian detachment or Delphic omniscience. These choices are personal. They reflect our views as historians faced with the difficult tasks of trying to cover such a vast subject. We hope our decisions on what to include and how best to cover it prove as stimulating for the readers as they have done for the writers, and that they can be seen as individual (as all history is), but not eccentric. It is important for the reader to be aware that what is here, how it is treated and organized, and what is omitted reflects a process of choice. The past is viewed differently and these differences should lead us to more searching questions about what is being discussed and about the process of writing history. This is most apparent and valuable when discussing the recent past. Then reading any work of history necessarily throws light on both subject and process.

All periods of history centre on the interplay of change and continuity, an interplay that is sometimes dramatic but always as insistent as the rhythm of the seasons and the course of generations. The nineteenth century was a century of striking changes and a great pressure of change. It was a modern age, not the modem age of the twentieth century, but, nevertheless, an age that was radically different to what had come before. This process of change is the major theme of the book. The text reflects this emphasis, but the organisation is thematic, not chronological. This is the best way to tackle the range of human experience. One aspect of change after all is that the range that invites attention is now far wider than for a scholar writing in 1799 or 1899 about the recent past. In particular, far from being confined to politics, economics and 'society', the idea of history is now widely defined and due attention is also paid to cultural history, culture understood as music hall as much as the orchestral works of Sir Edward Elgar. Furthermore, the environment, both natural and human, is now seen as an important topic.

This broadening of range became more apparent in historical writings particularly the twentieth century, and we hope this has influenced the design and methods of this book. For example, it became less convincing to discuss social structure in terms solely of class or occupation – based criteria. Instead, it became increasingly clear that issues of gender and ethnicity played a central role in social structure and, furthermore, that they could not be discussed simply as adjuncts to class-based analysis. More generally, an analysis or narrative that focused on Westminster and Whitehall, the centres of national politics and government, could no longer be seen as the defining feature of modern British history. Such a broad range can be handled only in a thematic fashion, for that prevents a repetitious discussion of, for example, the impact of the railway or public health in chapters devoted to periods of time, such as the 1860s and 1870s. Furthermore, the use of thematic chapters, rather than continuous narrative, will enable students to use the book in response to specific subject needs. It is sometimes, however, easy to get lost if a chronological framework is missing. As a result, the text is preceded by a Chronology – a list of key dates – with a separate, more detailed, listing of Prime Ministers. Readers who may prefer to begin with a political narrative should turn to Chapters 8 and 9 on 'The Political World'. These chapters have deliberately not been put first, because, although political developments are central, they are generally over-emphasised in books of this type. Instead, preference is given to issues such as demographic (population) history, or social structure. These were obviously affected by government policy, as in public health legislation. Yet, it is important not to focus excessively on such government interventions at the expense of wider social movements.

Furthermore, a stress on government policy can lead to a focus on domestic/internal factors and a notion of 'exceptionalism' that under-rates the extent to which the broad thrust of the period's history was not restricted to Britain. For example, industrialisation, secularism, and the growth of class consciousness were all general trends in the western world. As a consequence, the narrative and exposition of change has to be aware of factors outside the scope and control of Britain's government. In addition, it is necessary to remember that political history should be understood in a wider fashion than Prime Ministers and elections. Politics is about the nature, distribution and use of power, and thus involves an understanding of developments in society, the economy and public culture, for example the decline of the landed interest. These developments are covered throughout the book but more particularly in Chapters 2–5.

A note of explanation on the use of the term 'Britain' is required. The Act of Union of 1800 with Ireland created the state termed the United Kingdom (UK) of Great Britain and Ireland. After southern Ireland became the Irish Free State (from 1937, Eire) following the Anglo-Irish treaty of 1921, the United Kingdom became the United Kingdom of Great Britain and Northern Ireland. 'Great Britain' therefore refers to England, Scotland and Wales. However, neither 'United Kingdom' nor 'Great Britain' lend themselves to use as adjectives, and the term 'Britain' is frequently applied to both. This may be misleading, but it captures the degree to which there has been a central governmental thrust coming from the government in London throughout the century. Throughout this book, the term 'Britain' is then used to refer to the United Kingdom.

The organisation of the chapters also requires some understanding. The book should be read sequentially, moving, after an introductory chapter on the eighteenth-century background, from the 'structural', or fundamental, factors of demographics (population), the environment and material culture, to a treatment of economics, society, transport, ideology, government and politics, the major parts of the British Isles, Britain and the wider world, and British culture. Such an approach offers a framework for understanding the analysis and seeing the text as a whole. Each chapter begins with an Introduction, an outline of its major themes, and a list of the key issues that are discussed in the chapter. At the end of each chapter, there is a summary, a list of point to discuss, and suggestions for further reading. Additional material is provided throughout the text in the form of text and profile boxes, and definitions of key concepts. But, also remember the vast range of information offered by oral history, the legacy of the built environment, and the massive amount of relevant material on radio, television and film.

This book will work if it makes you think. It is possible to suggest different subjects, other themes, and contrasting approaches and organisations. It would be worrying if this was not the case. The past is not fixed, a monolith capable of only one interpretation. If you disagree, good, but think why. What do you disagree with: observations, analysis or explanation? Readers should consider how *they* would organise the book and approach writing about the nineteenth century as an active part of studying the period. The historian is not a magician figure able to unlock the past, but a guide who stimulates you to see with your own eyes.

July 2002   JEREMY BLACK and DONALD MacRAILD

Acknowledgements

We have incurred a number of debts whilst writing this book and we wish to acknowledge them here. Any general survey such as this one inevitably leans on a huge body of scholarship which we hope is in some way noted in our suggestions for further reading. Particular mention must be made of four scholars who acted as anonymous readers for the publisher. Each of them spent a great deal of time reading the draft very closely. Their observations were both erudite and fair. Our publisher, Palgrave Macmillan, has been a model of patience as we struggled to produce the final typescript. The book has been several years in the making and several editors have come and gone from the Foundations Series. However, we would like to record our special thanks to Suzannah Burywood and Keith Povey whose support and encouragement helped us along the final stretch. None of these people, anonymous or otherwise, is responsible for any errors that remain.

The authors and publishers wish to thank the following for permission to use copyright material: HMSO Crown Copyright material is reproduced under class licence number CO1W0000276 with the permission of the Controller of HMSO and the Queen's Printer for Scotland.

Photographs and illustrations: AKG Berlin/Archiv Für Kunst: p 228, Ann Ronan Picture Library: pp. 3, 60, 72, 89, 129, 130, 139, 154, 156, 157, 160, 163, 175, 181, 214, 269, 287, 290, 303, 308, 316.

Chronology of Key Events

Year	Event
1775	Outbreak of the American Revolution
1776	Adam Smith's *The Wealth of Nations published*
1777	American Declaration of Independence
1778	France enters war on American side
1779	Wyvill's Association movement
1780	Gordon Riots in London
1781	British army surrenders at Yorktown
1783	Peace of Versailles, fall of the Fox–North coalition, Pitt the Younger becomes Prime Minister
1784	Pitt wins general election
1788–9	Regency Crisis
1789	Outbreak of the French Revolution.
1790	Edmund Burke's *Reflections on the Revolution in France*
1791	Thomas Paine's *The Rights of Man*
1793	Outbreak of war with Revolutionary France
1796	Vaccination against smallpox introduced
1797	Naval Mutinies at Spithead and The Nore
1798	Irish Rising, income tax introduced, Malthus' *Essay on Population*,
1799	Napoleon seizes power in France
1800	Act of Union with Ireland
1801	First British census, Union with Ireland begins
1802	Peace of Amiens with France
1803	War with Napoleon resumes, General Enclosure Act
1805	Nelson's victory at Trafalgar
1806	Death of Pitt
1811	George, Prince of Wales made Prince Regent, 'Luddite' disturbances
1812	Earl of Liverpool brings ministerial stability
1813	East India Company monopoly ends
1815	Wellington triumphant at Waterloo, Corn Law passed
1819	Peterloo Massacre
1820	George IV succeeds George III
1821	Stockton and Darlington railway opens
1829	Catholic Emancipation
1830	William IV succeeds George IV, Liverpool and Manchester railway opens
1831	Swing riots
1832	First Reform Act
1833	Factory Act to regulate child labour
1834	Parish workhouses, Tolpuddle Martyrs
1835	Municipal Reform Act

1837	William IV dies, Queen Victoria succeeds
1837	Anti-Corn Law League founded
1839	Chartist disturbances
1840	Penny Post established
1844	Royal Commission on Health of Towns, Bank Charter Act
1848	Public Health Act
1851	Great Exhibition
1854	Northcote–Trevelyan civil service report
1854–6	Crimean War
1857–9	Indian Mutiny
1859	Charles Darwin's *Origin of Species*
1860	Anglo-French treaty helps free trade
1861	Death of Albert, Prince Consort
1862	Limited Liability Act
1867	Second Reform Act, Dominion of Canada Act
1882	Third Reform Act
1886	Gladstone introduces first Home Rule Bill for Ireland, Liberal Party splits
1887	County Councils Act leads to elected county authorities
1888	London dock strike
1893	Second Home Rule Bill rejected by the Lords. Independent Labour Party founded
1898	Battle of Omdurman, crucial to conquest of Sudan
1899–1902	Second Anglo-Boer War
1900	Formation of Labour Representation Commuittee (precursor to the Labour Party), Commonwealth of Australia Act
1901	Death of Victoria; accession of Edward VII
1902	Balfour's Education Act
1904	Anglo-French Entente
1905	Liberals replace Conservatives in power
1906	Landslide Liberal win in general election
1907	Lloyd George's budget rejected
1911	Parliament Act curtails power of the House of Lords; Lloyd George's National Insurance Act
1911–12	Railway, mining and coal strikes
1914	First World War begins

A detailed chronology of Anglo-Irish political issues is in Box 10.1 (pp. 168-9).

Prime Ministers

Name	Period in office	Party
William Pitt the Younger	1783–1801	Tory
Henry Addington, 1st Viscount Sidmouth	1801–4	Tory
William Pitt 'the Younger'	1804–6	Tory
William, Lord Grenville	1806–7	Whig
Spencer Perceval	1809–12	Tory
Robert, 2nd Earl Jenkinson (Lord Liverpool)	1812–27	Tory
George Canning	1827	Tory
Frederick, Viscount Goderich	1827–8	Whig
Arthur, 1st Duke of Wellington	1828–30	Tory
Charles, 2nd Earl Grey	1830–4	Whig
William, 2nd Viscount Melbourne	1834	Whig
Arthur, 1st Duke of Wellington	1834	Tory
Robert Peel	1834–5	Tory
William, 2nd Viscount Melbourne	1845–41	Whig
Robert Peel	1841–6	Tory
Lord John Russell	1846–52	Whig
Edward, 14th Earl of Derby	1852	Tory
George, 4th Earl of Aberdeen	1852–5	Whig
Henry, 3rd Viscount Palmerston	1855–8	Whig
Edward, 14th Earl of Derby	1858–9	Tory
Henry, 3rd Viscount Palmerston	1859–65	Whig
Lord John Russell	1865–6	Whig
Edward, 14th Earl of Derby	1866–8	Tory
Benjamin Disraeli	1868	Tory
William Ewart Gladstone	1868–74	Liberal
Benjamin Disraeli	1874–80	Tory
William Ewart Gladstone	1880–5	Liberal
Robert, 3rd Marquess of Salisbury	1885–6	Conservative
William Ewart Gladstone	1886	Liberal
Robert, 3rd Marquess of Salisbury	1886–92	Conservative
William Ewart Gladstone	1892–4	Liberal
Archibald, 5th Earl of Rosebery	1894–5	Liberal
Robert, 3rd Marquess of Salisbury	1895–1902	Conservative
Arthur James Balfour	1902–5	Conservative
Henry Campbell Bannerman	1905–8	Liberal
Herbert Henry Asquith	1908–16	Liberal

The Eighteenth-Century Background

CHAPTER 1

If the emphasis in our study of nineteenth-century Britain is on change, it would be all too easy to present the earlier age as one of stability. This is particularly so because those who direct or affirm change generally see, or at least describe, what came before as static, in need of reform, and, thus, in some fashion undesirable. This chapter, in contrast, sets out to show the *dynamism* of late-eighteenth century Britain, and to discuss its rapidly changing economy, society, culture and politics, in order to provide both a background for the remainder of the book, and an explanation of important aspects of the early decades of the nineteenth century. It is important to read this chapter because it helps to explain the origins of important trends and problems in the twentieth century, and provides the context for judgements of what came later. It is also necessary to underline the extent to which there was not one Georgian or eighteenth-century 'age' nor one set of influential beliefs, against which the nineteenth century can be seen as developing.

Key issues

▶ What was the nature of late eighteenth-century Britain?

▶ What were the principal pressures for change, and what developments occurred?

▶ How successfully were the political and social systems coping with change?

▶ What was the importance of Britain's imperial position?

1

1.1 Society and state in the eighteenth century

In 1776 Britain's most populous colonies in North America declared independence; Adam Smith, a Glasgow professor of economics, published his *Inquiry into the Nature and Causes of The Wealth of Nations*; Edward Gibbon, an enlightened MP, brought out the first volumes of his *Decline and Fall of the Roman Empire*; and, in 1777–9, the world's first iron bridge was erected at Coalbrookdale in Shropshire. Each was an aspect of modernity. The American Declaration of Independence made it clear that the revolution that had begun the previous year was to lead to a new state that would destroy the unity of the British empire. It also asserted a set of principles that suggested a radically different political system and culture. The *Wealth of Nations* provided the basis for modern economic theory and argued the case for the free trade that was to become the ideology of the nineteenth-century British state, and the cause of much prosperity, as well as much hardship. In place of a cyclical theory of history, Gibbon's *Decline and Fall* suggested that progress was possible, and that it was not inevitable that a fresh wave of barbarians would destroy Britain as it had done Rome. The Coalbrookdale bridge, designed in 1775 by Thomas Farnolls Pritchard, showed progress in action. It had a 120-foot span, and carried the road on arched ribs springing from the bases of two vertical iron uprights. The construction details were worked out by experienced iron-founders. Wrought iron had long been a valued decorative material, but the replacement of charcoal by coke smelting meant that reliable and precise cast iron became available.

Change was certainly coming from a series of developments that are collectively known as the 'Industrial Revolution'. The development of industry and trade, agricultural improvement, and the construction of canals and better roads, led to a growth in national wealth and a gradually emerging new economy. The percentage of the male labour force employed in industry rose from 19 in 1700 to 30 in 1800, while, because agricultural productivity increased, that in agriculture fell from 60 to 40. The British economy developed powerful comparative advantages in trade and manufacturing and greatly impressed informed foreign visitors. A sense of economic change and the possibilities of progress was widely experienced in the later eighteenth century and can be glimpsed in depictions of industrial scenes, such as Coalbrookdale. Heroic paintings were produced in praise of scientific discovery and technological advance, for example by Joseph Wright of Derby. In the Frog Service that Josiah Wedgwood designed for Catherine the Great of Russia, each piece of china was painted with a different British scene. These included not only aristocratic landscapes, such as Stowe, but also the Prescot glass works on Merseyside. From the 1730s and 1740s, the majority of British commentators argued that modern achievements were superior to those of former times, especially the ancient world. A culture of improvement lay at the heart of much innovation and the diffusion of new techniques and machinery, although art, architecture, furniture, and much else in the cultural world, all used classical designs.

What kind of society and state were these changes arising from and impacting upon? As with any other period, it is possible to present diverse views, and indeed there has been considerable diversity in recent treatment. Two major themes can be defined. The first focuses on aspects of modernity, rationality, secularism and change; while the second offers a more conservative account stressing continuity and, in particular, the continued

Adam Smith (1723-90)

The founder of modern economics and Professor of Logic at Glasgow University in 1751. He is famous for his *Inquiry into the Nature and Causes of the Wealth of Nations* (1776). This argued the case for free trade that was to become the ideology of the nineteenth-century British state, and the cause of much prosperity as well as hardship.

impact of a more traditional religious world view. The first view is generally 'optimistic'. It sees a rising middle class and an age of reason, a polite and commercial people, aristocratic ease and elegance, urban bustle and balance, a land of stately homes and urban squares: Castle Howard, Blenheim, Bath, the West End of London, Dublin and the New Town of Edinburgh.

Different images and views can also, however, be stressed. Serious disease played a major role in what was a hostile environment. Although the plague epidemic of 1665–6 was the last grave attack in Britain, there were still other major killers, including a whole host of illnesses and accidents that can generally be tackled successfully in modern Europe. Smallpox, typhus, typhoid, measles and influenza were serious problems. Although progress was made in tackling smallpox, the facts of life remained grim, and disease was a subject of anxiety and bewilderment. Primitive sanitation and poor nutrition exacerbated the situation. Glasgow, for example, had no public sewers until 1790, and the situation thereafter remained inadequate for decades. There and elsewhere the limited nature of the housing stock led to the sharing of beds, which was partly responsible for the high incidence of respiratory infections.

Problems of food storage and cost ensured that the bulk of the British population lacked a balanced diet even when they had enough food, which many of them did not. Poverty remained a serious problem. The Workhouse Test Act of 1723 encouraged parishes to found workhouses to provide the poor with work and accommodation, but too few were founded to deal with the problem, especially as the population rose from mid-century. Gilbert's Act of 1782 gave Justices of the Peace (JPs) the power to appoint guardians running Houses of Industry for the elderly and infirm. Workhouses, however, remained less important than 'out relief': providing assistance, and sometimes work, to the poor in their own homes. Under the Speenhamland system of outdoor relief introduced in 1795, although never universally applied, both the unemployed and wage-labourers received payments reflecting the price of bread and the size of their family. Payments to families were made to the man, a measure that was in keeping with the male-centred nature of society and specifically the role of the man as head of the household (see Chapter 14).

Social structures and attitudes were not challenged by the educational system. The majority of children did not attend school, the distribution of schools was uneven, and the curriculum of most seriously limited. It was generally argued that education should reflect social status and reinforce the status quo, and thus that the poor should not be taught to aspire. The educational opportunities of women were particularly limited. Illiteracy was widespread, being more pronounced among women than men, and in rural than in urban areas.

The inegalitarian nature of social and educational structures was mirrored in the judicial system. Crime was linked to hardship, with bad winters sending theft figures up. The criminal code decreed the death penalty, or transportation to virtual slave labour in colonies (from 1788, Australia) for minor crimes. The game laws laid down harsh penalties for poaching and permitted the use of significant force by landlords. Many who were transported died under the harsh conditions of their long journeys, a counterpart to the treatment of Africans sent as slaves to Britain's colonies in the New World.

1.2 Political and religious tensions

A feeling of insecurity helps to explain that, in so far as there was an aristocratic and establishment cultural and political hegemony, it was in part bred from elite concern, rather than from any unchallenged sense of confidence or complacency. Aristocratic portraits and stately homes in part reflected a need to assert tradition and superiority and to project images of confidence against any potential challenge to the position of the elite.

Indeed, there were bitter political and religious tensions. Union with Scotland and, more generally, the Settlement which followed the Glorious Revolution, was put to the test in 1714–16. William III's sister-in-law and successor, Queen Anne (1702–14), had numerous children, but none survived childhood. By the Act of Settlement of 1701, the house of Hanover, descendants of James I through his daughter, were promised the succession, and this led to George, Elector of Hanover, becoming George I in 1714. This was not immediately contested, but discontent rapidly developed in both England and Scotland. George replaced Anne's Tory ministers by a Whig ascendancy that left the Tories no place in government service. This reflected George's distrust of the Tories, whom he saw as sympathetic to Jacobitism – the cause of the exiled Stuarts – and also the difficulty of operating a mixed Whig–Tory ministry, although he also saw the danger of being a prisoner of a Whig majority.

The Jacobite rising of 1715–16 was the most serious response. Although it centred on Scotland, there was also a rising in North-East England in 1715. This led to an advance on Preston where the Jacobites were defeated, as the Scots had been in 1648. Thereafter, Jacobitism remained a threat, but not one that was central to political life. Indeed, until the next Jacobite rising in 1745, divisions among the Whigs took precedence. They focused on competition for ministerial office as well as on differences over foreign policy. The most powerful Whig in this period was Robert Walpole, a Norfolk gentleman landowner. Although he led those Whigs who were in opposition in 1717–20, thereafter he was in office until his fall and retirement in 1742. In 1720–2, Walpole benefited from the fall-out of the South Sea Bubble, a major financial scandal in 1720 that compromised leading ministerial figures, and also from the unexpected deaths of his two leading Whig opponents, Stanhope and Sunderland. He swiftly rose to dominate politics.

Walpole was invaluable to George I (1714–27) and George II (1727–60) as government manager and principal spokesman in the House of Commons, and as a skilful manager of the state's finances. He also played a major role in the successful elections of 1722, 1727 and 1734. Aside from his policies, Walpole was skilful in parliamentary management, and in his control of government patronage. He helped to provide valuable continuity and experience to the combination of limited monarchy with parliamentary sovereignty. While Walpole maintained a Whig monopoly of power, he took more care than his predecessors not to support policies that would alienate Tory opinion. In particular, his refusal to extend the rights of Dissenters contributed to a lessening of religious tension. As Dissent came to be seen as less of a threat, so it became easier to lessen tensions between Whigs and Tory clerics.

The Walpolean system had its defeats, most publicly the failure of the Excise Scheme of 1733, a plan to reorganize indirect taxation, but it lasted until 1742, the longest period of stable one-party rule in a system of regular parliamentary scrutiny. Then, Walpole succumbed to a combination of hostility from the reversionary interest – the active opposition of Frederick, Prince of Wales – and a sense that he was somehow losing his grip. Against Walpole's wishes, Britain had gone to war with Spain in 1739 – the War of Jenkins' Ear – and he was blamed for the failure to win hoped-for victories.

Walpole's fall led to a period of political instability as politicians vied for control, but, from 1746, Walpole's protégé, Henry Pelham, 1st Lord of the Treasury since 1743, was in a position to pursue Walpolean policies: fiscal restraint, unenterprising legislation, maintaining a Whig monopoly of power and the status quo in the Church, and seeking peace. If this political system maintained social inequality, that was very much what those with power expected. This was a society that took inegalitarianism for granted, although there was a certain amount of social criticism. In *The History of the Life of the late Mr. Jonathan Wild the Great* (1743), Henry Fielding offered a satirical indictment of false greatness: 'the Plowman, the Shepherd, the Weaver, the Builder and the Soldier, work not for themselves but others; they are contented with a poor pittance (the Labourer's Hire) and permit us the GREAT to enjoy the Fruits of their Labours.' The blatant corruption of the political system led to considerable criticism. In John Gay's *The Beggar's Opera* (1728), Walpole was referred to as if a crook with a series of aliases: 'Robin of Bagshot, alias Gorgon, alias Bluff Bob, alias Carbuncle, alias Bob Booty … .'

The religious establishment could similarly be probed both for effectiveness and for failure, some of it self-serving. Alongside pluralism, non-residence, appointments due to patronage, and a very unequal system of payment of clerics, there was conscientiousness and the provision of regular services in most parishes. Methodism developed in the 1730s, but this, and other, aspects of religious enthusiasm reflected not so much a failure of the Church of England as the contradictions inherent in a national body that had to serve all as well as enthusiasts. In addition, there was an international dimension to Protestant evangelicalism, so that it is not explicable solely in English terms.

1746 also saw the final crushing of Jacobitism. In 1745, Bonnie Prince Charlie – Charles Edward Stuart, the elder grandson of James II – had successfully raised much of Scotland for the Stuarts. In November 1745, he invaded England. The Jacobites did not only want a Stuart Scotland, not least because a Hanoverian England would not allow the existence of a Jacobite Scotland. Carlisle fell after a short siege, and Charles Edward then advanced unopposed through Lancaster, Preston and Manchester, reaching Derby on 4 December. Opposing forces had been outmanoeuvred. However, this was very much an invasion. The Highland chiefs were discouraged by a lack of English support (as well as by the absence of a promised French landing in southern England). They forced Bonnie Prince Charlie to turn back from Derby on 6 December. This may well have been a defining moment in English history. Had the Jacobites advanced they might have won, ensuring that the new state created in 1688–9 and 1707, with its Protestant character and limited government, would have been altered. Although Jacobites called for a restoration of liberties, and a balanced constitution, Jacobite victory might have led to a Catholic, conservative, autocratic and pro-French England/Britain, or, in turn, such a state might have provoked a violent reaction akin to that of the French Revolution.

Instead, Charles Edward was eventually heavily defeated by William, Duke of Cumberland, the second son of George II, at Culloden near Inverness on 16 April 1746. The Whig Ascendancy was not to be overcome from outside. Thanks to this victory, as well as to a growing economy, an expanding population, and a powerful world empire, there was strong feeling of national confidence and superiority. This replaced seventeenth-century anxiety and a marked sense of inferiority *vis-à-vis* Louis XIV's France. Whig confidence broadened in mid-century into the cultural moulding of the notion and reality of a united and powerful country. It was no coincidence that 'Rule Britannia' was composed in 1740. Cultural nationalism and xenophobia were other aspects of growing assertiveness. In part, this was a continuation of earlier anti-Popery and, in part, involved a response to cosmopolitan influences. Thus, John Gay's English-language ballad-operas, such as *The Beggar's Opera* (1728), were a response to Italian opera. In addition to the new cult of Shakespeare, the Royal Academy, founded in 1768, and its long-serving first president, Sir Joshua Reynolds, advanced the dignity of British art.

Britishness was one response to the need to create a political culture to accompany the new state formed in 1707 by the Act of Union. Sympathetic Scots made a major contribution. Yet Britishness was also in many respects a product of English triumphalism and, in part, a vehicle for it. Conceptions of Englishness, not least of the notion of a chosen Protestant nation, and of a law-abiding society, were translated into Britishness. There was a sense of superiority over Scotland, Wales, Ireland and the rest of the world. Although, in the period 1714–45, many people thought England was being ruined by the rising national debt and becoming corrupt and weak under the Hanoverians, mid-century victories helped to produce a self-confidence in England's destiny. The English dimension of Britishness is one that for long received insufficient attention, but was highlighted by separatists in the twentieth century. They, however, emphasized the extent to which the creation of Britain rested in large part on military conquest, and underplayed the vitality of England as a model. In part, the skill of the concept of Britishness rested on its ability to draw on assessments of Englishness but not to associate them too closely with England. Alongside Britishness, there were still vigorous senses of local, provincial and national identities.

Englishness/Britishness was contrasted with Continental Europe. It was argued that the English were free, and this contributed to a public myth of uniqueness. The Common Law was seen as a particularly English creation, was contrasted with legal precepts and practice in, above all, France, and enjoyed marked attention. Liberty and property, and freedom under the law were cried up as distinctly English. Foreign commentators observed a lack of deference to the King and to aristocrats in elections and in the life of counties, even though the reality was that, as the century progressed, wealthy aristocrats grew richer and controlled more and more boroughs. The Whigs in power grew complacent and intellectually bankrupt. They forgot the demand made in the 1680s by the 1st Earl of Shaftesbury and the Exclusion Whigs for a freeholder franchise in all boroughs.

The defeat of Jacobitism was one stage in a struggle with France that led to fighting in 1743–8 and 1754–63 (although war was declared only in 1744 and 1756). They ended with the Thirteen Colonies on the eastern seaboard of North America, and the British possessions in India secure, with Canada and the French bases in West Africa and the West Indies captured, and with the Royal Navy unchallengeable at sea. Key victories included three in 1759, the 'year of victories', James Wolfe's outside Québec and the naval victories of Lagos and Quiberon Bay. Two years earlier, the East India Company, an English private company, was established as the most powerful power in Bengal when Robert Clive defeated the Nawab of Bengal at Plassey.

Imperial conquest does not conform to the mores of the late twentieth century and there is profound ambivalence, not to say amnesia, towards Britain's imperial past. At the time, however, victories and conquests abroad were deplored by few. Britain was ruled not by Quakers, but by a political elite determined to pursue national interests and destiny across the oceans of the world, and this resonated with the aspirations of the wider political public. Truly a world that is lost, but one that cannot be disentangled from the history of the period.

1.3 Towards the Industrial Revolution

It was not only Britain's global position that was changing. There was also a series of developments in the economy and society that contributed to the move towards what has been subsequently termed the 'Industrial Revolution'. Neither economy nor society were static, and for centuries the pressures of an increasingly insistent market economy had encouraged change, a process facilitated by the availability of investment income and the absence of internal tariffs. The amount of coal shipped annually from the Tyne rose to 400,000 tons by 1625 and to well over 600,000 in 1730–1, much of it going to London. Coal represented a major development as a fuel source. It gave a more predictable heat than timber. Coal was the main fuel in sugar refining, brewing, glass-making, salt-boiling and brick-making by 1700. The ability to create and apply power was increased with the steam engine. The first one was developed by Thomes Savery in 1695, and improved by Thomas Newcomen, with his Atmospheric Engine of 1712. This pumped water out of coal mines and Cornish tin mines.

The initial value of the steam engine was specific to particular locations. Population trends were far more widespread in their impact. After population growth from 1500, the English population fell between 1660 and 1690, probably, in part, due to enteric fevers and gastric diseases, but, thereafter, the population began to pick up. The population for England and Wales probably rose from 5.18 million in 1695 to 5.51 in 1711 and 5.59 in 1731 and, despite a serious demographic crisis in 1741–2, 6.20 in 1751. Thereafter, it rushed ahead, to 8.61 million in 1801.

Average age at first marriage fell from the 1730s to the 1830s, particularly from the 1730s to the 1770s. Infant mortality rates fell in the second half of the eighteenth century, maternal rates throughout the century, and adult rates particularly in the first half of the century. Marital fertility among women aged 35 and over rose from mid-century. The rise in marital fertility was probably the consequence of a fall in stillbirths, and this can be seen as evidence of rising living standards.

The rising population affected both rural and urban England. In the countryside, where the bulk of the population lived until the mid-nineteenth century, rising demand for foodstuffs benefited landlords and tenant farmers, not the landless poor. Agricultural wages remained below fifteenth-century levels in real terms. The position of the rural poor was further hit by enclosure. About a quarter of England's agricultural land was directly affected by enclosure through Acts of Parliament, of which there were 5,265 for England alone in 1750–1850. Much of the Midlands in particular was enclosed during the century. Enclosure made it easier to control the land, through leases. Rents and land values rose to the profit of landowners. Enclosure also made it easier to control people, as many peasant farmers became labourers. Enclosing landowners created wide disruption of traditional rights and expectations, common lands and routes. The propertyless lost out badly, especially with the loss of communal grazing rights. This was not a rural society of simple deference and order, but one in which aristocratic hegemony was seen as selfish by many, as custom was displaced by harsh statutory enactments. Landed society celebrated its position and spent its money on splendid stately homes and on surrounding grounds which increasingly developed away from geometric patterns and towards a naturalistic parkland style that was developed by 'Capability Brown'. This was to become part of the visual character of Englishness, a counterpoint to the hedgerows of the enclosed worked landscape. Both reflected the power relationships of the period.

Some of the rural population migrated to the towns, helping to counter the impact of the higher death rates there. The percentage of the population living in towns, defined as settlements with more than about 2,000 people, rose from about 17 in 1700 to about 27.5 in 1800. The most important by far was London. In 1700, it had more than half a million people and in 1800 more than a million, making London by then the most populous European city and over ten times larger than the second city in England. As a result, London established notions of urban life. Through its central role in the world of print, London shaped news, opinion and fashion. It was the centre of finance and government, law and trade. The West End of London established the 'classical' style of Georgian town-building. London was disproportionately important to the character of England, in so far as such a concept can be used. It helped promote the interaction of bourgeois/middle-class and aristocratic, urban and rural thinking and values, and also helped secure the influence of commercial considerations upon national policy. Furthermore, London helped to mould a national economic space, although it is clear that specialisation for the London market was accompanied by the persistence of more local economic patterns.

London was the Britain/England visited by most foreigners who praised its constitution and society and held them up as a model. Institutions and practices such as trial by jury, a free press, Parliamentary government and religious toleration were widely praised, although their problems and limitations could be overlooked.

The extent to which London offered different prospects to those of landed society was captured by George Lillo in his play *The London Merchant* (1731). This deliberately focused on ordinary people. 'A London apprentice ruined is our theme' declared the prologue. In the dedicatory preface to the printed version, Lillo claimed that tragedy did not lose 'its dignity, by being accommodated to the circumstances of the generality of mankind … Plays founded on moral tales in private life may be of admirable use'.

Other towns also expanded and played a major role. In 1700, there were only five English towns with more than 10,000 inhabitants: Norwich, Bristol, Newcastle, Exeter and York. By 1800, the number (27) included important industrial and commercial centres in the north and midlands, such as Manchester, Leeds, Sheffield, Sunderland, Bolton, Birmingham, Stoke and Wolverhampton. Smaller towns also expanded.

Urban economies were helped by the growing commercialisation of life and by the rise of professions such as law and medicine. The infrastructure of, and for, money transformed the nature of the domestic market and of townscapes. New covered markets and shops were opened, as were banks and insurance offices. In a world of 'things', where increasing numbers could afford to purchase objects and services of utility and pleasure, towns played a central function as providers of services as much as of commercial and industrial facilities. Theatres, assembly rooms and subscription libraries, matched shops. Parks and walks replaced old town gates and walls. This helped bring renewed cultural activity to provincial centres. The dynamic character of urban life was seen in the number of town histories published – 241 between c.1701 and 1820. This was civic pride with a purpose. Town life was presented as the cutting edge of civilisation. Towns were crucial to provincial culture and also to the vitality of the middling part of society, which was subsequently to be known as the middle class.

Towns were also the nodes on the transport system. This expanded greatly with the creation of turnpike trusts, authorized by Parliament to raise capital and charge travellers in order to construct turnpike roads. By 1770 there were 15,000 miles of turnpike road in England, and most of the country was within 12.5 miles of one. Although turnpike trusts reflected local initiatives, a national system was created. Travel was made faster and more predictable by the development of stagecoach services, the cross-breeding of fast Arab horses, the replacement of leather straps by steel coach springs, and the introduction of elliptical springs. The time of a journey from Manchester to London fell from three days in 1760 to 28 hours in 1788.

Speed was less important for the coal moved by the new canals developed from the 1750s. They cut the cost of transporting bulk goods. By 1790, the industrial areas of the Midlands were linked to the Trent, Mersey, Severn and Thames. This was not new technology, but the rate of canal construction reflected demand from a rapidly burgeoning economy as well as the availability of investment and a sense that change was attainable and could be directed. The last was most important to what is known as the Industrial Revolution. A belief in its possibility and profitability fired growth.

This was a case not only of more of the same, important as that was, but also of changes in the nature of the economy, society, and culture. The relative importance of industry as a source of wealth and employment rose, and England became less agricultural. Industrialisation contributed powerfully to a culture of improvement, a conviction that modern achievements were superior to those of former times, and an, at times, heroic exultation of the new world of production, seen for example in paintings of industrial scenes such as Coalbrookdale.

Coal and steam power were increasingly important. Coal was not only a readily transportable and controllable fuel. It was also plentifully available in many areas, although not in most of south or east England. Combined with the application of steam power to coal mining, blast furnaces, and the new rolling and slitting mills, this led to a new geography of economic activity. Industry was increasingly attracted to the coalfields, especially to the north-east, to south Lancashire and to south Staffordshire. James Watt's improvement to the steam engine made it more energy efficient and flexible. In the 1790s, developments in metallurgy made it easier to produce malleable iron. Other industries, such as textiles, also benefited greatly from technical developments which increased productivity, and created a sense of ongoing improvement. In his *Inquiry into the Nature and Causes of the Wealth of Nations* (1776), Adam Smith regretted expenditure on successive wars but continued:

> though the profusion of government must, undoubtedly, have retarded the natural progress of England towards wealth and improvement, it has not been able to stop it. The annual produce of its land and labour is, undoubtedly, much greater at present than it was either at the Restoration [1660] or at the Revolution [1688]. The capital, therefore, annually employed in cultivating this land, and in maintaining this labour, must likewise be much greater. In the midst of all the exactions of government, this capital has been silently and gradually accumulated by the private frugality and good conduct of individuals, by their universal, continual, and uninterrupted effort to better their own condition. It is this effort, protected by law and allowed by liberty to exert itself in the manner that is most advantageous, which has maintained the progress of England towards opulence and improvement in almost all former times, and which, it is to be hoped, will do so in all future times.

This assessment of economic progress as dependent on freedom, the rule of law and limited government was to be very important to the English conception of national history and development. It failed to give much attention to the social problems arising from economic growth.

1.4 Challenges and political failure

While it is important not to exaggerate the scale of economic change, especially the number of factories, it was more extensive in Britain than elsewhere in Europe or the world. Industrialisation was to make Britain's the most powerful economy in the world, but this did not prevent a series of major political failures in the last third of the eighteenth century, including the loss of the Thirteen Colonies in the War of American Independence (1775–83) and defeat at the hands of Revolutionary France in 1793–5. The first reflected widespread, although far from universal, American suspicion of the policies and intentions of George III (1760–1820), and a British failure to adapt parliamentary sovereignty to the needs and aspirations of colonists. The British government under-estimated the extent of opposition and then found it difficult to conduct the war successfully.

Major American towns, such as New York in 1776 and Philadelphia in 1777, could be captured, but decisive victory eluded the British, and in 1777 they lost one army at Saratoga. Furthermore, after France (in 1778) and Spain (1779) entered the war, the British were in a more vulnerable position, as these powers could contest British control of the sea. In 1781, the army in Virginia was surrounded and forced to surrender at

Yorktown. This led to a collapse of confidence in the war, the fall of Lord North's government, and a willingness to concede independence. This was done in 1783. The British also had to cede territory to France and Spain.

The loss of America raises questions about the effectiveness of British government, but it was far from easy to govern transoceanic empires in a flexible fashion. It is more instructive to note the essential political stability of Britain in the 1750s–1780s. This description may seem surprising, as this was a period noted for constitutional disputes, especially in the 1760s, 1782–4 and 1788–9, and also for extra-parliamentary action, some of it radical, for example the Wilkesite agitation of the 1760s and the Yorkshire Association movement of the 1780s. However, discord was compatible with a stable political system, although a degree of ambivalence towards the notion of a loyal opposition helped to blind many contemporaries to this. Ministries were stable as long as they could avoid unforeseen problems and retain royal confidence. They did not lose general elections. Lord North, Prime Minister 1770–82, won the elections of 1774 and 1780, but was brought down in March 1782 by his inability to secure a satisfactory solution to the American Revolution.

William Pitt the Younger, Prime Minister 1783–1801 and 1804–6, won the elections of 1784, 1790 and 1796, but nearly fell in 1788–9 due to George III's apparent madness, and resigned in 1801 because he could not persuade George to accept Catholic emancipation, giving votes to Catholics as part of a process of extending full civil rights. Pitt the Younger brought an important measure of stability after the political chaos and general loss of confidence of 1782–3. He revived government finances and helped ensure a revival of British international influence. In 1787, British-encouraged Prussian intervention in the United Provinces (the modern Netherlands) overthrew the pro-French Dutch government.

More generally, British government relied on co-operation with the socio-political elite, and lacked the substantial bureaucracy and well-developed bureaucratic ethos that would have been necessary had they sought to operate without such co-operation. This co-operation extended to newly prominent social and economic interests. They were incorporated into the state, while those who were not offered incorporation in large part found their aspirations contained and their interests treated in terms of elite paternalism..

The major challenge to this system came from the French Revolution. This began in 1789, and aroused widespread interest in England. As the revolution became more radical, very clearly so from 1791, most of this interest became more hostile to the Revolution. The French threat to Britain's Dutch ally in the winter of 1792–3, led in 1793 to the outbreak of war. Both the domestic response and the war itself caused major problems. Radicalism was encouraged by the example of France. This led both to government action and, from 1792, to a wave of loyalism in England. The government sought to suppress radical organisations. Habeas Corpus was suspended, radicals were tried for sedition, and their newspapers suffered from the rise in newspaper duty. The Treasonable Practices Act and Seditious Meetings Act of 1795 sought to prevent denunciations of the constitution, and large unlicensed meetings. These measures hindered the radical societies.

Radicalism was weakened by its association with France. Parliamentary reform, which had been widely supported in the 1780s, was not pressed forward. The francophile and increasingly radical Earl of Shelburne, who had been Prime Minister in 1782–3, found that his ideas were increasingly unpopular. In 1787, he had written, 'it is the Public which decides upon measures with us'; but this public was not identical with the population. In 1790, the total electorate in England was only about 300,000. In 1791, Shelburne praised the French National Assembly for determining that the right of making peace and war came from the nation, not the Crown, and he urged the British government to 'follow the example of trusting the people'. In 1798, Shelburne pressed the Lords for parliamentary reform 'while it could be done gradually, and not to delay its necessity till it would burst all bounds'. Yet, the political world had become more conservative and cautious thanks to the Revolution. Reform was retarded. Signs of popular agitation were increasingly viewed with suspicion. Trade unions were hindered by the Combination Acts of 1799 and 1800.

These moves owed much to the acute problems of the war years. The cost and economic disruption of the war led to inflation, the collapse of the gold standard of financial exchange which supported the issue of paper currency by the Bank of England (1797), the introduction of income tax (1799), the stagnation of average real wages, and widespread hardship, particularly in the famine years of 1795–6 and 1799–1801. These problems were accentuated by the benefits that others, such as farmers, drew from the economic strains of the period. Aside from serious food rioting, there were also, in 1797, naval mutinies that owed much to anger over pay and conditions. The mutinies threatened national security.

Yet, despite this, the country did not collapse. The greater popularity of George III in the 1790s helped. He cultivated the image of being a father to all and did not inspire the negative feelings that focused on his French and Spanish counterparts. The association of radicalism with the French also helped to damn it for most people, not least because of the anarchy, terror and irreligion associated with the revolution. Patriotism received a new boost in the lengthy struggle, which was less divisive than the War of American Independence. In response to the French Revolutionaries and their allies, nationalism was defined in a conservative fashion, and conservatism was increasingly nationalist in tone and content. War with France was justified on moral grounds. Loyalism was a genuine mass movement. The widespread volunteer movement helped raise forces to repel any planned invasion. In the 1800s, *God Save the King* came to be called the national anthem.

The war sorely tested Britain. In July 1791, London audiences applauded the final lines of George Colman's new play *The Surrender of Calais*:

> Rear, rear our English banner high
> In token proud of victory!
> Where'er our god of battle strides
> Loud sound the trump of fame!
> Where'er the English warrior rides,
> May laurelled conquest grace his name.

This was not to be the experience of British forces when war broke out in 1793.

In 1794, the British were driven from the Austrian Netherlands (Belgium), in 1795 the French over-ran the United Provinces, and from 1796 Britain was threatened by invasion. Despite important naval victories, especially the Glorious First of June (1794), Cape St Vincent (1797), the Nile (1798), and Copenhagen (1801), in 1802 the government had to accept the Peace of Amiens which left Britain isolated and France dominant in western Europe.

The abortive Irish rising of 1798 and the unsuccessful French attempt to intervene encouraged an Act of Union between Britain and Ireland in 1800; the Act came into effect on 1 January 1801. Following the 1707 Act of Union between England and Scotland, it created a single state for the entire British Isles, although it was to have only limited success in producing a lasting primary British identity. Alongside such an identity, national allegiances remained, particularly in Ireland.

Napoleon had seized power in France in 1799, and in 1803 distrust of his aggressive expansionism led to a resumption of the conflict. In the face of preparations for invasion, volunteer units manoeuvred along the south coast. In 1805, the French tried to achieve a covering naval superiority in the Channel, but their complex scheme was mishandled and thwarted by an alert British response. Cancelling his invasion plans, Napoleon turned east to attack Austria. En route from Cadiz for Italy, the Franco-Spanish fleet was intercepted off Cape Trafalgar by Horatio Nelson on 21 October 1805, and heavily defeated, with the loss of 19 ships of the line, in the greatest of all British naval victories. Nelson, however, died in the moment of triumph.

Trafalgar did not prevent Napoleon from defeating Austria (1805) and Prussia (1806). French control of much of Continental Europe helped encourage a sense of British distinctiveness and superiority. Napoleon then sought to exclude Britain from European trade. This proved impossible, but indicated the threat posed by French dominance. Napoleon's attempt to impose control on Spain and Portugal provoked bitter resistance from 1808 which was aided by British troops. Initially, the British struggled to protect Portugal, but they were increasingly able to challenge the French position in Spain. By late 1813, the Duke of Wellington was leading the British army into south-west France. By then, Napoleon had been defeated in Russia (1812) and Germany (1813). With France invaded in early 1814, Napoleon was forced to abdicate. He sought to regain power in 1815, but on 18 June was defeated at Waterloo by an Allied army under Wellington in which the British played a key role. By then Britain was dominant through much of the transoceanic European world.

1.5 Conclusion

Countries do not change overnight at the passing of one century and the beginning of another. Indeed, many of the key aspects of change that we associate with the nineteenth century had their roots deep in the previous period; there were also key continuities. Urban and industrial growth and social change had begun to make themselves felt prior to 1800. For ten years or more either side of that same date, Britain was consumed by a sense of unease, born from the long-running effects of the French Revolution but also from the demands for reform of its own people. The French Revolution was accompanied by fears that the same forces might be at work in Britain; even following Napoleon's final exile in 1815, the British state continued to act as though revolution was a possibility. Peterloo in 1819 and the Cato Street Conspiracy (1820) were just two of many events which added a certain authenticity to these fears. As we shall see the book unfolds, however, the revolutionary threat in Britain was limited; change was a feature of life but so too was a high degree of social stability and what we might call 'managed' change. Government would grow; popular participation in politics would become a feature of life; the urban world would expand massively; Britain's Empire would straddle the globe. It is important to remember, however, that the men and women of the eighteenth century had (admittedly reduced) experiences of these very same things, too.

Summary

◆ It is possible to offer very different accounts of eighteenth-century Britain.

◆ Alongside a stress on the rise of a rational, genteel 'middle class' society centred in and on the growing towns, less optimistic facets can be emphasized.

◆ The political background was not as stable as is sometimes thought, but Britain avoided revolution.

◆ The century closed with defeat abroad and social tension at home.

◆ Aspects of continuity as well as of change mark out the eighteenth and nineteenth centuries.

Points to discuss

◆ How far was there major change prior to the nineteenth century?

◆ How stable was the eighteenth-century political system?

◆ Why did Britain avoid a revolution comparable to that in France?

References and further reading

J.M. Black, *Britain in the Eighteenth Century, 1688–1783* (2001).

J. Cannon, *The Fox–North Coalition: Crisis of the Constitution, 1782–84* (Cambridge, 1969).

M. Duffy, *The Younger Pitt* (2000).

D Eastwood, *Governing Rural England: Tradition and Transformation in Local Government, 1780–1840* (Oxford, 1994).

F. O'Gorman, *The Whig Party and the French Revolution* (1969).

R. Price, British Society, *1680-1880: Dynamism, Containment and Change* (Cambridge, 1999).

A. Smith, *Inquiry into the Nature and Causes of the Wealth of Nations* (1776).

P. Thomas, *Lord North* (1976).

The Industrial Revolution (1750–1850)

CHAPTER 2

Contents

Introduction

Imperial state; industrial power. These were the two aspects in which nineteenth-century Britain made its greatest impact on the world and its sense of history. Industrial power grasped the contemporary and historical imagination largely through machines. Yet, far more than that was at stake. The emphasis can be placed on socio-politico-economic fundamentals, rather than simply on manufacturing industry, as crucial to the rise of the economy. A relatively stable political system, legal conventions that were favourable to the free utilisation of capital, especially secure property and contracting rights, a social system that could accommodate the consequences of economic change, and an increasing degree of integration and interdependence, were all fundamental factors. Belief in the stability of political and economic arrangements encouraged the long-term investment that was crucial in many spheres of the economy. In addition, taxes on manufacturing industry and transport were low or non-existent. Thus, economic growth benefited from, and acted as a focus of, a range of the characteristics of British society in this period.

Key issues

▶ What was the role of new technology?

▶ What was the pace of economic growth?

▶ What were the regional consequences of economic growth?

▶ How was economic growth organized?

Progress took many forms, but the most important was a belief in the prospect and attraction of improvement. From 1759, there was a marked increase in the number of patents, testimony to an interest in the profitable possibilities of change. Industrial development led to more specialisation, as well as a greater division of labour and the growth of capital. In parts of the economy, there were important changes in the experience and intensity of work, the organisation of labour, and in material conditions. There was a greater emphasis on the need for constant and regular labour. New working practices and technology required a more disciplined work-force. The Derby clock- and instrument-maker John Whitehurst (1713–88) designed the first factory time-clocks; although most workers never saw one in the mid-nineteenth century, and time remained an indistinct concept until railways and factory buildings incorporated clocks. Although by the end of the eighteenth century fewer than 2,000 steam engines had been produced, they each represented a decision for change. The cumulative impact of often slow and uneven progress was impressive by the end of the century, and, by then, the rate of industrial growth had risen markedly. The harnessing of technological change eventually led to an economic transformation of the country, not least as a consequence of the benefits of readily available capital and labour and the burgeoning markets of growing home, colonial and foreign population.

2.1 Coal

For rapid industrial growth, the essentials were capital, transport, markets and coal. Coal, a controllable fuel, but bulky for transport purposes, was useful even in the preparatory stages of traditional manufacturing methods, such as soap-boiling, let alone as a power source in factories. Coal replaced wood, which, with its greater bulk for calorific value and less readily controllable heat, was a poor basis for many industrial processes, as well as for the development of large new industrial populations, with attendant demand for bricks, pottery and all the other fuel-consuming ancillaries of towns. Coal was *the* fuel of industrialisation, and Britain led in its production. Widespread use of the abundant and easily-worked British supplies of coal to fuel mechanical power freed the economy from its earlier energy constraints, reducing costs and increasing the availability of heat energy. This was exploited in a host of industries such as soap production, glass works and linen bleaching, which congregated where coal was available. As a consequence Newcastle became a major centre of the chemical industry, as did other Tyneside towns, such as Jarrow, Hebburn and Gateshead.

Coal had to be mined and transported, and both these requirements acted as spurs for innovation and activity, especially the construction of canals and of railways along which horses pulled barges and wagons, respectively. Without transport, coal was of scant value, but coal with transport could serve as the basis for the creation of buoyant mixed-industrial regions with large pools of labour and demand, and also specialist services. Faced by the costs of moving coal three miles by pack horse and barge from his colliery at Middleton to Leeds, in 1758 Charles Brandling secured an Act of Parliament 'for laying down a Wagon-way, in order for the better supplying the Town and neighbourbood of Leeds ... with coals', the first Act to authorize the construction of a railway. In 1780, a Newcomen steam engine was installed at Middleton, and, by the close of the century, the

Box 2.1

Industrial Revolution

A term, first coined in the mid-nineteenth century to capture the economic transformation of the period which spread from Britain to other countries. What is particularly understood by the term is a major shift from an organic economic to a mineral-based economy, with coal replacing wood as a major source of power to drive new steam engines, etc. Equally associated with this concept are the emergence of specialised factories, widespread urban growth, deep social change, migration from the land, and the development of a language of class. During this period, mass-produced textiles, metal smelting, and, later, chemicals, engineering and iron (then steel) ship-building are all taken as indicators of change. The term has been hotly disputed by historians; many have stressed continuity over dramatic change. However, revolutions need not necessarily be quick so long as they are thorough. In this respect, considerable change did occur in the areas described.

pit's average annual output was 78,500 tons. In 1776, Brandling had installed a steam engine at his pit in Felling, east of Gateshead, following up with the opening of a deep pit.

The increased demands for coal set challenges for those who produced it, masters and workers. Many of the most formidable obstacles were technological. As quantities of coal increased, deeper mines became more common. This raised issues of safety and logistics, quite separate from the problem of transporting new quantities of the fuel. Deeper mines required ventilation to avoid explosions and asphyxiation; deeper mines also invariably risked flooding and so new methods of pumping water were required.

The north-east was, in the 1850s, the pre-eminent coal-producing centre in the world, as it had been since the seventeenth century. That its major mines were close to two rivers – the Tyne and Wear – played an important role in assuring this predominance. The region produced twice as much coal as Scotland (15.4m tons as against 7.4m, according to 1854 figures), and almost twice that of its nearest competitors, Lancashire and South Wales, which accounted for some 9.9.m tons and 8.5m tons, respectively. The North-east dominated the London trade, as it had done for centuries. In 1827, London received 1.9m tons of coal in total, much of which came from Newcastle upon Tyne and Sunderland. This close relationship between the metropolis and the Great Northern coalfield can be seen in the fact that, in the same year, the two North-east ports despatched a total of 1.4 m tons of coal on to collier boats – but only 82,000 tons of that went overseas.

2.2 Iron

Iron was a integral part of the industrialisation process of this period. Railways, machinery, tools, and a variety of other goods and industries relied on new supplies of cheap iron. By the mid-1850s, iron production had reached approximately two-thirds of its nineteenth-century maximum: 10m tons against the 18m produced in 1880 and 1882. The main problem for iron production was that smelting techniques had to be developed to keep pace both with demand and with miners' potential to dig the ores. Traditional furnaces used charcoal, not coal, because it produced fewer impurities in the final metal. The blast furnace techniques needed to removed impurities could not be used with charcoal and iron because the blast of hot air used in the process would crumble the fragile fuel.

Most iron produced in the later eighteenth- and early-nineteenth centuries was pig iron, a brittle substance with a high carbon content, some of which went into the manufacture of pots, cannon, railings and similar products. Pig-iron could be improved, and much of the impurity removed, by further heating and working in a hot forge. By removing further carbon elements, iron-workers could then turn pig-iron into wrought or bar-iron. This type of iron was used for more refined products, such as nails, pins, locks, guns, etc. It should be noted that, in this period, when a very high grade of iron was required, Swedish and Russian iron was imported (these countries benefited from the availability of wood for charcoal). When iron production was small-scale and not factory-based, the centres of production were different from the later period. Places with freely available wood were often associated with iron production in the early industrial period. The Forest of Dean, and other parts of the south west of England, provides a good example. The Backbarrow Company had iron forges in the Furness District of North Lancashire as well as in the Highlands of Scotland long before the Industrial Revolution period.

The manufacture of iron was thus limited by the technologies which predominated in its industry. More than that, steel production, which required even greater refinements of the iron, was also locked in a 'technology gap'. The gap was not closed until the 1860s and 1870s when new methods, such as the Bessemer Converter, were produced which allowed high-grade steels to be produced from pig-iron. This is discussed in Chapter 3.

2.3 Technology

Steam engines were the icons of the new age. Thomas Jefferson visited the Albion Mill, a steam-powered corn mill, when he went to London in 1785. Although most power generation at the end of the century was still by traditional methods, steam engines offered an alternative source of power. They were best suited to enterprizes where substantial quantities of energy were required for long periods, such as pumping water out of mines. Steam engines were also used for winding and, by the end of the century, for driving machinery. Continual change and the search for improvement were an important part of the process of the Industrial Revolution, and the Newcomen engine was improved as the casting and boring of cylinders developed, particularly thanks to the new boring machines produced by John Wilkinson in 1774 and 1781. This enabled the steam engine to become more efficient in its fuel use and more regular in its operation. In 1769, James Watt, the first to perfect the separate condenser for the steam engine, patented an improved machine that was more energy-efficient and therefore less expensive to run, although more expensive to buy. In 1782, Watt patented fresh innovations that gave a comparative uniformity of rotary motion, and thus increased the capacity of steam engines to drive industrial machinery. In 1779, James Pickard, a Birmingham button-manufacturer, had fitted a crank and flywheel to his Newcomen engine in order to use its steam power to drive a mill that could grind metals. This innovation greatly enlarged the market for steam engines which was exploited by the partnership of Watt and the Birmingham industrialist Matthew Boulton. The Wheal Virgin steam engine of 1790, produced by Boulton and Watt, could do the work of 953 horses. In 1802, Richard Trevithick patented beam engines powered by high-pressure steam, such as those near Redruth. They were used for pumping water out of mines and for winding up men and ore to the surface. As a mobile source of energy, the steam engine enabled industry to move away from previous locations, particularly the fast-flowing rivers important for water-driven mills. Industry could be concentrated on coalfields, near the new energy source, but also in towns: coal could be transported.

2.4 Sectors of expansion

There were also important developments in metallurgy and textiles. Coke replaced charcoal for smelting iron and steel. Henry Cort's method of puddling and rolling, invented in 1784, but not adopted until the 1790s, produced malleable iron with coal more cheaply than the charcoal forge and refinery.

Combined with the application of steam power to coal mining, blast furnaces, and the new rolling and slitting mills, these changes led to a new geography of economic activity. Steam power freed industries from having to locate near riverine sites where water power could be obtained. Instead, industry was increasingly attracted to the coalfields. This was true, for example, of South Staffordshire, and also of South Wales, which also attracted copper-smelting. Coastal shipping and canals helped overcome communication problems. The copper works in the lower Swansea Valley depended on sea-borne supplies and used Cornish, Irish and Welsh copper. The valley dominated the non-ferrous smelting industry in Britain.

Demand for iron helped stimulate mining. The national production of iron rose from an annual average of about 27,000 tons in 1720–4 and 1745–9, to 80,000 in 1789. The production of coal rose from about 3 million tons in 1700 to 5.2 in 1750, 8.8 in 1755 and 15 by 1800, with the rate of growth accelerating from mid-century. Coal also became more important to the national economy as mining developed outside North-East England, which had been the most important coalfield in 1700, and which continued growing. From mid-century there was also major growth in South Lancashire, South Wales, Cumberland and South Staffordshire.

Demand for coal, copper and iron helped to bring great wealth to landowners. George Hunt of Lanhydrock benefited hugely from tin and copper mining on his Cornish estates. The Gibside estate in County Durham was improved on the coal wealth of the Bowes family. Plas Newydd was improved by Henry Paget, 1st Earl of Uxbridge and 1st Marquess of Anglesey, thanks to the coal in his Staffordshire estates and his Welsh copper mines. The 3rd Marquess of Londonderry created the harbour and town of Seaham to export from 1831 the coal from his Durham pits.

2.5 Textiles

Coal and canals were vital to the industrialising regions of Britain, but there were also other important changes. This was particularly, but, not only, true of textiles, an industry that benefited from the growing consumerism of the period. There a series of technological changes attracted and continued to attract attention because they dramatically altered what individual workers could achieve and transformed the organisational basis of industry. John Kay's flying shuttle of 1733 increased the productivity of handloom weavers by making it possible both to weave double-width cloths and to weave more speedily, although it took half a century before it came into general use. Woollen textile manufacturing was greatly changed by the early machinery that raised the productivity of labour, such as James Hargreaves' hand-powered spinning jenny of 1764. The same period also saw developments that produced machine-spun cotton yarn strong enough to permit all-cotton cloth. These included Richard Arkwright's water frame of 1768, which applied the principle of spinning by rollers, and Samuel Crompton's mule of 1779 with its spindle carriage. In 1773, Arkwright produced a cloth solely of cotton, and two years later he patented a process enabling yarn manufacture on one machine.

Machine-produced yarn was smoother and more even than hand-spun cotton. This encouraged the move of spinning from home to factory production. From 1771, Arkwright and his partners built a number of water-powered cotton-mills in Lancashire and the Midlands that displayed the characteristics of the factory system, including the precise division of labour and the continual co-operation of workers in the different manufacturing processes. The first worsted spinning mill was erected in 1784, and in 1790 Arkwright erected a Boulton and Watt steam engine in his Nottingham mill. The cylinder printing machine invented in 1783 transformed the basis of calico-printing industry. The following year, Samuel Greg opened Quarry Bank Mill to spin cotton south of Manchester. Six years later, he built the Apprentice House for the pauper children from the workhouses who made up about a third of the work-force.

While it is important not to exaggerate the scale of economic change, especially the number of factories, it was, nevertheless, more extensive in Britain than elsewhere in Europe or the world. Furthermore, a new economic geography of Britain, of expansion and decline, winners and losers, was being created. By the 1790s, industrial change had a clear regional pattern that was reflected in indicators such as expenditure on poor relief by head of population. Seasonally unemployed labourers, many of whom worked in farming, were a major call on poor relief, although the poor elderly also required relief. In 1801, the average figure per head for England and Wales was 9s 1d (45p), but in the industrial counties it was far lower – 4s 4d in Lancashire and 6s 7d in the West Riding of Yorkshire – while counties with hardly any industry, such as Sussex, or with declining industries, such as Essex, Norfolk and Suffolk, had to pay far more than the average. The Suffolk yarn industry had collapsed by 1800, unable to compete with the uniform quality and lower prices of machine-spun yarns from the West Riding of Yorkshire. De-industrialisation was due to far more than the absence of coal. Bruton in Somerset had been a major centre of silk production, with the largest manufacturer employing 700–900 hands on about 15,700 spindles in 1823, but, due to foreign competition, by 1831 he was down to 230 hands, 7,000 spindles and a four-day week. Winners and losers could also be seen in so far as the manufacturing process was concerned. New technology brought skilled jobs for some who managed and worked the machines but others were very much subordinated to the machines and 'deskilled'. Furthermore, previously acceptable customary working practices, for example machine hands taking a portion of the produce for themselves, were made illegal.

Much of Ireland's economy remained basically pre-industrial. Although there was an important expansion in textile production in some areas, principally linen-weaving in east and south Ulster, the economy of coal, iron and metallurgy was absent. Scotland, with a more self-sufficient and mixed agricultural sector, coal, and more favourable political, financial and social circumstances than Ireland, developed considerably from the mid-eighteenth century, especially in industry and banking in the central Midlands.

Slumps in manufacturing and mining also occurred in expanding or buoyant areas. They could lead to severe conditions, especially given the limited nature of social welfare. In March 1800, William Jenkin, land agent at Lanhydrock in Cornwall, reported that the local copper miners had been hard hit:

> There are a great number of families in this neighbourhood who never provide themselves with any kind of food but Barley Bread, Potatoes and Salt Pilchards from one week to another, with which they sip what they call Tea, little better than warm water without milk or sugar.

Industry became especially important in central Scotland, in England in the North and the Midlands, and in South Wales; in all cases in and near coalfields. The population rose rapidly in such areas: in County Durham from about 70,000 in 1700 to 150,000 by 1801. Lancashire, Yorkshire and the West Midlands were the principal centres of industrialisation. In contrast to an annual average increase in population in England and Wales in 1750–70 of 0.75%, the percentage for the West Riding of Yorkshire was 1.7%. In addition, urban manufacturing was very important, with towns such as Derby, Newcastle, Nottingham and Stockport becoming major centres of activity. The national population shot up, especially in such centres – in the borough of Liverpool from 83,250 in 1801 to 375,955 in 1851, in Stockport from 3,144 in 1754 to 4,975 in 1779 and 14,830 in 1801 (for a detailed discussion see Chapter 5). The relationship between urbanisation and industrialisation became closer, with the growing cities closely associated with manufacturing or with related commerce and services.

Yet economic change was not restricted to the major cities and the coalfields. Furthermore, the whole country was affected by a greater degree of economic integration. Higher levels of information flow were one characteristic of this process. For example, *Woolmer's Exeter and Plymouth Gazette* of 30 November 1809 provided not only London grain, meat and butter prices, but also Salisbury, Basingstoke, Devizes, Newbury, Andover and Warminster grain prices. The *Sherborne Mercury* in 1837 offered reports on Smithfield as well as the local cattle market. Pressure for such material was noted in the *Dorchester and Sherborne Journal* of 27 November 1801:

> In compliance with the request of many of our readers, and it being our wish to render our journal as extensively useful as possible, we have inserted the current prices of all the leading articles of merchandize, which we mean to continue weekly; and as the greatest care will be taken as to accuracy, we have no doubt it will prove highly interesting to merchants and traders of every description.

The press frequently reported new developments in industry and mining, Particular attention was devoted to details of new machinery. There was similarly little criticism of new developments, as a marked contrast to the position over agriculture, where the issue of a free market in grain aroused strong feelings.

Political changes encouraged this process of industrialisation. The reopening of the crucial export trade to America in 1783 encouraged a boom that was particularly important for cotton production. War with France from 1793 led to far greater demand for metallurgical products and greatly encouraged the development of iron production, especially in South Wales. By 1796, there were 25 furnaces in South Wales, including three at Cyfarthfa and three at Dowlais, where development had begun in 1759. By 1811, there were 148 furnaces in South Wales and, due to the use of coke (rather than charcoal) and the steam-engine, their yield increased. In 1810 a furnace at Ynys Fach, near Merthyr, produced what was then the record of 105 tons a week. The production of pig iron in South Wales rose from 5,000 tons in 1720 to 525,000 by 1840: 36 per cent of the British total. The tremendous industrial expansion in Monmouthshire and east Glamorgan, at for example Ebbw Vale and Merthyr Tydfil, created numerous jobs and helped lead to a permanent demographic shift. The largest town in 1801 was Merthyr Tydfil, no more than a hamlet in 1750, but now the leading centre of the coke and blast-furnace-based iron industry of South Wales, and the leading centre of iron production in the world. Throughout Britain, war also encouraged efforts to increase agricultural production, most prominently by the enclosure of wasteland.

2.6 The British Economy

The global context is worth grasping before turning to consider developments within Britain itself. There, again, it was the pace of technological innovation and economic development that was most powerful. These phenomena deserve attention ahead of domestic politics and imperial expansion. Britain set the pace in technology, and the ideology and thrill of modernization, not least with the dramatic development of the railway. Technological change brought the outer world closer, enabling the more rapid and predictable movement of messages, people and goods. In 1821, the Dover–Calais packet service was converted to steam. Thirty years later, the first messages were sent through the new submarine cable between Dover and Calais. The telegram was the Victorian equivalent of the internet in speeding up communications. More generally, the harnessing of technological change contributed to an economic transformation of the country, as did the benefits of readily available capital, an increasingly productive agricultural sector, and the burgeoning markets of a growing home and colonial population.

The British economy became dramatically different to that in the rest of Europe, encouraging a sense that Britain was exceptional. A crucial ingredient of industrialisation, the annual average production of coal and lignite, in million metric tons, amounted to 18 for Britain in 1820–4, and two for France, Germany, Belgium and Russia combined; and the comparable figures for 1855–9 were 68 and 32. The annual production of pig-iron in million metric tons in 1820 was 0.4 for Britain and the same for the rest of Europe; in 1850 2.3 and 0.9; again a larger gap. Behind these figures, there was a vivid reality. The radical journalist William Cobbett wrote from Sheffield in January 1830:

> All the way along, from Leeds to Sheffield, it is coal and iron, and iron and coal. It was dark before we reached Sheffield; so that we saw the iron furnaces in all the horrible splendour of their everlasting blaze. Nothing can be conceived more grand or more terrific than the yellow waves of fire that incessantly issue from the top of these furnaces ... Nature has placed the beds of iron and beds of coal alongside of each other, and art has taught man to make one to operate upon the other, as to turn the iron-stone into liquid matter, which is drained off from the bottom of the furnace, and afterwards moulded into blocks and bars, and all sorts of things. The combustibles are put into the top of the furnace, which stands thirty, forty, or fifty feet up in the air, and the ever-blazing mouth of which is kept supplied with coal and coke and iron-stone, from little iron

wagons forced up by steam, and brought down again to be re-filled. It is a surprising thing to behold; and it is impossible to behold it without being convinced that ... other nations ... will never equal England with regard to things made or iron and steel ... They call it black Sheffield, and black enough it is; but from this one town and its environs go nine-tenths of the knives that are used in the whole world.

Other sectors of the economy also boomed. Raw cotton consumption in thousand metric tons was 267 for Britain in 1850 and 162 for the rest of Europe. The British economy benefited from the rising demand of a growing population (excluding Ireland: 1801, 10.5 million; 1831, 16.3; 1851, 20.8), and from its ability to export to less dynamic economies, but more was at stake in British growth. The application of technology was fundamental.

The availability of capital for investment was also crucial. The development of Penshaw Colliery in County Durham, for example, cost £60,000 in 1816. The financial system improved in 1826 when the Bank Charter Act permitted the formation of joint stock banks more than 65 miles from London, thus spreading risk. Later Acts in 1833 and 1844 brought considerable improvement by giving the Bank of England a central role in the issue of notes. Changes in banking were an important aspect of the institutional dynamics of economic development.

Alongside major changes, however, it is also appropriate to stress the two-tier, gradual and evolutionary nature of the Industrial Revolution (see also Chapter 6). Technological change was generally slow in the early decades of the nineteenth century, and there was great variety between and within industries. Water rather than coal, for example, continued to provide much of the power for Scottish industry before 1830. Handloom weaving persisted on an appreciable scale in the leading textile county of Lancashire into the 1840s. London and Birmingham were primarily cities of workshops, not factories. Despite the railway, much of Britain remained a horse-drawn society. More generally, it is necessary to be cautious in arguing direct from economic to social change. For example, the chronologies of the growth in the use of steam power and in urban population do not tally.

Allowing for these points, the notion of an Industrial Revolution is still justified. The potential and character of much of British industry changed dramatically. Many of the fastest-growing cities of the early nineteenth century were centres of industrial activity, for example Bradford, Dundee and Merthyr Tydfil. The population of the first climbed from 16,012 in 1810 to 103,778 in 1850, as the city became the global centre of worsted production and exchange. Factory horsepower in the town rose 718 per cent between 1810 and 1830. Mechanisation there brought profit, larger factories and a wave of immigrants. Innovation was continual in Bradford as elswhere. The mechanisation of yarn spinning was followed in 1826, despite riots by hostile workers, by the spread of machinofacture into worsted weaving. By 1850s the work formerly done in Bradford by thousands of handloom weavers, working in the countryside, was now performed by 17,642 automatic looms contained in factories and mass-producing women's dress fabrics. By 1821 Manchester had over 5,000 power looms, and by 1850 Sunderland was the greatest ship-building town in the world.

The same process was repeated on a lesser scale in smaller towns. The population of Carlisle, a centre of cotton manufacture, rose from near 10,000 in 1801 to over 35,000 by 1841. Carlisle also saw the development of biscuit manufacturing. Jonathan Dogdson Carr adapted a printing machine to cut biscuits, replacing cutting by hand, and then, helped by

Carlisle's position as a major transport junction, sold his product through the country by rail. Companies and towns that wished to stay at the leading edge of economic development had to become and remain transport foci, as long-distance economic exchange was increasingly involved in manufacturing. Mills located earlier to benefit from fast-flowing streams in upland areas, such as the western Pennines, faded because they lacked the access enjoyed by large-scale steam-driven urban mills.

New technology affected almost every aspect of the economy and social life. As we will see in Chapter 4, transport innovations new and improved roads, canals, railways, and so on – were vital in this respect. But technological innovation was diffused far and wide, affecting specific activities, such as the press. In 1814, the largest-selling newspaper, *The Times*, switched to a steam press, which allowed the production of 1,000 impressions an hour, as opposed to the 250 per hour from an unmechanized hand-press. The machinery was secretly prepared to prevent the opposition of workers, who had already mounted a strike in 1810. On 29 November 1814, *The Times* announced 'the greatest improvement connected with printing since the discovery of the art itself'. The new machinery allowed *The Times* to go to press later, and thus to contain more recent news than its competitors, and also to dispense with duplicate composition on the larger number of presses required before the switch to steam, and this cut wage bills. Koenig's steam press, which could produce 400 items per hour, was eclipsed in 1827 with the arrival of Augustus Applegarth's press which produced 4,000 impressions per hour. However, there was no rush elsewhere to introduce steam presses. Instead, the Stanhope press, introduced from 1800, and with the use of an iron frame, permitting a clearer impression and slower rate of production, sufficed. The type was on an iron bed or carriage, that was moved into and out of the press by human effort. It was not until the 1820s that some titles began to follow *The Times*, for example the *Morning Herald*, in 1822, the *Manchester Courier*, in 1825, and the *Manchester Guardian*, in 1828. Other papers followed far more slowly. Web rotary presses, which were able to print directly onto continuous rolls, or 'webs', of paper were introduced in Britain from the late 1860s. The Walter press was first used by *The Times* in 1869 and by the *Daily News* in 1873, while the *Daily Telegraph* purchased the American Bullock press in 1870, a sign of growing competition from the United States which was a feature of the later period. Steam power was also used in book publishing. When in 1832 Oxford University Press opened its new site in Walton Street, it introduced a steam engine to power the works. Older industries such as brewing were also affected by new technology.

2.7 Conclusion

In 1851, the Great Exhibition expressed Britain's economic potency. Planned in 1849 by Queen Victoria's husband, Prince Albert, a keen moderniser, the Great Exhibition was intended as a demonstration of British achievement and a reflection of the country's mission, duty and interest to put itself at the head of the diffusion of civilisation. The Exhibition was a tribute to British manufacturing skill and prowess. Joseph Paxton's iron and glass conservatory, the Crystal Palace in Hyde Park, London, the central space of the Exhibition, was 1850 feet long, 460 feet wide and 108 feet high. A 24-ton block of coal was placed by the entrance. The symbolism was clear. Coal had powered a new world and the Victorians had the technical expertise to mine and to transport such a huge item.

Summary

◆ Coal, steam power and new technology were crucial to economic growth.

◆ The pace of economic growth varied greatly by sector.

◆ Economic growth led to the de-industrialisation of much of southern England, but expansion on the coalfields.

◆ Much, *but not all*, economic growth was located in factories. Private enterprise, not state control or planning, prevailed.

Points to discuss

◆ Why did the Industrial Revolution occur first in Britain?

◆ Could the Industrial Revolution have occurred without coal?

◆ How far were there coherent regional economies?

◆ What was the geography of economic development?

References and further reading

A. Birch, *Economic History of the British Iron and Steel Industry, 1784–1879* (New York, 1967).

N.F.R. Crafts, *British Economic Growth during the Industrial Revolution* (Oxford, 1985).

R. Church, *The History of the British Coal Industry III: 1830–1913: Victorian Pre-Eminence* (Oxford, 1986).

F. Crouzet, *The Victorian Economy* (1981).

M.J. Daunton, *Poverty and Progress: An Economic and Social History of Britain, 1700–1850* (Oxford, 1995).

D.A. Farnie, *The English Cotton Industry and the World Market, 1815–1896* (Oxford, 1979).

M.W. Flinn, *History of the British Coal Industry, 1700–1830* (Oxford, 1983).

R. Floud and D. McCloskey (eds), *The Economic History of Britain since 1700* (2nd edn, 1994).

C.H. Lee, *The British Economy since 1700: A Macroeconomic Perspective* (Cambridge, 1986).

P. Mathias, *The First Industrial Nation: An Economic History of Britain, 1700–1914* (1983 edn).

J. Mokyr, *The British Industrial Revolution: An Economic Perspective* (Boulder, CO., 1993).

G. Von Tunzelmann, *Steam Power and British Industrialisation to 1860* (Oxford, 1978).

E.A. Wrigley, *Continuity, Chance and Change: The Character of the Industrial Revolution in England* (Cambridge, 1988).

The Industrial Revolution (1850–1914)

CHAPTER 3

Introduction

The formative years of *industrialisation* generally receive more attention than the less dramatic second stage. Furthermore, books of this type usually devote only one chapter to this topic, and thus present a unitary account. By dividing the subject into two chapters, we intend to focus attention on shifts in the economic fortunes of the country. These were important not only for its economic history, but also for other aspects of British history.

Key issues

▶ What were the major shifts in industrial activity in the second half of the century?
▶ Is the term economic decline an exaggeration?
▶ What was the regional geography of economic change?

3.1 Economic growth

Britain was the workshop of the world, and was happy to see itself in this light. In 1880–4, the annual average production of coal and lignite in million metric tons was 159 for Britain, and 108 for France, Germany, Belgium and Russia combined, that of pig-iron in 1880, 7.9 for Britain and 5.4 for the rest of Europe, and of steel 1.3 and 1.5; while raw cotton consumption in thousand metric tons in 1880 was 617 for Britain and 503 for the rest of Europe. Increased production interacted with expanding trade. This led to an expansion in merchant shipping, ship-building and new docks. In London, the leading commercial and industrial centre in the country, and, by far, the most populous city, the Poplar Docks, opened in 1852, were followed by the Royal Victoria Dock (1855), Millwall Dock (1868), Royal Albert Dock (1880) and Tilbury Docks (1886). Ships bringing goods from all over the world docked in London; most of them were British-owned.

Growth remained most pronounced in and close to the major coalfields. Thus in Wales, growth was centred on the South Wales coalfield was also important. Welsh coal was suited for coking for iron furnaces and for steamships, and Welsh anthracite coal was ideal for the hot blast process for the iron and steel industry which had developed on the coalfield. Equally, Scottish industrial capacity, which reached its zenith in this later period, was focused on the central belt area (between Glasgow and Edinburgh, and including their hinterlands) where coal reserves were extensive.

Economic growth put pressure on communications, not least because coal and iron were bulk products. The Glamorgan iron-masters encouraged the construction of a road from Cardiff along the Taff Valley, and in 1793–4 of the Glamorgan Canal which provided inexpensive bulk transport. The mountainous terrain, however, meant that most of Wales was particularly badly suited for canal construction. This made the possibility of digging the Glamorgan Canal especially important, but also ensured that the railway would have even more of an impact than it did in the English Midlands. The development of the port of Cardiff by the Marquess of Bute and the spread of the railway, especially the Taff Vale line between Cardiff and Merthyr Tydfil (1841), permitted the movement of large quantities of coal. In the decade after 1856 exports from South Wales led to the opening of three new dock developments, the Bute East, Roath Basin and Penarth docks, all linked to the Taff Vale Railway, which brought the coal from the Glamorgan coalfield. Production of coal in million tons rose from 1.2 in 1801 to 10.25 by 1860, 13.6 by 1870 and 57 by 1913. Improvements in mine technology, especially in drainage and ventilation, made possible the working of deeper seams and thus a rapid expansion of the coalfield and a rise in production. The major area of mining in the eighteenth century had been in the Neath and Swansea area, but in the early nineteenth century there was major expansion in the copper valleys of the Rivers Taff and Cynon, and from the 1860s in the Rhondda Valley and the eastern section. Not only was more coal dug in South Wales, but its importance in national output rose: from about 2.7% in 1750 to 15% in the 1830s, 17.08% in the 1890s, and 19% in 1900–13, the last a percentage reduced by the 1910–11 mine strike.

Most of the coal was exported and the coal industry employed about a third of the Welsh male labour force. Coal furthered industrialisation, especially the emergence of Cardiff as the Welsh metropolis: its population rose from fewer than 2,000 in 1801 and 10,000 in 1841, to 200,000 in 1921; that of the coalmining Rhondda from under 1,000 in 1851 to 153,000 in 1911.

The presence of coal encouraged the development of metallurgical industries. Founded by John Vivian from Truro in 1809, the Hafod works in the lower Swansea valley were developed under the management of his son John Henry Vivian into one of the largest and most up-to-date metallurgical enterprises in Europe. Copper smelting was the core of the Vivian business, but, by the mid-1870s, they also ran nickel, cobalt, silver, alkali and phosphate works, collieries and an iron foundry. North-east Wales was also a region of significant economic growth, in which coal and metallurgical enterprises played major roles near Wrexham. Like Swansea, Flint was a centre for alkali manufacture, an important early stage in the chemical industry. The presence of coal was important, but so also was Cheshire salt and North Wales limestone. Other chemical plants in the 1880s were found near Cardiff and on Anglesea.

Economic growth changed the rest of the economy, creating, for example, new markets for agriculture. The processes of machinisation, steam power, and a willingness to search for and try new methods that were characteristic of major industrial regions could also be seen throughout the economy. Thus, for example, mills that had been hitherto powered by water were converted to steam. This was true of the New Mills cotton manufactories of north-west Derbyshire in the 1860s. Local economies were transformed as transport links improved. Thus, after the Banbury to Cheltenham Railway came to the Oxfordshire village of Hook Norton in 1887, agricultural facilities changed. As a result of this new communication link, a monthly cattle market was opened near the station, while it became practical to exploit the area's low grade ironstone, which began in 1889. A processing works was built and the product was transported to Staffordshire, which had previously lost out in competition with Cumbrian and Cleveland iron, and also to South Wales. To complete the transition, terraced housing was built for the workers (Tiller, 2001). Power was also applied to agriculture. After the 1856 Royal show of the Royal Agricultural Society of England (a body founded in 1838) great interest was shown in the steam plough demonstration. (Scantlebury, 2001).

Britain's industrial strength faced challenges, however. The very pace of change required investment in new processes, and international competition was becoming more acute. This was especially so after America had recovered from the Civil War of 1861–5, and after the unification of Germany in 1866–71. Britain's unprecedented economic dominance of about 1870, her near monopoly of manufacturing, was unsustainable. In terms of productivity, in many industries, Britain's rivals were catching up with best practice. Many British companies were unable to respond. Established practices were not discarded rapidly enough, and there was considerable caution about investing in new technology.

A widespread economic crisis, especially in farming and in some traditional industries, was apparent in Britain in the last quarter of the century, the so-called Great Depression. Coal-mining, the key activity of the steam age, and the source of power for Britain and of much export wealth, was hit from the 1870s. By the 1880s, one of the leading coalfields, that in County Durham, had passed its peak and miners were leaving the county. Yet, we must remember that the highest ever total of miners in Britain was not reached until 1911, when more than one million were thus employed.

3.2 Decline, or was it?

Nevertheless, the mid-Victorian boom of the third quarter of the century gave way to a long period of depression thereafter. Whereas before the 1870s, Britain had enjoyed a free run on world markets, with little or no competition, this was to change. Following the American Civil War (1861–5) the opening up of the prairie states gave American access to untold agricultural riches, much of which found its way to European markets, thanks to sound investment in railways and new technologies, such as the McCormick's reaper (a combine harvester). Free trade encouraged Britain to become reliant on overseas grain,

Table 3.1 Total number of coal-miners in Britain, 1841–1911 (000s)

1841	1851	1861	1871	1881	1891	1901	1911
218	383	457	517	604	751	931	1,202

Source: B. R. Mitchell and P. Deane, *Abstract of British Historical Statistics* (Cambridge, 1962)

and this came in from America and also Canada, where large expanses of land were falling under the plough. American industry became focused and far-sighted in a way that Britain's was not: focused, in the sense that it met the needs of a huge and expanding home market; far-sighted, in that it also tapped into key markets in Britain and elsewhere. By 1914, too, American firms such as Ford and Westinghouse were establishing outlets in Europe in a way which echoes today's world economy of inward investment by other nation's companies.

America's comparative advantage over Britain lay chiefly in its size and potential. Britain could never have competed, toe-to-toe, with American capital. However, the Americans were additionally successful at maximising what potential they had through the effective deployment of new technologies. Following the Civil War, the use of inter-changeable parts – first in munitions, later in farm machinery and sewing machines, etc – gave America a lead over Britain, where highly skilled craftsmen were still being used to make precision parts as unique one-offs. This tells us more about the comparative labour position of the two economies than it does about inherent strategic strengths and weakness, however. America had always had a shortage of skilled labour, so it made sense to invest in machines; in Britain, labour was plentiful and therefore to use relatively cheap skilled labour was no more than commonsense. The classic, oft-cited, example of this is in the textile industry. Whereas American mill-owners invested in new ring-spinning technologies, the existence of a plentiful supply of skilled male spinners justified the continuance of old technologies.

The Americans did, however, assume the place once held by the British—as entrepreneurs and inventors. Many of the most important new technologies of the period were of American design and implementation. The Yale lock (1855), the machine gun (1865) and the new development on an older design, Singer's sewing machine (1850), were all resoundingly American. The United States led the way in the machine tool industry, too. Machine tools were machines used for making other products out of metals. The universal milling machine (1861) and the automatic lathe (1870s) were but two of these. When coupled to the manufacture of hard drill bits and cutting implements for fitting on the machines (these were made of alloys, such as tungsten-carbide, so as to be harder than steel) they enabled the rapid and large-scale cutting and shaping of steel products. The development of automated systems also led naturally to larger units of production. The Americans did not invent the production line, and the British were not entirely absent from this sphere of industrial endeavour, but the former led the way and achieved far greater success in this way. Systematic organisation, large factories and scientific management techniques (developed by F.W. Taylor and known as 'Taylorism') were all exemplified in the American way of doing things. Even in heavily manual forms of labour, such as in the meat packing industry, technologies such as the moving conveyor belt, widely in use in Chicago by the 1890s, held out new possibilities for economies of scale.

Yet in Britain, too, the 1880s were a period of larger and more concentrated units of production. The development of iron and then steel ship-building also precipitated the development of large shipyards. The yards of the Tyne, Wear, Clyde and Mersey, as well as at Belfast and Barrow all grew significantly in this period. It was not uncommon to have yards with 5,000 men employed under a single series of roofs. This had a major impact on urban residential patterns, with streets around factories crammed with people who did the same work, or who at least worked in the same place. Cotton textile factories also became concentrated in this period, with steel sheds, engineering factories, and so on, becoming larger, too. At the same time, much of the British economy continued to be dominated by hand labour and took place in relatively small places of work.

Manufacturing in Britain was hit hard from the 1880s, and it was this that prompted both contemporaries and historians to question the management skills of British industrialists. This was true both of the national economy as a whole and of the centres of heavy industry. In the Sunderland shipyards, there were empty order books and wage cuts in the 1880s. The same was true of the yards of the Clyde. Iron and steel had been central to manufacturing, but this sector was affected by severe problems and serious bankruptcies. The iron industry was hit by the exhaustion of easily worked deposits of iron ore, which necessitated more difficult deeper workings, and by competition from more easily worked foreign deposits. Furthermore, while the invention of the Bessemer steelmaking process had given Britain a comparative advantage, the development in the later century of new systems, such as the Siemens open hearth furnace, posed serious problems of obsolescence, leading to the need for investment. Bessemer converters required high-grade ores, such as the haematite iron produced in west Cumbria, which could be up to 60 per cent pure. Later technologies could mass produce steel from much inferior ores.

Many furnaces were thus shut and there was much disruption and hardship in the 1870s and 1880s. Problems continued. In Gateshead on the Tyne the major ironworks ceased trading: Hawks, Crawshay in 1889 and Abbots in 1909. Elsewhere, the West Cumberland Iron and Steel Company closed in 1891, and many workers emigrated to America or South Africa. The Britannia Foundry at Derby also closed in 1910. When iron-masters in the North-East of England were faced with a choice between competitive modernisation and market-rigging and price-fixing collusion, they opted for the latter. As a result, British iron continued to be puddled and rolled in increasing ancient mills. Long after competing nations had opted for efficient new methods of smelting steel, the British continued to rely on old Bessemer converters: 1860s technology was still at work on the eve of the Second World War. To some extent, British iron-masters protected themselves from each other with price-fixing cartels; but this did not preclude the import of cheaper European or American metals.

Equally, it would be inappropriate to ignore signs of continued expansion in established industries. Thus, in Lincolnshire there was a synergy of iron industry, steel manufacturing, and railway expansion, as there was in other areas, for example, west Cumberland. From 1860, ironstone was mined in north-west Lincolnshire in and close to modern Scunthorpe. Initially, it was moved to processing works in Barnsley: by rail to the Trent, then by water, and again by rail. In 1866, the Trent was bridged. By then there had been an expansion in iron-working in the area, with the Trent Iron Works built in 1862–4, and then the Frodingham Iron Works. By 1880 there were 21 furnaces in the area, of which 15 were blast furnaces. The first steel furnaces followed in 1890. Further south, the Holwell Iron Works near Melton Mowbray was built in 1878–81.

In 1902, Arthur Benson's words for 'Land of Hope and Glory', the first of Edward Elgar's *Pomp and Circumstance* marches, were first heard as part of the Coronation Ode for Edward VII. They promised a steadily 'wider' empire. The empire, was indeed the most extensive and populous in the world, and was still expanding rapidly. It also dominated the production of many important goods. Gold and diamonds came from South Africa, and helped to drive British expansion there. Copper and wheat came from Canada, tin from Malaya, cocoa from Ghana, palm oil from Nigeria, lamb, mutton and wool from Australasia. Imperial products were processed, manufactured and marketed in Britain, and it was from there that the finance for their exploitation and transport came. To a certain extent, however, the existence of the empire lessened the pressure to improve the industrial base in Britain in order to succeed in more competitive markets, especially in Continental Europe and the United States. The Empire also provided direct competition for much of British agriculture.

Aggregate figures of British economic growth concealed and reflected a regional geography of great contrasts and variations, again a pattern that persisted during the twentieth century, and one that was true of other industrial countries. As industrialisation gathered pace and became more normal, so did the contrast between industrialised regions and the rest of the country, between, for example, Clydeside and South-West Scotland. In the industrialised regions, the experience and world of work changed. By the mid-nineteenth century, fewer than 10 per cent of those employed in the Scottish central-belt counties of Lanark, Midlothian and Renfrew worked in the traditional activities of agriculture, forestry and fishing.

In such areas, the landscape changed. The mining gear of coal and other mines, the slag heaps of mining and industrial waste, and the smoking chimneys of industry, came to dominate visually, while metal-beating and the hiss of steam swamped natural sounds, and coal smoke became the prime smell as well as a major restriction on visibility. Paintings such as Myles Foster's *Newcastle upon Tyne from Windmill Hills, Gateshead* (c. 1871–2) showed formerly prominent buildings – the castle keep and the cathedral – now joined by sites of the new industrial world: factory chimneys and the railway bridge. Atmospheric pollution exacerbated respiratory illnesses.

The population of regions experiencing industrial growth rose rapidly, far more so than in other parts of the country. The population of County Durham, a centre of coal mining and heavy industry, rose from 390,997 in 1851 to 1,016,152 in 1891, that of the iron and steel centre of Workington from 6,467 in 1861 to 23,749 in 1891, and that of Newcastle from 28,294 in 1801 to 215,328 in 1901.

Major increases in population were only achieved by migration. The dislocation of extensive migration was part of the pattern of economic growth, essential to provide labour, and yet disruptive for individuals and communities and the source of many difficulties. Migration within Britain was a central feature of the social fabric of Victorian Britain and, was again, a trend that continued into the twentieth century. It contributed to a powerful sense of fluidity, and to the decline of established patterns of social control. Areas with limited economic growth, such as Cornwall and Ireland, produced large numbers of migrants, who were soaked up by growing cities. Glamorganshire and Monmouthshire, the key zone of Welsh mining and industrialisation, had about 20% of the Welsh population in 1801, but 57.5% by 1901, in part because of migration from the more rural areas of Wales, especially from Central Wales, but also from Ireland and South-West England. 11% of Swansea's population in 1901 had been born in south-west England. London, Britain's largest industrial city, drew heavily on East Anglia and the West Country, both areas with limited economic growth, especially that created by industrialisation, and with serious problems in their traditionally important agricultural sector. There was a general flight from the land after about 1870.

Industrial regions that failed to maintain earlier growth rates, for example the Staffordshire coal and iron area, also provided migrants. Staffordshire and Shropshire iron-workers were partly responsible for the expansion of the population in County Durham. Changes in the location of industrial expansion reflected transformation in the economy. Engineering, ship-building and chemicals became more prominent, rather than the textiles and metal smelting of earlier decades, although both the latter remained important.

Thus the regional character of industrialisation changed. This was not due only to the rise of new industries, but also to changes in the location of existing ones. Thus, new coal and iron-ore deposits were worked, in part because railways made it more economical to transport relatively low-value bulk items like coal and iron from hitherto to unworked or lightly worked deposits. For example, the Durham coalfield expanded as a result of the opening of the Stockton and Darlington line, the Clarence, and other railways, leading to the abandonment of other forms of trasnport forms, such as waggonways built to riverside staithes (wharves). Equally, Workington on the Cumbrian coast developed as a major centre of iron and steel production from 1857, but, initially at any rate, much of the local ore was sent to Scotland for processing. Railways built in the 1840s and 1850s had created ready access from Whitehaven and Workington to nearby iron-ore fields and to the coke supplies of Durham, and so, gradually, local ores began to be turned into iron in the region itself. It was in the later part of the century that capacity and potential was reached, both in Cumbria and more generally within iron centres elsewhere in the country.

The nature of the industrial base varied greatly between the individual manufacturing and mining regions. For example, from the outset, the industrial revolution in South Wales had been limited in scope and without the development in heavy engineering, shipbuilding and locomotive manufacture seen in North-East England or of textiles seen in Lancashire and Yorkshire. This had social as well as economic consequences. For example, job opportunities for women were relatively limited in South Wales compared to Lancashire and Yorkshire. In Scotland, two-thirds of all textile workers were women.

The organisation of economic activity also developed. Mechanisation was crucial to uniformity, the production of low-cost standardised products. As a result, brands of mass-produced goods, such as chocolate and soap, could be consumed and advertised nation-ally. This development was linked to the growth of the railway system, which provided rapid, predictable and, as far as the urban population was concerned, comprehensive delivery, and to the growth of the national press. The resulting opportunities for economies of scale were grasped by entrepreneurs. They also led to consolidation in manufacturing and retail. Public limited companies developed. They used their borrowing capacity to fund expansion and consolidation. Products, such as beer, that had produced a degree of local identification, were replaced by regional or national brands as local breweries were taken over. The number of breweries in Scotland fell from 220 in 1860 to 125 in 1900. In the 1890s and 1900s, there was a concentration of ownership and production in the Northumberland and Durham brewing industry, accompanied by the emergence of the public limited company. At the same time, the brewing industry serves as a good example of how much industry was not located on the coalfields or in major manufacturing areas. Thus, Stratford-upon-Avon's largest employer was a brewer, Flower and Sons. Furthermore, far from being a rural relic made redundant by big breweries located on major industrial centres, the Flower and Sons business expanded, exported and helped to support local concerns, such as timber merchants and the brewers' chemists, Kendall and son, which became a profitable and innovative leader in the field (J. Reinaz, 'Kendall and son, Stratford-upon-Avon: the business of a brewers' chemist in the nineteenth and twentieth centuries', *Warwickshire History*, 11, 3, 200, pp.9–11).

There was a similar process in retail and services. Big retail chains became important. By 1900, J. Sainsbury had 47 provision stores, by 1906 there were over 500 shops in Julius Drewe's grocery chain, and by 1914 another grocer, Thomas Lipton, had 500 shops. Banks amalgamated. In 1896, twenty private bands merged to form Barclays. Strongest in East and South-East England, the bank spread by amalgamating with the Consolidated Bank of Cornwall in 1905. When Nevile Read and Co. merged with Barclays in 1914, it ended nearly 140 years of private county banking in Berkshire. In 1909, the London and County Bank had merged with the London and Westminster. More generally, middle-class professions developed to 'service' the new and expanded manufacturing and retail spheres. New professions, such as accountants emerged, as did new 'industries', such as leisure and tourism.

The impressive growth of American and German competition and the relegation of Britain to third place in the industrial world by 1914 has prompted historians to develop a cultural critique of British business, with British entrepreneurs blamed for their eclipse by the competition. Begun by contemporaries, such as A. Shardwell, and developed by more recent Marxist historians such as Eric Hobsbawm, the loss of entrepreneurial energy is seen as a class-ridden inevitability. Shardwell, in his critical study, *Industrial Efficiency* (1906), writes:

> England is like a composite photograph, in which two likeness are blurred into one. It shows traces of American enterprise and German order, but the enterprise is faded and the order muddled. They combine to a curious travesty in which activity and perseverance assume the expression of ease and indolence. The once enterprising manufacturer has grown slack, he has let the business take care of itself, while he is shooting grouse or yachting in the Mediterranean.

Hobsbawm (1968) argued that in the 1880s and beyond, while 'it was no doubt inevitable that British pioneer industries should lose ground relatively as the rest of the world industrialised, … this purely statistical phenomenon need not have been accompanied by a genuine loss of impetus and efficiency'. However, he also accepted that something of this was inevitable, given Britain's comfortable place in the world:

> It is equally true that British business lacked a certain non-economic spur to enterprise; a nation which is already at the top politically and economically, and tends to look down on the rest of the world with self-satisfaction and little contempt inevitably does. Americans and Germans might dream of making their destiny manifest; the British knew that it had manifested itself already.

Two of the most influential relevant recent studies are Martin J. Weiner, *English Culture and the Decline of the Industrial Spirit* (1981) and W.D. Rubinstein, *Capitalism, Culture and Decline in Britain, 1750–1990* (1990). Weiner agrees with Hobsbawm that there was a failure of entrepreneurs. He, too, blames that failure on the social and mental structure of Victorian England. He argues that the English upper and middle classes were essentially hostile to industrialism; that they saw it as vulgar, rude, somehow beneath them. He also stresses the ease with which the industrial middle classes channelled their wealth and energy into apeing the aristocracy. The sons of money preferred hunting and shooting to book-keeping and wage-bargaining, and there was, we are led to believe, no drive, no zest, to find new ways of doing things. Public schools and the class system – wherein the nouveaux riches learned their snobberies – are really to blame in Weiner's thesis. What we must remember is that there are more conventional economic explanations for decline – or, rather, relative economic decline. More recently, Rubinstein has taken issue with the 'cultural critique. He says the critique goes thus:

> The most common view of modern British economic history may be put concisely, but not inaccurately, as follows: Britain was the first nation to experience an industrial revolution, which began around 1760, and, by 1850, had transformed Britain into the 'workshop of the world' …
> After Britain's short-lived zenith (1850–70) Britain experienced a relentless period of economic decline, now lasting for 120 years, wherein it not merely lost its industrial hegemony but was surpassed by virtually every other western nation.

Rubinstein stresses that there is plenty of evidence, both empirical and anecdotal, to suggest decline. But he refutes that it was 'cultural'; and he stresses that it was relative. The clearest evidence is actually economic, but Rubinstein does pay due reverence to some of the cultural factors. First, Britain had too much money riding on old technology – but new technology was expensive, unless, like Germany or the United States, industrialisation was at an early stage of development. Secondly, too much British investment went overseas. This created an investment gap at home. Thirdly, too many men of substance became *rentiers*; that is, they invested their gentlemanly capital and lived a nice life off the modest pickings of their investments. They weren't 'piratical entrepreneurs'; they didn't take risks any more. Fourthly, the British stuck to the family-firm ethos and avoided the corporate structure adopted overseas. Fifthly, the old boy network dominated, and, therefore, stifled British industrial management. British industry needed technocrats; what it got were pinstriped civil-service types.

One of Rubinstein's central planks is this: that we must not under-estimate the incredible extent to which the United States had become an economic superpower. In many respects, Britain was the second-placed player; although, in trade, and with her navies, she was the premier queen of the high seas. Where she fell back – in iron, coal, etc – she was placed third behind Germany and the United States. Several historians suggest that Britain was not finished as a major economic (even industrial) power in 1913, but that it was the First World War, not least in the related and necessary sale of stock, and the subsequent loss of invested wealth, that finished her. But even this perspective raises Rubinstein's ire as he points out that the inter-war period wasn't 'unrelievedly black'.

For Rubinstein: 'The most objectionable feature of the "cultural critique" – and, indeed, of many other lines of criticism of Britain's economic performance during the past generation – is its obsession with manufacturing industry, its manufacturing fetishism.' This is something raised by Cain and Hopkins (1993), in their suggestion of the import-ance of 'gentlemanly capitalism'. Rubinstein puts its more bluntly, though: 'There is nothing privileged or preferable about manufacturing industry as compared to the services: a pound is always a pound, a dollar is always a dollar.' He also adds that far from being anti-industrial, British society emphasised 'positivism and rationality to a remarkable degree'; that it had a culture 'based on reason and ratiocination which is fully congruent with its economic comparative advantage as an economic and financial power'.

Rubinstein, like Sidney Pollard (1988) before him, also takes issue with the claim that the British education system failed to produce people of the calibre of the Germans or Americans. He states that German technical education has been massively over-rated and that while there had been too much emphasis on the classics in British universities, this was being eroded by the 1920s. Like Pollard, he also stresses the development of technical education in Britain, a sector of training and skills which was unmatched elsewhere. However, whereas Britain was producing apprenticed tradesmen who went on to technical colleges for night-school classes, the Americans were producing technically adept graduates from within blue-collar ranks who went on to become industrial managers.

Moreover, decline in manufacturing industry was relative, and not absolute. Some businesses answered the problems they had by importing American managers to revamp their businesses on American lines. The service sector was crucial to the economic strength of late nineteenth-century Britain, for invisible earnings more than offset the deficit on trade. Thanks to her prominence in submarine telegraphy, Britain was also at the centre of the world's communications. Britain was still a leading economy. Her share of world trade had fallen, in particular due to American and German competition, but that trade was now far larger. Britain was the largest overseas investor in the world, and able, therefore, to benefit from economic growth elsewhere. Moreover, we must stress that the decline was only a decline in world share; it was not an absolute fall.

Britain was the greatest merchant shipper in the world: in 1890, Britain built 90 per cent of the world's ships; in 1914, the proportion was still 60 per cent. In addition, Britain was the centre of the world's financial system, and benefited from the expansion of the service sector. This was to remain very important throughout the twentieth century. Global commodity prices, shipping rates and insurance premiums were all set in London, the prime site of what Cain and Hopkins have dubbed 'gentlemanly capitalism'. Indeed, this emphasis on invisible power – the power of investment, money flow and trade – has led economic historians radically to reappraise the importance of Britain's industrial base. Industrial power was of course important, and it was up-front and prestigious. It was more tangible and more impressive to watch the *Aquitania*—all 40-odd thousand tons of her—slide into the purposely deepened and widened river at Clydebank in 1913, than the stock reports in the *Financial Times*. But Scottish-dominated business such as the Royal Niger Company, for example, which specialised in palm olive for soap manufacture, was worth far more in monetary terms than any ship built at home in Scotland.

Aside from her major and frequently leading role in the production of traditional goods, such as coal, textiles, steel, iron and ships, Britain was also playing an important part in the development of new sectors: in the growth of production in chemicals, and in new consumer goods, such as motor cars and telephones. The sheer scale of activity was impressive. The cotton industry was already well established, but, in addition, in 1900–9, 15 m spindles (35%) was added to the capacity of the industry. Founded in 1903, the Glasgow-based North British Locomotive Company was the largest private locomotive-builder in Europe. 1910 was the peak year for the number of collieries in South Wales: 688 in all. Despite pressure in particular sectors, Britain was doing well in the liberal international economic order, but that order was greatly challenged in the First World War.

Management, its quality and ambitions, is a controversial subject. It has been argued that this bears a large part of the responsibility for Britain's relative decline. Managers, of course, varied, but it has been claimed that, on the whole, they lacked the necessary calibre and vision, not least compared to their American and German counterparts. Instead, they have been seen as drawn from a narrow section of the community, poorly educated for their task, and complacent. For decades, many managers were gentlemen and amateurs, rather than being equipped with the necessary technical understanding to encourage, and respond to, innovation. This failing became more important as the pace of innovation increased and as British industry dropped behind. The maintenance of the economic status quo was not enough, and the failure of managers, bankers and trade unionists to appreciate this was serious. These attitudes became strongly entrenched throughout much (but by no means all) of industry in the second half of the nineteenth century, and they became normative (the norm that conditioned the response to new circumstances). As a consequence, the domestic economy performed poorly, encouraging British investment abroad.

The relative poorer performance of the domestic economy was exacerbated by the First World War (1914–18), but the war did not cause it. Difficulties before the war encouraged many economic interests to support protectionism and the development of the empire as a secure zone for British exports. This was not, as it turned out, an economic strategy that addressed the problems of productivity that handicapped the domestic economy. Politicians, union leaders and managers all failed to address the latter, especially over-manning and restrictive practices. Too little effort was devoted to raising the educational attainment of managers and workers, specifically the lack of sufficient vocational training, particularly apprenticeships. In industries such as coal mining, there was a failure to match the rate of technological and organisational change shown by foreign competitors. This can be attributed as much to a managerial failure to adopt, and invest in, technological innovation as to an unwillingness on the part of miners to respond to change. There was also a failure to restructure the industry by amalgamating the large number of mines, many of which were uneconomic.

Management failure has been linked to mistaken investment strategies, both within companies and more generally in the economy. It has been argued that the institutional providers of investment in the City of London, especially the banks, shared in a culture of complacency and gentlemanly amateurism. This has been traced to a series of inter-related cultural norms and practices, such as a suspicion of expertise and technical skills, that inhibited efficiency and encouraged false patterns of investment. Difficult to prove or quantify, such analyses suffer from an inability to demonstrate that the whole interpretative structure they give rise to can account for particular facets of the British economy.

More specifically, it has been suggested that there was a preference for investing in well-established companies, rather than in developing sectors. Risk or venture capital was thus insufficient and too expensive: interest rates were too high. Furthermore, aside from this pattern of industrial investment, there was also a preference for non-industrial investment, both on the 'money markets', for example in British and foreign government bonds, and in housing. Even when there was investment in industry – old or new – it has been argued that much of it was poorly directed, because of an absence of sufficient professionalism in information flows within the capital market. Furthermore, much British investment was short-term, responding to myopic institutional shareholders unwilling to commit sufficiently to long-term investments. In contrast, it has been suggested that American and German capital markets were more effective in providing large flows of investment income for technologically advanced industries, such as cars, chemicals and electrical engineering, before the First World War.

3.3 Conclusion

In his novel *Great Expectations* (1860–1), Charles Dickens describes Pip's journey down the Thames and its

> tiers of shipping. Here, were the Leith, Aberdeen and Glasgow steamers, loading and unloading goods ... here, were colliers by the score and score ... here ... was tomorrow's steamer for Rotterdam ... and here tomorrow's for Hamburg ... again among the tiers of shipping... hammers going in ship-builders' yards.

Later, in his poem *Cargoes* (1903), John Masefield was able to present the three ages of marine trade through a 'Quinquireme of Nineveh', a 'Stately Spanish galleon', and, lastly, a 'Dirty British coaster', carrying a cargo of British exports.

This was reality as well as image. It needs to be set alongside the late-Victorian sense of economic decline. There was indeed decline in particular spheres. For example, the British dominated the chemical industry at mid-century, but had then been surpassed by the United States and Germany, both of which made more effective use of new techniques, such as electro-chemical processes. By the last quarter of the century, there was a strong sense that Britain was falling behind. She no longer had important cost advantages in factors of production, especially labour and resources. Nevertheless, the British economy was still far stronger in absolute terms than it had been fifty years earlier and Britain was one of the leading three economies in the world and, in some spheres, the foremost. Modern British leaders would be happy to be in this situation.

Summary

- Britain experienced absolute growth but relative decline.
- National marketing became more important and contributed to a degree of consolidation in industry and retailing.
- The quality and ethos of management were a problem in many companies.

Points to discuss

- Was the British economy in decline?
- Why was so much investment directed abroad?
- What was the relationship between industry and trade?

■ References and further reading

D.H. Aldcroft (ed.), *The Development of British Industry and Foreign Competition, 1870–1914* (1968).

C.R. Byatt, *The British Electrical Industry, 1875–1914* (Oxford, 1979).

P. J. Cain and A. G. Hopkins, *British Imperialism: Innovation and Expansion 1688–1914* (1993).

P. J. Cain and A. G. Hopkins, *British Imperialism: Crisis and Destruction 1914–1990* (1993).

B. Collins and K. Robbins (eds), *British Culture and Economic Decline* (1970).

R. Church, *The Great Victorian Boom, 1850–1873* (1975).

C. H. Feinstein and S. Pollard (eds), *Studies in Capital Formulation in the United Kingdom, 1750–1920* (Oxford, 1988).

R.C. Floud, *The British Machine Tool Industry, 1850–1914* (Cambridge, 1976).

E. J. Hobsbawm, *Industry and Empire: The Birth of the Industrial Revolution* (1968).

D. McCloskey, *Enterprise and Trade in Victorian Britain* (1981).

D. McCloskey, *Economic Maturity and Industrial Decline: British Iron and Steel, 1870–1913* (Cambridge, Mass., 1973).

S. Pollard, *Britain's Prime and Britain's Decline: The British Economy, 1870–1914* (Cambridge, 1988).

W. D. Rubinstein, *Capitalism, Culture and Decline in Britain*, 1750–1990 (1990).

H. Scantlebury, 'The 1856 Royal Show at Chelmsford', *Essex Journal*, 35, 2 (Autumn 2001).

A. Shardwell, *Industrial Efficiency* (1906).

S. B. Saul, The Myth of the Great Depression, 1873–1896I (2nd edn, 1985).

K. Tiller, 'Hook Norton – an open village', *Cake and Cockhorse*, 15, 2 (2000).

M. J. Weiner, *English Culture and the Decline of the Industrial Spirit* (1981).

Transport and Communications

CHAPTER 4

Contents

Introduction

The key area of change was in *communications*. This was important not only for the end result but also as a process. A sense of continuous change characterised communications in this period and that powerfully contributed to a sense of a changing world. Not only did it have direct consequences on everything from settlement patterns (the creation and spread of suburbia) to agriculture (the growth of foreign competition), but changing communications also became a symbol of the age. This book deliberately devotes much space to the issue because it is important in its right, affected much else in Britain and joined centre and locality in a common process that can be charted with considerable precision.

Key issues

► What was the situation before rail?
► How did the rail system develop?
► What happened to other transport systems?
► What was the impact of rail on the economy?
► How did road transport develop towards the close of the period?

The transport revolution of the nineteenth century – the focus of this chapter – followed another in the eighteenth. This requires discussion here because it was important in its own right, dominated communications in Britain in the early decades of the nineteenth, and provided the background and competition for the rail revolution. The eighteenth-century revolution centred on canals and improved road transport. Canals were more important for economic development, but we shall begin with road transport because it came first, and because canals developed in large part owing to the deficiencies of the road system.

4.1 The Roads

The road system was very poor at the beginning of the eighteenth century. The techniques of road construction were deficient, maintenance was inadequate, and the road system both magnified the effects of distance and imposed high costs on economic exchange. The quality of the roads reflected the local terrain, in particular drainage and soil type, and the ability and determination of local communities to keep the road in good repair. The resistance of the road service, generally loose and rough, to bad weather or heavy use was limited, but frequent repair was expensive in terms of money and manpower. As a result of the Statute for Mending of Highways of 1555, each parish in England and Wales was responsible for the upkeep of roads, but the duty was generally not adequately carried out, certainly not to the standards required by heavy through traffic. Travellers complained about the number of pot-holes. Poorly constructed roads often enforced the use of light carts, or panniers on a horse or mule. Pack-horses were still very common in Britain's advancing areas, even in the 1800s, and the construction of good roads could offer a major increase in loads.

The roads were built by Turnpike Trusts, the first of which was authorised in 1663. They were allowed by Parliament to raise capital for such purposes and to charge travellers on the roads. Thus, as later with canals and railways, the road system came in part to reflect the degree of dynamism of individual companies (in this case trusts), and the ability of particular routes to produce revenue. This was a consequence essentially of the strength of the regional economy and the role of the route in intra-regional communications. Parliament oversaw the system through renewal and amendment Acts that reflected the strength of local interests.

Although trusts reflected local initiatives, a national turnpike system had been created by 1750, and in the 1750s and 1760s a major expansion of the system took place with leading provincial towns becoming the centre of local networks. By 1770, there were 15,000 miles of turnpike roads in England and most of the country was within 12.5 miles of one.

These roads proved the basis of a major improvement in the transport of people and goods. Carrying services improved. By 1783, there were 25 coach departures a week from Norwich to London, as well as two departures of stage wagons. By 1788, the Pickford family was sending a wagon from Manchester to London every day except Sunday. The *Birmingham Chronicle* of 9 January 1823 carried an item from the *Sheffield Independent* about a new coach service between the two cities.

However, the road system still had many deficiencies. It was not until the 1780s that John McAdam began experiments on improving road services, by consolidating a layer of small, broken hard stone to form a very hard surface with a camber for drainage, although McAdam did not publish his major works on the subject until 1819–20. Road accidents were frequent, particularly the overturning of coaches.

Nevertheless, road improvements were a major feature of the nineteenth century. Pioneers such as Metcalfe, McAdam and Thomas Telford developed new types of roads and did much to improve the resilience of road surfaces as well as expanding the network. Transport improvements played a major role in improving, and in many cases creating, economic integration and efficiency. Transport improvements did not only affect mining and heavy industry. Instead, they produced a higher-tempo economy everywhere. For example, in the *Taunton Courier* of 23 January 1828, there was an advertisement for a tri-weekly coach service from Tauton to Bath, connecting there for London. The paper commented:

> As we ourselves have experienced the advantages of the improved communication which has been effected between London and this town and neighbourhood … we feel much pleasure in calling the attention of our readers to the advertisement in this day's paper. A regular and cheap communication to the markets of the metropolis being equally important to the manufacturer and agriculturist, for the disposal of their produce, as it is to the tradesman and shopkeeper, for the purchase of their stock, we trust and feel confident, that the public will support an undertaking which has been begun and is now carried on with so much spirit!

4.2 Canals

The difficulties and cost of road transport helped to ensure that much was moved by sea or river. Water was favourable for the movement of heavy or bulky goods, for which road transport was inadequate and expensive. It cost 33s 4d (£1.67 in modern currency, but probably three times the then average weekly wage) a ton to move goods by road from London to Reading in 1792, but only 10s (50 pence) by water.

However, the river system was not always helpful. Many rivers were not navigable, transport was often only easy downstream, rivers did not always supply the necessary links, and many were obstructed by mills and weirs. The canalisation of rivers and the construction of canals was the response to problems with the river system. It represented a determined human attempt to alter the environment and to make it operate for the benefit of man. As with the turnpikes and again unlike elsewhere in Europe, private enterprise and finance were crucial. If the development of such a costly and inflexible transport system faced numerous problems, it also increased the comparative economic advantage of particular regions or interests within them and was therefore actively supported. Landlocked countries found their relative position transformed. Canal-building was especially active in the 1770s and 1790s.

Demand for coal helped to drive the growth of the canal system. The Sankey Brook Navigation of 1755 carried coal from St Helens to Liverpool, and stimulated both the development of coal-consuming industries on Merseyside and the expansion of Cheshire's salt industry which depended on coal-fired salt pans. James Brindley planned the canal by which, from 1761, Francis, 3rd Duke of Bridgewater moved coal from his Worsley mines to nearby Manchester. By 1792 freight traffic on the canal was worth £80,000 a year.

Bridgewater's role is an instance of the co-operation between the landed order and commerce, as was that of Sir Roger Newdigate in Warwickshire. He sought to link the coal mines developed by his father to Coventry by canal, and also actively promoted the Oxford Canal and the Coventry to Leicester turnpike road. Similarly, Thomas Anson supported Brindley, the great canal engineer, and one of his canals bordered his estate at Shugborough Park. The building of the Staffordshire and Worcestershire Canal between 1766 and 1770 enabled the movement of Staffordshire coal and iron to the Severn, and thence to the sea. The new town of Stourport was built at the junction of the canal and the Severn. The first coal barge arrived in Birmingham on the new Birmingham canal in 1772. The Trent and Mersey Canal, known as the Grand Trunk, and Brindley's most important canal, was completed three years later. The Coventry Canal brought coal to Coventry from the 1780s, and the opening of the Monkland Canal in 1793 stimulated the development of the Lanarkshire coalfield in order to serve the rapidly growing Glasgow market. Delayed, in part, by the need to build many locks, the Birmingham to Worcester Canal was finished in 1815.

Canals were not separate to the process of industrial change, but integral to it. The location of new mine shafts, factories and wharves responded to the possibilities of canal transport. When the Britannia Foundry was established in Derby in 1818, to produce quality cast-iron products, it was sited on the banks of the River Derwent, and linked, via that and the Derby Canal, to the Midlands' canal system and the sea. *Smart's Trade Directory* for 1827 noted that from Pickfords' canal wharf in Wolverhampton, a leading centre for the manufacture of iron products, goods could be sent direct to 73 towns including Bristol, Liverpool, London and Manchester.

Canals made it easier to transport bulk goods, although only on a wharf-to-wharf basis. Unless the water froze, canals had a particular advantage over roads in the winter, as many of the latter were then impassable. This was especially true of routes across the Midland clays. Canals were also more predictable than coastal shipping. Today canals are noted for leisure activities; it is a little difficult to visualise the major changes that they brought. There was a new geography, as landlocked counties, such as Derbyshire and Staffordshire, found their relative position transformed. Totally new links were created. Isolation was lessened. This was not only true of industrial and mining areas. The opening of the canal between Aberdeen and Inverurie in 1805, for example, made it easier for the Leith Hall estate to sell and deliver goods.

It is appropriate that the eighteenth century is known for canals, as the nineteenth is for railways, and the twentieth for roads. Each transport system was the product of the socio-political systems of the age and were central to economic transformation and to shifts in attitude. Each also led to geographical change, as new nodes emerged, although, unlike rail and road, canal was crucial to freight, but not passenger traffic. The centre of passenger traffic, London, was not central to the canal system. Instead, thanks to the mutually stimulating interaction of canals and their industries, the West Midlands, South Lancashire and South Yorkshire became more important to communications within the country.

Canals, however, were expensive and faced problems, not least preventing leaks and securing an adequate water supply. Owing to financial problems, the 38-mile Forth–Clyde Canal, which had 39 locks, was begun in 1768, but not finished until 1790. Most goods and people in the British Isles continued to move by road. The canal network was sparse, somewhat fragmented and especially limited in Scotland, Wales and Ireland. Nevertheless, the Lagan Navigation, the Tyrone Navigation and the Strabane Canal were all completed in Ulster by 1796, while the Grand (1756–1805) and Royal (1789–1817) Canals linked Dublin to the Irish midlands.

4.3 Coastal trade

Coastal trade remained more important than is generally appreciated. Thus, Bristol received copper for smelting from Anglesey and Cornwall, China clay from Cornwall, and iron, coal and naval timber from the Forest of Dean. More generally, the Irish Sea formed an economic zone held together by marine links based on major ports, such as Bristol, Belfast, Dublin, Lancaster and Liverpool, as well as now-forgotten or tiny ports, such as Parkgate in the Wirral, for long the major port for passenger traffic en route to and from Dublin (its role was to be taken by Holyhead once road and rail links to Angelesey had been improved). Thanks to sea transport, Ireland's fuel shortage was met by coal from Cumbria and, to a lesser extent, Ayrshire. The east coast of England was also an important coal route: from Newcastle to London and intermediate ports, such as King's Lynn and Great Yarmouth. They offered transhipment on to river systems.

There was scant improvement in the condition of marine transport. It still remained heavily dependent on the weather. The seasonal variation of insurance rates reflected the vulnerability of wind-powered wooden ships, which had not yet reached their mid-nineteenth-century levels of design efficiency. Sea travel was very slow compared with what it was to become in the age of steam. However, it was the cheapest method for the movement of goods, and sea brought together regions, such as south-western Scotland and eastern Ireland, whose road links to their own hinterlands were poor. Inland towns might be most accessible via their nearest ports rather than by long-distance overland routes. A widespread improvement in docks and harbour facilities benefited domestic as well as international trade. Mineral owners developed ports such as Maryport and Whitehaven in Cumbria to ship coal. Similarly, ports were developed or improved in North Wales to ship slate: nearly 250 cargoes alone from Caernarfon in 1793.

4.4 Before steam

Turnpikes and canals were clearly of considerable importance in shrinking distance and developing intra-regional links. New and improved transport links required large amounts of capital and led to increased employment. Transport costs were reduced, thus helping to increase and extend consumption and markets. The increased speed and frequency of deliveries also improved the integration of production and consumption, and furthered the development of the market; it became easier to dispatch salesmen, samples, catalogues, orders and replacements.

Transport links helped to provide comparative advantages: the British iron, pottery and textile industries benefited from cheaper transport costs and more reliable links than their French counterparts. Regional specialisation increased, because regions that could produce goods cheaply were now better able to compete in areas with higher-cost local production. This was crucial to economic development, because division of labour was effective only with a high volume of production, and thus with a large market.

Yet, it is important to place changes in the 'pre-steam' period in perspective. Road construction usually followed existing routes, and the balance between land and sea transport did not alter significantly. Much of the dense network of local routes changed little in quality, direction and type of use, although levels of use increased with greater economic activity. Exciting technical developments, such as iron railways along which horses could pull wagons, or the hot-air balloons of the 1780s, had scant immediate effect. In the 1730s, the first railway bridge in the world, Causey Arch, was built for the movement of Durham coal towards the Tyne. It had the largest span of any bridge built in Britain since Roman times, and the architect had to work from Roman models. However, it was not until the application of steam power that such railways could develop into anything other than feeders to existing water links and, in particular, become a long-distance network of their own.

A quantum leap beyond the legacy of turnpikes and canals was necessary for major economic advance. Yet, it would be mistaken to imagine that the transport system was stagnant prior to the application of steam to communications. It is true that the canal system did not expand greatly after the 1790s, although there was still fresh construction. For example, the Lancaster Canal linked Kendal to Preston in 1819, and the Caledonian Canal was constructed in 1822. Canal-building continued to involve major feats of engineering and encouraged a sense that there were solutions to every problem. Telford's cast-iron aqueduct at Pontcysyllte, built in 1805, carried the Ellesmere Canal over the Dee at 127 feet. Nevertheless, most feasible opportunities that had been perceived had already been exploited.

Instead, it was land transport that improved most in the early nineteenth century. A series of often quite small-scale improvements greatly improved the system. Thus, in Devon, the Honiton and Ilminster Turnpike Trust constructed a new road from Yarde to near Ilminster in 1807–12 and the Cullompton Turnpike Trust another from near Broadclyst to near Cullompton in 1813–16. There was also a process of improvement to existing routes. In the 1820s and early 1830s the worst routes of the Exeter Turnpike Trust were replaced. These led to smoother and more level roads, and thus to an ability to pull heavier loads. There were important improvements in many regions before the steam railway reached them. Non-suspension bridges had been opened over the estuaries of the Teign and the Plym in 1827, opening up much of South Devon to road traffic; the former was then the longest in Britain. The widening of Devon roads in the 1820s also helped in the replacement of packhorses by wheeled traffic. Steam and chain floating bridges followed at Dartmouth, Saltash and Torpoint. Such improvements served to integrate regions into the national economy, and to create demand for further such development. Journey times and, thus, costs fell. R.W. Newman, an Exeter MP of the 1820s, told a House of Commons Select Committee that 'since the roads have been improved ... a very large amount of the economy of the county is daily sent from Devon to the Metropolis [London]'. That decade, the turnpike through the Snake pass from Glossop to Sheffield helped open up the Northern Peak District. By then, London mail coaches could reach Manchester in one day. More generally, many roads were improved by resurfacing. In Cheshire, the Wirral did not get most of its turnpike roads until after 1820, although other parts of the county were better served early on. Coastal shipping also improved. Steamships were introduced to carry passengers in the Thames estuary in 1815.

More generally, road transport of freight had improved thanks to the introduction in the 1760s of fly wagons. Thanks to changing teams of horses, these could travel day and night, covering 40 miles every 24 hours.

There was also some important bridge-building which did much to improve the efficiency of the road system. In London, Westminster bridge in 1750 was followed by new bridges across the Thames at Blackfriars (1769), Vauxhall (1816), Waterloo (1817) and Southwark (1819). The iron Wear bridge, built by Rowland Burdon in 1796, was the new lowest crossing-point on the river and the first bridge in Sunderland. It was crucial to the development of the town and was regarded as a great achievement of the age. Sunderland also acquired docks 1837 and, more substantially, 1850. The construction of specialised docking facilities and the associated infrastructure was part of the process by which in Victorian Britain acitivities were organised and regularised and their efficiency increased and regimented by means of permanent facilities.

4.5 The railway

The British led the way with the technology and practice of rail traffic. Wagonways had existed for many years, with horses drawing wagons along rails, especially from the collieries to the coal-loading staithes on the Tyne and Wear, but also elsewhere. Other products, such as stone, were also carried. The Surrey Iron Railway Company, the world's first railway company and public railway, operated between Wandsworth and Croydon from 1803. Self-propelled steam locomotives changed the situation, not least by making long-distance movement possible. In 1804, Roger Hopkins built a tramroad between Pen-y-darren and Abercynon in South Wales upon which Richard Trevithick tried the first steam railway locomotive engine, essentially a mobile beam engine.

Locomotive technology achieved a breakthrough in the 1820s. The development of the locomotive from the stationary steam-engine provided the technology for the rail revolution, and industrialisation supplied the necessary demand, capital and skills. George Stephenson opened the Hetton Railway in 1822. The more famous Stockton and Darlington Railway followed in 1825, opened with a ceremonial journey from Witton Park colliery to Stockton; the Manchester and Liverpool Railway in 1830. Economic considerations were foremost. Thomas Meyneel, a wealthy merchant who was a leading promoter of the Stockton and Darlington Railway, had argued that a railway was preferable to a proposed canal, as it was likely to yield a better return. The 40-mile long line was designed to transport coal from the coalfields near Bishop Auckland to the port of Stockton. The Stockton and Darlington was extended to Middlesbrough in 1830 and a suspension bridge took the line across the Tees.

When Goldsworthy Gurney's steam-jet (or blast) was applied to Stephenson's *Rocket* locomotive in 1829 speeds rose from 16 to 29 miles an hour. *Rocket* won the Liverpool and Manchester Railway's locomotive trials at Rainhill. Direct drive from the cylinders and pistons to the wheels increased efficiency, as did an engine design that boiled water more rapidly. The development of wrought-iron rails in the 1820s and 1830s was also very important. The Union Chain Bridge, opened over the Tweed near Berwick in 1820 for the Berwick and North Durham Turnpike Trust, was the first British suspension bridge able to carry loaded carriages. Turnpike roads focused on new crossing places, such as the suspension bridge across the Tees at Whorlton opened in 1831.

The Conwy Suspension Bridge, built by Thomas Telford (1757–1834) and completed in 1826, replaced the ferry that had previously been the sole way to cross the river. It was part of an improvement to road transport that helped open up North Wales, ensuring that Holyhead became a more important port for Dublin. In the same region, bridges also replaced ferries at Porthaethwy (1826), Beaumaris (1830), and Abermenai (1840s). There were also improvements to open up the slate mining district, especially in the 1820s. In the early 1840s, a regular coach service was established from Caernarfon to Harlech. Telford was also responsible for the construction or improvement of 1,200 miles of road in the Scottish Highlands. The poet Southey called him 'the colossus of roads'.

The cause of suspension bridges was put back in 1830 when the newly completed one over the South Esk at Montrose partially collapsed, when 700 spectators rushed from one side to another during a boat race. As a result, the proposal to build a suspension bridge across the Tamar was abandoned. Nevertheless, suspension bridges were still built. The design submitted in 1831 by Isambard Kingdom Brunel (1806–59) for a suspension bridge over the Avon at Clifton below Bristol was accepted as the most mathematically exact of those tendered. Brunel was appointed engineer and the works were begun in 1836, but unfinished in his lifetime owing to a lack of funds. The bridge was eventually completed according to Brunel's plans, and using chains removed from the Hungerford suspension bridge which he had constructed over the Thames in 1841–5.

Railways offered new links and cut journey times for both freight and passengers. Initially, the railways were mostly small-scale, independent concerns providing local links. The movement of coal was crucial. The first public railway in the Midlands, the Leicester and Swannington Railway of 1830, was designed to move coal to the expanding Leicester market and to undercut canal-borne supplies from Nottingham and Derby. The company paid an 8% dividend in 1839. Other lines, such as the 1838 Carlisle–Newcastle line, were important for more than local reasons. Glasgow and Edinburgh were linked by rail in 1841.

With time, bolder trunk schemes were advanced and financed, and, in addition, already existing lines were linked to create long-distance networks. Services from London reached Birmingham in 1838, Southampton in 1840, Bristol and Brighton in 1841, Oxford in 1844, Norwich in 1845, Portsmouth and Plymouth in 1847, and Banbury and Holyhead in 1850. A formidable amount was invested in building the rail system. The London to Brighton line, including the spur to Shoreham, alone cost £2,569,359. Rivers were bridged, and the Menai Straits in 1849. Tunnels were blasted through hills: the Kilsby tunnel (1834–38) between London and Birmingham, and the Woodhead tunnel (1839–52) between Manchester and Sheffield. The Railway Clearing House created in 1842 established standard rates and apportioned through revenues. Three years earlier, Thomas Edmondson developed what was to become the standardised type of ticket.

Canals and coastal shipping now faced significant competition, especially as the rail companies developed processes and policies to handle through freight movements. When it came to carrying bulk items before the steam age, water-borne transport systems had been vital. In 1800 London received more than one million chaldrons (25.5 cwt per chaldron) of coal by sea, principally from collier boats sailing from Newcastle. Even in the 1850s, when the rail network was becoming well established, sea-borne coal was far more important to the capital than that brought across land: in 1855, for example, when tons were used as measurement, it was 3m as against 1.2m. Only in 1869 was coal brought by sea matched by that moved by rail. Yet, in 1879, although 6.6 m tons was transported to

London by rail, some 3.5m still entered the Thames by vessel. The victory of the railways was thus hard-fought and occurred over a long period. Improvements to the infrastructure for sea-borne trade continued, with new facilities and improved lighthouses. The fourth Eddystone lighthouse, for example, was built between 1878 and 1882 and cost £59,250 – a sum that indicated the expense of such undertakings.

Unlike canals, rail was quicker than its competitors. The mass canal-building craze stopped in the 1830s, although specialist projects such as the Manchester Ship Canal (1894) were put into place much later. In general terms, canals would be eclipsed by rail, and, in an effort to meet the competition, canal companies drastically cut tolls in 1840. The use of steam tugs, instead of horses, speeded up canal transport. Nevertheless, rail was more flexible, and, in some cases, railways directly replaced canals. The opening of the Buckinghamshire Railway in Oxford in 1851 brought severe competition to the Oxford Canal Company, and, in the year ending 1 October 1853, the canal carried 24,079 tons of coal to Oxford against the railway's transportation of 51,608 tons. In Plym Bridge Woods the railway was built on the canal towpath, to bring stone and peat from Dartmoor to Plymouth. The canal from Carlisle to Port Carlisle closed in 1853 and was converted into the Port Carlisle Railway. The Kennet and Avon Canal sold out to the Great Western Railway. The railway also hit river traffic. The opening of the railway to Barmouth in 1867 wrecked the lighterage carriage up-river to Dolgellau: 167 ships entered and left the port in 1866, but only eleven in 1876.

Major bridges, such as the Britannia Tubular Bridge across the Menai Straits and the bridges across the Tay (1877) and Forth (1890), and tunnels, such as that under the Severn (1886), dramatically hit ferry traffic. This was a major change in the geography of the country. With ferries, major routes had been exposed to the impact of wind and tide, and this remained the case even when steam replaced sail. Railways, in contrast, were all-weather, an ability celebrated on canvas by J.M. Turner. The bridges that took them across the Dee and the Tamar, the Solway Firth and the Tay, and other rivers and estuaries dramatically altered both local and national geography.

The process was not without serious problems. The Tay bridge completed in 1877 was a triumph of Victorian technology, specifically iron-working. Nearly two miles long and consisting of 85 wrought-iron lattice-girder spans resting on cast-iron columns, it was designed by Thomas Bouch, and he was knighted by Queen Victoria when she crossed it in the summer of 1879. However, on 28 December 1879, 74 people died when part of the bridge collapsed during a storm as a train was crossing. The resulting inquiry highlighted problems in design, construction and maintenance, for which much of the blame was allocated to Bouch. This is a reminder both of the problems that were an aspect of Victorian engineering achievements, and yet also of their ability to learn from mistakes. This was necessary, as they were at the forefront of new techniques. The replacement Tay bridge (1887) was better built and steel was employed for the Forth bridge.

A related problem was that of aligning technology with practical considerations, not least profitability. This was true of Brunel's work on the Great Western Railway and also of his massive steamships, the *Great Western* (1837), *Great Britain* (1843) and *Great Eastern* (1858), the last the largest ship built before the twentieth century.

The new rail links that were created had a major impact on the economy. The volume of freight carried rose from about 38 m tons in 1850 to 513 m in 1912. Much continued to focus on coal, a crucial source of investment income. The Taff Vale line between Cardiff and Merthyr Tydfil was opened in 1841 and, in conjunction with the development of the port of Cardiff, this permitted a major increase in the export of coal from South Wales. Other products and industries were also greatly affected. Use of the railway from the 1840s enabled the brewers of Burton-upon-Trent to develop a major beer empire, and also helped speed North Wales slates towards urban markets. The Ffestiniog Railway of 1836 linked the slate mines with Porthmadog harbour, and the rail network in the area improved from 1867. The press also took major advantage of the rail system: London newspapers could be transported rapidly round the country. In the 1870s, the railway companies opened up urban markets for liquid milk, encouraging dairy farmers to produce 'railway milk', rather than farmhouse cheese. Many of the 6 million visitors to the Great Exhibition in 1851 came on rail excursions. Horse-race meetings, such as those at York and Stockton, benefited from 'specials' and came to enjoy a national or regional following. Gladstone used the railways to campaign nationally in the 1870s and 1880s, Queen Victoria and the royal family used the railways to visit Balmoral and to see more of Britain than their predecessors. No eighteenth-century monarch had visited Scotland and George IV (r.1820–30) went there only once. Victoria, however, was able to go there frequently.

The impact of rail was also psychological. 'Space' had been conquered, time cut. Attitudes to, and perceptions of, distance were transformed. The horse ceased to define the possibilities of land travel. The journey time from London to Holyhead was cut to 9 hours 35 minutes compared to 40 hours by rail coach; speeds unknown to human nature became not only possible but common. New sounds and sights contributed to a powerful sense of change, and this was overwhelmingly seen as progress. Railway stations, such as Sir Gilbert Scott and W.H. Barlow's St Pancras (1873), Thomas Prosser's York, Queen Street (1877), and Isambard Kingdom Brunel's Paddington, were designed as master-pieces of iron and glass, and many, such as John Dobson's Newcastle Central (1846), were planned with bold, often classical, facades. Trains were also celebrated in art with paintings such as William Frith's *The Railway Station* (1862). So also were the impressive engineering feats that took railways across viaducts and through mountains, for example, in John Wilson Carmichael's *Early Viaduct, the Newcastle and Carlisle Railway* (1836). Musical scores that sought to mimic the rhythms of steam locomotion were produced, and train travel left its mark on popular song as with 'Oh, Mr Porter', a song greatly popularised on the music halls by Marie Lloyd, the chorus of which ran:

> Oh! Mr. Porter, what shall I do?
> I want to go to Birmingham
> And they're taking me on to Crewe,
> Send me back to London as quickly as you can,
> Oh! Mr. Porter, what a silly girl I am!

The railway also left its mark in the world of children's games and toys. In cultural as well as economic terms, then, this was 'the age of steam'.

The opening of new links and facilities and attendant celebrations provided plenty of copy for the press. The general attitude was that of praise for new developments, and a sense of opportunities, tempered by criticism of schemes deemed inappropriate. The *St James's Chronicle* of 30 March 1847 provided a lengthy report on the completion of the rail link between London and Paris and discussed the impact of rail travel on the human body; the issue of 26 October 1847 provided details of the opening of the Gloucester and

Cheltenham Railway. The *Staffordshire Advertiser* of 14 October 1848 reported the open-ing of the Crewe branch of the North Staffordshire Railway 'which will give the district an outlet to Liverpool, Chester and Holyhead as well as … Manchester and the north'.

Trains swiftly came to play a role in fiction, killing the villain Carter in Dickens' *Dombey and Son* (1846–8). This matched the reality of numerous deaths in accidents, most famously the politician William Huskisson during the 1830 trials on the Liverpool and Manchester. Huskisson is widely accepted as the first man to be killed by a train. In addition, numerous rail workers died in construction and maintenance accidents. This was part of the harsh cost of economic change, while the world of railway work with its labour discipline, quasi-military uniforms (thus enforcing corporate identity) and well-regimented hierarchy and command system reflected a labour process and organisation ethos that was very different to traditional ones. The railways, in more than one respect, were ultra-modern in the 1840s or 1850s. The railway's system of work was designed so that employees would respond rapidly and predictably to orders.

The railway was seen as better than the canal, not just another form of transport. It helped bring uniformity. Time within Britain was standardised, and the station clock became an authoritative symbol and means of precision. The railways needed standard time for their timetables, and, in place of the variations of time from east to west in Britain, adopted the time set by the Greenwich Observatory as railway time. Clocks were kept in time by the electric telegraph that was erected along lines. News and fashions sped round the country. A travelling post office ran between Birmingham and Warrington from 1838 and a system to pick up and drop off the mail at stations without braking was speedily introduced. In 1840, the Penny Black, the world's first postage stamp, was released as part of a system that set a uniform postal rate based on weight in place of a postal tariff system based on distance. In 1848, the first of what was to be the network of W.H. Smith railway bookstalls was opened at Euston Station. Libraries of books created to be read on trains were sold at such bookstalls. W.H. Smith made a fortune and embarked on a political career that was satirised in Gilbert and Sullivan's *HMS Pinafore* (1878) with its account of a First Lord of the Admiralty who did not like to go to sea. In fact he was competent and popular, and when he died in 1891 both First Lord of the Treasury and the Leader of the Commons.

Commuting developed, and London and other major cities spread: the railway helped to create suburbs and suburban environments. Rail services from London Bridge reached Deptford in 1836 and Greenwich in 1838. The London to Croydon line opened in 1839, followed by lines to Margate in 1846, and to Southend in 1856. The spread of suburbia inspired the Commons Preservation Society, founded in 1865, and a campaigning base of figures who were instrumental in the foundation of the National Trust in 1893–5, especially Octavia Hill and Robert Hunter. In 1875, Hill failed in a campaign to save Swiss Cottage Fields from development.

The shape of towns was changed as lines both joined and bisected. There was much demolition work to be undertaken in order to build lines, for example in Birmingham. Urban street patterns focused on railway stations, and commercial patterns changed. Pubs were built near stations, as was the case with the Crown Liquor Saloon in Belfast, origin-ally the Railway Tavern across the street from the terminus of the Great Northern Railway. The impact of the train can be seen in numerous pub names, especially the Locomotive, The Station or premises named after particular engines, for example The Rocket. In its process of transformation, the railway also brought much destruction. Construction destroyed or damaged many of the most prominent sites of the past, including Berwick and Newcastle castles and Launceston Priory. The geography and townscape of London was changed by the train. In 1862, Gladstone joined the directors of the Metropolitan Railway on the first run over the full length of their underground railway in London.

The impact of the railway was local as well as national. Sunderland was reached by the Durham and Sunderland Railway in 1836, the Newcastle and Darlington Junction Railway in 1852, and the Londonderry Railway in 1854. On the northern bank of the Wear, branches of the Brandling Junction Railway reached Wearmouth and North Dock in 1839. The same railway reached Gateshead in 1839, a year after the Newcastle and Carlisle. Railways competed. The Clarence Railway offered a shorter route for West Durham coal to the coast than the Stockton and Darlington, and was, in turn, likewise challenged by the Great North of England, Clarence and Hartlepool Junction Railway. The West Durham Railway was laid from Crook to Byers Green to compete with the Clarence line. The speculative schemes of George Hudson, the 'Railway King', whose frauds caused the financial crisis that hit the railways in 1849, were important in the development of rail routes in the region. The large number of companies led not only to competition, but also to different services supplementing each other, as at Carlisle where seven railway companies operated. This availability furthered the general use of the rail system.

Both locally and nationally, railways also contributed to industrialisation. Demand for ironwork grew. It encouraged the industrialisation of Gateshead, with the major growth of Hawks' ironworks, so that it employed over 1,000 workers by 1841, and also the opening of locomotive works in 1839 and 1852. On the Newcastle side of the Tyne, locomotives were made at Forth Banks. Train works and employment for the railway were very important in a number of other towns, such as Brighton, Carlisle, Crewe, Darlington, Derby, Horwich, Shildon, Stratford (London), and Wolverton. Existing ironworks also began to produce for the railway. The Gaunless Bridge in York was the first example of an iron railway bridge. The Britannia Foundry at Derby came to make railway bridges and turntables, carriage wheels, locomotive tenders and steam engine castings. The Foundry was linked by sidings to the Great Northern Railway, and another site for the Foundry linked to the Midland Railway system was built.

For reasons of topography and economics, other areas had less rapid development. This was especially true of agricultural and upland areas. The former initially seemed to offer only limited traffic, while the latter also posed the problems of gradients. Predominantly rural Suffolk was slow to acquire rail links. The railway reached Ipswich and Bury St Edmunds only in 1846, and Newmarket in 1848. In 1852, there was still no link between London and Cornwall, and there was none between London and Aberystwyth until 1864.

A national network was not really in place until mid-century, but, by 1845, it was possible to travel via the Newcastle and Carlisle and Maryport and Carlisle Railways from the North to the Irish Sea. There were about 4,600 miles of track by 1848, but the main-line system was not completed until the early 1870s, and many local and branch lines were built thereafter. Across the Pennines, the original cross-country Carlisle–Newcastle link of 1838 was not supplemented until the line from Durham to Barrow-in-Furness in 1861 and the Carlisle-Settle line of 1876. The first took Furness iron east and Durham coke west, helping the iron and steel industry on both sides of the Pennines.

The new national network was very important in integrating Scotland and England. Earlier road and shipping links had been significant, but the two competing rail links on either sides of the Pennines, via Newcastle and Carlisle, dramatically cut travel time, and improved the predictability and regularity, as well as the speed, of the transport of both passengers and freight. The impact of such a development can be charted in terms of line-opening and travel times, but it is as appropriate to consider the psychological consequences. Britain became the unit as far as rail traffic was concerned. Edinburgh and Glasgow were now closer to London, an extension of a network for which York and Manchester were merely stages.

In addition to new lines, existing ones were improved, and the railway system as a whole became more durable and effective in meeting both freight and passenger needs. Wooden bridges were replaced by iron, as on the North Midland Railway at Belper. New stations were built. The first in the Wolverhampton area, opened in 1837, was at Wednesfield Heath, because the line did not come into the town centre; passengers had to take a cab. This changed in 1852, when the London and North Western Railway opened the High Level Station, followed in 1854 by the Great Western Railway's Low Level Station.

There were important improvements in the quality of rail transport. Early rails were not strong enough for heavy steam locomotives, but by 1820 wrought-iron rails, that were less brittle than cast iron, were being rolled successfully. The far more resilient steel rails were introduced from 1857, creating a permanent way that could bear heavy weights. This made it possible to invest in more powerful locomotives that were able to pull heavier loads. As a result, more freight or passengers could be carried on individual trains, thus raising the efficiency and capability of the system. These improvements are a reminder of the need, when considering technology, not to focus solely on the original breakthroughs, the 'heroic' stage, but, instead, to consider the extent and impact of subsequent changes, many of which are far more obscure. These changes were driven forward by the productive synergy of the Victorian economy, specifically the availability of fresh investment capital and the determination to seek and apply technological advances. The net result was more activity and employment. By 1873, there were 274,000 rail-workers. The joint-stock companies created to finance railway construction were larger than any hitherto.

In areas with limited rail penetration, such as Cumbria or North-West Devon, scheduled country carriers remained very important. In many respects, their business supplemented the rail system, providing cartage focused on railheads. The railway encouraged the development of feeder carriage and cart services. Even so, rail links spread. The Eden Valley Railway (1862), the Cockermouth, Keswick and Penrith Railway (1864–5), and the Cleator and Workington Junction Railway (1880), all aided the development of the West Cumberland iron industry. Railways were also planned into the Lake District, to further quarrying in Borrowdale and into Ennerdale and Ullswater. William Morris complained, 'You will soon have a Cook's tourist railway up Scawfell – and another up Helvellyn – and another up Skiddaw. And then a connecting line, all round', this being a reference to the expanding activity of the first national travel agent, the Quaker Thomas Cook. This was overly pessimistic. A public campaign, launched by Hardwicke Rawnsley, one of the founders of the National Trust, and backed by the Commons Preservation Society, blocked the Borrowdale, Ennerdale and Ullswater plans.

Elsewhere, the arrival of the train led to the decay of existing routes and of related facilities. Food for horses had been a major cost of wagon and carriage services. Coal for trains was less expensive. Transport networks changed. Crawley had been an important town on the London to Brighton coaching route, but the train, instead, went via Three Bridges. The coaching town of Honiton was hit by the opening of a different rail route to Exeter via Taunton, only, in turn, to benefit when a new line from London via Honiton was opened in 1860. Some turnpikes were bankrupted, for example, in Dorset, the Wimborne to Piddletown by the Southampton and Dorchester Railway. The last Turnpike Act for Berkshire's roads was obtained in 1832, and by 1900 all the county's Turnpike Trusts had been wound up.

At sea, steamships put pressure on less expensive, but less reliable and slower sailing ships, and harbours were built or improved to benefit from steamships; Porthmadog harbour being opened in 1824 to export slates from North Wales. But for the railway, more freight within Britain would have gone by steamships. Instead, they were linked to railways at ports, such as Hartlepool, Lowestoft and Penarth, and the two developed together. In 1882, the Great Eastern Railway introduced a through train from the north of England to the newly opened Parkeston Quay at Harwich. This was an example of the way in which the train created new routes. Coastal shipping, however, remained important for some carriage.

Rail travel reflected a social system stratified by wealth. There were three classes, with different conditions and fares. On the London to Brighton line, the 3rd class carriages lacked roofs until 1852, and were thus exposed to the weather and the hot ash from the engine. Return fares on the line in 1845 were 21 shillings (£1.10p) 1st class, 9 shillings (45p) 2nd, and 5 shillings (25p) 3rd. Brighton developed as a popular resort thanks to the train. So also did other coastal towns. The timing of development was often linked directly to the train, as at Littlehampton in 1863.

This was true of commuting as well as holiday resorts. The building of a direct route from London to Southend via Upminster avoiding the Tilbury detour, opened in 1888, cut the express journey time from 95 to 50 minutes, and was followed by an alternative route via Shenfield opened in 1889. Commuting from Southend rose rapidly. The same process could be seen with other cities. Thus, the opening of a line from the coast to Newcastle led to the development of towns such as Whitley Bay. Some resorts sought to preserve the tone by keeping the railways out. This was true, for example, of the Devon coastal resort of Sidmouth. When such resorts finally had to accept the train, they ensured that the station was some way inland in order to deter day-trippers.

The rail system continued to spread into the following century. By the early 1900s, all except 5 per cent of British rail passengers were travelling third class; an affordable system of rapid, mass transport had been created. The last main line to London – the Great Central – ran through to London only in 1899. Branch lines linked the network to towns that it had passed. In Berkshire, branches were built to Faringdon (1864), Abingdon (1873), Wantage (1875), Wallingford (1886) and Lambourn (1898).The line that killed river traffic on the Tamar on the Cornwall–Devon border was opened in 1859. Light railways in Essex to Tollesbury and Thaxted were opened in 1907 and 1913. However, most of these later lines were never very profitable, the Grand Central being a case in point. By 1914, the system was very largely complete with about 21,000 miles of track in Britain. Subsequent expansion was to be minor, and was to be greatly outweighed by contraction. The system served society in ways that had not been imagined when the *Rocket* won its trials.

4.6 Car and aircraft

In 1887, Britain was still adjusting to an expanding rail system, and the bicycle craze had begun in 1885. By 1918, the internal-combustion engine had brought lorries and tanks, as well as buses and the motor car; there were also electric trams, submarines, aircraft and airships. There were 132,000 private car registrations by 1914. What had been on the drawing board in 1887 had become commonplace. Distance had changed. 'Britain is no longer an island' reflected the press baron Lord Northcliffe as the American Wright Brothers achieved the first successful powered flight in 1903 and Blériot flew across the Channel in 1909. In January 1904, Leo Amery emphasised the onward rush of technology when he told the Royal Geographical Society that sea and rail links and power would be supplemented by air, and then

> a great deal of this geographical distribution must lose its importance, and the successful powers will be those who have the greatest industrial basis. It will not matter whether they are in the centre of a continent or on an island; those people who have the industrial power and the power of invention and of science will be able to defeat all others.

The creation and spread of electric tram system in Britain's cities had more of an impact on ordinary people, and was affecting rail receipts from commuting by the early 1900s in cities such as Newcastle where the first electric tram ran in 1901. However, it was the motor car that was to be more important for the future. In 1886, Parliament repealed the legislation that had obliged cars to follow a man carrying a red flag, and, instead, allowed them to drive at up to 14 mph. The first original, full-size British petrol motor was produced in 1895 and the first commercial motor company was established at Coventry in 1896. Motor buses were introduced in about 1898 and by 1914 there were 51,167 buses and taxis on the road. Legislation and government action aided the spread of the new legislation. The Motor Car Act of 1903 extended the rights of the motorist, the motor bus was introduced in London in 1905, and four years later the national Road Board was founded to lend energy and cohesion to road construction.

4.7 Conclusion

It is a truism to say that this was far distant from the situation a century earlier. Yet, like most truisms, it is worth dwelling on the remarkable pace of change and on its impact throughout society. Britain and the British were linked as never before. The construction of the transport systems revealed much about the nature of British politics. In particular, although parliamentary legislation provided the enabling framework, these systems were not state-planned or directed. There was no equivalent to the role of Continental governments and no ministry of transport. Instead, the investment capital and planning decisions were private.

The consequences were both good and less fortunate. Reliance on private capital ensured that transport investment did not have to fight for its share with other calls on the national purse. In addition, it proved possible to tap national wealth. This was far less possible if reliance was placed on state support, not least because taxation was low. Reliance on private capital also made it easier to transfer from canal to rail. A state transport system might have been more concerned to protect the earlier investment in canals. There were also major problems arising from the absence of central planning. For both canals and rail, mixed-gauge development lessened the possibility of effective integration. There was also competition between the railway companies of which there were 366 in the mid-1860s, and still, despite amalgamation, over 100 in 1900. Competition led to wasteful duplication, not least of railway stations, a step that discouraged integration. By 1900, there were four termini in Manchester. The absence of effective integration combined with competition helped lessen profitability and thus the possibility of fresh investment. Nevertheless, the efficiencies gained from rail transformed the transportability of goods and passengers, and altered the mental as well as the physical landscape.

Summary

◆ Transport changed considerably in this period with multiple effects.

◆ The first stage – turnpikes and canals – was most important in the late eighteenth century.

◆ The second stage – steam-powered rail transport – was particularly effective from the 1840s when long-distance routes and a national system developed.

◆ At the close of the century, a mature rail system began to be complemented by a revival in road transport using the internal combustion engine.

Points to discuss

◆ How important were changes in transportation?

◆ How was the effectiveness of different transport systems assessed?

◆ How did transportation in your area develop in the nineteenth century?

◆ How did the railway affect British society?

References and further reading

W. Albert, *The Turnpike Road System of England, 1663–1840* (Cambridge, 1972).

P. S. Bagwell, *The Transport Revolution from 1770* (1974).

M. J. Freeman and D. H. Aldcroft (eds), *Transport in Victorian Britain* (Manchester, 1988).

M. J. Freeman and D. H. Aldcroft (eds), *Atlas of British Railway History* (Beckenham, 1985).

T. R. Gourvish, *Railways and the British Economy, 1830–1914* (1980).

G. R. Hawke, *Railways and Economic Growth in England and Wales, 1840–1870* (Oxford, 1970).

J. R. Kellet, *The Impact of Raiways on Victorian Cities* (1969).

P. K. O'Brien, *Railways and the Economic Development of Western Europe, 1830–1914* (1983).

T. S. Williams, *River Navigation in England, 1600–1750* (Manchester, 1964).

Population and Migration

Contents

Introduction

Overall, population history is one of the most debated areas of historical inquiry. Like contemporaries at any given time in the past, historians are concerned with the progress of population. Friedrich Engels, in *The Origins of the Family, Private Property and the State* (1884), said population was central to history since it captured the most basic social reality. He wrote:

> According to the materialist conception, the determining factor in history is, in the last resort, the production and reproduction of immediate life. But this itself is again a twofold character. On the one hand, the production of the means of subsistence … on the other, the production of human beings themselves, the propagation of the species.

Looking back on population profiles in the past, we can see that from the eighteenth century the number of people in Europe began to rise dramatically. Why, then, did population stagnate, fall or else grow slowly in the seventeenth century and grow (with notable exceptions like France, where it grew slowly) on a steep upward curve in the nineteenth century? Schoolchildren's textbooks of twenty years ago, still driven by the 'Great Men' approach, tended to stress human endeavour and scientific improvement. Thus the health of nations and the growth of population were contextualised in terms of this or that medical improvement: smallpox vaccines, antiseptics, X-rays, the fight against tuberculosis. Later generations of historians have moved away from this approach, again using sophisticated quantitative techniques, to look at mortality and fertility patterns and age-cohort performances – measuring, therefore, not simply growth but the velocity of growth across different regions, nations, occupations and age-groups. As a result of such work, our understanding of human history has been changed.

Key issues

▶ What were the main patterns of population growth?

▶ Why did population grow so sharply?

▶ What were the main patterns of migration?

▶ What effect did labour migration have on the population, economy and society of the nineteenth century

5.1 Population growth

British population growth in this period was astounding. During the eighteenth and nineteenth centuries, the population of Great Britain grew at a previously unparalleled rate and to an unprecedented size. In 1750 the population of England and Wales stood at approximately 6 m, with Scotland having around 1.3 m and Ireland 3 m. In 1801, as Table 5.1 demonstrates, three of the four countries had grown significantly: England and Wales, together, had nearly 9 m, Ireland had about 5 m, whereas Scotland's population had grown by only 300,000 to 1.6 m. By 1901, the growth rates had been even more dramatic in England, Wales and Scotland – but not so for Ireland, where the picture was distinctly mixed. By that date, England and Wales totalled some 32.5 m people and Scotland nearly

Table 5.1 Population growth in England and Wales and Scotland, 1801–1901 (000,000s)

Year	England and Wales	% increase	Scotland	% increase
1801	8,893,000		1,608,000	
1811	10,164,000	14.3	1,806,000	12.2
1821	12,000,000	18.1	2,092,000	15.8
1831	13,897,000	15.8	2,364,000	13.0
1841	15,194,000	9.3	2,629,000	11.2
1851	17,928,000	18.0	2,889,000	10.0
1861	20,066,000	11.9	3,062,000	5.6
1871	22,712,000	13.2	3,360,000	10.0
1881	25,974,000	14.4	3,736,000	10.1
1891	29,003,000	11.7	4,026,000	7.8
1901	32,528,000	12.2	4,472,000	11.1

Source: Reports on the Census of England and Wales; Census of Scotland (1951)

4.5 m. Ireland's growth rate had continued to rise until 1841; then the disaster of the Famine killed nearly around 1 m people, pushed the same number again into emigration, and altered attitudes to reproduction in such a way that by 1901, in a pattern unique in European population history at this time, Ireland's population had shrunk from 8 m on the eve of the famine to 4.5 m in 1901. These contrasting fortunes tell us much about history under the Union (although this is discussed in a separate Chapter on Ireland, see Chapter 10). The purpose of this chapter is two-fold: first, to explain this phenomenal growth in population; secondly, to consider how migration, as well as the absolute growth itself, led to a re-ordering of population.

Although population grew at different rates in different decades, no census recorded a fall in population in either England, Wales or Scotland. Growth was remarkably evenly spread. In the eighteenth century, population had increased at no more than two-thirds of 1 per cent per annum; in the nineteenth, an average of 1 per cent per annum – or 10 per cent per decade – was the mean growth rate. This fast rate of expansion was maintained till the 1920s, since when developments have been much more modest.

Throughout the century, women outnumbered men. Industrial accidents and wars took a heavier toll on men and accentuated the statistical fact that live female births were anyway more numerous than male. Table 5.2 reflects this.

The most important work on English population history, written in recent times, is that of Wrigley and Schofield (1981). In a monumental study covering more than 400 individual parishes, they have shown that while births, marriages and deaths grew in the eighteenth and nineteenth centuries, the proportion of births over deaths was rising more dramatically still. This was the result of increasing fertility: people were marrying earlier (shown by a reduction in the mean age of marriage) and were thus having more children. That they married earlier in a time without widespread use of contraception meant that, on average, the population *must* produce more offspring. The relationship between birth-

Table 5.2 The ratio of men to women in England and Wales and Scotland, 1801–1901 (000)

	England and Wales			Scotland		
	Females	Males	F : M	Females	Males	F : M
1801	4,638	4,255	109 : 100	869	736	118 : 100
1811	5,291	4,874	109 : 100	980	826	119 : 100
1821	6,150	5,850	105 : 100	1,109	983	113 : 100
1831	7,126	6,771	105 : 100	1,250	1,114	112 : 100
1841	8,137	7,778	105 : 100	1,378	1,242	111 : 100
1851	9,146	8,781	104 : 100	1,513	1,375	110 : 100
1861	10,290	9,776	105 : 100	1,612	1,450	111 : 100
1871	11,653	11,059	105 : 100	1,757	1,603	110 : 100
1881	13,335	12,640	106 : 100	1,936	1,799	109 : 100
1891	14,942	14,060	106 : 100	2,083	1,943	107 : 100
1901	16,799	15,729	107 : 100	2,298	2,174	106 : 100

Source: Reports on the Census of England and Wales; Census of Scotland (1951)

rates and death-rates, and the mean age at marriage, are central to the population history of any given country. While live births must outnumber deaths for significant growth to occur, and though an increased average age at death will obviously contribute, too, the most important single factor in explaining population growth is the age at which couples married. This applies to periods when contraception was not widespread, and works on the basis that people were more or less celibate before marriage (bastardy rates give the lie to this, but it is true that, in the nineteenth century, an overwhelming proportion of births occured from the union of married partners). Put simply, then, the earlier people married, the more time they had to produce children. Despite this knowledge (which is in any case lacking in sensitivity to subtle variations in cultural practices), historians are still not able to explain precisely why changing patterns occurred.

Why did more people marry younger in the 1800s than in the 1600s? The answer usually given relates to social and economic opportunity: this is premised upon the notion that, when planning marriage and families, young people were making rational economic choices which revealed what they thought were their opportunities for the future. It is certainly true, for example, that in something of a golden period for Irish agriculture in the late eighteenth and early nineteenth century, with war-time demand and English population growth stimulating the Irish economy, the population there rose sharply – from around 4 m in 1780 to more than 6 m in the 1820s. That the Irish population grew more slowly thereafter, reaching 8.2 m in 1841, before dramatically halving by 1891, was due to a series of staggering economic blows, not least of which was the Great Famine (1845–51).

Population growth in Victorian Britain cannot be attributed to the inward movement of people from other countries. Throughout the nineteenth century, though the intensity varied according to the business cycle and was affected by wars, emigration *from* the British Isles outstripped immigration. The British Empire, the English-speaking colonies of Canada and Australasia, but most of all the United States, presented a magnetic attraction to Britons in search of better lives. The Irish and Scots were among the world's most mobile people; in European terms, only the Norwegians and Germans came close to matching their rates of exodus; even the English, despite coming from the world's wealthiest country, maintained a high level of mobility. Thus, in every year from 1876 to 1914 (for which period statistics are most comprehensive) the United Kingdom had a net outward migration, ranging from a low of 31,000 in 1876 to a high of 268,000 in 1912. In the lean years of the 1880s, the difference between immigration and emigration resulted in a net outflow of more than 1.5 m.

Despite the enormous importance which people from the British Isles played in peopling developing parts of the world, immigration was an important feature of life in this period. During Victoria's reign, Britain became more cosmopolitan than at any time since the waves of invaders following the decline of the Roman Empire. More than half a million Irish lived in England and Wales in the 1850s, and other immigrants, such as Jews, Italians and Germans, also found their way to Britain. Large numbers of Russian and Polish Jews immigrated from the 1880s until the Aliens Act (1905). There was also a substantial Chinese immigration at the end of our period, especially to ports such as London and Liverpool. Nevertheless, immigration did not have a fundamental effect on overall population size. This is partly due to emigration rates; but it is also due to the fact that immigrant populations were not anything like as important in Britain in the 1800s as they are today.

It is not admissable to suggest that medical interventions had a decisive effect on the growing population. Lives were certainly saved by improvements to medical care or the development of vaccines, but the overall structure and size of the population could be but little affected by scientific invention or good medical practice. To explain population growth we need to look to changing marriage patterns and longer life expectancy. Patterns of earlier marriage are seen as an indicator of the opportunities and rising prosperity of the Industrial Revolution in Britain, and of the lack of opportunity in pre- and post-Famine Ireland. Though the thesis cannot be proved in a quantifiable sense (how can we read the minds of the dead?), as a hypothesis it has much to recommend it. Moreover, we can certainly see the effects of economic opportunity that prompted young men and women to marry earlier. In Victorian society, early marriage meant more children. A couple who married when the woman was 23 years old had five years more of that woman's fertile period than if they had married when she was 28 years old. Thus, if people married earlier, their unions would yield more children on average. The fact that births outstripped deaths, and this offset even the appalling social conditions in major cities such as Manchester in 1830s, where the average age at death was less than 20 years of age (this, though was a figure pushed downwards by the incidence of infant mortality), also helped to explain the upwards movement of the British (but not Irish) population. A combination of improving diet – particularly after 1850 – and the survival of more young people offset the fact that, in the 1890s, the average male death-rate was in the mid-forties.

Population grew dramatically in this period without famines (except in Ireland and in parts of north-western Scotland); in other words, without the 'positive checks' on population which were seen as so vital by the Reverend Thomas Malthus (1766–1834), one of the most important political economists that Britain has produced (see Profile Box 5.1). Malthus, writing in the 1790s, was appalled by the speed with which population was growing: he feared cataclysmic problems as population grew to outstrip food-supply. Not only a population theorist, but also an environmentalist and cleric, Malthus combined his interests to attack the profligacy and fecundity of the poor. He viewed population growth as the great evil of his day: it threatened the environment by consuming too many precious resources, and he worried that food production could not keep pace with the rate of population. Whereas food production, he averred, increased on an arithmetic scale – 1, 2, 3, 4, 5, 6, 7, 8 – population grew at a geometric rate – 1, 2, 4, 8, 16, 32, 64, 128, and so on. As we can see, when food supply had increased by eight times, according to Malthus, the population would be 128 times bigger! This would have meant the direst imaginable food shortages, famine and death, and thus a self-regulation that would restrict population growth. Malthus' famous *An Essay on the Principle of Population* (1798) was very acutely a work of its time, given that it addressed an issue, population growth, in a way that was, in England at any rate, to be superseded by the realities of the subsequent century. His concerns about population growth were part of a wider political concern about the use of poor rates to supplement low wages in the poorer rural areas – this was the great criticism of the 'Speenhamland System' of outdoor poor relief employed in the Berkshire village of that name. Malthusian principles were certainly part of the logic of the reformers who pushed the Poor Law Amendment Act (1834) through Parliament.

Malthus' prophesies of a population crisis never occurred. This is because, although Malthus has been described as Britain's most original social scientist, he was effectively using historical examples to forecast future trends. The past had indeed seen population

Thomas R. Malthus

(1766-1834) A cleric, social critic and population theorist, who wrote *An Essay on the Principle of Population* (1798), a critique of utopian notions of the perfectibility of humanity. He expressed concern that society was under threat from the natural desire of humanity to reproduce itself at a rate out of proportion with food and other resources. Although the Malthusian nightmare of widespread starvation was avoided in England, despite continuing growth in the population, his treatise was perhaps most important at the time for the effect it had in supporting demands for a more punitive poor law system to encourage the poor to exercise restraint.

disasters: the Black Death in the mid-fourteenth century had killed around one-third of the 6 m-strong population of England and Wales. One hundred years later, the population stood at between 2.5 and 3 m. It took until the sixteenth century for the population to recover its medieval demographic position.

The world which Malthus looked back on had been ravaged by disease, famine, long wars and other factors that impact heavily on demography. But his own time was one of improvement, despite the fact that Britain was fighting a protracted war. Malthus could not forecast it, but urban work opportunities, the development of overseas markets and suppliers of food, and most of all the increasing food production engendered by the Agricultural Revolution, made any 'positive check' both unnecessary and ineffectual. This period was the first point in human history where, in terms of food production or the ability to buy food, it could be said that the British population had overcome the perils of nature.

The great fertility decline after (approximately) 1870 is another instance of huge endeavours shedding new light on the old problem of population performance. Once it was presumed that the fertility decline – the reduction in the number of live births and/or family size – was a uniform experience which began with the middle classes and trickled down to affect working-class sexual practices. A study by Simon Szreter, *Fertility, Class and Gender in Britain, 1860–1940* (1996), has radically changed accepted views of a fundamental feature of human life. Szreter reappraised the once commonly upheld idea that the fertility decline of the period in question was nation-wide and undifferentiated. By drawing upon and marshalling a huge array of quantitative material, including the 1911 fertility census, Szreter is able to show a vast array of fertility regimes differentiated by occupation, gender and region. The fertility decline, which is at the heart of Szreter's study, led at the time to great anxiety among commentators and politicians, and poor population growth rates were seen to threaten the position of one nation against another. Thus, the French feared that the newly unified Germany, with its greater and growing population, would outstrip France in both economic and military terms, and such fears were duplicated elsewhere.

Something as crucial as population inevitably affects other facets of life. Falling fertility in the later nineteenth century, for example, led to debates about emigration being reopened. Whereas in the period 1820 to the 1870s British political economists had believed emigration was a panacea for overcrowding, unemployment and population boom, and had encouraged emigration to Australasia and Canada, the fall-off in fertility rates prompted a return to the eighteenth-century idea that emigration was a drain on human resources because it prompted only the industrious and intelligent to leave. On the eve of the First World War, the fertility decline was tied into wider pessimism about Europe as a spent force, and has been linked by historians to increased militarism and aggression among European nations on the eve of the war.

The related questions of family, fertility and population are obviously of enormous importance. Although they cannot be adequately covered in just a few words, the impression of their importance can still be gleaned. Historians are concerned with problems and debates in the field of population history; at the same time, the magnitude of this phenomenon suggests it will always be a contentious area.

5.2 Conceptualising migration

Population growth, industrialisation and urbanisation encouraged, and was encouraged by, great population movement, both internal migration and external emigration. Between 1815 and the Slump of the 1930s some 50 m Europeans crossed the Atlantic for new lives in the United States. In 1815–65, 1,273,000 people emigrated from the British Isles to North America, with another 905,000 to Australia and New Zealand. Millions of people also moved within Europe, especially in the north where the lure of work encouraged a drift towards the North Sea. With population growth and redistribution, a new social fabric unfolded in both Europe and America. The declining importance of the countryside was paralleled by the rise of great urban centres, symbols of the industrial age.

The study of migration can be dated to seminal works by E.G. Ravenstein in the 1880s. In more recent times, Brinley Thomas (1954) advanced the understanding of migratory patterns by identifying a link between the building cycle and both internal migration and emigration from Britain. He noted peaks and troughs in migratory patterns of approximately 20 years' duration, aligning broadly with high and low points in investment and construction. Thomas suggested that the export of capital from Britain to America led to falling internal migration within the former and an increase in emigration to the latter. Like population growth itself, therefore, labour migration is a sensitive and important economic indicator.

Historians no longer regard migration as a first-time once-and-for-all shift from rural to urban areas, with overseas emigration similarly presumed to have occurred between the rural regions of one country and the urban centres of another (say, from Wiltshire to America's east coast). It is now agreed that the majority of emigration actually occurred from urban areas, having been preceded, in the case of rural workers, by short-distance 'step' migrations within the country of birth. This was as true for Scots crofters as for Devonshire farm-hands. As Arthur Redford showed in his important work, *Labour Migration in England, 1800–50* (1926), the process of migration from the land to the town occurred in a 'complex wave-like motion'. This motion began in earnest in the mid-eighteenth century and peaked after the 1840s when comprehensive nationwide transport links, especially the railways, were put in place. Some of this motion occurred from early industrial towns, for example in east Lancashire and west Yorkshire, to newer centres, in the same counties, but most came from rural areas. Although rural depopulation is difficult to measure, owing to the crudeness of calculations of long-run change based on decennial census returns, it is clear that surplus population in the countryside fed in to the towns and cities. Many of the great urban-to-urban transatlantic migrations – from Liverpool or Glasgow to New York or Boston – involved people who had moved from countryside to town in their own country before emigrating to North America and Australia.

Although it has long been common to stress the increasing integration and homo-genisation of economy and culture in the nineteenth century, more recent research has offered a number of alternative perspectives, in particular regionally distinct patterns of development. In relation to the question of migration, for example, it has been suggested that increased population mobility encouraged an outgrowth, a diffusion from a core, of local customs and practices. This type of regionalisation helped to enforce local identities, and some types of customary behaviour, rather than destroying them. The nature of migration certainly suggests that such a regional perspective is plausible. Most initial population movements occurred over short distances. Among rural tradesmen – carpenters, coopers, blacksmiths and the like – the drive to leave the home village or small town was generated as much by the prospect of holding on to their trade as of changing it. Return migration also was quite common, with migrants drifting back and forth from their place of birth. This was certainly the case with many Welsh migrants and with peripatetic Irish seasonal labourers. The Welsh, for example, often clung on to a distinct rural culture long after arriving in new urban settings, and then maintained close contact with the home country. Certainly, rural migrants helped to promote the image of towns as loosely-connected 'ethnic villages', where different regional or national groups per-petuated pre-industrial culture and customs. Therefore, while migration can be seen as a process of 'uprooting' – an undertaking by sometimes desperate and reluctant villagers – it also has been viewed as a rational response to new opportunities for self-improvement which increasing numbers of both rural and urban workers embraced as the century wore on.

5.3 Urbanisation and mobility

In the early phases of industrial and urban growth, towns and cities experienced large two-way flows of population, with natural increase unable to meet the labour demands of local industries. The ratio between natural increase and migration-fed growth is difficult to ascertain and many estimates are misleading. It is a received wisdom to suggest that early urban growth (that is, pre-1850) was sustained by rapid in-migration, while growth thereafter tends to be explained by the fertility levels of a largely young urban population. Research by Baines (1985), however, suggests that the role of migrants in the later period is often under-estimated when most growth is attributed to natural increase. Migrants, too, were mostly young, and Baines calculated that they accounted for around two-fifths of urban population increase in this period. What is more, in certain areas, for example the Highlands of Scotland, kinship and clan ties were such that migrants usually travelled in small family groups that included members of the right age for marriage. These ties were remade once favourable economic circumstances had been achieved in the towns and cities of the Scottish central belt.

Britain's big cities attracted labour from far afield. The impact of Irish migration in Liverpool, Manchester and Glasgow was particularly striking. Liverpool had nearly 50,000 Irish-born in 1841 and almost 84,000 in 1861; Manchester's Irish-born population ranged between 33,490 and 52,076 in the same years; and Glasgow's peaked at 68,330 in 1871. With what the demographers call age-cohort heaping (in this case, clustering in the 15–35 age-group), and the predominance of young males in the migratory flow, it is possible to suggest that Irish labour may have accounted for around one-third of the male work-force in these great centres. While a family from Buckinghamshire might find their way to Manchester, cities like this tended to obey a more fundamental law of migration by deriving the majority of their labour supply from the surrounding countryside. Thus, Lancashire and Cheshire were dominant in the cases of Manchester and Liverpool, with the Welsh also prominent in the latter. Moreover, a high proportion of the Lancashire-born in the two cities were sons and daughters of recent arrivals. A more striking example of such local networks of migration can be seen in Sheffield, a city whose isolated and semi-rural character impacted upon the profile of its labour migrants. In 1861, three-quarters of the city's 185,172 population had been born in Yorkshire, with the neighbouring counties of Derbyshire and Nottinghamshire and Lincolnshire next in the list. Although the arrival of the railways meant that steel-workers and miners from Lancashire, the north-east of England or Wales could find their way to the growing 'steel city', migrants from distant points of departure such as Ireland and Scotland constituted less than 5 per cent together. Short-range migration from the counties of Northumberland, Durham and Cumberland predominated among migrations to Newcastle recorded in the 1851 census, but there was also considerable migration from further afield, and more so than in earlier periods. In 1851, about 54 per cent of the population of Newcastle had been born outside the city.

On a larger scale, it is appropriate to ask, what accounts for Scotland becoming the urban–industrial economy with the highest incidence of out-migration in Europe? One of the first points to note is that the Scottish Highlands emitted a constant flow of migrants to both Scotland's central belt and to Canada, America and Australasia. It is important to recognise that the Scottish economy was particularly reliant on the export sector, and thus to economic fluctuations. Moreover, Scotland lacked the tertiary service sector which buffered England's industrial economy against further recessions. In addition, by the 1860s a majority of emigrations from Britain to America were part of a Europewide urban-to-urban shift, driven by the fact that skilled workers' wages were so high in the New World and by the fall in transport costs. It is also important to remember that huge, but uncounted, proportions of Scots workers moved in continuous, and largely unreciprocated, labour migrations to the big towns and cities of England, where, throughout the nineteenth century, wages were higher than in Scotland. If European emigration by the 1870s was a complex mixture of old and new factors – rural hardship and urban opportunity – then Scotland was uniquely placed to send forth masses of people on both counts. Even then, its urban and industrial growth might be seen as a positive factor which prevented an Irish-type problem permeating areas other than the Highlands and Islands.

5.4 **The rural world and migration**

During the Industrial Revolution there was a highly significant linkage between rural depopulation and urban growth, particularly in the 30 years after 1820. During the French Wars (1793–1815), the effects of rural population growth were absorbed by the prospect of steady work and of increasing wages. With a slump in post-war demand, increasing commercialisation, and the move to larger farm units (via enclosures and the like) the pull of the town and the push from the land exerted a complementary force on the increasing pool of unskilled farm labour. By 1831, there were five landless labourers in England and Wales to every owner-occupier, a ratio that had doubled since the 1690s. As agriculture became more efficient, with more food being produced by fewer workers, rural labour demands became more seasonal. Consequently, under-employment was added to the problems of this landless class. While farm-workers in Lancashire or Warwickshire could make their way to Manchester or Birmingham, the effects of the agricultural revolution were felt most acutely in those regions where alternative work, whether rural or urban, was not available in remote places like Dorset or the Scottish Highlands.

Patterns of population change in rural areas between 1851 and 1911 show that there was a broad band of decline. It reached from Cornwall, Devon and Dorset in the south-west of England through to the Fens of East Anglia in the east; it cut across the middle and northern parts of Wales to the Vale of York in central-northern England. From there, it cut north along the Pennines to the Borders region of north Northumberland. Norfolk's population decreased after 1851 and it was not until about 1880 that it returned to the 1851 level. In more detail, much of the county experienced a population fall in the second half of the century, as growth was concentrated on major towns. The loss of population in the countryside reflected the difficulties of farming as well as of village handicrafts. There was a similar pattern in Lincolnshire, with growth in urban areas such as the county town of Lincoln and the rural impact of agrarian depression. Other areas that grew reflected particular economic developments such as tourism at Skegness and metallurgy at Scunthorpe. Similarly, in Berkshire there was a depopulation in some agricultural areas, while other parts of the county from which people could commute to London, such as Bracknell and Maidenhead, grew.

Migration tended to move in a wave-like motion. Rural incomers to towns came first and foremost from the immediate countryside, usually in the same county. The motion of migration then carried in waves of people from more distant points. This has been demonstrated, for example, in Charles Withers' study of Highland migration to Dundee, Perth and Stirling. Overall, rural population depletion was consistent and general through the Victorian period, falling only after 1901 when there was an economic upturn.

Migration from rural areas was both more frequent and shorter in distance than movements between urban areas. There had long been a degree of short-distance mobility among rural workers, notwithstanding the rigours of the Elizabethan Poor Law and the various Acts of Settlement which were aimed to restrict population movement. Indeed scholars now recognise that there was significant pre-industrial labour migration, with young people from far and wide finding apprenticeships and work in domestic service, especially in London. The highest levels of rural out-migration occurred in short hops, especially from the immediate hinterland of large cities such as Liverpool, Manchester and

Leeds and around closely situated new towns, as in Durham, west Cumberland, the west Midlands and Clydeside. The rural hinterlands of major urban centres usually had higher wages than was the case in other rural areas; but the major towns also offered the highest industrial wages. Thus, although nearby industrial activity is thought to have forced up agricultural wages, differentials remained relatively balanced in a regional context so that rural-dwellers still migrated. For this reason, even farmers in prosperous regions were concerned about their inability to hold on to hired labour. Transient, well-paid workers, such as navvies, carried the message and example of occupational as well as physical mobility to the envious farm-hand. The disturbing effects of progress were felt long and hard in the shires. Commentators feared urban and industrial growth when they lamented the emptiness of rural communitites. In *The Condition of England* (1907 edn), C.F.G. Masterman captured the foreboding of what was a common viewpoint:

> Outside this exuberant life of the cities, standing aloof from it, and with but little share in its prosperity, stands the countryside. Rural England, beyond the radius of certain favoured neighbourhoods, and apart from the specialised population which serves the necessities of the country house, is everywhere hastening to decay. No one stays there who can possibly find employment elsewhere. All the boys and girls with energy and enterprise forsake at the commencement of maturity the life of the fields for the life of the town.

In the Victorian period the rural population declined in absolute and relative terms. However, while the absolute number of rural-dwellers fell only by around 11.5 per cent, the large rise in the overall population meant that the proportion of rural dwellers had declined by more than half. In the former year, 9,936,800 people (49.8 per cent), lived in rural areas; in 1911 the figure was 7,907,556 (22.9 per cent). Significant out-flows occurred in the 1850s, which, although stemmed in the 1860s, were greatly increased in the 1870s and 1880s, with the end of Britain's so-called agricultural 'Golden Age', and the beginning of a period of agricultural depression. Although there was considerable return migration, the overall trend was one of permanent contraction and decline. Between 1851 and 1871, the total number of agricultural workers fell by more than 250,000. However, most of the loss from rural areas – which, between the 1850s and 1890s, occurred at around 75,000 per annum – was offset by the natural increase of high birth rates.

The decision to migrate from the rural areas was not taken lightly. The first link forged in the chain of migration or emigration was often made by farm-workers whose ancestors had worked the land for centuries. Once the process had been initiated, however, future movements became more likely. Further stimulus was provided by the success stories of previous generations of migrants. As early as 1833, the Petworth Emigration Society had produced a one-shilling booklet of letters from previous emigrants to Canada. The letters were re-issued within a year. Poor Law officials and private charities also sometimes assisted overseas migration or emigration.

Departures from the poor rural south were slow. Earlier in the period, laws of settlement still bound men and women to their parishes. If they fell on hard times while tramping to other places, they risked removal to their place of origins (as occurred in Liverpool in the late 1840s when many Irish migrants were forcibly returned to Ireland, despite the likelihood that death would befall them). The financial outlay of labour migration was also significant and rural workers tended to lack the complex networks and institutionalised support systems – other than those provided by family and friends – that facilitated the often peripatetic lifestyles of skilled migrants.

A brake was also applied by what might be termed the 'rural mentality'. Rural folk, especially in the most isolated communities, were particularly suspicious of strangers and hostile to change (Box 5.1). To them, London might have been on the other side of the world, while a journey of just 20 miles was more than an adventure – it meant the trauma of uprooting. These people may have seen trains but probably had not travelled on them. They undoubtedly knew of nearby towns and cities but may not have visited them. They listened to their religious leaders who sometimes preached of the immorality, vice and unhealthy living conditions that awaited for the unsuspecting country folk. Then, again, more enlightened individuals acted as facilitators of migration, with some clerics encouraging the outward flow. Canon Girdlestone organised the migration of labouring families from Halberton, Devon, to Kent and the northern counties in the late 1860s and early 1870s, and had to do everything for those who departed. As F.G. Heath, in *The English Peasantry* (1874), recalled:

> their luggage [had to be] addressed, their railway tickets taken, and full and plain directions given to the simple travellers. The plan adopted when the labourers were leaving for their new homes, was to give them, as Canon Girdlestone did, plain directions written on a piece of paper in a large and legible hand. There were shown to the officials on the several lines of railway, who soon getting to hear of Canon Girdlestone's system of migration [whereby he acted as *de facto* agent], rendered him all the assistance in their power by helping the labourers out of their travelling difficulties.

The image conveyed is one of a pathetic group almost incapable of helping themselves. Indeed, some were so ignorant of geography that they even asked if they were travelling across the sea. Yet these same rustics were keen enough to take their families from a backward region where wages were no higher than 8s per week to northern towns in Lancashire where they earned not less than 13s.

Rural out-migration greatly increased in the 1880s, which caused an upturn in the economic conditions of those left behind. However, workers in the towns became increasingly restive at the sight of so many agricultural labourers moving in to search for work, citing the depressing effect upon wages and worsening overcrowding in what became a new assault on the problem of rural depopulation. Observers in the shires also noted the depletion of population, lamenting its economic origins and its social effects. Smallholdings Acts were passed in 1892 and 1907 in an attempt to encourage the rural population to hold its place. This legislation offered landless labourers a stake in the land they worked, but, as Chambers and Mingay pointed out, 'more than Acts of Parliament were needed to turn a centuries-old rural proletariat into a race of peasant cultivators' and 'the drift from the land continued to disturb observers of the rural scene. From census material of 1901 it can be inferred that fewer than half the farmworkers aged 15–24 a decade earlier remained in the industry.' Over the duration of our period, the share of the population engaged in agriculture, horticulture and forestry in England and Wales had declined from around 50 per cent to about a much-diminished, though still significant, one-third. The agricultural 'Great Depression' of the last quarter of the century led to the Duke of Bedford in 1897 to write about his 'ruined' estate.

The distinction between urban and rural areas became less clear as the century progressed. Indeed, an element in the depletion of the most rural regions can be accounted for by the transformation of rural districts into semi-rural or partially urban ones. West Cumberland, around Whitehaven, south Northumberland, just north of

Box 5.1

Rural isolation

Sir Gilbert Scott (1811–78), a famous architect, recorded of his native village, Gawcott, a hamlet a few miles from Buckingham:

The inhabitants of Gawcott were a very quaint race. I recollect my father [Thomas Scott (1780–1835)] saying that when he first went there to reconnoitre he found the road to it rendered impassable by a large hole dug across it in which the inhabitants were engaged in baiting a badger; a promising prelude to an Evangelical Ministry among them! However he succeeded in bringing the place in due time into a more seemly state as to externals though the old leaven remained and a certain amount of poaching and other forms of rural blackguardism, though there grew up amongst all this a good proportion of really excellent people, some of whom had at one time belong to the previously more normal type!

Source: *Recollections of Nineteenth-Century Buckinghamshire* (Buckinghamshire Record Society, 1998), p. 16

Newcastle and North Shields, and large areas of the West Midlands, provide useful examples of this change; mining districts in general became much less rural as 1914 approached. Very few genuinely rural districts existed in the early twentieth century, beyond the south-west of England, central Wales, the northern Pennines area, the Lake District and north-western Scotland.

5.5 Migration between rural regions

Labour migration occurred between rural areas, even if by the 1860s the majority of labour migrants moved between towns. Part of the reasoning behind the Elizabethan Poor Law had been a fear of migration (much of which was rural-to-rural) because of the burden which itinerant workers could place on their parishes of residence when times were hard. For Elizabethan society migration had been a potentially socially unsettling influence, and administrators sought to curb it. Although the nineteenth century is characterised as an age of urbanisation, this does not mean that rural areas were static. In 1871, for example, almost one-fifth of inhabitants in the isolated rural area of Furness and Cartmel, in the Lake District, had been born in other counties There were also backward flows, from established urban centres to developing ones. The earliest examples of work-related mobility came in the rural agricultural world. Here, when the mechanisation of labour activity, enclosures and greater efficiency in farming techniques increased the demand for seasonal labour while diminishing the need for a permanent static work-force, workers often had no option but to seek out new occupational pursuits, often in different places. From the early 1800s, in Ireland, the Highlands of Scotland and in the south west of England, farm-workers increasingly came to the market-place looking for casual employment, and there was often friction between them as they struggled to command work opportunities.

Rural poverty and displacement created a valuable supply of needy workers, but it also led to increasing pauper migration. In this particular form of migration, those from the very poorest areas, especially Highland Scotland, the west of Ireland and the southern Uplands of England, predominated. Irish seasonal harvesters – spalpeens – were the single largest group, finding their way into a range of agricultural economies across a wide arc of Britain, from the potato-growing regions of Scotland to the hop-picking areas of Kent. Seasonal passage became a key part of both Irish and British life in the mid- to late eighteenth century, and continued, particularly in Scottish potato fields, until the 1960s. The most important period, however, was between the Famine of the 1840s and the 1880s, when threshing machines and other such labour-saving devices were being very widely employed. Irish seasonal migration has been seen by some historians as a precursor of permanent settlement; yet the evidence suggests that it was, in fact, a parallel movement.

Population growth and commercialisation in agriculture also affected small farmers in northern Scotland. In the early part of the nineteenth century there were effectively two Scotlands: the Highland region and the industrialising central belt. Both were undergoing significant changes, and in the more traditional north population increases were significant in the period from 1750–1830. The Highland Clearances of the early 1800s marked the final destruction of the clan system, which undermined an economic as well as as a cultural system. With enclosures underpinning the shift towards larger farm units and with more landowners bringing in sheep, thousands of peasant cottars and their black cattle were driven closer to the sea and nearer to a subsistence crisis. New farming practices in the Highlands led to increased demand for seasonal agricultural labour, and this also undermined the traditional peasant proprietor. As in Ireland, Tom Devine (*The Great Highland Famine*, 1988) has shown us, the famine of 1845–51 exacerbated these problems, especially in the far north-west where dependence upon the potato was most significant. The concept of labour migration took a savage twist at this point as many landlords used the famine as an opportunity to rid their estates of surplus tenants. There were horror stories about entire families sent forcibly to Canada and Australia.

5.6 Industrial migration

Labour migration was not an undifferentiated movement of agricultural workers to urban work, though this aspect was important. Some movements were contrived by employers, providing the starkest possible evidence of Brinley Thomas' argument that labour flowed after capital and investment. In March 1843, for instance, as W.H. Chaloner points out in his *Social and Economic Development of Crewe* (1950), between '750 to 900 persons living in different parts of Liverpool were suddenly uprooted from familiar surroundings and placed together in the semi-rural district of Crewe' because it suited their railway employers' new investment plans. The building of railways generally led to a large increase in the numbers of itinerant industrial workers travelling about the country. Much social commentary was written to deride the behaviour of these wild navvies. Migration often occurred between particular places, and, over time, developed as an historic tradition. Thus, in the 1870s, considerable labour migration was taking place between south Wales and Middlesbrough, with iron-masters and their workers taking part in a regular movement from one iron region to another. An even more striking case of directed labour migration occurred in the 1880s when the firm of Cammells dismantled its Derbyshire steelworks and moved it all the way to Workington, west Cumberland, where iron deposits were rich and plentiful. As a result, between 1881 and 1891 some 1800 iron-workers uprooted from Dronfield and moved to Workington.

During the 1840s, the so-called period of the `railway mania' saw around 200,000 roving navvies working on lines up and down the British Isles. This was one of the most notable migrations in Victorian history. The navvies' work was very ardous but well-paid; their living conditions were primitive, but their leisure culture was intense and ribald. They were responsible for some of the most impressive feats of civil engineering in the Victorian period: the Tring and Edge Hill cuttings, the Forth rail bridge and the Ribblehead viaduct are just some examples. More importantly, they added fluidity to the construction industry labour market: many years after the zenith of the 'railway age' these men were still building roads, digging new canals, and excavating huge docks – providing muscle and no little skill wherever they were needed.

Labour migration was common among skilled, often unionised, workers. Indeed, it was an important cultural practice among artisans; tramping provided an outlet for excess labour. It was a sign of solidarity, efficiency and of the effectiveness of the union which funded and supported such migrations. Tramping represented a broadening of horizons and a deepening of skills. It also was extremely intricately organised. Workers were sent forth with documents from the union attesting their good character and detailing their paid-up union subscriptions. Many received route maps, names and locations to head for. On arrival in a new town they headed for a `house of call', an 'unofficial labour exchange', often a pub, where they received food, sometimes beer, accommodation, and the chance of a job, if one was available. If not, they received more money and directions to the next town. This went on till they found work or were forced to return home, which could mean, as E.J. Hobsbawm has argued in *Labouring Men* (1964), a round trip of 2,800 miles for compositors in the 1850s! Recent studies have suggested that localised economic conditions were the main cause for this form of labour migration, and that the development of a more integrated national economy reduced the possibility of avoiding unemployment in particular trades simply by moving to other regions. The national slump of the 1840s exposed the inadequacy of the tramp and led unions to replace or supplement it with a system of unemployment pay.

Migration remained a characteristic of the skilled worker's response to dearth. Declining regions and older, waning industries often experienced a steady outflow of skilled labour. Thus, we find that a significant number of the iron-workers in Cumberland in the 1840s and 1850s had migrated from declining iron centres such as Staffordshire. Similarly, mining communities in South Wales, West Cumberland and Lanarkshire benefited from the outflow of Cornish copper and tin miners. In the 1850s, many miners in the haematite iron industry of north Lancashire were men displaced by industrial decline in Cornwall. These men brought many valuable skills into the region and, with their families, formed distinctive social enclaves. The descendants of these same workers must have been within the steady of flow of iron-miners leaving the Cumbrian coalfields for the South African gold and diamond mines in the 1880s. Cornishmen were also prevalent among the hardrock miners of North America, just as Irish miners from Cork were very heavily concentrated in the copper mines of Butte, Montana, in the later nineteenth and early twentieth centuries. In Cornwall, serious falls in the prices of copper and tin in the late 1860s and 1870s, in part due to growing world competition, led to a fall in the number of mines being worked, and to heavy out-migration, both overseas and to newer mining settlements in the north of England. By 1891, the Cornish diaspora amounted to 210,000, roughly 42 per cent of all the Cornish-born population. About 45 per cent of these were living in England and Wales, but the rest were spread over much of the world, mostly in Australia, North America and South Africa, where they continued to work in mining.

Skilled female labour also comprised an important part of the migrant streams between certain areas and industries. Women textiles workers from Ulster were more important in the Dundee flax and jute industry than were men. Highland women also found work in similar circumstances, and, like their Irish counterparts, came to outnumber male migrants in towns such as Perth. For unskilled or less-skilled women, migration was also an option. Domestic work traditionally attracted young girls from outlying rural districts to the nearest town, although there was something of a reversal of this trend in the later nineteenth century when holiday-making and hotel-building in rural settings resulted in many young girls moving from towns to the countryside for 'live in' work as household servants, chambermaids, cooks and so on.

The trade cycle, temporary downswings in production and available work, affected export-orientated trades, such as ship-building, and clearly helped to forge a culture of migration among shipyard workers, though the situation was complicated by regional divisions of labour and increasing degrees of specialism in particular yards (for example, ocean-going liners in Belfast and submarines – as early as the 1870s and 1880s – in Barrow). Ship-building workers thus flowed fairly frequently between the major industrial centres: the Clyde, Tyneside, Wearside, Merseyside, Barrow and Belfast. This movement of workers was in contrast with the early nineteenth century, when skilled workers such as shipwrights had sought to protect members of their union from competition by eliminating geographical mobility. A similar motivation was thought to be behind the Sheffield outrages of the 1860s, when violence and murder were sparked by competition from undercutting, less-skilled labour, some of which was thought to have come from outside the city.

By the turn of the century, however, high levels of mobility led to a more integrated approach to labour issues by both masters and workers. In shipbuilding, for example, union men in Barrow and Belfast attempted to follow the wages patterns and conditions of employment experienced by their counterparts on the Clyde. Most of the skilled men had been trained in Scotland and this provided a vital flow of information about procedures and practices. Even in the larger centres of Tyneside and Wearside the Scots' influence was significant, because the men had 'very largely come as young shipwrights from Dundee, Montrose, Aberdeen', as S. Pollard and P. Robertson have shown in their *British Shipbuilding, 1870–1914* (1979). This was a good example of the integration of the British economy.

Economic fluctuations meant that many workers spent months, even years, without work, or else in a state of under-employment. Yet, despite regular migratory rhythms among the men, ship-building afforded no opportunity for skilled workers to transfer from one trade to another – not even temporarily and certainly not at a comparable rate of pay. Thus migration occurred between yards, or from shipping to engineering (but within the same trade), and this was the main coping strategy for skilled workers pressed by economic recession or industrial conflicts. Even in the good times, the turnover of labour was high. As John Marshall, has shown, in *Furness and the Industrial* Revolution (1981), the shipbuilding town of Barrow grew from 47,292 to nearly 64,000 between 1881 and 1911, but in the same years there was a total permanent loss from the district of 11,800.

High levels of mobility among skilled workers was a characteristic of some workers' experiences because it acted as a form of labour control, ensuring, where possible, that local markets were not saturated. Just as men sought to regulate the flow of apprentices into their trades, their unions also encouraged workers to pack their bags and to head for areas with a shortfall in the job market. This consequently lowered (but did not eliminate) regional wages differentials in the industry, also resulted in a high turnover in unskilled labour, most of which was Irish Catholic and hailed from Ulster. Skilled Welsh migrants to England, were attracted to industrial centres which offered mainly male work – places like Tyneside, Sunderland, Middlesbrough, Portsmouth and Plymouth. Cities of regional importance, such as Liverpool, Birmingham and Bristol, also drew Welsh migrants, mainly from the Welsh counties nearest to them. Similar patterns can be observed among the Irish, although the Welsh in Liverpool in 1871 were distributed more evenly across the labour market than the Irish; the Welsh were under-represented in unskilled work and over-represented in the ranks of the skilled and semi-skilled.

5.7 Irish labour migrants

Irish migration provides examples of a variety of migrations (Box 5.2). Irish workers, because of the nature of the Irish economy, were overwhelmingly rural-to-urban migrants, passing from one of Europe's most pastoral nation into certainly its most industrial setting. The Irish were a marginal, migrating people, shunned by native workers who feared for their jobs, reviled because of their Catholicism (even though many were Protestants), but embraced by employers looking for cheap and flexible manual labour. The Irish maintained unusually high levels of mobility; many viewed Britain as a stop-gap measure – as a part of a deliberate plan to move on to North America or Australasia. While many achieved this goal, most lived the rest of their lives in Britain, sometimes at the margins of subsistence, always drifting to where work was available. Irish migration provided British capitalists with one of their most important, resourceful and flexible labour forces. Attracted by opportunity and driven from their homeland by pressure upon unevenly distributed resources, low wages, under-employment and a failure to industrialise, thousands of Irish labourers entered, and sometimes unbalanced, the British labour market at particularly important moments, for example during the Famine crisis of the later 1840s and early 1850s.

Irish settlement in Britain emerged as a particular problem in the years after 1815 when a collapse in Irish agriculture led to a significant increase in pauper migrants. By the 1820s, local authorities, especially in the coastal districts from Glasgow to Wales, were beginning to complain bitterly about the costs of maintaining the peripatetic poor of Ireland. The clamour undoubtedly influenced poor law reformers and led to calls for the introduction of an English-style Poor Law for Ireland. The Poor Law (Ireland) Act (1838), however, had no discernible effects on the rate of migration from Ireland, where population pressure continued to mount. By the early 1830s the Irish were fully spread across the established industrial regions of Britain. Apart from in London, the Irish were most prevalent in Lancashire, west and central Scotland, the north-east, Yorkshire and the west Midlands. As Table 5.3 indicates, the Irish-born community in Britain was already sizeable in 1841 but grew most rapidly in the 1840s and 1850s, as a direct consequence of

Box 5.2

Irish migrants

Until the advent of 'New Commonwealth' immigration after the Second World War, the Irish were the largest migrant group in Britain. They were not always welcomed and violence sometimes erupted between them and the 'indigenous' population. However, they played an important role in the Industrial Revolution and were central to the renaissance of Catholicism in Britain in the nineteenth century. Table 5.3 gives an indication of the way the Irish population grew. Note the bulge which followed the Famine (1845-51). The illustration shows Irish immigrants embarking for America – at Waterloo Docks, Liverpool (July 1850).

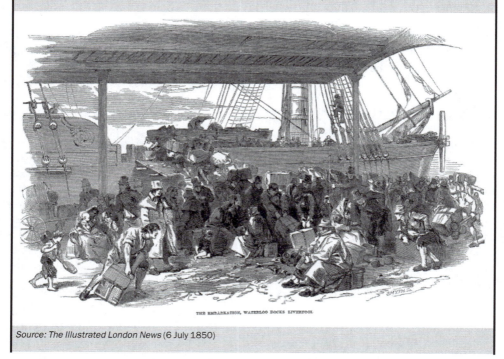

THE EMBARKATION, WATERLOO DOCKS LIVERPOOL

Source: The Illustrated London News (6 July 1850)

the Great Famine (1845–51), when, due to the 'Potato Blight' (a fungal infection of the crop) and attendant hunger and disease, emigration reached flood proportions. Liverpool alone received more than 500,000 arrivals in 1846 and 1847, and all centres of settlement noticed considerable increases in the numbers of destitute Irish incomers.

The pattern of Irish settlement changed as the century wore on. Throughout the period, Irish harvesters remained important to British farmers and found work as far afield as Sutherland, in northern Scotland, and Kent. Permanent settlement was noticed first in London; then in the Scottish textile towns of Ayrshire, Wigtownshire and Dumfriesshire, and in early industrial Lancashire. By the 1840s other places were experiencing large-scale influxes of Irish labour migrants. While the migrants accounted for anything up to 30 per cent of the male work-force in the big cities – such as Liverpool and Glasgow – they were if anything more prominent in smaller Scottish towns such as Girvan or Dundee. By the 1870s Tyneside and west Cumberland were as important, in

Table 5.3   The   Irish-born   population
of Britain, 1841–1911

Year	England and Wales	%	Scotland	%
1841	289,404	1.8	126,321	4.8
1851	519,959	2.9	207,367	7.2
1861	601,634	3.0	204,083	6.7
1871	566,540	2.5	207,770	6.2
1881	562,374	2.2	218,745	5.9
1891	458,315	1.6	194,807	4.8
1901	426,565	1.3	205,064	4.6
1911	375,325	1.0	174,715	3.7

Source: Census of England and Wales, 1851, 1871;
Census of Scotland, 1851, 1871

proportionate terms at least, as these other more familiar Irish centres. Irish workers also showed an unusually high degree of mobility within Britain, and they were probably more mobile between types of work as well. The Irish were under-represented in the skilled trades and were over-represented in the worst kinds of hard manual labour (chemical works, dock labour, etc.), though perhaps not as much as was once believed. Although the highest levels of Irish settlement occurred between the early 1830s and the mid-1850s, there was still a regular flow of Irish labour into Britain on the eve of the First World War and beyond.

In terms of labour effect, the impact of Irish settlement is difficult to assess and historians disagree as to the wider economic implications of what contemporaries regarded as a flood of Irish settlers. The nineteenth-century view was quite clear: whether for good or ill, Irish workers were thought to have played a decisive role in the Industrial Revolution. Irish labour was commonly held to have checked the upward pressure on wages; native workers considered the Irish to be a threat to their livelihoods because of an alleged willingness to work harder, longer and for less pay. Yet Irish labourers were not alone in being accused of undercutting wages or strike-breaking. In fact, all forms of rural–urban migration posed some sort of threat to established workers. John McEwen, a Perth millowner, said in 1834 that the children in his employ were Highlanders who worked for lower wages and kept out their Perth-born counterparts. In Disraeli's 'Condition of England' novel, *Sybil: Or, the Two Nations* (1845), it was Suffolk 'hagri-cultural labourers ... sold out of slavery, and sent down by Pickford's van into the labour market to bring down our wages', who drew the venom of Mowbray's hard-pressed workers. In Gaskell's *Mary Barton* (1848) striking Manchester mill-workers were moved to violence by the threat from workers who were 'weary of starvation'; 'foot-sore, way-worn, half-starved' imports from the outlying textile towns. As if to emphasise the ambiguities of this issue, Gaskell's, *North and South* (1854–5), revolves around a factory in which there occurs a strike in which local workers riot because of the introduction of Irish 'knobsticks'.

Historians are divided on the issue of Irish labour and its impact on wages and conditions. E.H. Hunt (1973) considered that Irish workers played a decisive role in the economy, going as far as to argue that the volume of migration was so great that it slowed out-migration from the poor agricultural districts of England, thus increasing hardship in these areas. A more recent econometric interpretation by J.G. Williamson (1986), however, contends that Irish numbers were not large enough to influence wage rates, although this argument founders because it under-plays the regional features of the early Victorian economy and of Irish settlement. Irish labour may have been well spread across the west of Britain, and eastwards into London, Yorkshire and Durham, but it was also very densely compressed in key areas, such as south Lancashire, where its effects were likely to have been considerable. As with other questions relating to wages and standards of living, the absence of comprehensive data suggests that a complete picture will never be known to us.

The Irish presence was important for the social, economic and cultural development of modern Britain – though nowhere was that impression so considerable as in Scotland where the Irish presence was proportionately larger than in England and Wales. During the nineteenth century, thousands of Irish workers flocked into the expanded centres of Scottish industry. Scotland eventually developed an Irish-born population that, in proportional terms, was far more important than its equivalent in England and Wales. Glasgow was to become the focus of the Irish settlement, with around 10 per cent of all the Irish-born in Britain in the middle of the century. But this was not simply a big city settlement. The outlying towns and villages of Lanarkshire and Ayrshire also attracted a large number of settlers from Ireland. Edinburgh, Leith and every town in the central belt from the Forth to the Clyde developed an association with these immigrant workers. Irish labourers quested as far north as Aberdeen in search of work. Further south, on Tayside, the Dundee flax and jute mills attracted one of Scotland's highest proportional Irish populations, the majority of whom were female textile workers.

Many of these Irish were poor and desperate refugees from a rack-renting, hard-bitten economic environment that offered few prospects for improvement. Some were skilled workers, valued as human capital, although ship-builders, blacksmiths, masons, clerics and even the odd captain of industry, were lost in the sea of opprobrium that met swamped paupers and famine victims.

While Scotland, by virtue of its close cultural and geographical links with Ulster, attracted far more Protestant Irish settlers than any other part of the British Isles, it was the Catholicism of the majority which did most to influence Scottish views of the immigrants. A small but vibrant community in the Hebrides had long provided Catholicism's greatest number of adherents in Scotland, but it was the huge influx of Irish Catholics, mainly from Donegal, that transformed the faith. The needs of Irish Catholics, for example, led to a massive urban church-building programme in this period, and from that foundation emerged a vibrant social and spiritual Catholicism. The arrival of so many Catholics also stoked up ancient anti-Catholic sentiments in Scotland. As in other parts of the Protestant world, Irish settlers in Scotland met with hostile responses, not least from the established church. Echoes of this live on in Scottish culture today.

Although many Irish harvesters came to Scotland looking for seasonal labour, the salient feature of Irish migration to Scotland at this time was its permanence. The Irish-born population grew rapidly in the eighteenth century, as labour supply matched the rhythms of industrial demand, and was well spread throughout the south-western counties of Wigtownshire, Kirkcudbrightshire, Ayrshire, Lanarkshire and Renfrewshire.

Like all immigrants, these Irish brought with them a distinctive cultural baggage, most notably the Orange Order. The first lodge north of the border appeared in Maybole in 1799 or 1800, with soldiers returning from Ireland after the 1798 rising and incoming Ulster weavers providing the initial impetus. Important Orange traditions also developed in Wigtown, Tarbolton, Airdrie, Beith, Kilbirnie, Ardrossan, Port Glasgow and other places on the Clyde. The Orange Order, which survives still in Scotland, was to provide a formidable obstacle to Catholic integration.

At the turn of the century, then, migration patterns were beginning to solidify with growing towns attracting increasing waves of Irish. The most densely packed Irish-born populations outside Glasgow were to be found in textile towns of the western Lowlands. In 1831 another Ayrshire town, Girvan, had a population of 6,430, three-quarters of which had been born in Ireland. Most of these were employed as handloom weavers, outworking for Glasgow merchants. In Kilmarnock (which between 1831 and 1841 grew from 12,768 to 18,093), a large numbers of Irish migrants worked as labourers, stones-breakers and weavers.

Central Scotland rapidly developed into one of the most highly industrialised regions in the world, and Irish labour was drawn in by the availability of steady work, often in the most unpleasant industries such as salt-works, tanneries and chemical factories. This period also saw the development of craft controls which affected incoming ethnic groups, most notably in coal-mining, where Irish workers were often restricted to less well-paid surface work. However, the experience of the Irish in the West of Scotland suggests these early settlers were able gradually to break the native stranglehold on coal hewing.

Epithets such as 'swarming' and 'herding' were commonplace in the 1830s as Scots sought to describe the expanding Irish immigration. An already deep-seated hostility was enormously increased by the desperate immigration of the Great Famine era (1845–51). Although the poor of Ireland were suffering an unimaginable calamity, the *Glasgow Herald* showed bitterness in describing the effects on the great port city. 'The streets of Glasgow', it claimed, 'are at present literally swarming with poor vagrants from the sister kingdom, and the misery of these can scarcely be less than what they have fled or been driven from at home'. Religious passions were also fomenting with the age-old spectre of 'Popery' raised in explanation of the Irish influx. Indeed, the city's *Witness* newspaper went as far as to blame the very famine itself on 'a religion of dependency and indigence'. The 33,267 Irish who landed in Glasgow between June and September 1847 were without exception either wholly dependent upon charitable help or 'in the last stages of wretchedness'. Disease, and with it death, had become a part of migrant stream into Glasgow. As elsewhere, this hardened public opinion from a position of pity or sympathy to one of fear and worse. Between 1845 and 1846 there was a doubling of the death rate in Glasgow. Whereas the cholera outbreak of 1832 had claimed 3,005 Glaswegian victims, the same disease carried off more than 2,300 in December of 1847 alone. The poor rate rose in line with the increased burden of Irish paupers and the spread of disease among the poor. Critics blamed the Irish, but the medical inspectors were more concerned at 'Those frightful abodes of human wretchedness which lie along the High Street, Saltmarket, and Bridgegate . . . the bulk of that district known as the "Wynds and Closes of Glasgow"... [where] all sanitary evils exist in perfection.'

The famine transformed the size and nature of Irish immigration to Scotland and intensified negative reactions to it. Coming on top of growing tensions between workers in the Hungry Forties', anti-Irish feeling was increased still further by the re-establishment in 1850 of the Papal Hierarchy in England (what the London *Times* dubbed the 'Papal Aggression'), as we shall see in chapter 12.

5.8 Conclusion

Population growth was one of the most important features of British society in this period, with England in particular seeing rapid rates of development. Britain also became the world's first large-scale urban and industrial society. In Ireland, however, the situation was quite different from that in Britain, not least because of a failure to industrialise and the effects of rural poverty, and, in the 1840s, of the Great Famine. Not only did population grow, but the very character of population in England, Scotland (and to a lesser extent Wales) also changed beyond recognition. If population increases in size many times over it was also redistributed to an enormous degree: new towns developed, cities expanded and the the north of England and Scotland became economically much more important than had previously been the case. Industrialisation and labour migration together turned Britain from a mainly rural to an overwhelmingly urban place. Important rural areas remained, but the dominant experience, as we shall see in Chapter 6, was urban. A range of factors contributed to population growth in this period, the most important of which was the reduced age at marriage and an increase in the surplus of births over deaths.

Summary

◆ Britain was the world's first industrial and urban power.
◆ Development was not uniform.
◆ Population was redistributed as well as growing in absolute terms.
◆ Migration, urbanisation and population growth are interlinked.
◆ Ireland's population history followed a unique path in UK terms, with decline and massive migration outstripping examples elsewhere.

Points to discuss

◆ Why did population in Britain grow so rapidly?
◆ Why did growth tail off and decline in the later period?
◆ Why did so many people emigrate from the British Isles in this period of population growth?
◆ Why was Ireland's population history in the nineteenth century so different from that of England?
◆ What part did migration play in re-orientating the British population?

References and further reading

A. Armstrong, *Farmworkers: A Social and Economic History 1700–1980* (1988).

B. Thomas, *Migration and Economic Growth: A Study of Great Britain and the Atlantic Economy* (Cambridge, 1954).

D. E. Baines, *Migration in a Mature Economy: Emigration and Internal Migration in England and Wales, 1861–1900* (Cambridge, 1985).

W. H. Chaloner, *Social and Economic Development of Crewe* (Manchester, 1950).

C. E. Chambers and J. D. Mingay, *The Agricultural Revolution, 1750–1880* (1966).

T. M. Devine, *The Great Highland Famine: Hunger. Emigration and the Scottish Highlands in the Nineteenth Century* (Edinburgh, 1988).

F. Engels, *The origins of the Family, Private Property and the State* (1884).

F. G. Heath, *The English Peasantry* (1874).

E. J. Hobsbawm, *Labouring Man* (1964).

E. H. Hunt, *Regional Wage Variations in England and Wales, 1850–1914* (Oxford, 1973).

J. Langton, 'The industrial revolution and the regional geography of England', *Transactions of the Institute of British Geographers*, 9 (1984).

R. Lawton (ed.), *The Census and Social Structure* (1977).

R. Lawton and C. G. Pooley, *Britain, 1740–1950: An Historical Geography* (1992).

D. M. MacRaild, *Irish Migrants in Modern Britain, 1780–1922* (Basingstoke, 1999).

T. R. Malthus, *An Essay on the Principle of Population* (1798; Cambridge, 1992), edited with an introduction by D. Winch.

J. Marshall, *Furness in the Industrial Revolution* (Beckermet, 1981 edn).

C. F. G. Masterman, *The Condition of England* (1907 edn).

S. Pollard and P. Robertson, *British Shipbuilding, 1870–1914* (1949).

C. G. Pooley, 'Welsh migration to England in the mid-nineteenth century', *Journal of Historical Geography*, 9 (1983).

E. G. Ravenstein, 'The laws of migration', *Journal of the Statistical Society*, I: 48 (1885), II: 52 (1889).

A. Redford, *Labour Migration in England, 1800–1850* (Manchester, 1926).

J. Saville, *Rural Depopulation in England and Wales, 1851–1951* (1957).

S. Szreter, Fertility, *Class and Gender in Britain, 1860–1940* (Cambridge, 1996).

J. G. Williamson, 'The Impact of the Irish on British Labour Markets during the Industrial Revolution', *Explorations in Economic History* (September 1986).

C. W. J. Withers, *Urban Highlanders: Highland–Lowland Migration and Urban Gaelic Culture, 1700–1900* (Edinburgh, 1998).

E. A. Wrigley and R. S. Schofield, *The Population History of England, 1541–11871: A Reconstruction* (1981).

6 Living Space

Contents

Introduction

Although an economy can be urban without being industrial, and vice versa, in practice, in the modern western world, the two have gone hand in hand. What we can say, then, is that *urbanisation* was both companion to and corollary of industrialisation. The population of Britain changed dramatically during the long nineteenth century. It became far larger, in absolute terms, and more concentrated in terms of where the people lived. In the mid-eighteenth century, Britain had one huge city, and a number of small ones. None of them (apart from London), even in 1801, numbered more than 100,000 inhabitants. By 1914, big cities, large towns and a multitude of smaller towns had sprung up: more than that, great swathes of former agricultural regions had become heavily urbanized, as town boundaries melded into each other. The green spaces between towns such as Oldham and Rochdale, South Shields and Jarrow, or Birmingham and Wolverhampton became smaller or else completely disappeared. In almost every case, the emergence of an urban centre was coterminous with the type of industrial developments that we associate with the Industrial Revolution. Lancashire registered the most startling growth; the north-east of England and central Scotland became two of the most industrial and urban societies in the world; Yorkshire, the west Midlands and South Wales grew into major regional and then world centres of commerce and industry. By the time hostilities broke out on the Western Front, in 1914, Britain had 35 cities and towns of more than 100,000 population: from a mainly rural society, the country had been transformed into the most urban place on earth.

In this chapter, then, we seek to sketch the patterns of urban development in Britain during the period 1801–1914. We also attempt to evaluate the importance of urban development, offering some explanation of the ways in which it affected the lives of ordinary people.

Key issues

▶ How did urban Britain grow?

▶ How did people in urban society live?

▶ What was the effect of urban growth?

▶ Where did people live?

▶ How important was rural society?

6.1 Patterns of urban development

Of the nature of urban centres, several observations can be made. First, established urban areas continued to grow. Cities such as Norwich and Bristol, which had been important in the eighteenth century, expanded again in the following hundred years, although not as impressively as in previous years. Secondly, Britain saw huge growth in the size of its great commercial and manufacturing towns. From the mid-eighteenth century, Glasgow, Liverpool and Manchester began to seize urban predominance, after London, from established cities such as Exeter, Bristol or Norwich. Thirdly, sizeable, but previously unremarkable centres, such as Bradford and Merthyr, burgeoned enormously. Fourthly, and perhaps most impressively, the Industrial Revolution fostered economic and urban growth of a quite remarkable order in little-known towns, some of which had been mere hamlets in the early nineteenth century: towns such as Barrow-in-Furness, Crewe, Doncaster and Middlesbrough.

It is difficult to exaggerate the extent to which urbanisation affected British society in the nineteenth century. Indeed, the growth of towns or cities, and the radical overhaul of the balance of population between rural and urban worlds that this indicates, is one of the most sensitive indicators there is of the emergence of a modern industrial state. A country may be urban without being industrial, and certain sorts of industry can occur without large urban centres, but the scale and nature of Britain's economic development during the long nineteenth century suggests that urban growth was fundamental to it.

If any single social experience can be said to have typified the living arrangements and the new working experiences of the majority of the British people, then it was urbanisation. Although growth rates were uneven, varying by region, several key centres experienced rapid growth in the early industrial period. Big town or cities such as Birmingham, Liverpool and Manchester doubled in size in the third quarter of the eighteenth century, though none contained many more than 50,000 people – a figure that by 1901 would be matched even by such places as Luton. By the 1830s, Glasgow, Liverpool and Manchester had more than 200,000 inhabitants.

The measurement of urban development, and of urban centres, was exceptionally crude. This was reflected in migration patterns as well as in the distribution of population in the industrial regions. Census enumerators were told to regard settlements of over 2,000 as towns, even though many of these were far from obviously urbanized. By 1851 just over 50 per cent of the people of England and Wales lived in urban centres of this size or greater (see Table 6.1).

This, however, masked a more subtle reality. The simple division between urban and rural hides some important aspects of nineteenth-century spatial geography and culture. In the coalfield regions of south Wales and County Durham, both rural and urban characteristics – such as open spaces yet cramped housing – existed in parallel long after the classic period of the Industrial Revolution. In 1821, the majority of Durham and Northumberland colliers lived in settlements of less than 2,000 people, in places such as Crook or Tow Law. In these regions, even much later, towns tended to be small and dispersed, and were un-nucleated, having no recognisable central business districts. The scattered nature of mining meant that factories, centres of commerce and administrative buildings were absent from these towns, most of which were simply linked villages. Such urban areas were thus amorphous; they were towns only inasmuch as someone chose to label them 'census enumeration districts' or 'urban sanitary districts'. There was a world of difference between physically compressed towns such as York and Carlisle, with their medieval walls, and the scattered settlements of the coal-mining Rhondda Valley in South Wales; yet both were defined in later century censuses as 'urban'.

6.2 London, world capital

London has a rich history of urban development. From the fifteenth century it was the largest city in Europe, with people from across the continent finding their way there. It was (and remains) a cosmopolitan place; a magnet for an admixture of different people from Britain and further afield. Jews and Irish, Scots and Welsh, for instance, formed noticeable and commented-upon ethnic clusters prior to the eighteenth century. Distinct crafts and religions led to the settlement of German tailors and Protestants escaping the

Table 6.1	Urban and rural populations of England and Wales, 1851–1911 (m)				
	Total	**Urban**	**Urban %**	**Rural**	**Rural %**
1851	17.93	8.99	50.2	8.94	49.8
1861	20.07	10.99	54.6	9.11	45.4
1871	22.71	14.04	61.8	8.67	38.2
1881	25.79	17.64	67.9	8.34	32.1
1891	29.00	20.86	72.0	8.11	28.0
1901	32.53	25.05	77.0	7.47	23.0
1911	36.07	28.16	78.1	7.91	21.9

Source: Census of England and Wales, 1911, vol. I, p.xv

persecution in Europe's Catholic countries, notably the French Huguenots. Labour migration was seen as a challenge to the stability of the social fabric in the medieval period, but events such as the Black Death in the fourteenth century, and increasing demand in growing towns, meant that restrictions had to be slackened. As a greater flow of people developed, much of it was drawn to the burgeoning capital, mainly from the southern counties. This influx more than compensated for London's high death rate; by the twentieth century some 20 per cent of all English-born people were resident there.

London's population was dynamic, with a steady but uncounted flow of people passing in and out of its boundaries. Between 1861 and 1911, it burgeoned from 2.8 m to 4.5 m inhabitants. While much of this was due to net in-migration, natural increase accounted for 85 per cent of all growth by the end of the century. Yet, London, while not a centre of industry or of large factories in comparison with the great northern cities, did nevertheless have a richly variegated economy. Few of its businesses employed large quantities of labour; workshops and small concerns prevailed, and 86 per cent of employers in 1851 had fewer than ten employees. Women out-numbered men, because, according to Philip Waller, 'domestic service and the prospect of marriage were the prevailing forces'. This coincided with a reduction in labour opportunities for rural women: in 1851, 229,000 women were employed in agriculture; by 1901, this had fallen to 67,000. This decline was especially noticeable in places where urban industrial development was least apparent, for example, in the shires of southern England and East Anglia. Like their counterparts else-where, migrants to the metropolis were young, mainly in their twenties. Rural migrants tended also to avoid London's inner city, where three-quarters of residents were London-born, and many others were Irish and (especially later in the century) Jewish and Italian. Although it peaked in 1851 at 108, 548, the Irish population remained an important presence until well into the twentieth century.

Mobility was highest among casual labourers, whose job security was lowest. Once in London migrants did not necessarily stay put, and the social investigator, Charles Booth, who conducted extensive research into poverty in London's East End, in the 1880s, discovered that 40 per cent of families in Bethnal Green had moved within one year. In general, migrants from other counties were attracted to London in inverse proportion to their distance from the south-east of England. Among these migrants, turnover was high, with a large part of the working-class populace occupying the same housing for only a few months.

By the later nineteenth century London had cemented its position as the world largest metropolitan centre. It was a magnet for people, a centre of political life, a place whose cultural elite had European pretensions but whose businesses were of world importance. As the administrative centre of Britain, London was also the hub of the world's greatest empire. Its waterfront thrived on a huge commercial traffic which saw London con-ducting European and Empire traffic in a way that dwarfed even Liverpool's dominance of transatlantic commercial activity. London's waterfront housed at any one time more vessels that any other port in the world. A cosmopolitan maritime population – Chinese, Lascars (East Indians), Americans, Europeans – crowded the dock front embarking on, or disembarking from, vessels. This was very much an environment moulded by man. In 1913, Arthur Sarsfield, a London crime reporter who, under the pseudonym Sax Rohmer, published *The Mystery of Fu Manchu*, described a journey down the Thames, the 'oily glitter of the tide', and 'on the Surrey shore a blue light … flicked translucent tongues against the night's curtain … a gasworks'.

The people of London lived in a multitude of different types of dwellings, dependent upon their status and social class. As London sprawled outwards, areas of countryside were swallowed up by new suburban areas. Although Ford Madox Brown's Hampstead was still surrounded by suburban greenery when he painted it in *English Autumn Afternoon* (1852–4), it had been fully rural thirty years earlier when John Keats had lived there. Twenty years later it had itself been engulfed by more suburban places. As London's boundaries rolled out into the Home Counties, too, small towns and villages were swallowed up by its progress.

6.3 Other urban centres

The large cities

In the growing cities of the industrial north, especially in Glasgow, Liverpool and Manchester, large industrial and commercial enterprises were far more common than in London. In Manchester, mills and factories to some extent, and warehouses in a far more wide-ranging way, encapsulated the newer industrial way of life (even if they were located mostly away from the immediate city centre). This differed from Liverpool, where the dominance of the docks meant that work was casual and that factories were uncommon, although food-processing concerns, for example Tate and Lyle's sugar refinery, became more apparent as the period progressed. Glasgow's economy rested on a number of enterprises. As a commercial port, Glasgow, like Liverpool, had risen quickly in the eighteenth century. Textiles, engineering and shipbuilding all became increasing important in the second half of that century. Glasgow was the hub for a cluster of growing Clydeside towns, places where ship-building and engineering would earn an international reputation for scale and quality. Additionally, the Clyde's thriving dock frontage afforded thousands of jobs that were similar to those on Merseyside – casual, hard and organized into small and localized territorial units. These three cities represented important peaks in the vista of labour mobility and in-migration. Their patterns of growth were remarkably similar in pace and extent, even if founded on very different economic bases. In 1801 Liverpool's population stood at 82,000; within fifty years this had grown to 376,000. The corresponding figures for Manchester were 75,000 and 303,000 and for Glasgow 77,000 and 357,000 (See table 3.2).

Manchester – 'shock city' of the Industrial Revolution, Liverpool – the British empire's second port (behind London), Glasgow – a major empire port, Scotland's principal population centre, and a major British centre of engineering and shipbuilding, all epitomize the enormous effects of urban development in the high age of British economic development.

All three cities experienced remarkable periods of growth between 1811 and 1851. In only one recorded instance during that time (in Manchester in 1841) did the decennial growth rate fall below 30 per cent. Moreover, in Manchester (1831), in Glasgow (1821) and in Liverpool (1831) growth rates reached 45 per cent or more.

Table 6.2 Population growth in the major northern cities, 1801–1911 (in 000s)

	Liverpool	% inc.	Manchester	% inc.	Glasgow	% inc.
1801	82	–	75	–	77	–
1811	104	26.8	89	18.6	101	31.6
1821	138	32.7	126	44.9	147	45.5
1831	202	46.4	182	44.4	202	37.4
1841	286	39.6	235	29.1	275	36.1
1851*	376	31.5	303	28.9	357	29.8
1861	444	18.1	339	11.0	420	17.6
1871	493	11.0	351	3.5	522	24.3
1881	553	12.2	462	31.6	587	12.5
1891*	630	13.9	505	9.3	658	12.1
1901	685	8.7	645	27.7	762	15.8
1911	753	9.9	714	10.7	1,000	31.2

*Highest figure recorded in years when boundaries changed
Source: Reports of the Census of England and Wales; Census of Scotland, 1851–1921

These major cities followed the known rules of migration because they gained the majority of incoming labour from surrounding towns and rural areas. Lancashire and Cheshire were dominant in the cases of Liverpool and Manchester, though the high proportion of young people among migrants suggests that many of these Lancashire-born residents were actually the sons and daughters of recent arrivals. Irish workers also featured prominently in these populations, as we saw in the previous chapter.

Industrial and commercial towns

Victorian statistics – censuses and the like – indicate quite clearly that the urban experience began not with great cities but with more modest towns. While compared to European nations at the time, Britain had numerous large cities and a huge urban population, most of the urban population lived in more modest-sized towns. The number of very large cities in Britain was (and remains) quite low compared to the patterns that have emerged in the United States since the 1880s. Britain's large cities in the nineteenth century (outside the capital) were Liverpool, Glasgow and Manchester. Others, such as Bristol and Leeds, though large by the European scales of development, were much smaller than American cities such as Chicago. The importance of the myriad smaller centres – both cities and large towns – cities such as Newcastle, numerous mill towns in Lancashire and Yorkshire (Bradford, Preston, etc.), was far greater than that of the big three or four cities.

While towns became larger and more numerous, those of between roughly 10,000 and 200,000 constituted a much more typical social experience for the emerging working class. Textiles centres such as Bury, Bolton and Bradford grew tenfold in the years 1780–1830; the wool capital, Leeds, grew seven-fold to more than 120,000; and industrial centres, such as Sheffield and Wolverhampton, experienced five-fold increases. Similar patterns of development were observed in the medium-sized towns of south Wales, the Black Country, Tyneside and central Scotland.

Britain's other cities were small in comparison to London. They were, nevertheless, important regional centres. By the 1850s, Birmingham, with a population of more than 230,000, had become a major urban centre and the focal point of the increasingly densely populated and industrialized West Midlands region, drawing in labour migrants from Warwickshire, Worcestershire, the West Country and Wales, as well as from further afield. Newcastle, which in 1831 had a population of only 54,000, expanded massively over the following decades to reach 267,000 on the eve of the First World War.

Newcastle was at the heart of the north-east's ship-building, mining and heavy engineering region. It centred on a district that included many other major towns along the Tyne and Wear rivers (North and South Shields, Wallsend and Howdon, Gateshead, Hebburn, Jarrow and Sunderland) as well as the smaller industrial towns and mining villages, fanning out between Ashington, Barnard Castle and Easington.

Further to the north, by the 1850s, Edinburgh had become a major commercial city as well as a long-standing national centre of government and law. Its hinterland, which combined rural pursuits, such as farming, and semi-industrial developments, for example mining, lacked the dramatic growth rates and sheer size of Clydeside's urban areas, but, with Leith fast becoming a major port, the area was of both regional and national importance. The same could be said for Leeds, the dynamic and fast-growing centre of the worsted industry, which proved to be a major recipient of local and distant labour alike. To the south, Bristol, despite passing its heyday in the eighteenth century, continued to be a magnet for rural in-migrants from some of the poorest parts of England.

Most of Britain's cities were at the centre of thriving regional economies, which included agricultural lands and smaller, often quite specialized, towns. There were several other regions of urban population, however, which lacked the focal point of a large city. The Potteries centred on Stoke-on-Trent and had no town to compare to Birmingham; Sheffield, in the 1850s, was unlike Manchester or Liverpool in being an isolated and semi-rural string of urban villages rather than a great city (though its near-neighbour, Rotherham, nurtured exceptional growth in the 1860s). Sheffield's isolated setting was reflected in the profile of its labour migrants, most of whom came from the city's rural hinterlands. In 1861 more than three-quarters of the city's 185,172 population had been born in Yorkshire, Derbyshire, Nottinghamshire and Lincolnshire. Although the arrival of the railways meant that steel-workers and miners from Lancashire, the north-east or Wales could find their way to the growing 'steel city', migrants from distant points of departure such as Ireland and Scotland together constituted less than 5 per cent.

Perhaps the most impressive developments in the early Victorian period occurred in Lancashire, where commercial, industrial and factory developments were at the forefront. This county, the seat of cotton manufacture, and the leading sector of the Industrial Revolution, saw unparalleled urban growth and labour migration. The earliest and most striking developments occurred in mill towns, such as Bolton, which grew from around 18,000 in 1801 to 181,000 in 1911; Oldham (12,000 to 147,000) and Preston (12,000 to 117,000) were also to the fore. At the same time, the county's coal and engineering industries also stimulated considerable population redistribution and absolute growth. Wigan expanded from 11,000 to 89,000 between 1801 and 1911. Other major industries, such as glass and chemicals (along with coal) also gave rise to urban growth in Lancashire. This was certainly the amalgam of stimuli that prompted the population of St Helens to grow from 15,000 in 1851 to 97,000 in 1911.

The nature of towns, and of the industries within them, clearly influenced patterns of migration. While women in search of domestic work had a good chance of finding it quite close to home, men were often compelled by the demand for their skills to travel much further. Male mobility was determined by the economic specialisation of many regions: thus, whereas women's domestic work was universally available, employment opportunities in many skilled trades were not. Skilled Welsh migrants to England, for example, were attracted to industrial centres which offered mainly male work – for example, Tyneside, Sunderland, Middlesbrough, Portsmouth and Plymouth. At the same time, cities of regional importance, such as Liverpool, Birmingham and Bristol, also drew Welsh migrants, mainly from the Welsh counties nearest to them. Similar patterns existed among the Irish, although the Welsh in Liverpool in 1871 were distributed more evenly across the labour market than the Irish; the Welsh were under-represented in unskilled work and well represented in the ranks of the skilled.

Scotland and Wales

The Industrial Revolution turned Scotland into one of the mostly starkly divided countries in the world. The maintenance of strong agricultural districts in the lowlands and borders, and in the north-east counties of Fife and Angus and further north on the east coast, and the perpetuation of traditional 'peasant'-type culture in the Highlands ensured that much of Scotland would contrast sharply with the developing central belt. Here, between Edinburgh in the east and Glasgow in the west – in a narrow band some 40 miles wide and 20 miles deep – there developed one of the most industrial and urban regions in the world. Textiles, mining, metal manufacture and shipbuilding ensured that by the 1880s, few places in the world were as densely populated. Dozens of large villages, small towns and more substantial urban centres ensured that this was in general a crowded region. Although most of the population of Scotland lived in this urbanised region in 1900, very few of the towns in this area appear in lists of large towns. Thus, although Glasgow was a city to compare with any in Britain or the world at this time, and Edinburgh, though smaller, was an important capital city, the majority of the central belt population were found in satellite towns that fanned out from the major rivers (the Clyde and the Forth) or were studded throughout coal- and iron-fields. The largest urban centres in Scotland (after Glasgow) are indicated in Table 6.3.

As we can see from tables 6.2 and 6.3, there is a significant drop from Glasgow (which had topped 1 m in 1911) to Edinburgh, which was half its size. While the fall to third and fourth placed towns, Dundee and Aberdeen, is even more striking, the fact that neither of the fifth and sixth towns of Scotland, Greenock and Paisley, was more than 100,000 strong indicates something of the nature of Scottish urban society. While towns of more than 100,000 were more common in England, places below that size – particularly those of between 30,000 and 40,000 inhabitants – were more representative of the British spatial experience in these years than were either cities or very large towns. Those in the Scottish central belt were likely, for example, to live in linked mining villages or small towns: places such as Hamilton, Airdrie, Wishaw, Bathgate.

Table 6.3   Five largest urban centres in Scotland (after Glasgow), 1851–1911

Year	Edinburgh	Dundee	Aberdeen	Greenock	Paisley
1851	202,000	79,000	72,000	37,000	48,000
1861	203,000	91,000	74,000	43,000	47,000
1871	244,000	119,000	88,000	58,000	48,000
1881	295,000	140,000	106,000	67,000	56,000
1891	342,000	154,000	125,000	63,000	66,000
1901	395,000	161,000	154,000	68,000	79,000
1911	424,000	176,000	164,000	75,000	84,000

Source: Census of Scotland, 1911

The urban scene in Wales bore some similarities to the pattern of development in Scotland. Central, north and western Wales remained very rural, and many of the villages in these areas were isolated places. Hill farming tended to be common and relatively primitive, as it was in the Lake Counties of England or the Scottish Highlands.

Urban growth in Wales, as we can deduce from Table 6.4, was unremarkable in a British context, although a number of qualifications should be offered. The notion that urban growth simply means the development of very large towns and cities is too unsubtle a characterisation for the Welsh case; secondly, Welsh urban growth was striking enough in the context of what was a thoroughly rural society in the eighteen century.

The main urban developments in Wales were regionally very specific, occurring in the south around Swansea in the west, and further east, focusing on Cardiff and the Rhondda coal region in the valleys that raked down towards the Welsh capital like the indentations from a tiger's claws. Other coastal centres such as Newport were also important. In the

Table 6.4   The three major urban centres in Wales, 1831–1911

Year	Cardiff	% rise	Newport	% rise	Swansea	% rise
1831	6,000		–		20,000	
1841	10,000	66.7	10,000	–	25,000	25.0
1851	26,000	160.0	19,000	90.0	31,000	24.0
1861	33,000	26.9	23,000	21.1	42,000	35.5
1871	40,000	21.1	27,000	17.4	66,000	33.3
1881	83,000	107.5	38,000	33.3	76,000	15.2
1891	129,000	55.4	55,000	44.7	91,000	19.7
1901	164,000	27.1	67,000	21.8	95,000	4.4
1911	182,000	11.0	84,000	25.4	144,000	51.6

*Highest figure recorded in years when boundaries were changed
Source: Reports of the Census of England and Wales; Census of Scotland, 1851–1921

valleys near Cardiff, Merthyr Tydfil was the largest town, but, as in the north-east (another prominent coal mining region), urban development comprised many small towns and linked villages rather than in bigger conurbations. For every town such as the iron manufacturing centres of Merthyr Tydfil or Dowlais there were dozens of small villages and towns in which were housed one of Europe's largest mining work-forces.

Growth in Wales's urban centres occurred in a number of noticeable bursts: this, too, can be seen in Table 6.4. Cardiff was a coal metropolis; its patterns of growth offer a very sensitive indicator of what was happening to the north in the valleys that fed its docks and commercial centre. In 1801, Cardiff was a tiny town of merely 2,000 strong – a figure which remained the same 10 years later. Doubling in size to 4,000 in 1821, reaching 6,000 in 1831 and 10,000 in 1841, Cardiff then went on to record what, from this base, were quite staggering rates of growth, with particular bursts of activity in the 1840s and the 1870s and, to a lesser extent, the 1880s. The first explosion came as a result of developments in coal but, to a greater extent, iron-ore. The 1840s were when the iron towns of Merthyr and Dowlais recorded their first and greatest periods of population growth. The second phase of growth, in the 1870s and 1880s, was when South Wales – compared to the north-east of England, a late arrival to the world market – became the synonym for coal that it was to the Edwardians.

6.4 Varieties in the urban world

As we shall see, changes to the way people lived affected all classes; but is workers' living environments that traditionally attracted historians. This is because the housing conditions of the urban working class is an emotive subject. Contemporary commentators have left us with the impression that one of the most awful effects of industrialism was the degeneration of housing, caused by a huge increase in the size of the urban population. Writers such as James Kay, the Manchester doctor, educationalist and social reformer, in his influential study, *The Moral and Physical Condition of the Labouring Classes in … Manchester* (1833), enforced the view, still held by many social historians, that living conditions at mid-century were one of the most significant brakes upon the improvements of the standards of living of ordinary working-class people. Kay portrayed the social environment of the Manchester labouring class as a product of poor housing and living conditions; although he suggested these factors were exacerbated by the allegedly immoral and unrestrained attitudes of immigrant groups such as the Irish.

The living conditions and housing of the urban working class varied greatly and it would be impossible to encapsulate the entire experience here. A number of general observations can, however, be made. The speed of urban growth in most towns tended to catch out local builders and speculators. It was very difficult to forecast how successful an industry, or series of industries, was going to be, and thus spurts of in-migration to towns almost always led, first, to a serious shortage of housing and then, secondly, to acute overcrowding. The key issue was whether acute overcrowding should become chronic. On the whole local entrepreneurs were aware of the need for housing – without it, a town would engender a high turn-over in population which destabilised the workforce and thus affected businesses.

Some of the worst living conditions are associated with the early part of our period when industrial development and urban growth occurred on a scale without precedent (Box 6.1). The worst conditions occurred, moreover, in towns with a high proportion of higgledy-piggedly seventeenth- or eighteenth-century housing which was wholly unsuited to nineteenth-century populations. This was certainly the case in Liverpool, where the Victorian problem of overcrowding, poor sanitation and disease were at least predicated upon the fact that so much of the housing had been built for an eighteenth-century population. Here, many urban dwellers were probably crammed into old, airless, damp and sometimes dilapidated accommodation. By 1841 Liverpool and Manchester were the mostly densely populated urban spaces in the world. Population density for England and Wales averaged 275 persons per square mile, whereas the figure for Liverpool was 138,224 and for Manchester 100,000. Dr Duncan of Liverpool – the country's first Medical Officer of Health – calculated in the mid-nineteenth century that certain streets and alleys in the city had a density equivalent to 657,963 people per square mile. Perhaps unsurprisingly, mortality rates were also fearfully high. In 1840 Liverpool's death rate was 34.4 per 1,000; the figure for Manchester was 33.3 (compared to 27 in London). The average age of death, moreover, was 17 years in Liverpool and 20 in Manchester (compared to 26.5 in London). The conditions of the labouring classes were hardly much better in Glasgow, Newcastle, Leeds, Birmingham and many other towns and cities; nor was this just a problem in such large centres. Old walled towns, for example, were particular inappropriate for coping with increased populations; examples included the old parts of Edinburgh, Hull, London and York. This is why Norwich was so badly affected by the smallpox epidemic in 1870-2 which killed 45,000 people in England and Wales.

Throughout this period, the average number of persons per house was 5.45 nationally, although this figure does not account for the desperate overcrowding experienced by many working-class people. The physical shape of these communities was, however, contested ideological ground. For those who lived two or three families to a house, overcrowding was simply a question of poverty and the lack of personal space. For philanthropists and reformers, overcrowding compromised hygiene and morality by encouraging unnecessary familiarity between people of both sexes. Yet few families could afford homes which met with the approval of moral guardians. For example the social investigator Joseph Adshead pointed out in his *Distress in Manchester: Evidence ... of the State of the Labouring Classes in 1840–2* (1842) that 'there are children of both sexes, *mere decency* requires *four rooms,* – three for sleeping and one for daily use' (emphasis in the original).

The poor conditions of these new urban communities were often merely caused by pressure on money, space and time. Lodging-houses provided many young migrant workers with rudimentary places to rest, and contemporary writers cashed in on the lurid fascination of their audiences whom they regaled with sordid tales of beds occupied day and night by rotating shift-workers, entire families crammed into single rooms, drunkards and criminals lounging in the doorways, and prostitutes lurking on every stairwell. Not all lodging houses were corrupted, and some aspired to be more than glorified brothels. However, Henry Mayhew, in *London Labour and the London Poor* (1861–2), his classic sociological investigation, estimated that 10,000 of London's 70,000 lodging houses were of the lowest sort, by which he meant places in which criminals and prostitutes resided. One Whitehaven surgeon told a team of government investigators under Robert

Box 6.1

'Coketown'

The urban landscape described by Charles Dickens in *Hard Times* (1854). Coketown was a fictitious place thought to have been based on Preston. The illustration is an engraving of London in 1872, entitled: 'Over London by Rail'. Coketown, to which Messrs. Bounderby and Gradgrind now walked, was a triumph of fact ...

It was a town of red brick, or of brick that would have been red if the smoke and ashes had allowed it; but as matters stood it was a town unnatural red and black like the painted face of a savage. It was a town of machinery and tall chimneys, out of which interminable serpents of smoke trailed themselves for ever and ever, and never got uncoiled. It had a black canal in it, and a river than

ran purple with ill-smelling dye, and vast piles of buildings full of windows where there was a rattling and trembling all day long, and where the piston of the steam-engine worked monotonously up and down, like the head of an elephant in a state of melancholy madness. It contained several large streets all very like one another, and many small streets still more like one another, inhabited by people equally like one another, who all went in and out at the same hours, with the same sound upon the pavements, to do the same work, and to whom every day was the same as yesterday and tomorrow, and every year the counterpart of the last and the next.

Source: *Hard Times* (Hazel Watson and Viney Ltd, n.d.), p. 522

Source: Gustave Doré and Blanchard Jerrold, *London: a Pilgrimage* (London, 1872)

Rawlinson, who worked for the Chief Medical Officer of Health, John Simon, in 1849 that the town's high incidence of fever was due to overcrowding in local lodging houses: 'nearly all the cases in Ribton Lane were from two lodging houses which are always crowded with Irish', he claimed. Even the more reputable ones were thought to be choked with young single males – which usually equated with drunkenness, crime and a pool of demand for other vices – and were overcrowded to a dangerous degree. But some buildings, especially large town houses, could fall into the lodging-house trade almost by accident when they became part of the multiple room-letting syndrome from the landlord's desire to maximize the value of his utility.

Multiple occupancy was not something that workers and their families chose. They avoided it where they could; but it was absolutely a fact of life among the majority of working-class households, even in 1900. It was a necessary condition of existence for the poorer or transient groups, many families chose to ignore the fact that they had lodgers. Lodgers, in fact, could be shadowy characters: although usually young men, often fellow migrants from the same town or village, they were, nevertheless, tangential to family life. Lodgers provided income but also generated more washing and required feeding. They often represented the mother's best chance to earn income while small children played at her feet; but they also added to the hard-work and drudgery of the domestic scene. Equally, respectable families also could be found in overcrowded tenement houses, which might be difficult to distinguish from lodging-houses but offered families a room for as little as 1s 6d a week.

The worst of all urban accommodation was the cellar: in these were found the down-at-heel, the old, infirm, single mothers, and Irish immigrants were found. Some cellars were ventilated by windows or pavement high grates that also afforded natural light, but the majority were dark, damp, miserable and overcrowded. Their sole advantage was low rent, though their relative disadvantage was compounded by cheapness, while the poorest members of the working class lived in them, they were often intially rented, and then sub-let, by the more prosperous working-class families occupying the houses that sat above such subterranean accommodation. The factor of cost undoubtedly encouraged the Irish to congregate in them, sometimes more than one family to a room. Commentators such as Peter Gaskell on Manchester wrote of the 'loathsomeness' of these Irish cellars, made worse by the residents' 'domestic companion, the pig'. Kay also regarded the pig with horror, while Angus Bethune Reach, writing for the *Morning Chronicle* in 1849, reckoned he had seen the worst cellar in Manchester. Besides the usual dampness, darkness and overcrowding, and scenes of drunkenness and dissolution, Reach was shocked to find 'a well-grown calf' sleeping next to a fully clothed man. While as many as one-fifth or more of the working populations of Liverpool and Manchester lived in these lamentable dwellings, cellar living-space tended to be a feature of older residential areas in most towns and cities. Whitehaven, a once buoyant eighteenth-century port which dominated the colonial trade with the Americas, had many of these dwellings. The cellar was not, however, a universal form of accommodation, and it was deliberately avoided in new towns. In Liverpool, where cellar accommodation was a true social menace, the authorities actually tried to prevent people living in them: however, during the Irish Famine, half-a-million starving immigrants descended on the city and simply tore boards from cellar doors and skylights and began to re-occupy them *en masse*. It was in these dwellings that diseases such as typhus were propagated and many starving Irish, such as Sarah Burns, expired. Burns had complained of head and chest pains before she died. The inquest heard how she had eaten only one piece of bread in the two days before her death, and the coroner and members of the jury visited the cellar in which she had lived. The *Liverpool Mail*, 26 December 1846 depicted the scenes they found:

> A person could not stand upright in it, the floor was composed of mud; and in that hovel there were seventeen human beings crowded together without even so much as a bit of straw to lie down on. We felt convinced that if they were allowed to remain in their present condition, there would be two or three deaths before many days.

A verdict of 'died from disease of the lungs accelerated by the want of the common necessities of life' was passed on what was, for mid-1840s Liverpool, an all too common case.

One housing type that prospered across urban Britain was the back-to-back, described by John Burnett, as the 'speculative builder's answer to . . . mass demand'. Either two-up-two-down or one-up-one-down, these houses were relatively cheap and efficient in terms of materials and space. Despite their poor reputation, the better ones were a significant improvement on the majority of urban and rural housing for they were usually built with fire-places, staircases and cooking-ranges, and of solid materials, usually brick. Although the rooms were smaller than was normal with other houses, each dwelling was meant to be self-contained and private. Some had attic rooms and cellars, but the main focus of the house would have been a kitchen, another downstairs room and two bedrooms.

The worst examples of back-to-back building, however, compounded many of the worst effects of rookeries, courts and other overcrowded urban properties. Social reformers such as Edwin Chadwick complained that many back-to-backs which had sprung up by the 1840s were jerry-built, with too little brick work, too much rubble and straw, inadequate ventilation, and little or no drainage, which in turn led to poor sanitation. Chadwick suggested that the lack of space between the rows meant they actually re-created the old environmental problems associated with tightly-pressed court-dwellings. He also criticized the fact that 20 dwellings or more might share one wash-pump and a single privy. The back-to-back house was most common in Birmingham and in many towns across Lancashire and Yorkshire, with the West Riding having a particularly dense concentration. London, however, had proportionately less of this type of housing; instead, it had a vast array of housing types which was typical of a sprawling metropolis, built up over the centuries.

The classic terraced house – that utilitarian type of dwelling which still dominates large parts of most British towns and cities – was rare in the 1830s beyond the means of poorer working-class families. In the first instance, they had been intended mainly as artisans' dwellings. It was not until the 1860s that the terraced streets we know today were being built, and many date from after that. By the 1870s the most modest version of all working-class housing was the two-up-two-down 'through terrace' – with its access at both front and rear, sometimes with small gardens or back yard, and of solid construction and adequately ventilated. Increasingly, this was becoming the standard dwelling of urban Britain. Nevertheless, many of the poor and casually employed still lived in tenements, back-to-backs, rookeries and courts and would continue to do so until the Second World War.

The traditional terraced house was a great improvement on the back-to-backs, the lodging-house and the damp cellar. Many were built in the 1850s and 1860s at a time when covered sewerage systems and adequately piped clean water were also being provided by municipalities. These houses, with their separate rooms, enabled greater definition of the spheres of domestic activity, from chatting or reading to eating or sleeping. Town Improvement Acts laid down minimum standards of street access, open spaces, water supply, drainage, sewerage, earth or water closets, room height and window space. Bye-laws introduced by some local authorities to reduce overcrowding meant that builders and landlords faced a less than maximum economic return because the terraced houses used space less efficiently than either tenements or back-to-backs. Nevertheless, they were more efficient than the suburban semi-detached homes that became the vogue in the inter-war period; and, in any case, resourceful builders were able to improve on their efficiency by turning out flats modelled on the terraced principle. This was particularly evident on the north-east where 'Tyneside flats' – which effectively divided two-up-two-down terraced homes into two separate dwellings – became the region's most distinctive housing type. By the 1890s, up to 60 per cent of the populations of Gateshead and South Shields occupied such flats. These flats doubled the number of families that could be housed in a street, which had an effect on community life in such accommodation by pressing more people into the available space.

Terraced houses were usually built in straight streets. This replaced an earlier style of layout frequently described in terms of a warren. This earlier style had been difficult to keep clean or to light because it contained so many self-enclosed alleyways, closes or courts. In contrast, the straight streets of terraced houses, equally apportioned and relatively spaciously laid out, were easier to light and to provide with supplies of gas, water and drainage. This was true not only of areas, as a whole, but also of individual properties. This shift can be presented as making it easier to police neighbourhoods and thus contain the population, but it rather reflected a conflation of demand with entrepreneurial activity. Shifts in housing type are also a reminder of the variety that characterized the Victorian period. The expansion of housing led to a growth in brick, tile and slate production. The removal of the Brick Tax in 1850 was followed by major growth. Initially, brick-works were widely distributed, but from the 1880s large firms increasingly dominated production. They benefited from mechanisation in production and from railway movement of bricks. In the south-east, the Fletton process, using the Jurassic clays of the East Midlands, whose high carbon content cut the cost of firing, became increasingly important.

If working-class housing was major issue, in the nineteenth century, it was not the only sort of accommodation that was built in this period; nor indeed were working men, women and children the only ones to experience new ways of living in this period. The city or the town cannot be understood without reference to the development of the suburbs. Improved transport systems, including railways (later on, light railways), and particularly trams, omnibuses and later cars, opened up vast new areas where middle-class, professional and even artisanal households could reasonably live. Commuting was a feature of Manchester life as early as the 1840s, as Engels observed in his *Condition of the Working-Classes in England* (1845). By the later part of the century, suburbs had been joined by sleeper towns as modish places for the more affluent in society to live. Light railway systems in places such as Cullercoats and Whitley Bay on Tyneside enabled shipyard draughtsmen as much as city-centre businessmen to work in places such as Wallsend and Newcastle while living in the fresh air of the seaside. With railways, retirement centres and holiday destinations such as Brighton, Scarborough, and Weston-Super-Mare grew up and developed a more practical utility: not all of them were within easy commuter distance of the big cities, but many were ideal for weekend retreats and regular breaks. The ease of rail connections is one reason why, today, Windermere has so many middle-class villas, dating to our period, lining up along its shoreline.

The urban world was not, therefore, uniformly or solely for the compression of working people and their lives. Employers may have enjoyed the country life in their estates, but most also kept town houses. Large urban properties, far beyond the means of working people, were a feature of urban life. Much of today's poorer, multiple-occupancy urban accommodation began life in the nineteenth century as fine dwellings for the prosperous middle class: this is certainly true, for example, of the huge houses, many of them now derelict, around Liverpool's Sefton Park. Planned towns may have been designed to provide solid housing for workers, and adequate living space for all, but some part of the thinking was aimed at providing accommodation befitting the new wealth of industrial Britain. Bath's impressive town houses, and the striking crescents at the Haymarket end of Edinburgh, beyond Princes Street, are physical reminders of the type of house required by a wealthy family that might wish to spend weekdays in town near to the theatre, libraries, and their place of business.

To set these middle-class developments alongside the planned, mini-utopias built by philanthropic employers for their workers – Saltaire near Bradford, Port Sunlight on Merseyside, Bournville in Birmingham – is to note the increasing awareness throughout the century that urban development had its costs and others ways of living might entail general human benefits. The Garden City movement only really took off in the twentieth century, though it was mooted before. Places such as Welwyn Garden City – airy and with lots of green land around the dwellings – had their roots in a general rejection of densely packed urban centres – centres whose earliest rejection came in the form of suburbs.

A good deal of planning went into the development of suburbs; but the whole urban experience required the hand of government in a way not previously seen in the sphere of housing. Different authorities and localities dealt with the problems of urban communities in contrasting ways. From the 1830s, there were numerous national inquires into the physical and atmospheric environment of the towns, and various efforts were made to improve the lot of the labouring classes; this reformist zeal was stimulated by a combination of fears: about disease, moral decay and political agitation. The authorities in Liverpool – renowned as Britain's unhealthiest urban centre – tried to improve its urban conditions by closing cellars (as we have seen) and by becoming one of the first centres to sponsor municipal housing initiatives. In 1851–2, legislation was passed to enforce minimum standards in Britain's lodging-houses, though many dwellings went unchecked by the authorities. Liverpool was also the first place to embark on a comprehensive programme of municipal house-building. Elsewhere, bans on back-to-back building were gradually introduced and by 1875 (at the time of the Artisans' Dwellings Act, which provided local authorities with powers to clear slums and re-house inhabitants) few were being constructed. In Lancaster, house-building was left in the hands of small-scale private speculators, with larger firms playing no role in building, owning and renting working-class housing. Glasgow and Dundee builders chose to answer the need for accommodation by raising the sky-line towards the heavens, constructing large tenement buildings. Despite their forbidding, prison-like appearance, these constructions represented an efficient use of land. Many of these individual flats within these constructions were designed to be too small for multiple occupancy, and, though austere, the better models were significant improvements on the jerry-built back-to-backs or the ramshackle rookeries of previous eras when pressures were less.

6.5 The rural world

Urban space was far from uniform, despite the image of relentless and monotonous terraced housing. Equally, nor was the rural world characterized by anything approaching uniformity. The rural world remained important to the British people in every respect: this despite the historian's obsession with the urban world. Nor was the rural setting dominated only by the rural poor and the incredibly wealthy aristocracy. Towns and the countryside melded into each other. Urban workers could walk for only a few miles in order to throw a long-line into the sea or else to hunt rabbits. As towns sprawled, before planning and restriction came in to control that growth, it was common enough for farms to become virtually parts of towns and for rural labourers to be found living on the outskirts.

The rural world embraced an even wider range of dwellings than the town and also occupied a perhaps even more highly charged space in the nation's psyche. While the urban-dweller might reject the countryside as dreary, rain-soaked, repetitively green (as Lytton Strachey did on a trip to Skye in 1908), others lauded the rural idyll as the true English ideal, a world which was being lost. The lament for the land was not so much aimed at the pauper's hovel or the rickety, leaky cottage, endlessly patched up, which was occupied by the agricultural day-labourer. Then again, nor was it true that all rural dwellings were as poor as this. The truth is that social commentators and travel writers discovered examples of all kinds when they toured the British Isles. Some of the greatest disparities were between the huge estate houses – the mansions, halls and villas – in which resided the magnate landowners and the pokey, basic shelter provided for their tenants and labourers.

The land and industry never sat next to each other so clearly as on estates where mining provided for high levels of proletarianisation within spitting distance of the rustic labourers bent at the ploughshare. The south Northumberland estates of Lord Hastings provide a striking example of this. In the space of just a few square miles were found (and indeed can still be found) a number of small towns or pit villages – Seaton Delaval, New Hartley and Holywell – the fishing village of Seaton Sluice, the mining and port town of Blyth, broad acres of flat arable land, and the impressive estate of Delaval Hall. In a place such as this, miners, fishermen, estate managers, pit overseers, farmers, farm labourers, milkmaids, wholesalers, and a plethora of others, came into doubtless regular contact on a daily basis. And the complexity of social and spatial relations in the countryside was increasing as time went on. Each of the villages and towns mentioned here were serviced by railways that spurred off the main North–South line through Newcastle to Edinburgh. Hence, railway workers, signalmen, rail maintenance men – and their families – could also be found residing in a world which we might mistakenly see as solely inhabited by miners, fishermen and agriculturalists.

Far from merely being sites of ancient tradition, great estates were also places of enterprize. Fine botanical collections, highly treasured art collections and libraries, leisure pursuits such as hunting and fishing – these were just some of the things which made the aristocrat's mansion more than just a place in which to observe the idling rich. Lord Armstrong, of Tyneside ship-building fame, owned a magnificent estate house, Cragside Hall, in Northumberland, which aside from its gardens and finely decorated rooms, was also celebrated for its early example of electric lighting. This was more than just a sign of middle-class social climbing allied to aristocratic social tinkering – it was a sign of the inter-connectedness of urban and rural wealth and a sign that estates were far from unchanging. Indeed, by the 1880s, 25 per cent or more peers (men almost by definition normally associated with the countryside) held company directorships while more and more of them were embracing the very urban principles of modern business management in the running of their estates. New estates, new forests, deer parks, stocked fishing-waters, scientific breeding, exotic trees and plants sat alongside the maintenance of certain traditional values and the cherished, deferential position which rural society afforded to the country's noble-men. Equally, many of the middle class who aped their superiors fell well short of a wholesale adoption of upper-class mores. The deerstalker and twelve-bore shotgun might be standard fashion accessories, but it was not necessary to buy up 10,000 acres to enjoy the countryside. Many, indeed, bought the big house and a few acres, maintaining a balance of urban business interests and rural lifestyle.

The rural world, despite its poverty, hardship and out-migration, and in spite of its stark contrast of plutocracy and penury, nevertheless provided a model for so many critics of the town. Rural people tended to be healthier and stronger than their urban counterparts; the army wanted them for this reason, and the shock of the poverty of health among those who would join the army to fight the Boer War (1899–1902) right at the end of our period, did nothing to disabuse thinkers of the view that national efficiency might be better sought with a rural model to hand. But it was not merely a matter of physical health. The rural world was supposed to be characterized by good manners as well as good health, and a deference to accepted power structures which the average town-dweller was thought to lack or eschew. Cattle houghing, rick-burning and incidents of rural unrest – in the early 1830s and 1870s, for example – might cause us to question this ideal; the significant and continuous violence of Irish rural society would just about sink any notion of the harmony of landed relations. Perhaps, though, Ireland is a special case (Chapter 10). Rural society enjoyed a neighbourliness, a sense of community in which all members participated, which commentators feared was missing from the town. The rock of aristocratic privilege, the enjoyment of an age-old and solid social system, was thought to be the foundation of this allegedly superior rural world. The rural world also tended to be studded with smaller towns – sites of small-scale industry, market towns and the like. The fear of big towns was thus enforced by a seeming appreciation of the smaller town wherein the local elites had the magistracy, education and other bureaucratic and social services in their back pockets. As a kind of icing on the cake, too, villages were more likely to go to church than their urban counterparts – and they might even find themselves under the same roof as the local squire or other privileged members of their communities.

6.6 Conclusion

Urbanisation was undoubtedly one of the most remarkable features of nineteenth-century life. If any aspect of modern life was almost entirely created in that century of great change, then it is the fact that a significant majority of Britons now live in cities and towns, rather than in villages. Even those who today live in the countryside are never far from the busy and impersonal world of the town. Towns and cities also have a tremendous psychological impact on the people who live there. The physical state of working-class communities inevitably defined those who inhabited them. Behind the blackened walls, and amid the foul middens [refuse sites], were people whose shared experience of deprivation and squalor undoubtedly bonded them. These communities were physically and psychological inward-looking and defined as much by negative perceptions as by the shape of the streets. The neighbourhoods in which people lived were physical expressions of their class and status, not least in a period which witnessed the sustained suburbanisation of richer elements in society. Within these physical boundaries communities were forged and reforged, as people migrated in and out. Communities were not fixed – at least not in the sense that they comprized the same individuals and families from one year to the next. Yet there were continuities to the traditions and customs which captured the idea of community. Some of these were rehabilitated or imported from earlier lives in different places; some were new inventions based upon the needs of the urban world. In the end, though, people were at the heart of things.

Summary

◆ Urbanisation transformed the way a majority of Britons lived.
◆ Urbanisation affected the psyche as well as the living-place of people.
◆ The concept of community helps us to understand how people saw their world, but is nevertheless a problematical notion.
◆ Despite urban development, the rural world remained important for people of all classes.
◆ Suburbs were an important part of the redefined living arrangements of later Victorian Britain.

Points to discuss

◆ Why did urban Britain grow?
◆ What were the main features of urban growth?
◆ Which parts of Britain experienced most urban growth?
◆ What is a community? What problems do we encounter when applying this concept?
◆ What was the relationship between urban growth and industrialisation?

References and further reading

J. Adshead, *Distress in Manchester: evidence . . . of the state of the labouring classes in 1840–2* (Manchester, 1842).

J. Burnett, *A Social History of Housing, 1815–1970* (1980).

J. Cooper, *The Well-Ordered Town: A Story of Saffron Walden, Essex, 1792–1862* (Clavering, 2,000) (case-study of a market town, especially strong on the responses to poverty).

M.J. Daunton (ed.), *The Cambridge Urban History of Britain, Vol. 3, 1840–1950* (Cambridge, 2,000).

F. Engels, *Condition of the working-classes in England* (1845; New York, 1859 edn).

D. Englander, *Landlord and Tenant in Urban Britain, 1838–1918* (Oxford, 1983).

C. Hamlin, *Public Health and Social Justice in the Age of Chadwick* (Cambridge, 1998).

E. Gauldie, *Cruel Habitations: A History of Working-Class Housing, 1780–1918* (1974).

J. Kay, *The Moral and Physical Condition of the Labouring Classes in . . . Manchester* (Manchester 1833).

H. Mayhew, *London Labour and the London Poor* (1861–2).

I.C. Taylor, 'The court and cellar dwelling: the eighteenth-century origins of the Liverpool slum', *Transactions of the Historic Society of Lancashire and Cheshire*, 62 (1970).

P. Waller, *Town, City and Nation: England, 1850–1914* (Oxford, 1983)

People

Contents

Introduction

One of the most profound developments of the nineteenth century was the emergence and establishment of a *language of class*. While poverty and inequality had always been part of human societies, it was in this period that such relations seemed to become enmeshed into almost every aspect of life. It is not just that historians have invented class as a descriptor for the social relations that they considered to have emerged from the Industrial Revolution. It is also a fact that the people of the nineteenth century themselves began to use the word 'class' to distinguish groups in terms of their mores, lifestyles, experiences and expectations.

At the heart of this reordering of the language was the emergence of a mass, mainly urban, working class. What we mean by such a term is riddled with contradictions and is, in any case, imprecise. A bewildering range of people and experiences come under the umbrella 'working class', and it is sometimes true that descriptions of that class, or of its experiences, omit as much as they include. Nevertheless, it is vital that the student of nineteenth-century Britain is made aware of the experiences of what was, after all, a very large majority of Victorian society. Classes, and the working class in particular, are central to our understanding of the Victorian experience. The emergence of a mass society, in which classes stood out by their clothing, diet, modes of transport, living conditions, and leisure pursuits, was one important feature of this period. New commercial activity, industrialisation, and the development of dominant urban world (as we have seen in previous chapters) had an enormous influence on ordinary lives.

This chapter provides an introduction to some of the key issues in nineteenth-century history, dealing with issues associated with the rise of class. Linking with earlier chapters on industrialisation and on the urban world (Chapters 2, 3 and 6), this chapter seeks to explain not only how the working class emerged, and the world it inhabited and the lives its members lived, but also the emergence of a widespread middle class and the continued importance of an aristocracy.

Key issues

▶ Who or what was characterised as 'working class' in the nineteenth century?

▶ What is 'class'?

▶ What types of work were performed by these people, and how did patterns of employment change over time?

▶ Did the living standards of the working class improve over the course of the nineteenth century?

▶ What sort of cultural lives did the working class have?

▶ What were the political consequences of the emergence of a working class?

▶ Why did a middle class develop such importance in this period?

▶ How did the aristocracy survive the changing world of Victorian Britain?

7.1 An emergent working class

By the 1820s members of the ruling elite in Britain were beginning to express social relations in terms of class. In the growing towns and cities, employers, social commentators and others were increasingly of the view that they were surrounded by a working class. The literature of the day – works by such prominent writers as Charles Dickens, Benjamin Disraeli and Margaret Gaskell – contained numerous instances of the separation of classes, of strike activity, political discontent and of a growing sense of there being something loosely described as 'working class'. This new class (which in E.P. Thompson's (1963) conception had emerged, struggling against new technologies and a changing way of life, between the 1760s and the 1820s), struck fear into the hearts of wealthier onlookers. The working class came increasingly to be viewed as synonymous with the Stygian gloom of the new towns and cities; the unsanitary and unhealthy conditions of the towns were viewed partly as a product of the lack of moral fibre of these new town-dwellers. It comes as no surprise that at the very time when writers such as Thomas Carlyle were inventing the 'Condition of England' question, England's new working class was at its most pronounced.

7.2 Industrialisation and the formation of a working class

By 1830, industrialisation had made significant and irreversible progress, changing the lives of many people to such an extent that their way of life would have been unrecognisable to their grand-parents' generation. Not only was Britain becoming more urban (even if this was far from universal) and the rural world was becoming relatively less important. In the early stages of industrial and urban growth, prior to the social reforms of the 1840s and beyond, the environment of the urban world was more dangerous than would be the case later. Sewerage systems, housing stock, street lighting, policing – all these things were inadequate – or were perceived to be lacking – in the urban world

The increasing population mobility – especially the labour migration – that was discussed in Chapter 6 in many ways flowed against perceived social wisdom. The Elizabethan Poor Law had worked expressly to curtail movement because of the social upheaval that was thought to accompany radical changes in local population, especially in relation to the cost of relieving the poverty of the newcomers. In the eighteenth century, and especially in the nineteenth, workers travelled much more in search of work, and did so in far greater numbers, than had been the case previously. Employers resisted certain sorts of migration and often acted through a sense of fear about losing a stable labour force. We can see many instances of this. Masters and Servants' legislation, which was increasingly resisted by workers from the later eighteenth century onward, was designed expressly to tie labourers to their work with severe contracts (Box 7.1, 7.2). Government also sought to stem the flow of skilled artisans to the American colonies, especially after they gained independence. While population movement rates in the nineteenth century would suggest quite clearly that employers were losing this particular battle to hold on to their human capital, it is important not to underplay the degree to which there was a struggle between masters and men, over the issue of contracts. The legislation was still being used for this purpose by employers in the 1860s and 1870s. Moreover, some groups of workers, for example the miners in the north-east of England were tied even more firmly to long contracts in what was known as the 'bond system'. While they resisted what some saw as a semi-feudal system of labour relations, pit-owners nevertheless used all their powers to hold on to contracted workers. This meant going to magistrates, offering rewards for information of absconded workers, putting up posters, and so on. In the urban world, however, Thomas Carlyle's 'cash nexus' – a relationship at work based on money alone, and not loyalty, contract or honour – became increasingly prevalent as the century wore on.

In this way, and in others, pastoral Britain was giving way to the towns and industrial villages that came to typify early-Victorian society. Rural forms of life did not translate easily into the town and both workers and employers discovered this. Although urban dwellers were not quite a majority of the population in 1830, and the decline of the rural world was relative rather than absolute, large towns, such as Birmingham and Bradford, and the great industrial and commercial cities of Glasgow and Manchester, began to assume a dominant role in the nation's prosperity. The urban world also had a pyschological impact on the nation. Not only did towns and cities represent a different mode of life from the village and countryside, they also pressed upon the collective imagination of

Box 7.1

Worker action and the response

On 19 October 1815 the government issued a proclamation offering information to help employers break the seamen's combination in north-east England. This episode reflected both the strains of the post-war economy and official sensitivity about the radical implications of workers' organisations. Bear in mind that forming trade unions was illegal under the provision of the Combinations Acts (1799 and 1800), which were not repealed until 1824 and 1825.

October 19 1815

Proclamation –

Offer of information re seamen's combination

Whereas it has been humbly represented to His Royal Highness the Prince Regent, that a considerable number of people at Shields, Newcastle-upon-Tyne, Sunderland, and in the neighbourhood of these places, have unlawfully assembled themselves together in a disorderly and tumultuous manner, for the purpose of compelling the ship owners and others concerned in the trade of the above-mentioned ports, to comply with certain regulations prescribed by them with respect to the navigating ships and vessels to and from those ports; and have actually detained and prevented divers ships and vessels from sailing from the said ports, and have proceeded to other acts of violence: whereas it has been further represented to his Royal Highness the Prince Regent, that these misguided persons have formed themselves into committees, and have administered illegal oaths, with a view to the purposes before-mentioned; and have also upon various occasions used force or intimidation to compel persons to form such unlawful assemblies and to prevent their engaging with the said ship owners . . .

Source: Exeter, Devon Records Office, Sidmouth Papers

the people who watched them grow and who lived within them. In a sense, all periods are symbolised by some idea of change, some new aspect of life: in the nineteenth century, the place was undoubtedly occupied by urban and industrial development.

For the labouring classes of any society, at any time, work – whether in field or factory – could be tough, remorseless and sometimes dangerous. Working as a village blacksmith, a dock-side porter or a textile operative was similar insofar as the work was undertaken for remuneration in order to live. But there could be considerable differences between one working environment and another, the work of one period and another. There is little doubt that work patterns, overall, changed quite considerable in the nineteenth century, but this must not be over-stressed. Work was not entirely standardised in this period: the Lancashire textile trade alone counted more than 1,200 different job names, according to the census enumerators of 1841, a bewildering array that defied categorisation, except to say all were in some way or another connected with cotton-cloth production. But each trade carried its own customs, practices, experiences and rates of pay.

Moreover, until the 1840s, thousands of traditional handicraft trades had yet to die out, and toil was performed overwhelming by men and women working with their hands. Machinofacture was becoming a part of working life, especially in cutting-edge industries such as textiles, but muscle-power still provided more livings than the archetypal labour processes of factories as found in Lancashire and Yorkshire. The regimentation of people by machines did not achieve a majority position until the twentieth century. Machines were not even to dominate all aspects of the cotton trade until the second half of the nineteenth century. While spinning was mechanised long before weaving, powerloom weaving was not fully integrated into the factory system until after the 1850s. In the earlier part of the century, weaving remained a handicraft trade and the average cotton-mill employed no more than a couple of hundred workers. The technological gap between spinning and weaving was such that hundreds of thousands of handloom weavers continued to have work long after textile sheds appeared on the slopes of the Pennines. What is more, intricate types of production, for example, embroidery and lace-making, were still being created on handlooms because early-generation weaving machines were too crude for the working of very fine, fragile threads. As mechanisation spread, however, handloom weavers' wages tumbled. In 1800, these men could earn 30s per week; thirty years later, this was down to perhaps 5s or so.

Textile workers, not least the hard-pressed handicraft workers, thus became some of the first converts to militant agitation, trades unionism and other forms of protest. They also became noted recipients of poor relief and their distress became a noted aspect of working-class life in the 1820s and beyond. The most prominent cotton workers' leader, John Doherty (b.1799), spoke not just for displaced weavers but for most workers in his experience when he wrote his *Address of the Nation Association for the Protection of Labour* (1830), with its advocacy of trades union combination:

> FELLOW WORKERS, – The fearful change, which the workings of the last few years have produced in the condition of every class of labourers, summons you to a serious investigation of the cause. It warns you that the time is now come for you to make a stand ... in your downward course to pauperism ... Your power, as regards the operations of society, is omnipotent ... Let British operatives once become firm and united, and their unanimous voice of complaint will command respect.

Yet, with fierce reprisals from employers, and with communications between different workers so complex, much early trades unionism was fitful, fleeting and unsuccessful The following decades saw a further downgrading of the weavers' economic position and social conditions; so much so that their impoverishment continued to be a major social concern of the 1840s. It is interesting, however, that even when their position was so parlous, the handloom workers swam against the tide of social and economic change. They continued to protest against the demise of their way of life, and many clung to their trades rather than abandoning the way of life that they knew so well. When finally a weaver was forced to forsake his loom, a way of life was at an end and it caused great psychological trauma, which Benjamin Disraeli captured so well in his popular novel, *Sybil; Or, The Two Nations* (1845).

The average handloom weaver saw the tools of his trade as a sign of independence. Neither waged employees nor totally independent, these men had, nevertheless, once enjoyed a freedom that they were reluctant to give up. Some of them lived in the sorry hope that good times might return; others stuck to what they knew. But most clung to their trade because it was a way of life; it was more than simply a trade. In this case, their skills were a matter of pride. Work was not simply a measure of income: it was a kind of badge, it was membership of a club. Moreover, small-scale domestic production of this sort linked family members, who worked together, and was quite different from pursuing work that accrued weekly wages. Male weavers, for example, often had wives who were spinners; they also had children who could help their parents and so learn the trade. This undoubtedly had the effect of reducing the mobility of the worker and the family.

If the nineteenth century has been characterised by the remorseless progress of industrial society and the spread of weekly-paid regular employment, with work patterns

Box 7.2

Irish handloom weavers

The lot of the handloom weaver gradually declined with the introduction of new technology. English commentators also noted the negative influence exerted by Irish immigrant labour. This way, the reputation of the Irish for undercutting wages—one for which the evidence is at best sketchy— gradually strengthened:

The wages obtained by operatives in the various branches of the cotton manufacture are, in general, such, as with the exercise of that economy without which wealth itself is wasted, would be sufficient to provide them with all the decent comforts of life - the average wages of all persons employed in the mills (young and old) being from nine to twelve shillings per week. Their means are too often consumed by vice and *improvidence*. But the wages of certain classes are exceedingly meagre. The introduction of the power-loom, though ultimately destined to be productive of the greatest general benefit, has, in the present state of commerce, occasioned some temporary embarrassment, by diminishing the demand for certain kinds of labour, and, consequently, their price. The hand-loom weavers, *existing in the state of transition*, still constitute a very extensive class, and though they labour fourteen hours and upwards daily, earn only five to seven or eight shillings per week. They consist chiefly of Irish, and are affected by all the causes of moral and physical depression which we have enumerated. Ill-fed - ill-clothed - half-sheltered and ignorant; - weaving in close damp cellars, or crowded workshops, it only remains that they should become, as is too frequently the case, demoralised and reckless, to render perfect the portraiture of savage life. Amongst men so situated, the moral check has no influence in preventing the rapid increase of the population. The existence of cheap and redundant labour in the market has, only, a *constant* tendency to lessen its general price, and hence the wages of the English operatives have been exceedingly reduced by this immigration of Irish - their comforts consequently diminished - their manners debased - and the natural influence of manufactures on the people thwarted. We are well convinced that without the numerical and moral influence of this class, on the means and on the character of the people who have had to enter into competition with them in the market of labour, we should have had occasion to regret the physical and moral degradation of the population.

Source: J.P. Kay-Shuttleworth, *The Moral and Physical Condition of the Working Class*, etc. (Manchester, 1833), pp. 43–5

far more regimented and patterned than on the farm, we should not exaggerate the triumph of the factory and the town. Workers' resistance to change was uneven. Britain never experienced anything remotely approaching a revolution in this period and its strikes were never 'general', in the sense of bringing all or most of the country to a standstill. Agitators such as William Benbow advocated a grand national holiday (as he dubbed the idea of a general strike), but the unevenness of workers' responses was a measure of the equally variable patterns of hardship and desperation. The Chartist movement, formed in the winter of 1837–8 in order to advance the case of parliamentary reform so as to improve the workingman's lot, mainly attracted the most desperate workers. Handloom weavers and woolcombers – those in badly paid and disappearing trades – were more likely Chartist agitators than were well-paid coal-miners or mechanics.

The essential problem for working-class leaders was this variation in experience, which also transpired as a wide range of differences in pay. Every sector of the economy where workers were poorly paid was matched by one in which work was relatively highly remunerated. Agricultural labourers might earn between 5s and 12s, depending on where they were. Street hawkers and small-scale domestic workers who made brushes, and so on, could earn as little as 3s or 4s per week. Equally, miners, engineers and shipbuilders could at times take home over 20s per week. The urban unskilled also benefited from rates of pay that explain why there was a drift from the countryside: the Dorsetshire farm hand could expect to be paid in the 1830s little more than one-third of the 15s or so which a labourer in Liverpool could command.

The spread of urban and industrial development does not discount the fact that agriculture created the largest class of workers in Britain in the first half of the nineteenth century. Like many of their urban counterparts, they, too, were experience a rapid social change and downward economic pressures, governed largely by the consolidation of farm-holdings and the decreasing need for year-around labour. Consequently, some of the most important social unrest of the period occurred on the land, most notably with the 'Swing' Riots of 1831–2, which sent a spasm of fear through the governing class. The 'Swing' riots gained their name from the mythical 'Captain Swing', in whose names barns and hay-ricks were burned and livestock attacked. Concentrated mainly in the southern agricultural counties, these disturbances were meant to slow the rate at which labour-saving mechanisation spread, but there were also a myriad local grievances that were knitted together in what, nevertheless, remained a disparate series of actions. The riots were successful in curtailing the progress of certain machinery, and formed an interesting backdrop to the Great Reform Act of 1832. Equally, the government's commitment to the harsh Poor Law Amendment Act (1834) was undoubtedly influenced by what were seen as the excesses of agricultural workers. Cattle-maiming, rick burning, threats and physical violence remained as instruments for rural workers to express their grievances, even after the 1870s when trade union activity among such workers became more permanent.

While it is true that desperately poor weavers and hungry farm-hands engaged in some of the most violent forms of protest, this is not to say that there were not labour struggles among the higher-paid workers. Strikes usually occurred because of wage disputes, as was the case when in the 1840s North-east miners resisted changes in the nature of contracts and payment. There was, moreover, a general resentment at new notions of time discipline and alterations to payment, such as a regular working week or payment by the week or fortnight rather than by the month. The classic example of this type of struggle, however, is the desire of workers to to continue the age-old tradition of celebrating 'St Monday' (the idea of taking an extending weekend to drink and make merry) which continued long after 1830, even though employers increasingly opposed it.

7.3 Class: a useful concept?

What is 'class'? Class is both controversial and fraught with methodological and ideological difficulties. Can we take it for granted as some finite category of socio-economic status or as an objective measurement of the social relations of production? The term 'class', in its modern sense, was a creation of the nineteenth century and of two of the foremost social thinkers, and proponents of revolutionary change, Karl Marx (1818–83) and Friedrich Engels (1820–95). It also means far more than a simple socio-economic descriptor.

What do we mean when we apply such terms as 'social class' or 'class-consciousness'? There is disagreement, even among Marxists, as to what Marx and Engels meant by class. For some historians, class is considered to be the relationship between groups in society, objectively defined by those groups' relationship to the means of production – that is, their position in the productive system (e.g. workers or owners), and their share of the wealth created. Thus, class might be seen here as a structural thing; a condition born out of material circumstance, shared among individuals, making them into a class of common interest, resulting in shared values, outlooks and objectives.

To other historians – for example, E. P. Thompson – class is a creation of 'agency' not of 'structure'; an *historical* phenomenon' (Thompson's emphasis); 'something which in fact happens (and can be shown to have happened) in human relations'. At the same time, Thompson acknowledged, in *The Making of the English Working Class* (1963), how difficult it is to define examples of class: 'The finest-meshed sociological net cannot give us a pure specimen of class, any more than it can give us one of deference or of love.'

Thompson's analysis has been enormously influential in left-wing circles. Moreover, as his stance was deliberately anti-theoretical, and his methods of research were rigorous and intensive, Thompson provided a useful, accessible and relatively non-dogmatic intro-duction to Marxism and history. His work is also eminently readable: all in all, a good starting point for young scholars.

At the same time, however, we must acknowledge other viewpoints on the role of class in history. Recently, for example, historians of 'the linguistic turn' – those who emphasise the rooted and historical nature of language itself – have stressed the paradoxes inherent within usages of the very word 'class'. Gareth Stedman Jones, in what some have seen as the first move towards post-modernism in the field of labour history (*Languages of Class*, 1983), argued that because the term 'class' is a word 'embedded in the language' it should be considered in that 'linguistic context'. Jones then pointed out that because there were different 'languages of class', the term cannot be employed as an 'elementary counter of official social description'. Whether concerned with productive relations, 'culturally significant practices', or political and ideological 'self-definition', class, Jones argues, is locked into 'an anterior social reality'.

Of all the philosophical concepts raised in the writings of Marx and Engels, class has been welcomed as one of the most important and, conversely, criticised by many historians as one of the most controversial. In the eighteenth century, the term class was not used to represent an homogeneous social group of shared experiences and outlooks as it came to be used in the following century. In its Marxist connotation, in fact, class was not used at all. Social relations in the early modern world were framed in terms of 'sorts', 'orders' or perhaps 'classes', in the plural sense. These categories were, moreover, closely allied to both relative wealth and status; they were not necessarily ideological in the ways that social class was from the 1830s. In a semantic sense, 'class' – 'like 'industrial', 'bourgeois', 'liberal' or 'conservative', and a host of other terms – developed in response to the rise of a language of analysis, underpinned by the rapid modernisation and changing social circumstances of the period beyond the French Revolution.

By the 1840s Marx believed this graded division of society had become increasingly more sharply defined, in terms of the relations of production. Marx's laboratory for working out his ideas of class was Britain, where, according to his formulation, the Industrial Revolution was in the throes of creating the world's first authentic proletariat, defined by mechanised, factory and, above all, waged labour; by starker contrasts between owners and producers than had existed before; by social discord; and by deep-seated antagonism across class lines. This was the age of political agitation and socio-economic unrest; of Chartism and in Europe the years of revolutions (1830 and 1848). Moreover, this was the age through which Marx and Engels lived. Both of them spent most of their adult working lives in England. Engels' father had business interests in Manchester and Marx, who was unable to enter most European countries because he was viewed as a revolutionary, spent years working in the British Library in London. Therefore, the working class which they saw as rising up was one with which they were familiar (insofar as intellectuals can truly comprehend the lives of working men and women). Marx was not alone in believing this age was a chaotic one: writers on the right, such as Thomas Carlyle, shared Marx's observations, if not his resulting theories or panaceas. Equally, Marx under-estimated the innate and deep-seated stability of British society.

7.4 Beyond the working class?

The focus here has been upon the working class, or the lower order. This has been deliberate, for historians have disproportionately employed the term to consider the experiences and feelings of working men and women in our period – and they were far more numerous than their middle- and upper-class equivalents. That is not say that all the classes were working class, nor that only working-class people worked for a living. Without the existing of competing, antagonistic class (if we follow the Marxist line), then to be working class would have meant not very much. Equally as interesting as the rise of a working class was the simultaneous emergence of a middle class, Marx's bourgeoisie. Like the working class, however, the middle class was sharply differentiated. Working men's wages could vary from a low of 3s to 6s per week (for the agricultural labourer in Dorset or western Ireland) to a high of 50s (the sort of money paid to highly-skilled metal-workers, such as anglesmiths in good times in the ship-building industry). Equally, middle-class incomes range even more broadly than that: the owner of a shipyard or a cotton mill might have an annual income of thousands and an estate value of more than a million, whereas one of his clerks – a white-collar worker defined as different from the working class around him by the use of his brain not his hands – might received as little as £2 per week. The world of Victorian England contained many examples of middle-class wealth and prestige – both Robert Peel and William Ewart Gladstone came from earned rather than hereditary income, even if the earning had been done by their fathers rather than they themselves.

The aristocracy and gentry – those whose prestige and wealth came from the land – also had an enormously varying degree of experiences and incomes. A magnate with 10,000 acres might be a wealthy man; but a family such as the Londonderrys of county Durham and Ulster earned more in mining royalties than many massive landowners might ever have enjoyed from strictly rural incomes, rents, and so on. Moreover, while historians have focused on the imbalance in wealth and privilege noticed in the urban world, it would be hard to find a mill-owner and a factory hand as much separated in income and outlook as were some Anglo-Irish landlords and their poor tenants. Social stratification was indeed a feature of urban life: but it was rural as well as urban, *within* classes as much as between them.

The struggle for self-improvement that observers noted in the attitudes of working men and women was matched, in the case of the middle classes, by a desire to hang on to what they had. The closer to the working classes we make this observation, the more acute the struggle seems. There was little in our period that so clearly defined manners, customs and social attitudes as the desire of a petit-bourgeois (lower middle class) shop-owner or clerk retain what he had. The petit-bourgeoisie were thus jealous of their superiors and horror-struck at the thought of sinking back into the mass of their inferiors (some of whom had a higher take-home pay). The social and political conservatism of this bloc of people – a bloc which existed in every small town as well as every city – helped to ensure the character of Victorian society and political culture. Perhaps the embodiment of the world view of the petit-bourgeoisie is George and Weedon Grossmith's *The Diary of a Nobody* (1892). First published in *Punch* in 1891–2, this short novel tells of the story of a lower-middle-class clerk from Holloway, London. A cruel satire written in the first person, the book immortalised Charles Pooter and his wayward son, Lupin. The Pooters rent a house rather too close to the railway line (the landlord lets it go cheap because of the noise) and fill their lives with the snobberies they imagine to be typical of a slightly higher class. Delivery men and servants they can ill-afford are made to use the rear entrance of what is, in fact, a rather modest town house. The idea of maintaining an abode slightly too expensive for Pooter's salary typifies the anxieties of this much-parodied class. Despite the joke, Pooter's class did become large and influential in Victorian society. They tended to be physically settled ratepayers, which gave them access to the vote before many working men who might otherwise match their incomes; they also tended towards clubs, societies, civic events and local politics. While, in national terms, these people may have lacked the clout of the big capitalists and industrialists, the lower-middle classes were undoubtedly as important as they were numerous.

At the top of the pile, in 1880, were the aristocracy with their seeming monopoly on privilege and political power in, if not in earned wealth. The challenge they faced from the big bourgeoisie – capitalists and industrialists – was far from undifferentiated; and, in any case, the continued power of land, in both Houses of parliament (though especially in the Lords) made it clear that any transfer of power was an issue for discussion. Whilst we might expect the great industrialists to have seized political power without too much trouble, this is not actually the case. Research on the political parties at the time of Second Reform Act (1867) demonstrates that there was a increasing middle-class representation in politics; however, this amounting to a sharing, not a usurping, of power. The quest for political power was also complicated by the degree to which wealthy financiers, commercial entrepreneurs and industrialists bought into, rather than rejecting, the aristocracy. Alexis de Tocqueville, writing in the 1830s, had praised Britain's open aristocracy as a major cause of social cohesion and a major brake on movements towards social revolution. As a consequence, instead of seeking to destroy landed privilege, the middle classes, while not averse to weakening the hold upon power of the large magnates, instead sought out lands, estates and titles for themselves and their offspring. Salmon-fishing, hunting and other country pursuits gradually became as much as pastime of new money as of the old landed class.

The openness of England's aristocracy is not just a matter of myth. That there was no revolution in Britain in our period, and the fact of the monarchy's increasingly popularity later in the period (as opposed to its collapse or destruction) must come from a degree of approval for the system of governance as it existed. True, events such as the reform crisis of 1830–2 raised the spectre of usurpation by the forces of populism; but how real this was is open to debate. The likelihood of a successful mass uprising at this point is certainly questionable. The key issue, in politics, was the gradualist transition of a portion of power from aristocratic to middle-class hands. This did not amount to a wholesale abandonment of power nor a forcible seizure. By a clever yet simple process of occupying available spaces on the benches of power and an incremental expansion of the electorate and the development of something akin to urban democracy in the towns, Britain's elites maintained a high proportion of their actual power and almost all of their status. Between 1688, when Gregory King made is important study of the population of England, and 1803 when Patrick Colquhoun engaged in a similar process, England and Wales's aristocracy grew from almost 17,000 families to more than 27,000. The middle ranks grew in proportion, from 435,000 families to just over 630,000. The lower order, too, increased at a similar rate from 1.3 m to just over 2 m. While these surveys do not correspond to modern social science they are, in effect, as much as we have to make such calculations, and, when read in general terms, do no disservice to our attempts to explicate general principles. What we can see is that, while the poor expanded because population was growing, and the middle class developed because opportunity knocked at the door of the potential entrepreneur, this latter group, once they had made their money, could find a way on to the high table by buying an estate, title, etc. It was this fluidity between the middle- and upper classes that underpinned Britain's social stability. The radical, Richard Cobden, made a despairing reference in 1857 to the fact that 'the higher classes never stood so high in relative social and political ranks, as compared with the other classes, as at present. The middle class has been content with the very crumbs from their table.' The truth was slightly different: the ruling elite naturally dominated the House of Lords, but they also outnumbered all other groups in the Commons; and, while this was the case, the middle classes looked to a place at the aristocratic table – not merely the crumbs that fell from it. Middle-class politicians came into their own in the early twentieth century; but even then, the old families and those of landed wealth, or their sons, continued to be a significant portion of the office-holders at Westminster.

At every level, then, class is a complicated issue. There is no doubt that by the 1880s, a classic 'them and us' working-class mentality was in existence. Developed by social stratification, labour conflicts, struggles with employers, segregated living environs and by a more generalised, if diffuse, sense that working men and women were not enjoying their share of the industrial and imperial honeycomb, a high degree of social polarisation did emerge. However, that polarisation had its equivalents in country as well as town; within the middle class as well as between the classes; between new wealth and landed privilege.

The process of acclimatising the arriving middle class was not entirely simple; behind the statistical picture was layer upon layer of tradition: manners, customs, blood-lines, historical status. Land, alone, was not enough to guarantee acceptance into what was a social and culture as well as political elite. Many middle-class aspirants were ridiculed by those privileged by birth. However, second-generation landowners, the sons and daughters of the self-made mill-owner or commercial entrepreneur, could, through education and the right marriage, make a permanent mark. The super-elite aristocracy – those who had spent many generations working their way into the centres of power, bolstering huge estates with government service and work in the armed forces, etc – were relatively few. Aspirants and middle-rankers alike came and went; bankruptcy, scandal and the demographic dead-end of nurturing a child-less marriage could all signal the end of a family and, hence, an opportunity for someone rich in empire cash or mining royalties.

The aristocracy also showed a remarkable acumen for going with the economic flow. If land remained their vital spark, the source of the privilege as well as their wealth, hundreds of landowners were also able to share in the new privilege of industrialisation. The Lowther family of Whitehaven owed its initial power to the kingly patronage of Charles I, who granted them control of the harbour trust. With this came colonial wealth in coal and tobacco. In the nineteenth century, when Whitehaven mattered less as a port, the Lowthers, Curwens and others drew good living from mineral royalties in coal and iron. A striking example of how a large landowner could massively increase his wealth through mineral royalties can be seen in the shape of Lord Londonderry, whose Durham estates were as coal-rich as any in the world in the 1840s. He built his own port, Seaham Harbour, and ran his coal concerns like a feudal baron. The Duke of Devonshire and, to a lesser extent, the Duke of Buccleuch, made fortunes simply because they owned the land upon which the Victorian boom-town of Barrow in Furness came to be situated. Devonshire's man, James Ramsden, ran the Furness Railway Company (the town's *de facto* council until incorporation in 1867) and had shares in ship-building, iron and steel manufacturing, the steam corn-mill, and a variety of other interests. The seventh duke had completely reinvigorated the rather creaky English and Irish aristocratic empire that his uncle, the sixth duke, had bequeathed to him: benevolence towards his rural tenants in Derbyshire and Lancashire, however, was juxtaposed with the poor living conditions of his industrial workers in Barrow.

If Devonshire provides a good example of the landed entrepreneur, his right-hand man, the lowly-born Liverpool engineer, James Ramsden, whose rise to middle-class prosperity came on the back of his own entrepreneurship and Devonshire's patronage, provides an interesting model of the new social arrangements in the Victorian towns. The middle class did the day-to-day work: they became the mayors, they were the aldermen, they ran the councils, they owned ran the hospitals, they were the clerics, doctors and shop-keepers. But the middle class, as the listing in the previous sentence suggests, was a huge group. It ranged from the lowest clerk, who earned little more than the skilled man, to the factory-owning magnate. It included professional men of a huge variety, whether those employed in the service of God or the government, to those who designed ships, stamped customs' documents and others who designed cathedrals. An increasingly complex economy created an increasingly complex array of middle-class professions; an age of bureaucracy and burgeoning government created new jobs for the man with a good education, from town planning and sanitary engineering to factory inspection, and, later, health and safety. It might seem ironic, perhaps, but the emergence of a mass blue-collar trade union movement also led to a rash of clerking jobs, based in central and regional offices.

7.5 Standards of living

The issue that defined a person's class more than anything else was their spending power. In the nineteenth century, a person was working class if, like the majority of the population, he or she spent around 80 per cent of all income, and perhaps more, on the basic functional needs of the human being – food, shelter and clothing. That is one reason why the standard of living question has dominated so much of British social and economic history over the past two hundred years.

An apocalyptic vision of Britain in turmoil was influential during the crisis years of the 1830s and 1840s. The notion of questioning the socio-economic condition and position of the British people was a direct response to the upheavals of industrialism. It was considered, not inaccurately, that while the Industrial Revolution had created great wealth, and benefits for many, it had also produced victims. These were the displaced of society: handloom weavers, woolcombers and those who worked in a bewildering array of trades that were increasingly redundant in a modern economy.

The debate was, moreover, rejuvenated in the 1880s (at time when Britain's industrial hegemony was being challenged). A new generation of social commentators had replaced Thomas Carlyle who had studied the nature of industrial society and who, in the 1830s, coined the phrase 'Condition of England' (equally applicable, as it turns out, to South Wales and central-belt Scotland, too). This new generation of writers offered a devastating critique of the limited gains made by working men and women under the capitalist system. Their works, much more than those of the earlier generation, fed directly into political movements, especially through the Fabians, the Social Democratic Movement, and, later, through the emerging Labour Party. For Arnold Toynbee in his *Lectures on the Industrial Revolution* (1884), the Industrial Revolution was

> a period as disastrous and as terrible as any through which a nation ever passed; disastrous and terrible, because side by side with a great increase of wealth was seen an enormous increase of pauperism; and production on a vast scale, the result of free competition, led to a rapid alienation of the classes and to the degradation of a large body of producers.

The writings of Toynbee, and those of other reformers and social critics, such as Sidney and Beatrice Webb, and J.L. and Barbara Hammond, helped to bring socially-orientated labour history to the attention of both academics and a wide audience of concerned people. As the period of this book was drawing to a close, a debate raged over the question of whether or not the Industrial Revolution had a positive effect on the British working class. In this, the standard of living – the question of whether or not people had greater or less spending power than in the past – was of central importance. In some respects it represented a more systematic attempt to examine questions about the impact of economic change that had been discussed for several decades. While this is not the place to go into the massive literature on the standard of living debate, it is nevertheless important to acknowledge that visions such as those of Toynbee, developed at a time when Britain's economic pre-eminence was coming to an end. This tradition of writing remains deeply embedded in today's writings on labour history. Scholars of the working class and the Industrial Revolution, even if they reject a conflictual model of society, nevertheless still have to engage with the work of the contemporary commentators who shaped the initial debate in such apocalyptic terms.

While political economists were anxious to provide statistical evidence of almost everything – for the Victorian period was truly a statistical age – the question of workers' living standards was not thus treated. What little information we have on the subject has been put together by writers after the fact, drawing on incomplete (and thus unsatisfactory ranges) of material, none of which adds up to an entire statistical inquiry into the lives of the Victorian working class. Had the statisticians and political economists of the 1850s applied the credo of Mr Gradgrind to this issue ('facts are what I want'), then the standard of living issue might not today be one of the longest-running and most controversial sagas in British social and economic history. The heated debate which has, at least since the 1940s if not before, scorched the pages of *Economic History Review*, and other leading history journals, is in many respects a continuation of nineteenth-century modes of discussion. Since the 1830s, when Carlyle was working on the impact of industrialism, there has been an at times vituperative to-ing and fro-ing between often extreme positions. It was only in the 1920s, moreover, that what we might term 'proper historians' (people such as J.H. Clapham) became involved in the issue.

The question of poverty, and, thereby, of socio-economic improvement, exercised great minds long before the Industrial Revolution had reached its zenith. As early as the 1790s, Edmund Burke was castigating those who would denigrate poverty as though it was a condition from which all could escape. For Burke, poverty was a natural state for a proportion of any society. The condition of the growing urban working class was at the heart of discussions of poverty and hardship in society more generally. While rate-payers had no desire to expend more than was necessary on relieving the poor, it was appreciated that excessive hardship was a potential recipe for social disaster. The essence lay in getting the balance right. Ordinary people were exhorted to work hard for their living and for the well-being of their family members. The Bible was cited to remind workers than they broke bread by the sweat of their brow. Distortions in the market for labour were not tolerated in the early nineteenth century; until the middle of the century, indeed, political economists espoused the view that there was a fixed quantity of money in the economy for wages. Thus, if one person's wage was forced up in a bargaining victory over employers, another person's share would inevitably fall. Others challenged this view, not least Marx, who stressed the profits enjoyed by owners were simply the difference between what a worker's labour was worth and what he or she was paid. Whatever, the debate, however, working people regularly fell out of employment and often appealed to charity, the poor law and each other for help. At no point in our period did the state provide the degree of systematic benefits for the poor that are available at the present time; a more austere system, the Poor Law, nevertheless ensured the survival of many of society's poorest members.

Whether or not the nineteenth century saw improvements in peoples' economic lives to match their changing social world is a matter of some debate. Factories, town streets, urban housing, pressures upon space, and a lack of fresh air and green land may have come increasingly to typify the world of the worker, but it is not at all clear that the new wealth created at the time trickled down to the ordinary man, woman and child. Indeed, the standard of living debate continues to rumble on among historians. Part of the reason for this is that the data for measuring past economic life are partial and problematical. Historians simply cannot provide a definitive answer to the question 'did the Industrial Revolution increase the buying power of the working class?'

It is difficult, not to say impossible, to recreate the economic life of a past individual or family in its entirety. Any historian purporting to provide such answers would need to have access to information concerning aspects of life that appear to have gone unmeasured. We have no real idea about the regularity of wages in the Victorian economy. However, we do know that, in an export nation, the economy was susceptible to peaks and troughs of high activity or inertia. It is known that under-employment affected many trades, especially in agriculture, where work came in intense bouts – particularly at harvest time – only to drop off in the winter. Different regions, occupations and years or periods witnessed a variety of experiences with regard to economic performance. While male wages are relatively well charted, we know less about the methods and rates of payment for women, and the extent of child labour is problematical. While paid money wages were increasingly the norm for British workers at this time, many still took part of their pay in the form of perks and non-money payments, free produce (such as coal), and so on.

The emphasis on wages must be balanced against the cost of that basket of goods which all working families relied on. Staple food items for working-class families included flour, potatoes, cheap meats, tea, sugar and dairy products. Also vital was the rental cost of the family, which could fluctuate wildly, especially in boom towns where pressure on space was considerable. Clothing and basic furniture, pots and pans, limited quantities of cutlery, and vital commodities such as candles, all have to be factored in to the equation of what it cost for a family to live and whether or not their surplus income increased. The same should also be said for drinking, illness, old age and strikes – all of which reduced the ability of individuals and families to reach the necessary purchasing power for good health.

In recent years, historians have developed a method of research – dubbed anthropometric history – in order to study evidence of the changing physique of workers. While the incidents of data which include the measurement of the height or chest size of people in the past is limited (so far military and prison data have been most utilitised), this type of innovative approach has enabled the debate to move on from what was once simply a competition between incomplete registers of food prices and wage levels.

It is quite likely that the working family had more disposable income in 1900 than 1800. Probably wages doubled in the same period. But even in 1909, as Maud Pember Reeves famously asserted in her tract of this title, most workers took home 'round about a pound a week'. National income increased far faster than the individual's average share of that income. In other words, while the individual looks to have got a little richer (against increased wages can be set falling costs of living, especially in the last quarter of the century) the country overall got very much richer and much more obviously so. What this means is that if the average man and woman almost doubled their income while national income increased three or four times, then a smaller class of people enjoyed very much enhanced incomes and conditions of life.

Increases in wages were also uneven. In the early part of the century – taking into account the experiences of the then still proportionately important agricultural workers and those experiencing privation in dying trades (for example handloom weavers) – average wages probably fell. 'The hungry forties' was not a term used at the time. However, the term seems appropriate for an age of Irish Famine (1845–51), periods of general economic hardship, widespread problems faced by workers in hard-pressed trades, the mass social and political protests of Chartism and revolutionary ferment in Europe (1848), which swept away regimes.

Free trade, railways and resulting economic prosperity are said to have killed off Chartism in the 1850s. And there is little doubt that, if Victorian labour experienced anything of a 'golden age' it was in the years from the mid-1850s till the mid-1870s when those trades we really associate with Victorian mass production (iron- then later steelworking) flourished. The sense in which the period 1850–70 was one of general improvement is tempered by the fact that wages did no more than keep pace with rising costs in the 1850s and that it was not until the mid-1860s that improvements became clear. A fall in prices from the early 1880s, particularly in the price of food, then strengthened the buying power of the average wage. We must bear in mind, of course, that these generalisations hide a multitude of varying circumstances: unemployment, abandonment, drunkenness, and death of the breadwinner could have an enormous impact on individual families.

7.6 Working-class culture

Leisure

In our period, manual workers tended to work longer hours than is the case today. The legislation that protected them from exploitation was tiny by comparison with our own times. In 1800, there were few restrictions on the length of the working week. Most labouring people worked for six days a week and little time was left for leisure pursuits. During the early industrial period, when, in the eyes of many social commentators, Lancashire factories were seen to symbolise the excesses of hard work, reformers did press for working men and women to be granted more leisure time – so long as that time was spent in rational pursuits and individual self-improvement, not in drinking, gambling and idling. W. Cooke Taylor, in his *Notes of a Tour in the Manufacturing Districts of Lancashire* (1842), captured both the demand for leisure and also the need for the time to be well used:

> No one feels more strongly than I do the great but neglected truth that moral education, in spite of all the labours of direct instructors, is really acquired in hours of recreation. Sport and amusements are, and must be, means by which the mind is insensibly trained; the lectures of the school-room will be utterly ineffective when they are counteracted by the practical lessons of the playground.

By 1914, the working week was shorter: campaigns for 10-hour days, then nine and later eight all nibbled away at the amount of time a worker was expected to spend at the machine or in his place of work. Yet, even in the Edwardian period, those who found themselves in full-time employment could expect to work a far fuller week than is the case today. While the full six days had passed in favour of a shorter week, Saturday mornings remained a part of the normal working cycle, 50 hours per week, for manual workers, was not uncommon.

It is not surprising, therefore, that, with leisure opportunities so scant, men and women took their little freedom very seriously. Yet few observers – journalists, clerics, writers, and so on – could really comprehend the types of pursuits which working-class people found relaxing. The excessive use of drink, and the absence of a moral code to govern leisure-time activities, caused anguish. Much working-class recreation appeared mindless, without structure. There was, however, the occasional observer who understood the logic of what men in particular got up to. The rector of Bethnal Green in 1895, showed remarkable insight into working men's habits:

> a vast majority of the men in your district will have spent their Sundays for the last twenty-five years, and their fathers before them, in the following way: they will have lain in bed bed till about eleven or twelve, having been up early all week; they will then go round when the public-houses

open, which they do at one; they will have what they call a 'wet' till three ... they will then have dinner, the great dinner of the week, which the missus has been preparing all the morning. Then comes a lie down on the bed in shirt sleeves until five, with a pot of beer and *Lloyd's Weekly*; then follows tea, and after tea a bit of a walk round to see a friend or a relation; then fairly early to bed to make up for a very late Saturday night.

Some pastimes were deemed by moral reformers to be character-building and indeed 'rational'. Others, including heavy drinking and prize-fighting, were considered to be barbarous and degrading. As a result of this dichotomy between the 'rational' and the indulgent, Victorian commentators, and subsequently historians, viewed leisure as contested ground. Historians have disagreed over the extent to which leisure culture was created by, or was imposed upon, the working class. More recent research has offered a more fluid interpretation, with emphasis upon the division of 'rough' and 'respectable', irrespective of class or social status. The impulse to leisure time enjoyment remained constant throughout our period, even if the mode or sphere of that enjoyment may have changed. As Golby and Purdue (1984) remind us: '[i]f the nineteenth century saw a taming of its cruder and more violent manifestations ... many leisure pursuits remained in essence the same and were simply modified to suit a society that had become more prosperous, more humanitarian and less disorderly.' What this essentially means is that leisure pursuits did not necessarily change as rapidly as the society into which they fitted.

Criticism of working-class leisure were tied up with wider concerns about the nature of Victorian society. The way in which the working class passed their spare time was a source of great concern for middle-class observers. The apparent problems of leisure were linked to the way people felt about their changing world. Politicians and journalists alike were fearful of the social effects of urbanisation – the growth of whole areas of working-class population, beyond the control of priests and the authorities, where a 'mob' might quickly form. The same feeling that inspired the early Victorian evangelical revival also saw the middle classes promoting self-improvement for their inferiors while also demanding the constitution of an effective police force. Commentators alighted on the issue of popular culture, was part of a wider desire to transform society into a more civilised entity.

Men and women perceived leisure activities in an almost political way: governing free time was as important as controlling the work-place because, at some point, the two worlds touched each other. If a farm-hand or a miner could ensure a certain amount of leisure time, then it stands to reason that his working week could not be lengthened. In defending leisure time and particular sorts of pastimes, the working-class was stressing its independence. Thus, Liverpool dock labourers, like many other groups of casual workers, preferred to work harder longer days in order to maintain their leisure time. They resisted full weeks, cramming work into shorter spaces of time in order to enjoy long weekends of leisure. These men needed time to recover from the rigours of their toil; but they also liked to enjoy free time by drinking heavily. Casualism gave them an independence which was denied workers in other, more regimented trades.

The concept of St Monday (or even of St Tuesday or St Wednesday), which had been a feature of pre-industrial working patterns, remained fundamental to the work and leisure culture of many groups of workers in the mid-Victorian years, particularly those in small-scale workshops or who worked at home. Leisure was about control. But it was as much concerned with working-class self-control as well as with middle-class attempts to shape and improve the moral tendencies of the working man and woman. Most moral reformers, moreover, remained most concerned, not so much with the length of the leisure activity, but its content.

The extent to which the processes of industrialisation and urbanisation transformed people's lives is debated. Continuities and changes in popular leisure culture constitute an important part of any consideration. Pre-industrial popular culture is usually characterised as vigorous but not a threat to the social fabric. Rural leisure was intimately associated with local customs. It was shaped by the religious calendar (though this declined as time went by) and by the seasons. Many aspects of traditional culture declined due to the pressures upon common space exerted by enclosures and the commercialisation of agriculture, although great social occasions, such as the market town hiring fair, continued to bring together town and country in a ritual of widespread alcoholic indulgence. Mass football games were common across England. In many rural parts, violent sports, such as boxing, wrestling, and cudgelling were common-place as small-scale spectator sports, with gambling on the outcome also common.

Hunting and bloodsports, such as cockfighting, attracted gamblers, including local squires, who sometimes had considerable sums riding on the events organised by their tenants or labourers. These forms of rural leisure were often actively promoted and funded by local elites, in a marked contrast to the rather dismissive air exhibited by better-off townspeople in Victorian times. The rich and varied popular culture of 'Merrie England', with its emphasis upon participation and acquiescence by all tiers of the rural community, was in terminal decline in the eighteenth-century when the division between 'polite' and 'popular' culture became more apparent. In villages, though, traditions lived on. The country house continued to be a focal point of the rural community long after urbanisation shifted the balance of the population. Local landed families were intimately tied to the fate of the communities around them and the people were generally interested in how the prominent families of their area fared. This link between the common people and their social superiors, mediated through the great house, had an effect on the locals' leisure culture. Noblemen held parties and fêtes in their grounds, inviting local people to join in celebrations such as the coming of age of the eldest son. Lavish displays with music, fireworks and food enthralled the villagers roundabout. The death of a nobleman also offered people from across particular regions the opportunity to pay their respects. The fact that thousands of pounds were spent on individuals' funeral procession, or that more than 2,000 people filed past Lord Cardigan's coffin in 1868 gives us an idea of the role which the aristocracy could play in ordinary peoples' lives. The sort of public displays of loyalty given to royalty today extended to the ranks of the nobility in the Victorian period.

Certain aspects of rural culture maintained their importance in the town. Workers in Manchester kept pigs for the same reason as their rural counterparts: because pigs had economic value. For the Irish, the pig was 'the gintleman who pays the rint'. And in mining villages, where rural met urban, the pig was usually a welcome house guest, as Jim Bullock remembered in his autobiography (see Box 7.3). Similarly, while hunting rituals changed over time, and between town and country, long-lining for fish, hunting rabbits and poaching game were much the same in a village or on the outskirts of a town. The urban worker's company house sometimes came with small gardens, in which could be grown small amounts of vegetables for the family table. Some workers also rented allotments – often located on strips of land alongside railway lines – which provided scope for more significant of production of vegetables and flowers, as well as space to keep

Box 7.3

Killing the pig

Extract from Jim Bullock,
Bower's Row: Recollection of a Mining Village.

Jim Bullock, who grew up in a mining village, Bower's Row, near Castleford, Yorkshire, remembers how the killing of one of his father's pigs was a great social occasion for all his family's friends and neighbours. The ceremonial nature of the event emphasises a strong sense of community, and demonstrates how such events were embedded in the cultural and economic history of working-class life in the nineteenth and early twentieth centuries:

A big event in our family life was the killing of a pig. This was more than a family occasion, because the younger children would already have been round the village collecting orders for different joints of pork; so the whole village turned out to watch.

The pig to be slaughtered was chosen by my father, and the date it had to be killed was decided between my father and the village amateur butcher, the latter being the star of the occasion. He was always accompanied by his own team of six burly, strong miners, each of whom knew his job. They would arrive at the house carrying the 'scatch', a strong wooden platform with two handles at each end, standing on four stout legs about two feet high.

The butcher himself always wore a blue and white smock tied at the waist with a long piece of white tape. Carrying his bag of knives and killing instruments, he would come in and ask if the water was boiling. This water would be needed to scald the carcass so that the hair could be scraped away easily, and huge pans of it would be prepared by the neighbours.

When he was assured that everything was ready, the butcher led the procession to the pig sty. The chosen pig was hoisted bodily by the miners on to the scratch in a very similar way to a bull fight: everybody prepared for the kill, and the village butcher stood back like a matador, waiting to administer the final coup de grace, swiftly and skilfully.

Source: E.P. Publishing (Wakefield, 1976)

The economics of the times demanded that not a single part of the animal should be wasted, so the blood was collected in a bucket and used to make black pudding. When the boiling water arrived, carried by willing neighbours, the execution squad scraped all the hair from the carcass, which was then brought into the house and hung head downwards from a big hook in the ceiling.

Once the butcher had opened the pig, the intestines were taken by the next-door neighbour, Mrs Ingham. She used to clean and cook these, eating them as chitterlings, or else stuffed with minced scraps of meat as sausages. My mother would be busy cutting up the pig's heart and liver into small parcels to be given to those neighbours who in the past had sent scraps and potato peelings to help feed the pigs. The bladder was given to each boy in the family in strict rotation. This would then be blown up and put into a yeast bag or an adult's stocking, and it became the village boys' football until it was kicked to pieces.

Next day, the butcher would come back to our house and cut the pig up. We youngsters would deliver the various joints to those who had ordered them, collecting the cash and handing it over to my father, who then carefully counted it and placed it in the pig money box. He then calculated what the pig had cost to buy, what it had cost in feed, and whether that left any profit. This money was put towards buying another pig.

Every part of the dead animal was used, my mother doing all the preparation herself. The brains were fried, making what was considered a real delicacy in those days. The head and feet were boiled for brawn. The fat around the sides of the pig was rendered down and made into lard; the bits of fried left over were eaten with bread and called 'scratchings'. We kept one big joint of pork ourselves, and all the family, married or single, came home for that glorious meal. After killing a pig we lived for a few days just like lords. Oh, they were fortunate indeed those who kept a pig in the village.

chickens or a pig. Such larger-scale production provided green-fingered amateur gardeners with the opportunity to produce seasonal foods for their families perhaps with a little left for sale.

Leisure helped to delineate the community's physical space as well as defining differing moral positions: pubs were symbols of communities but also sources of conflict between indulgers and abstainers. In the towns, enclosures were also an issue, albeit less so than in the countryside, having the similar effect of proscribed certain leisure activities in the village. There were riots when urban spaces were enclosed. An example occurred at Plumstead Common in London in 1876.

There was much opposition to the more ribald forms of working-class culture. Drink, fighting and crime were seen as closely linked and became more noticeable in the confined spaces of the urban world. A key problem was the very nature of time itself, and the way in which it was divided up. Whereas numerous days of merry-making, carnival and indulgence were an accepted part of the pre-modern calendar, such apparent excesses could not be aligned with the regimented work rhythms of industrial life. The nature of public space was also contested in a similar fashion. Sprawling and violent games were suited to villages and fields; they became much less desirable, and indeed more dangerous, in the tighter confines of urban streets. Excessive public indulgence was impossible and undesirable in the town; rowdiness was amplified in built-up streets, and more people were disturbed by fights or drunken revelry if it occurred in places of dense population. As part of the general pressure exerted against what were considered ruinous forms of indulgence, gambling was often restricted by law (although this forced it underground). Common gambling houses were outlawed in the mid-1850s, but working-class communities continued to gamble on the street, in the home and away from the prying eyes of policemen.

Modern society considers many forms of gaming with animals to be cruel; yet in the past, cockfighting, bearbaiting and dogfighting were commonplace. In the nineteenth century, as a part of a wider sweep of moral reform, questions began to be asked about certain types of animal usage. Whereas the hunt was considered noble, and horse-racing attracted crowds from all classes of people, fights between beasts – especially those put on for the purposes of gambling – began to cause indignation. Laws were passed in 1822 and 1835 to prevent cruelty to animals. Although the Society for the Prevention of Cruelty to Animals (which became a 'royal' society only later) was founded in 1824, working men continued to orchestrate such things as dog fights and badger-baiting – but now they just did it secretly. Cockfighting was outlawed in 1839 but continued in the same fashion. Much of the impetus for a higher or 'rational' form of recreation came from the churches, many of which provided by the 1850s a whole range of organised pastimes to maintain eighteenth-century leisure attitudes and counteract the lure of the public house.

The churches occupied a somewhat ambiguous position in working-class communities. The religious census of 1851 (a one-off and crude attempt to measure faith through church attendance on a given Sunday) seemed to suggest that religion had never been less popular in British society. What is more, the established Anglican church suffered the most serious decline, while the few growth denominations included Catholicism, Methodism and Judaism (especially following the Jewish immigration from the Russian empire in the later nineteenth century). The degree of religious practice in society was declining steadily and this caused great concern for moral reformers. Most Britons, however, remained generally religious, even if church attendances were waning.

All churches concentrated on providing a comprehensive mixture of religious and social functions. An example of this latter occurred in 1887, when a Catholic priest founded Glasgow Celtic football club. Many other towns saw football teams of 'Hibernians', 'Harps' and 'Shamrocks' springing up at around the same time; and churches in most other towns provided a similar mix of the spiritual and the social in forming sporting societies and the like.

Much of the energy for the reform of working-class culture derived from the fear and loathing of drink. Churches organised tea parties and suppers at which alcohol was not permitted. Temperance societies, dedicated to a curtailment and then abolition of drink, became quite popular. Most towns had large halls which were built by public subscription to house The Band of Hope, the Ancient Rechabites, and other such temperance groups. These organisations produced tracts, held services, organised alternative leisure pursuits, such as day-trips to the country, and performed a missionary role in towns. Their aim was simple: to reform working-class culture and to improve ordinary peoples' lives by eradicating the demon drink.

Many leisure pursuits were fundamentally different in the towns. Generally, urban pastimes were marked by far greater organisation and had the capacity to be larger and more concentrated than in the shires. There also emerged a much more distinct division between participant and observer, especially in team sports, where spectators were becoming increasingly numerous. Sporting activities became more highly organised, competitive and commercialised – changes which derived part of their impetus from the public schools' new emphasis on the value of character-building and manly qualities of team sports. Certain types of leisure facilities needed urban populations to finance and sustain them, for example libraries, reading rooms, working-men's clubs and bath-houses. The same could be said for music halls, where the entertainment has been seen as epitomising the culture of urban workers. The music hall had a strong appeal because it offered a broad mixture of entertainment – singing, dancing, comedy – and because it was escapist. Music halls were generally large; all towns of any size had them; and most respectable working people used their facilities on a regular basis. Many music halls lost out to new technology, however, and were converted into cinemas. As early as 1914 there were around 4,000 cinemas.

While on the one hand, towns restricted the possibility for certain older forms of leisure, they also expanded leisure-time possibilities in other ways. This was particularly true of the sort of team sports that were favoured by the growing ranks of spectators. Football and cricket leagues could not have developed to the extent that they did without urban growth. They were clearly facilitated by the clustering of populations and by the spread of transport networks. Horse-racing remained consistently popular with the working class: this had, of course, developed much earlier in the villages, but it made the transition to the towns quite easily. It is claimed that around 100,000 people used to line the river Tyne in the 1840s to watch rowing races. In the early 1900s around 20,000 paying spectators were watching first round FA Cup matches.

A new phenomenon, governed entirely in its extent both by the existence of an urban population and development of transport connections, was the day-trip. Towns dedicated almost entirely to peoples' leisure – Blackpool, Morecambe, Southend-on Sea – could not have become what they were without the train and the cheap ticket. As time went by, cheap seaside holidays – longer breaks of a week or so – became a feature of the later

Victorian period. Between 1883 and 1914 the number of visitors to Blackpool increased four-fold to 4 m. Seaside centres such as Roker, Sunderland, Whitley Bay, near North Shields, and Portabello, Edinburgh, ensured that a day-trip to the seaside was within easy reach of thousands of workers. Walking on the beach, eating ice-cream and bathing in the sea all struck a pleasant contrast to the gloom of the coal mine or the hot, dry atmosphere of the dock-side warehouse.

Leisure was also political. The growth of socialism from the 1880s saw the development of a range of social organisations designed to attract converts and to strengthen the cultural aspects of class. Robert Blatchford's *Clarion* newspaper lent its name to an array of socialist leisure-time pursuits; there were Clarion cycling clubs in Glasgow, and Clarion ramblers in Sheffield. Labour churches and socialist Sunday schools became popular in this period, offering something more than religious instruction for all. John Maclean taught economics to working men in Glasgow, while institutional self-education was available through the Plebs League and London's Central Labour College. There is no doubt that the period 1880 to 1914 saw a great awakening in working-class political consciousness; much of it derived from the new-found organisational strength and voice of the unskilled workers. The skilled worker, however, remained at the heart of the labour movement's institutionals.

The development of youth organisations should also be seen as part of the self-improvment mission associated with many leisure forms, especially in the later nineteenth century. Football clubs, the Boys' Brigade, Baden Powell's Boy Scout movement, formed in 1908, and, later, the Girl Guides, represented a broad mixture of the disciplined, the quasi-military and the self-improving way in which the hearts and minds of working-class children were fought over. Sport, exercise and the great outdoors were increasingly thought to be an antidote to the problems of urban life; fitness of body was seen as an aid to fitness of mind; and a mentally alert, physically fit populace would bring its own rewards to the country at large. Indeed, the Edwardians held the view that their love of sport, and the qualities it bestowed, led to the successful management of their huge empire.

7.7 Protest and protection

In an age prior to the Welfare State, in which the Poor Law was the last hope of the hard-bitten workers' family, the working class went to great lengths to protect itself against the vagaries of employers and economy alike. On the one hand, Britain was, by 1914, the most highly unionised state in the world; equally, the British, like the Americans, built a huge and impressive structure of economically mutual organisations. Friendly societies, as these were called, including such famous examples as the Oddfellows and the Foresters, sought to protect members from unemployment, sickness or industrial injury. As the century progressed, coverage became more comprehensive, not least because legal protection against embezzlement, and so on, became more complete.

The first legislation to protect and promote friendly societies was passed in 1793. Many other acts were passed in the nineteenth century to assist people who wished to form friendly societies, and these were consolidated by a single, annually renewable act, the Friendly Societies Act of 1850, which was made permanent in 1875. This act outlined the basis upon which any number of individuals could form a society; it made rules concerning subscriptions, rules and registrations; most importantly, it also required treasurers to submit a bond to protect the society's funds from embezzlement.

The most important friendly societies were the affiliated orders. In the mid-Victorian years over 30 friendly societies had more than 1,000 members, and in all over 1.2 m people were affiliated. The Manchester Unity of the Independent Order of Oddfellows was the most powerful with 426,663 members; the Ancient Order of Foresters was in second place with 388,872. These affiliated societies were always strongest in the north of England. From the mid-century the declining membership in many of the industrial regions, can be explained by the formation in some towns of breakaway societies during the later 1840s when internecine conflict struck the Manchester Unity. The secession of lodges did not prevent the Oddfellows from continuing to prosper. By this point, friendly societies were part of the fabric of urban society, a reminder again of the mutualist aspiration of the working people. In 1874, there were 489,237 Oddfellows in Britain. By 1908, this had increased to 868,190, although the latter figure includes overseas members. In 1864, the Oddfellows drew in contributions for funerals and sickness totalling £278,971. At this time, the fund for such circumstances had reached almost £1.7 m, of which just over £200,000 was paid out. By 1908, the fund had reached £13,183,171 with some £462,026 being drawn by members or their families. These figures do not include the works of widow, orphan or juvenile societies which were an important part of all friendly society organisations.

The world of the friendly societies was colourful and convivial as well as financial and functional. The societies were clannish; new members were supposed to be mystified and astounded by what they might find on enrolment because this added to their aura. The meaning of the societies was quite clear, as this quotation from the inaugural lecture indicates:

> The duties of Oddfellowship will always teach you to stretch out your hand to a brother in distress; to offer up your warmest petitions for his welfare; to assist him with your best counsel and advice; and to betray no confidence he may repose in you.

The friendly society ideology even attracted converts among those seemingly least likely to be able to afford its costs. Poor Irish Catholic migrants, for instance, whose numbers increased dramatically at this time, found themselves pressured by the financial as well as the religious teachings of their church. Fearful of the secrecy and anti-religious message of many early trade unions, the Catholic church in Britain allied its vigorous anti-combination message for Catholic workers to a range of its own friendly-type services. Trade unionists were threatened with excommunication, and, at the same time, Catholic friendly societies were formed to promote a church-centred mode of self-improvement. By the late 1830s, almost all major urban centres in northern England had at least one Catholic friendly society.

7.8 Credit and debt

Most working people spent the majority of their wages on the essentials: food, shelter and clothing. The vast majority of Britain's labouring population had little to spare; others gave what little they did have to the local publican. The demands made on philanthropic bodies and the Poor Law provide indicate how tight life could be. In 1870, in England and

Wales, throughout the entire period, 1850–1914, the total of paupers receiving relief never dropped below 750,000. At the same time, mutual societies, such Scottish Widows, had life assurance funds running into millions. Those who could afford insurance took it out; those who could save, did so through the Co-Operative Bank or the Trustee Savings Bank. However, working-class savers were a minority; only in the 1930s was the labouring population significant among investors in banks. Few ordinary people could own their own homes in the nineteenth century, although building societies did develop as a lower-middle-class response to the need for cheaper, self-owned homes. Most ordinary folk simply struggled to make ends meet. This is why, for example, pawnbroking provides one of the most powerful images of credit and debt in the nineteenth century. For a respectable working-class woman – and women were usually lumbered with the job – a visit to what was commonly termed the 'pop-shop' was a humiliation. Overall, the management of the family budget was notoriously difficult when the balance of income and expenditure could be so fine. Critical factors, including death, unemployment or the birth of a child, could cause chaos for a family already finely attuned to the need for absolute frugality. While credit was something of a dirty word in the working-class argot, it was also a necessity for many. Mothers had to feed their families, and if the money caddy was empty two days before pay day, something had to be done. It is small wonder, then, that in early industrial towns, in the 1830s and early 1840s, prior to the spread of co-operative stores, chandlers' shops were very popular. Advancing goods on credit, these shops provided a bridge between one pay-day and the next. Many of the shopkeepers who ran these outfits were unscrupulous; debt held customers in thrall so that short-weight and adulteration were accepted with a mixture of reluctance and resignation. The truck system of payment added to working-class woes in this respect.

Like the friendly societies, the Co-operative Society had roots in an earlier period. Co-operation meant different things to different people, from workers' collectives and model communities to retailing for the common good on the other. The truck system had been roundly condemned before the emergence of the modern co-operative store, not least by socialists such as Robert Owen. Efforts to thwart the truck system also saw the advent of co-operative-type shops in these years but there were significant obstacles to their progress. Employers often opposed such manifestations of working-class independence, and threatened workers who sought to abandon truck stores which the employers themselves often owned. Truck wages were cheaper than money wages and the least well-organised workers were usually those who suffered most by its regimen. Thus women's wages were even more likely to be paid in truck than men.

The idea of the 'Rochdale Pioneers' was to buy good-quality foodstuffs at wholesale prices, cutting out the middle-man and obviating adulteration. Cash purchases were vital, because the early Co-operative could not provide credit. The idea caught on, and by the 1850s there were scores of similar societies. By the 1860s and 1870s virtually every industrial town had a co-operative store. The store was not exclusively the domain of the labour aristocracy, though its opposition to credit undoubtedly excluded many poorer members of the working class. The co-operative movement was particularly successful in the north and the midlands. By the end of the century co-operative stores were often the most impressive buildings on the main streets of most northern industrial towns. By this time, the co-operative store had expanded its trade to include coal, furniture and other household goods. A considerable departure had taken place in 1862 with the formation of the Co-operative Wholesale Society (CWS) which sought to enable bulk provisioning with even less of a threat from the middle-man. There were also other ventures on the production side, such as a biscuit and sweets factory at Crumpsall in Manchester, which was opened in February 1873.

7.9 Conclusion

The worlds of the worker was varied. It changed over time and was characterised by different experiences, depending upon time, place, the nature of employment and whether the individual concerned was a man, woman or child. Nevertheless, certain key aspects knitted working-class lives together. The fact that this term 'working class' came into existence does suggest, even if only on the most basic level, that there was some common experience linking ordinary people. The most obvious level upon which this might operate is work itself. By definition, a working man or woman toiled for some form of remuneration. Being working class also suggested a certain way of life, although this could be remarkably varied. While a day-labourer in rural Rutland was a worker, his life was very different from that of an Irish jute-worker in Dundee. The town and village were different; yet both had good housing and bad, poor people and rich, the able-bodied and the infirm. Working-class worlds were governed by a certain collective idea. It is probably accurate to state that, in say the 1850s, there was much more 'sticking together' or neighbourliness, than in today's world. This is partly because people perceived that, sooner or later, they would need someone's help, due to the possibility of unemployment, sickness or strike.

The working class may have been the most striking emergence of this century, but the growth and dynamism of the middle class, and the continued power and privilege of the aristocracy should not be downplayed and are equally as important. Working-class communities intersected with the classes above: employers, doctors, clerics, writers, journalists, magistrates, and so on, were of a higher social and economic status than the working people around them, yet the two came into regular contact. This is why, especially in the urban world, much of what middle-class people thought of working-class people concerned the need to reform their habits. Social improvement and moral betterment were each aspects of the Victorian ideal that impinged upon the working man and woman's perceptions of themselves.

Summary

◆ Class is an important, still valid, concept aiding our understanding of the structure of society.

◆ The emergence of a working class is a striking feature of our period.

◆ The increasing spread, sophistication and power of the middle class is also vital.

◆ The maintenance of landed privilege and power is a key to understanding the nature of British society.

◆ Classes, whichever they might be, shared a sense of community.

◆ Economic mutualism was a part of workers' lives.

◆ Leisure culture was a contested site.

Points to discuss

◆ What is class?

◆ Why did notions of class develop?

◆ What are the principal features of the three classes?

◆ What did the working class do to protect their own economic interests?

References and further reading

J.V. Beckett, *The Aristocracy in England, 1660–1914* (1986).

D. Birley, *Sport and the Making of Britain* (Manchester, 1993).

D.Birley, *Land of Sport and Glory: Sport and British Society, 1887–1910* (Manchester, 1994).

M. Body, *The Building Societies* (1980).

John Burnett, *Plenty and Want: A Social History of Diet in England from 1815 to the Present Day* (1979 edn).

G. Claeys, *Machinery, Money and the Millennium: The New Moral Economy of Owenite Socialism, 1815–67* (1987).

G. Crossick, *An Artisan Elite in Victorian Society: Kentish London, 1840–80* (1978).

R.G. Garnett, *Co-Operation and the Owenite Socialist Communities in Britain, 1825–45* (Manchester, 1972).

J.M. Golby and A.W. Purdue, *The Civilisation of the Crowd: Popular Culture in England, 1750–1900* (1984).

W. Cooke Taylor, *Notes of a Tour in the Manufacturing Districts of Lancashire* (New York, 1842).

P.H.J.H. Gosden, *The Friendly Societies in England, 1815–1875* (Manchester, 1961).

D. Fraser, *The Evolution of the Welfare State* (Basingstoke, 1984 2nd edn).

G. and W. Grossmith, *The Diary of a Nobody* (1982 edn).

J.F.C. Harrison, *Robert Owen and the Owenites in Britain and America: The Quest for the New Moral World* (New York, 1969).

G.S. Jones, *Languages of Class: Studies in English Working Class History, 1832–1982* (Cambridge, 1983).

P. Johnson, *Saving and Spending: The Working-Class Economy in Britain, 1870–1939* (Oxford, 1985).

T. Koditschek, *Class Formation and Urban–Industrial Society: Bradford 1750–1850* (Cambridge, 1990).

W.M. Knox, *Industrial Nation: Work. Culture and Society in Scotland, 1800–Present* (Edinburgh, 1999).

D.M. MacRaild, *Irish Migrants in Modern Britain, 1750–1922* (Basingstoke, 1999).

R.W. Malcolmson, *Popular Recreation in English Society, 1700–1850* (Cambridge, 1973).

H. Perkin, *Origins of Modern English Society* (1969).

S. Pollard, 'Nineteenth-century co-operation: community building to shopkeeping', in A. Briggs and J. Saville (eds), *Essays in Labour History* (1960).

M.E. Rose, *The Relief of Poverty, 1834–1914* (1972),

R. Samuel, 'The workshop of the world: steam power and hand technology in mid-Victorian Britain', *History Workshop*, 3 (1977).

F.M.L. Thompson, *The Rise of Respectable Society: A Social History of Victorian Britain, 1830–1900* (Cambridge MA, 1988).

E.P. Thompson, *The Making of the English Working Class* (1963; 1986 edn).

E.P. Thompson, *Customs in Common* (1991).

A. Toynbee, *Lectures on the Industrial Revolution* (1884).

D. Vincent, *Literacy and Popular Culture: England, 1750–1914* (Cambridge, 1989).

The Political World to 1851

■ Introduction

Traditionally books of this type and title would have concentrated on politics. Indeed they would have been mostly devoted to politics, with, maybe, an additional chapter on economics, another on society, and, just possibly, one on 'culture' that was designed to act as a catch-all for everything that had been missed out. Irrespective of the space devoted to the non-political topics, the central subject of the conventional textbook was politics and its intellectual interest and means of analysis focused on political questions and causes.

These were (and are) indeed important, but the agenda and method of this book are both very different. That still leaves the questions of how best to locate politics within the general scheme of the book, how to treat the political history of the period, and what form of analysis to employ. Our decision is not to focus on a detailed high political narrative. There is not the space available if we are to devote due attention to non-political topics. More seriously, such a narrative 'privileges' (gives a preference to) a particular definition of politics and understanding of how politics works that are of value to an understanding of high politics, but not to a wider assessment of the political process.

The two chapters on politics thus have two major tasks. It is necessary to provide a basic political narrative not simply for a discussion of the political process, but also because politics has a close relationship with the topics covered in other chapters, and it is necessary at some point to have a discussion that contextualises the politics of a specific period or the policies of particular ministries. Secondly, these chapters attempt to make general points about the nature of *political culture* in order to offer a comparable thematic approach to that in other chapters of the book. As a reminder of the extent to which politics recorded wider aspects of the public life, it is worth noting the report in *Jackson's*

Oxford Journal of 18 March 1820 about recent events in Banbury, in which the Corporation had been defied:

> On Friday the 10th inst. Being the day appointed for the election of a Member of Parliament for this borough, a large concourse of people assembled, and it being generally understood that the usual practice of distributing beer and ribbons to the populace was to be discontinued, the persons assembled soon began to shew strong symptoms of disappointment; by hissing, groaning, etc. and many of them paraded the streets with favours, made of deal shavings, in their hats. Whilst this was going on, a party proceeded to the White Lion Inn, and took possession of an old chaise, in which they placed a poor half-witted fellow, nick-named 'Old Mettle', and drew him to the Mayor's house, crying 'Mettle for ever! – No Legge [the man elected]'. A few stones were thrown through the Mayor's windows. The chaise was then placed in front of the Town Hall.

The report revealed an absence of deference alongside the usual public expression of exuberance of election time.

Key issues

▶ What was at stake in politics?

▶ What were the major political issues of this period?

▶ How serious was the crisis of the late 1820s?

▶ Why did the First Reform Act take the form it did, and why did it pass?

▶ How serious was dissatisfaction with the political system in 1836–48?

▶ What was the role of the press in the reform movements of the period?

8.1 Politics, society and revolution

Avoidance of revolution framed the political consciousness and was the dynamic of the political process in the first half of the century. The political imagination of both elite and non-elite was greatly affected by the French Revolution of 1789, especially by the violence and radicalism of 1792–4: the September Massacres in 1792, the execution of Louis XVI in 1793, and the Terror in 1793–4. This represented a present-day challenge to British political attitudes that was more immediate and credible than the principal issue earlier in the reign of George III (1760–1820), namely the extent to which it was possible to view him as a modern tyrant, or a latter-day version of the Stuart bogey-men of the British political tradition, Charles I (1625–49) and, more particularly, James II (1685–8). The expulsion of James and the consequent constitutional and political settlement had constituted the Glorious Revolution, the starting point for the definition of the Whig political system and identity.

The French Revolution led to a reconceptualisation of British politics. In crude terms, men of property rallied together to preserve the existing system, but, in practice, this rallying was a wider and deeper process. The combination of French and domestic radicalism was presented as a threat to religion, culture and identity as well as property.

Yet, while this rallying round was fundamental, it did not leave subsequent political strategies clear. Those who looked to France, the domestic radicals, were excluded from power, but, within the elite, there was a wide range of response. The two most important were an accent on conservatism and, on the other hand, interest in a measure of reform in order to prevent revolution. This remained the case after Napoleon brought a measure of order to France in 1799 and again after the fall of Napoleon in 1815. Concern about revolution and the specific impact of the French example was kept alive in 1830 by the 'July Revolution' there and then again by the overthrow of the French monarchy in 1848. Again, both had an impact on opinion within Britain. This tension, about how best to respond to potential revolutionary pressure, set the basic parameters of politics, and provided a continuity that cuts across the chronological barriers that might otherwise attract attention. All groups and interests that were part of the political process wished to avoid revolution and this also extended to most radicals.

Equally, these parameters operated as part of a dynamic political system that had to confront a series of challenges. Although seen as stable, even stagnant, the eighteenth-century British state had faced a series of challenges, including Jacobitism and the American Revolution. In addition, the Westminster Parliament was one of the sole successful representative assemblies of the period. By 1800, Poland had been partitioned and the United Provinces, Swiss Confederation, and Venice conquered by the French. Republican experiments in France had proved short-lived. Only in the United States did distance from powerful enemies permit the development of a decentralized representative system. In the British Isles, in contrast the Westminster Parliament was a great success. Not only did it continue, but it also extended to incorporate those of Edinburgh (1707) and Dublin, the latter effected by the Act of Union, which was passed in 1800 and came into effect on 1 January 1801.

This should not be seen in a triumphalist fashion, but it can be viewed as an increasingly distinctive feature of Britain in this period for other European states did not possess a powerful representative assembly. The relationship between centre and locality, state and population, sovereign and subject, was more, apparently and obviously, formally and informally, consensual than in most of the rest of Europe. Tension was integral to this relationship, but it brought important advantages and was fundamental to British political culture. In May 1810, William, Lord Grenville, who had been Prime Minister in 1806–7, wrote from his seat at Dropmore to Henry Brougham, an energetic Whig MP with a commitment to reform:

> This fine weather is not favourable to speculations about Parliamentary Reform and must at all events be my excuse for not having earlier answered the rational and well considered suggestions which you had the goodness to communicate to me. My general view of the situation is this. I continue to object strongly to the vague and undefined notions of reforming merely for the sake of reform. That is determining to make some change without previously considering its extent, its principles or its objects. I hold on the contrary side in equal reprobation the opinions in the other extreme, that on this point alone all change is to be rejected without examination, merely because it is a change. The just sentiment seems to be that in this as in every other matter in which the public interests are concerned the constant and vigilant superintendence of Parliament is required, neither adopting nor rejecting change in the abstract, but weighing each particular position in detail by the scale of probable advantage or mischief to the community ... all ideas should be disclaimed of extensive and as you justly call them wholesale plans of reform which are at once to strike out for us a new constitution of government and legislation.

Grenville was no Tory, but his letter makes clear that conservatism in this period was broadly based and not dependent on politicians termed, then or subsequently, Tory. The aristocratic liberalism of the Whigs, the other major political grouping, sought to link reform with a sense that aristocracy were natural leaders – trustees of the people – and also pressed for gradual reform that built on existing foundations: organic reform. This was scarcely the most radical of policies. There was little criticism of the electoral system, despite its multiple inconsistencies. For example, some settlements with very small populations were parliamentary boroughs, able to elect an MP. Cornwall was particularly over-represented as, more generally, was the south-west of England. Conversely, some major towns, including Birmingham, Bradford, Chatham, Falmouth, Leeds, Manchester, Sheffield and Whitehaven, were not parliamentary boroughs; although it is wrong to claim that were not represented; their votes did play a major role in county elections. Shifts in population did not lead to any redistribution of seats. Leaving growing towns in the Midlands and North unenfranchised was clearly anomalous and was bound, at some point, to result in sustained criticism.

In addition, many parliamentary seats were not contested at elections. A large number were 'pocket boroughs': controlled or at least heavily influenced by particular individual patrons or families. Even where they were not strictly 'pocket boroughs', powerful families could exert, by a combination of fear and favour, considerable control over the regularity and outcome of elections. Furthermore, many seats where there was no such control had no contested elections, either because one party was dominant or because the two parties had a compact to share power. There was thus no contest for the Nottinghamshire county seats between 1722 and 1832 or for those in Shropshire between 1722 and 1831, Dorset (1727–1806), Cheshire (1734), Lancashire (1747–1820), Staffordshire (1747–1832) and Oxfordshire (1754–1826). This matched the social politics of the country. Landed continuity on the part of the elite had political, social and cultural consequences, and contributed greatly to the exclusion by social status that was so important in politics, government and society more generally. This was a hierarchical society and its politics was essentially oligarchical, and there were very few challenges to the social assumptions that reflected and sustained this situation. Its political exclusions were justified by reference to the notion that the people at large were 'virtually' rather than 'actually' represented in parliament; and by the idea that independence of these unpaid (usually wealthy) MPs ensured their engagement with the needs of the people.

Nevertheless, despite a widespread conservatism, the stability of the political system was not some God-given national right, but, rather, owed much to success in war with France, especially the avoidance of invasion, to political leadership, and to social and economic developments. There was nothing inevitable in the transition that occurred from conspiracy and battlefield to elections and parliamentary government, a transition that in 1762 led the 'bluestocking' Elizabeth Montague to reflect that 'a virtuoso or a dilettanti may stand as secure in these times behind his Chinese rail as the knight on his battlements in former days'.

The nature, practices and purposes of parliamentary government were not accepted by all. This led to a series of crises, most obviously in the North American colonies in 1775, among British radicals in the 1790s and late 1810s, and in Ireland in 1798. However, the authority of the British state was overthrown only in North America. Elsewhere, the landed elite and their urban allies remained in control because of their shared interests

William Pitt the Younger (1759-1806)

Prime Minister 1783-1801, 1804-6. Became Prime Minister at 24, the youngest to hold the position in England. An effective peace-time leader, especially in reforming the public finances, his ministry was overshadowed from 1793 by war with Revolutionary (and after 1799) Napoleonic France. His support for Catholic Emancipation led him to resign office in 1801, the year he ushered through the Act of Union with Ireland, following opposition from George III. Pitt's long period in office helped to give coherence to cabinet politics.

Source: Engraving after Hopper

and confidence in their role, the lack of a widely accepted alternative, and, in Ireland, coercion. Governments that might be termed Tory, such as those of William Pitt the Younger in 1801 and 1806 (after Pitt's death), could fall without any sense that the essential continuity and conservatism of social structures and political practices were being compromised (see Profile Box and picture above).

Pitt's second ministry did not survive his unexpectedly early death in 1806, but the succeeding 'Ministry of All the Talents', led by Grenville, fell in 1807, in large part because of uneasy relations with George III over his determined opposition to Catholics gaining the vote. Grenville had an uneasy coalition of his own faction, the Foxite Whigs, and the followers of Henry Addington, who had been Prime Minister in 1801–4. This coalition had been responsible for the abolition of the slave trade, but its leading members were unwilling to promise the king that they would never again raise the Catholic question. This issue played a major part in Pitt's resignation in 1801. He had been determined to deliver relief to Catholics as part of the deal that helped drive through the Act of Union with Ireland, a country that was four-fifths Catholic. Overall, then, the whole issue was a reminder of how important eligion was in British politics. As a consequence, too, 'No popery', not the war, was the issue that dominated the 1807 general election. In 1807, the Pittite system returned in the shape of a ministry led by William, Duke of Portland and containing most of the leading Pittites, and the Whigs, thereafter, spent many years in opposition. The Whigs were unable to take advantage of the extent to which victory at Trafalgar had lessened concern about national security, nor could they capitalise on the unpopularity and divisions of the Portland ministry in 1809, especially the division between two of the most talented ministers, George Canning and Viscount Castlereagh. After Portland's poor health led to a protracted series of negotiations, the ministry was replaced by a government under the Evangelical and anti-Catholic Tory Spencer Perceval that continued on a Pittite base. An able financial manager, Perceval stood firm against Catholic Emancipation and in 1810 had Sir Francis Burdett, a prominent radical MP, sent to the Tower for his criticism of the government.

After Perceval was assassinated in 1812 by an embittered merchant, a firm and competent Pittite, Robert, 2nd Earl of Liverpool became Prime Minister, in large part

Robert, 2nd Earl of Liverpool (1770-1828)

A successful minister who held the major offices, as Foreign Secretary (1804–6, 1807–9) and Secretary for War and the Colonies (1809–12), during the long war with Napoleonic France. Prime Minister for nearly 15 years from 1812, he was not only a leader in war, his position accentuated by George III's ill-health and the Prince Regent's indolence and inexperience, but also in peace until he resigned after a stroke in 1827, the year of his death. Managed the difficult transition to peace, but seen as a reactionary by liberal critics. His position was eased, and his government less reactionary, in the 1820s.

because he enjoyed the support of most of the Pittites (see Profile Box 8.2, above). He held office until a major stroke in February 1827. The Whigs were not to triumph until 1832. In 1812 Brougham told Leigh that the press was the real opposition to Lord Liverpool's government; it was secure in Parliament, and indeed became more so from 1821. Liverpool was therefore the Prime Minister for both war and peace. He played a leading, but not the directing, role in the former, but once peace came in 1814, and, more definitely, 1815, he had to respond to the challenges of peace. These were very wide-ranging, from the attempt to reorganise government finances, after the cost of the most expensive war in Britain's history, to popular discontent with social and economic conditions.

8.2 Economic and social pressure

Economic change produced tension, as did social pressures. Both new industrial and agricultural technology and enclosures led to disturbances during the Napoleonic wars. For example, in Caernarvonshire in 1809, 1810 and 1812 enclosures led to disturbances. The loss of traditional rights greatly affected the livelihood of the poor and was also seen as an abuse of power. The response of the authorities was to deploy the coercive power of the state. In Caernarvonshire, the Riot Act was read, troops were used against enclosure rioters, and rioters were imprisoned and, on occasion, transported.

Post-war depression and demobilisation exacerbated the general situation from 1815. Population growth led to under-employment and unemployment, and, combined with low wages and limited social welfare, to poverty for those without work as well as for many of those who had. Difficulties were accentuated by poor harvests and pressure for political reform. Dominated by the landed interest, Parliament in 1815 passed the Corn Law, which prohibited the import of grain unless the price of British grain reached 80 shillings (£4) a quarter. This kept the price of food artificially high, leading to food riots amongst hungry agricultural labourers, with attacks on farmers and corn mills, and demands for higher wages. 'Bread or blood' was their call. Robert Sharp, a Yorkshire village school-master, complained in his diary: 'I have seen long and said often that the rage for enclosing open fields and commons was one great cause of the ruin or poverty of the rural population ... crowds of labourers, who now as a boon ask for employment and cannot have it, but at such a rate that hunger is always in their train.'

New machines threatened jobs, both on the land and in industry. Discontent and disorder were widespread. The most famous opposition was that of the Luddites – named after the mythical 'Ned Ludd' – who broke machines in South Yorkshire, Lancashire and the East Midlands in 1811–16. But far more was at stake. The replacement of hand-flailing by threshing machines led to machine-breaking, as in South Norfolk in 1812. The threat from John Heathcoat's patented bobbin net machines led to the riotous destruction of his Loughborough factory in 1816, and Heathcoat moved his machines to a disused Tiverton mill. In Carlisle, the handloom weavers rioted in 1819. Indeed, this opposition to machinery by workers fearful for their handicrafts continued sporadically throughout the 1820s and early 1830s

Political awareness was heightened by the growth of the press, an important development as it increased and underlined the public dimension of politics. The number of provincial papers rose from 50 in 1782 to over 100 in 1808, 150 by 1830, and over 230 by 1851. Publication began in new centres, and new titles were launched in existing ones. Cornwall's first paper, *The Cornwall Gazette and Falmouth Packet*, was launched in 1801; Warwick's first in 1806; the first in north Devon was established at Barnstaple in 1824. After two or possibly three failures in the eighteenth century, the continuous publication of papers in Plymouth began in 1808. The first newspapers in Wales were founded: Swansea's *The Cambrian* in 1804 and Bangor's *North Wales Chronicle* in 1808. In 1797, there was only one paper in Cumbria, the *Cumberland Pacquet*, but it was joined by the *Carlisle Journal* (1798), the *Westmorland Advertiser* (1811), the *Patriot* (1815), and the *Westmorland Gazette* (1818), all of which lasted into the present century, only the *Carlisle Chronicle* (1807–11) meeting with a speedy demise. In Herefordshire, the *British Chronicle, or Pugh's Hereford Journal*, launched in 1770 and lasting into the twentieth century, was joined by the *Hereford Independent* (1824–8) and the *Hereford Times* (1832 until the twentieth century). The number of Liverpool papers rose markedly between 1812 and the late 1820s.

Radical papers both attacked the government and focused on local issues, usually abuses, criticism of which could develop and elicit popular support. In 1812, the *Montrose, Arbroath, and Brechin Review*, a paper launched in 1811, began to publish attacks on local abuses, which revived the campaign for burgh reform and against self-elected corporations. In 1818, Montrose burgesses won the right to elect the magistracy. The paper also supported a wider franchise, education for the working class, liberal economics, and combinations (trade unions), and criticised Church patronage. The conservative *Nottingham Gazette* was launched in 1813 in order to stem 'the torrent by which the minds of the lower classes were being overwhelmed'. Charles Dibdin, junior, the proprietor of Sadler's Wells, claimed that year that

> there really is an impudence in the press of this age that does the country more disservice in disorganising the people than all the democratic leaders can do, I think; and I'm afraid it is sowing the seeds of a commotion that our children or grandchildren will feel the dire effects of.

By 1817 sales of William Cobbett's *Political Register*, a radical weekly, were estimated at 60,000–70,000. It was joined by Thomas Wooler's weekly, the *Black Dwarf* (1817–24), which pressed in clear and ringing tones for political and social justice, and by other papers that called into question the pretensions and prerogatives of the entire landed order, including the *Cap of Liberty* (1819–20).

Concern about popular disturbances has left many traces in the archives. For example, the papers of Henry Addington, who, as Viscount Sidmouth, was the Home Secretary in 1812–22, include for March 1815 the resolution of gentlemen members of the vestry of St Marylebone, London:

> Letters having been received from the magistrates at the Police Office in Marlborough Street recommending immediate steps be taken for the prevention of tumultuous meetings. And information which can be relied upon having been given to this meeting that it is the intention of a mob to destroy the houses of the members of both Houses of Parliament in this parish. Resolved that it is expedient that the Secretary of State should be applied to by a deputation from this meeting for a strong military force to act under the direction of the magistrates in this district.

The same month, Lord Rothes wrote in to say that the presence of the Yeomanry in Kingston had helped lessen the impact of an attempt 'by some of the most inferior class to raise a mob by carrying about an effigy of a farmer who had dismissed some of his labourers'. Sidmouth himself referred to 'fresh and lamentable indications of the turbulent spirit which prevails amongst the lower orders of the people of Nottingham'. (Exeter, Devon County Record Office, Sidmouth Papers 152M correspondence 1815 OH 3, 8.) Concern about radicalism also helped encourage pressure for the education of the poor. The reasons given for founding schools focused heavily on the wider issues of social control. Thus, for Warwickshire in the mid-1810s, one school was established because of the rising number of young delinquents and that, in it, 'the children have carefully been instructed in the first principles of religion … and initiated in the habits of industry'. In 1815, a school was opened in Warwick by the National Society for the Provision of Education for the Poor, a conservative Anglican body, so that children, would learn 'habits of industry, submission and economy' and would 'contribute to the diminution of crime … and our first aim is religious teaching. (D Fowler, 'Reading and writing in Warwick, 1780s–1830s', *Warwickshire History*, 11, 2, Winter 1999–2000, p.72.)

Meanwhile, public interest in reform rose. On 16 August 1819, about 60,000 people turned out in St Peter's Field, Manchester, to hear 'Orator' Henry Hunt demand parliamentary reform. The excited Manchester magistrates read the Riot Act and ordered the Manchester and Salford Yeoman Cavalry to seize the speakers, but the untrained, amateur cavalry also attacked the crowd, leading to eleven deaths and many injuries. There was public outrage at what critics of the government termed – in a contemptuous analogy with the Battle of Waterloo – the Peterloo Massacre. *The Times* deplored 'the dreadful fact that nearly a hundred of the King's unarmed subjects have been sabred by a body of cavalry in the streets of a town of which most of them were inhabitants, and in the presence of those Magistrates whose sworn duty it is to protect and preserve the life of the meanest Englishman'. Lord Liverpool himself, though a prime minister with a reputation for toughness, did not think the decision of the Manchester magistrates 'prudent'.

Government and elite attitudes in the 1810s, however, were hostile to the development of popular activism. Discontent and violence led to repressive legislation, most prominently the Six Acts of 1819, passed after Peterloo. Cobbett fled to America in 1817, when Habeas Corpus was suspended, and the Blasphemous and Seditious Libels Act and

Publications Act, both of 1819, were intended to limit press criticism. The Acts also increased the power of magistrates to search for arms to prevent reform meetings.

There were calls for revolution in Britain, but the radicals were divided and most, including Hunt, rejected the use of force as dangerous, counter-productive and undesirable. In the Cato Street Conspiracy of 1820 a small group of London revolutionaries, many of them cobblers, under Arthur Thistlewood, planned to surprise the Cabinet at dinner, kill them, and establish a republican government, but they were arrested; while a rising in Huddersfield that year was also unsuccessful. Tension in Scotland culminated in major strike action in 1820. There were also attacks on local privileges, attacks which reflected the volatile social relations of the period. Local opposition to the tolls on the bridge over the Tees at Stockton led to a riot that September in which the gates were pulled down and thrown into the river. The tolls were abolished in 1821.

Tensions lessened during the relatively prosperous years of the mid-1820s, as trade revived. The *Birmingham Chronicle* of 12 February 1824 suggested that prosperity was leading to a general 'apathy' about Parliament. In the late 1820s an industrial slump and high bread prices helped cause a revival in popular unrest. As an example of the unintended consequences of technological developments, the invention of friction matches in 1826 by the Stockton chemist John Walker, and their subsequent manufacture as 'strike anywhere lucifers', made arson easier. In 1830, 'Swing' riots affected large parts of southern and eastern England. Machine-breaking, arson and other attacks often followed letters signed by 'Swing', threatening trouble if job-destroying machines were not removed. Over 90 threshing machines were broken in Wiltshire. The identity of 'Captain Swing' is unclear, and the riots probably spread spontaneously, rather than reflecting central control. The diversity of protest, both social and economic, was a striking feature of the Swing Riots. Large farms were targeted for action, as small-scale farmers, who also opposed new machinery, attacked agrarian capitalists. 'Swing' brought unease to the owners of agricultural estates, a disquiet far from obvious to subsequent viewers of the splendid houses of the period. The building of such houses was helped by the higher prices and rents that flowed to landlords from the Corn Law and by the repeal in 1816 of income tax, seen as a temporary war-time measure. But there was also fear.

Living conditions for the bulk of the population led to complaint and discontent, but little violence. Cobbett wrote from Derby in 1829:

> The situation of the greater part of the operative manufacturers, in this county, in Nottinghamshire, and in Leicestershire, is said to be truly deplorable. There are supposed to be thirty thousand stocking-frames; and the wages of the weavers have declined to such a point, as to leave the poor creatures scarcely the means of bare existence ... one of the consequences ... their dress, their looks, their movements and the sound of their voices, correspond with their debasement with regard to their food. Potatoes appear to be the best of their diet. Some live upon boiled cabbage and salt ... And this is ENGLAND!

Popular discontent did not set the agenda for national politics, but it helped increase the volatility of politics in the early 1830s. In the late 1810s and early 1820s, Liverpool's government backed by the unsteady support of George IV (Prince Regent 1811–20, King 1820–30) had essentially contained the situation, firmly resisting both agitation and reform, but, in the late 1820s, religious issues focused and contributed to a sense of change. One of the most important developments of this time was the emergence of the charismatic Irish leader, Daniel O'Connell (1775–1847). O'Connell was a landowner and brilliant lawyer, but he became a symbol of the limitations imposed on Catholics and led a large Irish movement, the Catholic Association, dedicated to emancipation for Catholics. Later he became an advocate of home rule for Ireland (see Chapter 10).

Against the backdrop of O'Connellite agitation in Ireland, the Test and Corporation Acts that maintained the Anglican ascendancy were repealed in 1828 and Catholics gained the vote the following year, with the passing of the Roman Catholic Relief Act. Both were very contentious steps. In many areas, relations between the Church of England and Dissenters were difficult. The wave of petitions against equality for Catholics that flooded Westminster offered an acute sense, too, that ordinary people in the shires and far-flung towns were anti-Catholic by natural disposition.

Moreover, it was not just Ultra Tories who regarded equality for Catholics as a fundamental challenge to the Protestant constitution. The extent of petitioning, local meetings and newspaper agitation suggests that much of public opinion was firmly set against the concession to O'Connellism. Wellington, Prime Minister 1828–30, had had to press the obdurate George IV very hard to obtain his consent to the Roman Catholic Relief Act, a reminder of the continued role of the Crown in politics. The issue split the Tories, with the Canningites backing the measure, but the ultra-Tories seeing it as a betrayal. This division was important because it cut across the process of party formation that had been gathering pace. The number of those who voted rose dramatically from the 1826 to the 1832 election.

8.3 Pressure for political change

In the early 1830s, pressure for political change increased. This focused on demands for a reform of Parliament in order to make it more representative of the wealth and weight of the community, a view that reflected the notion of interests. Wellington's opposition to parliamentary reform was unacceptable to important circles of opinion. Aside from the issue of change in the franchise, there was also the question of a redistribution of seats to account for the shifting population of the country. This issue was particularly acutely felt in London, which people felt was under-represented, and, even more, in the major northern commercial and industrial cities, such as Manchester, Bradford and Leeds, which lacked seats of their own and were simply subsumed within country seats. This issue was important in shaping the contours of local political activism, not least because enhanced national representation was believed important in order to secure local goals. This was related to a process of social identification, as a self-conscious middle class was articulated, and the opponents of reform stigmatised as a redundant *ancien régime*.

Demands for change were far from limited to the world of high politics. An easing in political tension had reduced interest in political publishing for a popular market in the 1820s, but the situation altered in the early 1830s as parliamentary reform came to the fore as an issue. The protracted nature of the crisis, at once national and local, high-political and electoral, led to sustained excitement and a situation in which newspapers were obliged to take sides (see Box 8.1). The character and role of public opinion were much debated. Reports of reform agitation served to build up support, while disturbances such as the Bristol riots of 1831 encouraged alarm. During the riots that led in 1832 to the burning of Nottingham Castle, the windows of the office of the Tory *Nottingham Journal*

Box 8.1

Fear of sedition

The Exeter-based *Western Luminary and Family Newspaper: Agricultural, Commercial, and Literary Advertiser* (on 4 January 1831) commented as follows:

It will be observed by a paragraph in another column, that one of the rioters who was convicted of setting fire to a barn at Battle, and sentenced to death, has left it on record, in the confession of his guilt, that he ascribed his untimely end to Cobbett, who instigated him and others to these practices by his inflammatory lectures; and declares that but for this turbulent vagabond, he believed that there would have been neither fires nor mobs in that neighbourhood. We fear Cobbett has not been the only means of bringing about the disgraceful outrages which have been committed throughout the country. The fact is, the radical portion of the press have been labouring in their seditious vocation with increased fury, and wherever they have disseminated their doctrines, a spirit of insubordination and discontent has been conjured up which threatens to become fatal to existing institutions, and which even the Whigs will find exceedingly difficult to lay. It is impossible the country can enjoy peace unless the libellous demagogues [William] Cobbett, [Daniel] O'Connell, and [Richard] Carlile, and such like are put to silence.

were broken. In Wales the Merthyr Rising of 1831 was defeated by military action and its own divisions, with at least 20 rioters killed.

The Whig government of Charles, 2nd Earl Grey that took power in November 1830 from Wellington's Conservative government, after the general election that followed the death of George IV, supported reform, Grey thinking the situation 'too like what took place in France before the Revolution'. His was the first Whig ministry for 23 years. Rejected by the Commons in April 1831, the Bill passed in June after another general election had given the Whigs a clear majority, only to be thrown out by the Tory-dominated House of Lords in October 1831. Political division grew. In Cornwall, in place of the tradition of sharing representation, there was a full-scale political contest in the 1831 election and the Reform Act of 1832 was followed by a situation in which the parties sought to win all the seats allocated to the county. (B Elvins, '"A proud day for Cornwall. A deep univeral gloom has been cast over the county": the county election of June 1826', *Journal of the Royal Institution of Cornwall*, new series, 3, parts 3 and 4 (2000), p.122.)

During the crisis that ended with the Act of 1832, one staunch Tory, John, 1st Earl Brownlow, established and trained a militia to protect his seat at Belton from rioters; the feared attack did not come. The Lords gave way in June 1832, when George IV's brother and successor, William IV (reigned 1830–7), who was more willing to accept reform than his predecessor, reluctantly agreed that he would make sufficient new peers to create a majority for change. By giving way, they prevent the new creations that would have eroded for ever their position in the Lords. King William was influenced both by the widespread support for reform, by the view that the choice was between reform and widespread disorder, and by Grey's opposition to further changes, and thus the sense that the Reform Bill would not be followed by a total transformation of British politics. By offering his resignation to William after defeat in the Lords, Grey had forced William's hand, as he – William – did not wish to face another general election.

The First Reform Act of 1832 was the first major change to the franchise and political geography of England and Wales since the short-lived Interregnum constitutions of the 1650s. Separate Acts were also passed for Ireland and Scotland. The Reform Act franchise extended the franchise to sections of the middle class. A notionally uniform borough franchise, based on households rated at £10 annually, was established. The English electorate increased by 50 per cent, so that about one-fifth of all adult males could vote after 1832.

The distribution of seats was radically altered in order to reward growing towns that had not, hitherto, had their own MPs, such as Birmingham, Bradford and Manchester, and also under-represented counties. `Rotten boroughs', seats with a small population, that were especially open to influence, lost representation. Minehead, which had been a pocket borough of the Luttrells of Dunster Castle, was one such: in 1802, the unsuccessful candidates had alleged bribery and corruption by the Luttrells. Between 1734 and 1831 indeed half of all English and Welsh constituencies were contested three times or less, in large part because it was not thought worth challenging established interests. Many seats were controlled, to a varying extent, by prominent landlords. Thus, for example, Henry, Marquess of Worcester, heir to the Duchy of Beaufort, a solid Tory, was MP for Monmouth in 1813–32, and his brother Granville was MP for the county from 1828 to 1848 and another firm Tory. The loss of 'rotten boroughs' was a major blow to long-established interests. In addition, under the new franchise some long-established MPs, such as Charles Western, MP for Maldon since 1790, lost their seats.

The distribution of seats had been very unequal. Prior to the Reform Act, County Durham had had only four MPs, but the most heavily represented county, Cornwall had returned 44, many from pocket boroughs, although with none for the most populous town, Falmouth. In 1827–8, Manchester had failed in its efforts to secure the parliamentary seats of Penry. The Reform Act reduced the over-representation of the South-West and transferred seats to the North. For example, Durham gained an additional six MPs, including two for Sunderland and one each for Gateshead and South Shields. However, this process was not without controversy. Stockton, where the Tory Marquess of Londonderry was influential, remained without its own MPs, leading to accusations of bias against the Whig Earl of Durham, Grey's nephew, who had been influential in drafting the bill and was powerful in the north of the county where the towns gained representation. The passage of the Act helped sustained Whig popularity and they won the subsequent general election easily.

Although the changes in the Act were important, they neither amounted to a constitutional revolution, nor led to a social one. The political system remained under the control of the socially powerful, both directly and indirectly. John, Viscount Althorp, who became 3rd Earl Spencer in 1834, was Chairman of the Northamptonshire Quarter sessions from 1806 until his death in 1845. From 1803 until 1906 every heir to the Marquessate of Bristol sat at one time or another as MP for West Suffolk or for the borough of Bury St Edmunds, adjacent to the family seat of Ickworth.

This was not the end of pressure for reform. Critics of the Act said it would be the first, not the last, constitutional reform, and this is one reason why many feared it so much. From the opposite extreme, radicals who had fought for reform denigrated the final legislation as a half-way measure. The working classes, whom the middle-class radicals had abandoned as the deal for reform was done, received no benefit from the Act. Indeed, many who already had a vote under the old system actually lost out. A series of unstamped radical papers, including the *Prompter* (1830–1), *Republican* (1831), *Poor Man's Guardian* (1831–5), *Working Men's Friend* (1832–3), *Reformer* (1832), *Cosmopolite* (1832–3), and *Man* (1833), produced by bold and energetic publishers, such as Richard Carlile and Henry Hetherington, launched sweeping attacks on the Establishment, its pretensions, prerogatives, privilege and personnel. There was a call for action on behalf of the working class, including the right to vote. Radicals felt a sense of betrayal after their role in the extra-parliamentary agitation of 1830–2. The government responded with prosecutions, not least of the vulnerable news-vendors, but the expression of working-class radicalism was not staunched.

Reform continued, but not at the pace demanded by the radicals. In 1831, Henry Hunt told a Manchester meeting that he opposed the Reform Bill, as it would join the middle to the upper classes 'in order to raise yeomanry corps and keep up standing armies'. The Whigs, in fact, sought a stable civic society, serving progress and prosperity, not an uncertain situation vulnerable to disorder and demagogues. Such notions reflected a social stratification that treated the bulk of the population as prone to self-indulgence and a lack of wisdom. The middling orders, in contrast, were seen as a vital prop to society, and they and their interests benefited from the legislation of the period. Hobhouse's Vestry Act of 1831 was an important extension of their participation in the localities. The Municipal Corporations Act of 1835, passed by the Whig government of William, 2nd Viscount Melbourne, Prime Minister in 1834 and 1835–41, standardised the situation in England and Wales, replacing self-selecting oligarchic corporations, mostly run by Tories, and giving elected borough councils, based on a franchise of rated occupiers, control over the local police, markets and street-lighting. This change was to be the basis of an upsurge in urban politics, the party politicisation of corporations, and a wave of urban reformism. It was here – in the new urban centres – and not at the head of politics, in Westminster, that the middle classes first came to achieve freedom of political expression. Blessed with the historian's hindsight, then, we might argue that the Municipal Corporations Act was *the* crucial piece of legislation, with respect to political participation, in the early part of the century.

Other Acts of the period indicated the spreading role of reform agitation, the greater scope of legislation, and, also, the extent of accommodation with existing interests. In 1833, there was both a Factory Act and a Bank Charter Act. This gave the Bank of England new powers, renewed its charter for twenty-one years, and established its notes for sums of £5 or more as legal tender throughout England and Wales – a measure of national standardisation; but also added the accountability that was a steadily greater theme of public office: the Bank was required to publish its accounts on a quarterly basis. The abolition of the slave trade in 1833 was part of this wider reform drive. The reforming, Liberal middle-class culture of the period regarded slavery as abhorrent, anachronistic and associated with everything it deplored. However, it is necessary to note that the abolition of slavery was not totally an unambiguous step forward, for control over labour continued. So it did over labour flows. In place of slaves, therefore, the British West Indies imported Indian indentured labour.

The Poor Law Amendment Act, or 'New Poor Law' followed in 1834. It created a centrally controlled bureaucracy, rather than the earlier, varied system of local provision, although its provision initially concentrated in the south and did not spread to the big northern boroughs until 1837–8. Local parishes now had to join together into 'unions' to support workhouses, which were to replace home relief. It is useful to turn to a prominent example in order to see what the system meant in practice. The Thurgarton Hundred Incorporated Workhouse in Southwell, Nottinghamshire, which survives in the care of the National Trust and is the best preserved workhouse in England, was regarded by the Poor Law Commission as a model for the Union workhouses created under the 1834 Act. It was built by one of the leading writers on poor relief, the Reverend J.T. Becher (1770–1834), author of *The Antipauper System* (1828), who believed that a workhouse would deter the 'idle and profligate'. His workhouse, built in 1824 at a cost of £6,596 to house 158 paupers, became in 1836 the Southwell Union Workhouse, serving 60 parishes. Most of the inmates were younger women and older men. Initially, there was a punishment regime for reprobates of breaking stones and being locked in solitude, but this was dropped. The main block of the workhouse provided an architecture of control. Aside from the central hub for the master's accommodation, there were five wings for the three segregated groups, men, women and children. This design derived from prison groups and was shaped explicitly by Jeremy Bentham's idea of the 'panoptican', in which the central location for authorities allowed an eye to be kept on all inmates at all times. The stairs were also intended to extend the segregation to divide the idle and profligate poor from the blameless or the infirm, a segregation that also extended to the exercise and work yards.

This Poor Law Amendment Act was not seen as a reform by radical critics. The deliberate harshness of the workhouse regime – which was intended to be no better than that of the lowest class of labourer outside ('the principle of less eligibility') – was designed to deter need by encouraging individual thrift. This was a largely impractical goal, given the difficulty of saving money on low wages. The Act was also intended to cut the costs of poor relief overall. The discipline, sexual segregation and limited diet of the workhouse regime was unpopular and there was some opposition to the new system: the workhouse at Gainsborough, in Lincolnshire, was destroyed during its construction in 1837.

The Tithe Commutation Act of 1836 was another work of standardisation, while the introduction of civil registration of births, marriages and deaths in 1837 lessened the role of the Established Church. In 1839, state responsibility for elementary education was established. In addition, reform of the penal code ensured that the number of capital offences was greatly cut.

It would be misleading to stress the extent of reform after 1832, and to under-rate signs of conservative tendencies. There was a Tory revival in elections, although in part this was a recovery from Whig success. Nevertheless, in his Tamworth Manifesto of 1834 Peel captured a widespread concern with the pace of change in society. In elections in 1833–7 in County Durham, a largely Liberal county, the Tories gained three seats, and in 1835 all 12 in Shropshire, part of a swing in which they gained 98 seats in the general election of 1835 and another 40 in 1837. In Cornwall, the farmer–reformer alliance which had, in the 1820s, successfully forced issues to the forefront of political debate, fractured, resulting in the farmers realigning themselves with the protectionist Tories. Conservative tendencies were not only apparent at elections. In 1834, William IV turned out the Whig government, and, although Melbourne regained office in 1835, he was no radical, and held off radical rebels within Whig ranks.

William IV's dismissal of the Melbourne ministry was the last time a British ruler

Sir Robert Peel (1788–1850)

Prime Minister 1834–5 and 1841–6, he was an influential Home Secretary in 1822–7 and 1828–30 responsible for reorganising the role of the police force, originally named the 'Peelers'. As Tory leader, he helped to revive the party after the Great Reform Act (1832), which he had opposed, only to divide it by his decision to drive through repeal of the Corn Laws, in the teeth of the Irish Famine, in 1846. His political life was cut short by a riding accident.

Source: Engraving after a portrait by Lawrence

dismissed the government and called on other ministers. Contemporaries saw parallels with George III's dismissal of the Fox–North ministry in December 1783 and his appointment of Pitt the Younger, but the sequel was crucially different. Pitt won the 1784 election, while the Tory leader, Sir Robert Peel, lost the one in 1835. This dismissal was different to the image of William IV during the Reform Act crisis. Then, in the cartoon *The Reformers' Attack on the Old Rotten Tree*, which advocated electoral reform, William was portrayed on `Constitution Hill', applauding the process of reform. William IV was seen as seeking to be a 'constitutional' monarch, which he indeed sought to be. More generally, he had to, and could, adapt to political reform, and was, in the end, flexible over reform, unlike Charles X, who lost the French throne to a revolution in 1830. Somewhat eccentric, and prone to conversations going off on a tangent, William was popular and seen as having integrity.

William's reign began the process of monarchical revival that was to culminate in the development of imperial splendour under his niece, Victoria (reigned 1837–1901), and her son, Edward VII (reigned 1901–10). William's was not the cause of the ultras. Indeed, from William's reign, the British monarchy was not associated with the forces of political conservatism, as it would have been had his brother Ernest, Duke of Cumberland, been king. Instead, he became Ernest, King of Hanover on William's death, for Victoria, as a woman, was not eligible to succeed there.

Melbourne's ministry rested on Tory support and was acceptable to the Tories; indeed Peel has been seen as 'governing in opposition'. Melbourne was largely concerned to consolidate Grey's legacy, rather than to press on with radical reforms, while Peel, who was no Ultra Tory, was more comfortable with Melbourne that with many Tories. In 1841, the Tories under Peel won a comfortable majority in the general election, thanks to the support of the counties and the numerous small boroughs that it is all too easy to forget, not to the industrial towns. As Prime Minister, in 1841–6, Peel was to direct a major transformation in fiscal policy. He cut import and export duties, thus helping trade, and introduced the first peace-time income tax to make up the shortfall in government revenues. The Bank Charter Act of 1844 moved towards the centralisation of note issue in the Bank of England, a step that helped to further central control of the fiscal system.

8.4 Chartism

Peel's financial reforms constituted important changes, but he was not interested in assuaging popular demands for a radical extension to the franchise. He had opposed the Act of 1832 and he continued to maintain his implacable hostility to change. The bulk of the population was not offered the vote. Chartism, a variegated protest movement, developed, pressing, in the Six Points of the People's Charter, for universal adult male suffrage, a secret ballot, annual elections, equal constituencies, the abolition of property qualifications for MPs, and their payment (Box 8.2). The last two were designed to ensure that the social elite lost their control of the representative system.

Chartism enjoyed particularly strong support in industrial areas. It represented a powerful rejection of the ethos of the governing orders, and drew heavily on Christian radicalism and a sense that politics should be moral. A wave of strikes linked to Chartism has been termed the General Strike of 1842. Labour relations were volatile, not least because of the difficulties of creating and negotiating industrial relations and work practices in a rapidly changing situation. Nevertheless, it is necessary to put this militancy in context. Worker solidarity or unity was limited, trade unionism restricted, trade union organisation poor, and many strikes were specific to particular pits or factories. Moreover, commentators such as Samuel Bamford, the Lancashire handloom weaver and radical reformer, writing in the later 1830s and early 1840s when Chartism was emerging, tried to present English workers as reasonable, contrasting their style and intent with that of their continental counterparts, at the same time warning employers and politicians not to abuse their good sense:

> Above all things, be just towards them in respect of their civil rights, and fear not. You need not hesitate, they will never be like a French mob. There is more of an aristocratic spirit in the commonalty of England, than any other people; there is indeed too much of it. They are regularly stratified, as are the rocks of our island, and they wont be disrupted except by great, and long continued ill usage.

The leading Chartist paper, the *Northern Star or Leeds General Advertiser*, was launched in 1837. The initial focus of the paper was hostility to the Poor Law Amendment Act (1834); the replacement of outdoor relief with indoor help in the workhouse was presented as harsh and inhuman. Feargus O'Connor (1795–1855), the former Irish radical MP and ex-associate of Daniel O'Connell, who ran the *Northern Star*, made it the mouthpiece of Chartism. It helped increase Chartist cohesion, and at the same time disseminated its message. The commercial success of the paper, which sold 1,851,000 copies in 1839, allowed the employment of full-time political activists as its agents, an important strength for the Chartist challenge and quite beyond the possibility of earlier radical movements. If Chartist newspapers were characterised by a degree of social hostility to capital something similar was lacking in those that might be termed 'reform newspapers'; the latter, for example the *Leeds Mercury* and the *Manchester Guardian*, were critical of what they saw as the Establishment and of institutionalised abuses, but far less so of entrepreneurial capital and the world it was creating.

Parliament resisted Chartist mass-petitions in 1839, 1842 and 1848, and the Chartist uneasiness about any resort to violence ensured that there was no parallel to the Year of Revolutions on the Continent in 1848. Nevertheless, the scale of government preparation

Box 8.2

The Second Chartist Petition

One of the tactics of the Chartists was to present petitions to parliament, demanding reform. On this occasion (May 1842), Thomas Duncombe presented the petition, which was supported by John Fielden. The demand for reform was overwhelmingly defeated by 287 votes to 49. This extract is from *Hansard Parliamentary Debates*, 1842, vol. 62. It captures well the injustice which reformers felt at the inequalities of the electoral system and of society more generally.

...[Y]our noble house has not been elected by the people ... the population of Great Britain is at present about 26 million persons, and yet, out of this number little more than 900,000 have been permitted to vote in the ... election of representatives to make laws to govern the whole. The existing state of representation is not only extremely limited and unjust, but unequally divided and gives preponderant influence to the landed and moneyed interests to the utter ruin of small trading and labouring classes. The borough of Guildford with a population of 3,920 returns to parliament as many members as Tower Hamlets with a population of 300,000; Evesham with a population of 3,998 elects as many representatives as Manchester with a population of 200,000 ... these being but a few instances of the enormous inequalities existing in what is called the representation of this country. Bribery, intimidation, corruption, perjury, and riot prevail at all parliamentary elections to an extent best understood by the Members of your honourable House ...

In England, Ireland, Scotland and Wales thousands of people are dying from actual want; and your petitioners, while sensible that poverty is the great exciting cause of crime, view with mingled astonishment and alarm the ill provision made for the poor, the aged, and the infirm; and likewise perceive with feelings of indignation, the determination of your honourable house to continue the Poor Law in operation,

nothwithstanding the many proofs which have been afforded by the sad experience of the unconstitutional principle of that Bill, of its unchristian character and of the cruel and murderous effects produced upon the wages of working men ...

Your petitioners would direct the attention of your honourable house to the great disparity existing between the wages of the producing millions and the salaries of those whose comparative usefulness ought to be questioned, where riches and luxury prevail amongst the rulers and poverty and starvation amongst the ruled ... Your petitioners, with all due respect and loyalty, would compare the daily income of the Sovereign Majesty with that thousands of working men of this nation; and whilst your petitioners have learned that Her Majesty receives daily for private use the sum of £164 17s. 10d., they have also ascertained that many thousands of families of the labourers are only in receipt of 3 3/4 per head per day ...your petitioners have also learned that His Royal Highness Prince Albert receives each day ... £104 2s., while thousands ... exist on 3d. per head per day ... and your petitioners have with pain and regret also learned that the Archbishop of Canterbury is daily in receipt of £52 10s. per day, whilst thousands of the poor have to maintain their families on an income not exceeding 2d. per day ...

Your petitioners complain that the hours of labour, particularly of the factory workers, are protracted beyond the limits of human endurance, and that the wages earned, after unnatural application to toil in heated and unhealthy workshops, are inadequate to sustain the bodily strength and to supply those comforts which are so imperative after an excessive waste of physical energy. Your petitioners also direct the attention of your honourable House to the starvation wages of the agricultural labourer, and view with horror and indignation the paltry income of those whose toil gives being to the food of the people

for disturbances in 1848 was impressive. It benefited from modern technology, as trains and the telegraph greatly increased the speed and effectiveness of the government's response. The government had already showed its willingness to deploy troops against rioters as in 1842 when the 'Plug Plot Riots' in Scotland, Yorkshire and elsewhere brought soldiers into conflict with demonstrators protesting about wage cuts and unemployment (their name came from the removal of plugs from boilers to de-pressurise them and prevent machinery being driven).

Meanwhile, Peel had advocated the cutting and eventual ending of the Corn Laws, because he saw their continuation as likely to increase popular radicalism, as well as hitting the free trade that the exporting industries required. The Anti-Corn Law League was pressing hard on the issue. Founded in 1839, the League had been a product of middle-class dissatisfaction with the limits of 1830s reform, although Peelite conservatism was also important to a segment of the middle class. In 1842, Peel reduced the Corn duties and in 1845 he decided that the Corn Laws had to go. The advent of the potato blight in Ireland, and the subsequent famine, provided Peel's excuse, but, unable to convince the Cabinet, Peel resigned only to return to office when the Whig leader, Lord John Russell, could not form a ministry. Peel then pushed through the repeal of the Corn Laws in 1846, but it was carried in 1846 only thanks to the support of Whig MPs and with a majority of Tories voting against repeal. Having lost control of his party, Peel again resigned. This Tory baronet was seen as the figure who had given the people cheap bread, and had showed that the political system could satisfy public demands. When he died in 1850, Peel was commemorated in statues, engravings, street names and celebration mugs and plates. However, the Tory party was now divided.

There was considerable anxiety about the possibility of insurrection in the 1830s and 1840s. On 3 November 1839, a Chartist rising of over 5,000 men, in which many colliers, under John Frost, sought to seize Newport, South Wales, as part of a revolutionary uprising, was stopped when a small group of soldiers opened fire. The rioters dispersed and Frost was arrested. In Sheffield, a planned Chartist rising was snuffed out following collaboration between a local publican and the authorities. The ringleaders, among them Samuel Holberry, were arrested and imprisoned. While in prison, Holberry was walked to death on the treadmill and he died shortly after incarceration. At his funeral, held at Attercliffe, Sheffield, in 1842, George Julian Harney (1817–97), a radical agitator, and future editor of the *Northern Star* (1843–50), gave a melancholy but defiant speech:

> Our task is not to weep; we must leave the tears to women. Our task is to act; to labour with heart and soul for the destruction of the horrible system under which Holberry has perished. His sufferings are over; he is where the 'wicked cease from troubling and the weary are at rest'. He sleeps well; he is numbered with the patriots who have died as martyrs to the cause of liberty before him. His is the bloodless laurel, awarded him by a grateful and admiring people. How different to the wreath which encircles the brow of the princely murderer, and the conquering destroyer! Compared with the honest, virtuous fame of this son of toil, how poor, how contemptible appears the so-called glories that emblazon the name of an Alexander or a Napoleon! ... [Alongside][T]he [William] Tells and [Wat] Tylers of the earth, the name of Holberry will be associated, venerated, and adored. Be ours the task to accomplish by one glorious effort the freedom of our country, and thereby prevent for the future the sacrifice of the sons of freedom.

Riots and risings were not only threatened by urban workers. In 1839, in the same year as Frost and Holberry led their abortive actions, the 'Rebecca Riots' began in South West Wales: attacks on the tollgates that handicapped the rural economy. The riots persisted until 1844 and extended their targets to include attacks on unfair rents and workhouses. 'Mother Rebecca', the symbolic leader of the protests, with a white gown and red or black face, was named from the Rebecca of Genesis 'possessing the gates of them which hate thee'. The 293 crowd attacks on tollgates in 1839–44 reflected considerable social alienation, the product of the industrial depression of 1839–42, the inflation of land rents during the Napoleonic wars, and hostility to landlords, Church tithes and the loss of

Box 8.3

Chartist criticism of manufacturers

Under the headline 'Timid Law Makers and Powerful Law Breakers', an editorial in the *Northern Star* of 16 February 1850 declared:

The struggle for a Ten Hours Bill has to be renewed. After years of agitation, and large sacrifices of time, money and health, on the part of its advocates, the legislature, three years ago, at length recognised the justice of the principle they contended for, and embodied it in an Act of Parliament ... the millowners – who had resisted its enactment with all the strength of their part, while under discussion – determined to evade its provisions by means of a technical quibble. Remembering the old saying, that there never was an Act of Parliament yet passed, through which a coach and six might not be driven by those who had sufficient wealth and influence, they set to work to find, or make, the loop-holes which the legal verbiage always offers to the rich law breakers [and] introduced what is now known as the 'shift system'.

common land through enclosures. Violence was not restricted to Wales. *Besley's Devonshire Chronicle* of 25 January 1847 carried an item from St Austell in Cornwall about a JP using coast-guards to prevent demonstrating china clay workers from blocking the shipment of grain: 'We cannot be surprised that men, uneducated and ignorant as they are of subjects of political economy, should, when hunger presses on them and their families, adopt the first means that present themselves to make known their grievances.'

Under the County Police Act of 1839, Parliament enabled counties to raise uniformed police forces, although they were not compelled to do so. The number of constables was not to exceed one per 1,000 of the population. Purpose-built police stations were opened, that in Doncaster, for example, in 1846. The police force in County Durham, established in 1839, consisted of 65 officers under Major James Wemyss, a Waterloo veteran. This force was used to police the miners' strike of 1844, while troops were used against miners in St Helens and Wigan in Lancashire. By 1849, the Durham force consisted of 106 police officers, including the Chief Constable. Pressure for police and prisons reflected widespread concern over crime and disorder. An editorial in *Trewman's Exeter Flying Post* of 3 January 1856, calling for the establishment of a county police, noted correctly 'scarcely a week passes without our paper containing the record of numerous thefts, of a more or less aggravated character'. Aside from the police, there were also new county gaols.

Chartism collapsed as a result of its failure in 1848 and of a measure of growing prosperity, but many of its ideas, including democratic accountability, influenced popular Liberalism from the 1850s. Political pressures were not only expressed through violence. The developing socio-economic order created through industrialisation was one that sat ill with traditional hierarchies, allegiances and practices. This was true both of emerging working-class consciousness and of those who ran the new world of industry. The failure of the Chartist programme was followed not by an end in working-class activism, but by a growth of interest in the working class building up its own institutions, such as the co-operative society and a multitude of friendly societies and clubs, and in schemes for improving the physical and moral condition of the working people through education and temperance.

Chartism failed, but this was not due to the dominance of conservative ultras. Instead, officially sanctioned reform was the major theme in mid-century and moderate reformers were in power. From 1846 until 1852 the Prime Minister was the Whig – or, as it was increasingly known from the 1830s, Liberal – party leader, Lord John Russell, although he lacked a working majority in Parliament. Reform of the economic system was a major plank of the ministry. The repeal of the Navigation Acts in 1849 was designed to ensure free trade, as much a cause as a policy. Reform was linked to the growth in middle-class culture and consciousness, and was directed against what were seen as vested interests. In 1850, Royal Commissions were appointed to review the universities of Oxford and Cambridge.

A significant growth in accessible information also characterised the period. For example, the Tithe Commutation Act of 1836 reformed the tithe system and led to detailed surveys by tithe commissioners, valuers and map-makers. They provided comprehensive maps with accompanying lists of occupiers and details of land use. The 1851 census was far more thorough in its provision of information than its predecessors had been. For example, marital status, exact ages, and details of birth parish and county or town of birth were all specified. Clearer instructions were provided for the recording of occupations and the identification of households.

Reform was important to the appeal of the Liberals and to the movement of Whiggism to Liberalism, as, in acquiring middle-class support, the Whigs became a party fitted for the reformist middle class. The state educational grant to encourage schoolmasters to improve themselves was expanded from 1846–7 and the Public Health Act of 1848 was the first major item of compulsory health legislation. Russell also promoted those he saw as liberal, learned and energetic in the Church, while in 1847 the government established a new bishopric in Manchester, as an aspect of the response to the new geography of the country, and to what were seen as the social problems of the big urban centres. Russell also sought to introduce further reform in the franchise, but the cabinet was unsympathetic and the Peelites who gave the government important unofficial support in Parliament were opposed.

Russell fell in 1852, the momentum of his government lost. Its reformism was tempered and limited, certainly in comparison with that later under Gladstone. Nevertheless, the tone of British politics was different to that in the late 1830s. Reform was more obviously a central political topic, the landed interest had suffered badly from the repeal of the Corn Laws in 1846, and the middle-class was more politically aware, active and powerful than hitherto. Chartism had been averted, but change was to gather pace.

8.5 Conclusion

The first half of the nineteenth century saw a running debate about the nature of the political system. A desire to change the system was more prominent than the case made to raze it to the ground. The powers who would preserve the status quo were also of loud voice but, ultimately, the action that followed debate showed a clear balance in favour of those demanding change. Yet we can contrast the British experience with that continental Europe, where revolution silenced the voices of the *ancien régime* on more than one occasion. While British monarchs might oppose change – as George III opposed Catholic emancipation – none of them went the way of Charles X or Louise Philippe, both of France, in 1830 and 1848, respectively. The period was marked by legislation which demanded that those of landed privilege, and the new money of the commercial interest, as well as some of the large manufactures and important professions, should work together, providing just enough by way of reform to maintain the integrity of the system in the face of strong pressure for change. Violence in the towns and in the countryside was part of the general picture, but it is debatable how much of this was directly political. Machine-breaking and the acts of the Swing Rioters were economic in their origins; the abortive risings in Newport and Sheffield perhaps show the limited support for such activity. But we should not ignore the degree to which that agitation, often stirred by middle-class interest groups, helped to pressurise those in positions of power. Catholic emancipation (1829), the Reform Act (1832) and the Repeal of the Corn Laws (1846) demonstrated new configurations in politics. Such legislation, and the willingness to change (if only a little), created a platform upon which a popular politics would be built in the second half of the century.

Summary

◆ The threat of revolution was important to political thought in the first half of the century.
◆ The First Reform Act was intended by many to limit or end the pressure for reform, but renewed demands for change became more important in the 1840s.
◆ Middle-class political activism became stronger from the late 1830s.
◆ The repeal of the Corn Laws symbolised and represented the new social configuration of politics.

Points to discuss

◆ How strong were revolutionary pressures?
◆ What were the short and long-term consequences of the First Reform Act?
◆ Why was Chartism unsuccessful?

References and further reading

O. Ashton *et al.* (eds), *The Chartist Legacy* (1999).

R. Blake, *The Conservative Party from Peel to Churchill* (1970).

T.C. Blanning and P. Wende (eds), *Reform in Great Britain and Germany, 1790–1850* (Oxford, 1999).

M. Brock, *The Great Reform Act* (1973).

J. Cannon, *Parliamentary Reform, 1640–1832* (Cambridge, 1973).

B. Coleman, *Conservatism and the Conservative Party in Nineteenth-Century Britain* (1988).

D. Fraser, *Urban Politics in Victorian England* (Leicester, 1976).

N. Gash, *Reaction and Reconstruction in English Politics, 1832–1852* (Oxford, 1965).

N. Gash, *Pillars of Government, and Other Essays on State and Society, c.1770–1880* (1986).

D. Goodway, *London Chartisim, 1838–1848* (Cambridge, 1982).

P. Hollis (ed.), *Pressure from Without in Early Victorian England* (1974).

T.A. Jenkins, *The Liberal Ascendancy, 1830–1886* (1994).

H.S. Jones, *Victorian Political Thought* (2000).

P. Mandler, *Aristocratic Government in the Age of Reform: Whigs and Liberals, 1830–1852* (Oxford, 1990).

G.I.T. Machin, *The Catholic Question in English Politics, 1820–30* (1964).

F. O'Gorman, *Votes, Patrons and Parities: The Unreformed Electorate of Hanoverian England, 1834–1832* (1989).

R.J. Olney, *Lincolnshire Politics, 1832–1885* (Oxford, 1973).

J. Saville, *1848: The British State and the Chartist Movement* (Cambridge, 1987).

M.J. Turner, *British Politics in an Age of Reform* (Manchester, 1999).

D.G Wright, *Popular Radicalism: The Working-Class Experience, 1780–1880* (1988).

The Political World After 1851

Contents

▇ Introduction

The guests present being all English, it is needless to say that, as soon as the wholesome check exercised by the presence of the ladies was removed, the conversation turned on politics as a necessary result. In respect to this all-absorbing national topics, I happen to be one of the most un-English Englishmen living.

The appeal of politics referred to in Wilkie Collins' novel *The Moonstone* (1868) was not one that was allowed or readily accessible to all. Aside from the fundamental exclusion of women, who were deliberately formally denied any role in the political process, there was a social politics of containment. This was the uneasy response of a divided elite to the surge of social and economic change and, more specifically, their response to the fluidity of the expanding cities and the potential political challenge of the urban masses.

Key issues

▶ How far did the political system change?
▶ How were social pressures contained?
▶ What were the social politics of the period?
▶ What was at stake in politics?

9.1 Regulation and containment

Strategies of containment varied, and this was linked to different, not to say discordant, views about the process and ends of reform. At the 1852 Annual Meeting of the

Darlington Horticultural Society, the Reverend H. Harries pontificated: 'this society ... was calculated to improve and elevate the taste of all classes, especially the poorer classes, by withdrawing them in their leisure hours from grosser indulgences to a pleasurable and improving pursuit.' Such bodies provided opportunities for the dissemination of established views. The local political magnifico, the Marquess of Londonderry, told one of the Society's exhibitions in 1848 that 'by rallying round the throne and the constitution he entertained not the least doubt that the glories of England would continue to the end of the world'. So much for Chartism. Where it threatened powerful interests it got nowhere. Thus the Chartist Land Company, which had pressed for land reform so as to provide freeholdings for workers, faced opposition, although the naivety of its policies suggested anyway that it had little chance of long-term success.

The containment of the possible consequences of change proved central to the social politics of the period, while ideological and political strategies sought to confront what was seen as the troubling growth of democracy. These should be addressed before turning to the world of Parliament and ministries. Social politics, however, did not exist in a vacuum. Instead, they interacted with other shifts within Britain. Furthermore, it is far from clear how best to define links and ascribe causes. Take, for example, the crucial world of leisure. This can be seen in terms of social control, but clearly far more was involved. The new society of urbanisation and industrialisation created new needs. The development of urban working-class leisure, away from traditional customs, and towards new mass, commercialised interests was one response to the new society. Music halls and football-clubs were founded in large numbers. This was commercial and institutionalised leisure. As such, it was more open to regulation, so that it should not challenge the requirements of the established order, than earlier forms; but it is not clear how far this played a role in the development of the new leisure.

Regulation and containment were certainly at stake in the treatment of earlier forms of leisure. In 1854, pubs were forced to close at midnight on Saturday, and, except for Sunday lunch and evening, not re-open until 4a.m. on Monday. Complete Sunday closing was enforced in Scotland from 1853 and in Wales from 1881. Drinking was also affected by the 1869 Wine and Beerhouses Act and the 1872 Licensing Act. As pubs were central to working-class communal experience and alcohol lessened inhibitions, these changes were very much part of a more controlled society. Furthermore, governmental regulation, national and local, was crucial to the process.

In addition, alternative entertainments were scrutinised. Under the Vagrancy Act of 1824, and later laws, the police were able to arrest street entertainers. By the end of the century, they were figures of the past. Instead, popular activities were regulated and standardised; as, for example, with brass bands in the 1860s and 1870s. Public spaces were controlled. The new policing of the period was much concerned about the moral threat of the urban environment and sought to bring order and decorum to the streets. Though less thoroughly, the same process was at work in rural areas. This was particularly so with those that received working-class urban visitors. For example, the popularity of the Clent Hills with trippers from the West Midlands led to problems, not least due to drunkenness and disorder. In 1881, Conservators were appointed and they were given powers by Parliament to make bye-laws. This involved regulation, the licensing of the erection of booths, the sale of goods, and the hiring of horses and donkeys.

This was reform in the eyes of its supporters. The process might seem different to that involved in, say, Factory Acts, but in fact was part of the same development. Although the

individual components varied, what was crucial was an impatience with existing circumstances, an unwillingness to accept traditional methods, mores, and controls, an emphasis
on state regulation, and a belief in improvement, both in improvability (the capacity to be
improved) and in the need for, and duty of, improvement. This was the politics of mid-
Victorian Britain. It was linked to what has been seen as a mid-nineteenth-century
revolution in government that involved the extension of the role of central state government, a shift from permissive to mandatory legislation, and a change in the relationship
between central and local governments. This emphasis was linked to the dominance of the
mid-century decades by Whigs/Liberals.

9.2 Environmental regulation

Much of this regulatory regime involved the built environment. A sense of crisis had
inspired the Public Health Act of 1848, but this was only the start of a pressure for action
that helped to condition the politics and purposes of power in particular communities.
For example, Edward Cresy, a Superintending Inspector under the General Board of
Health, produced a critical report on Derby that led the Liberal councillors to embark on a
programme of works, including public baths and washhouses. The following year, George
Thomas Clark, another Superintending Inspector, was scathing about the situation in the
city of Durham, and William Ranger about Darlington where he found no adequate water
supply, deficient sewerage and overcrowding. Ranger recommended that the Public
Health Act be applied to Darlington, and, in 1850, a Board of Health was established there,
and a Medical Officer of Health appointed. As was common, outsiders were blamed for
the condition of the town: 'diseases are continually being imported into the town by the
vagrant population, who take up their quarters in these abodes [common lodging
houses].' Among those to blame, it was alleged, were 'Tramping tinkers, pedlars, drovers
and their dogs, singers, blind, maimed and deformed mendicants together with slatternly
women and precocious looking children' (K. Singlehurst *et al.*, *Aspects of Darlington,
1850–51* 1999, p.71).

With its population rising from just over 1m in 1801 to over 7m by 1911, London
presented the most serious health problem. However, from 1859, under the direction of
Joseph Bazalgette, Chief Engineer to the Metropolitan Board of Works, a drainage system
was constructed. Fully completed in 1875, this contained 82 miles of intercepting sewers
that took sewerage from earlier sewers that had drained into the Thames, and transported
it to new downstream outfall sewerage works. Storm-relief sewers followed in the 1880s.
Other aspects of Bazalgette's work showed how man-made constraints were being
stamped on the environment. He was responsible for the Victoria, Albert and Chelsea
embankments, each of which limited the river bank and lessened the risk of flooding.
Bazalgette also created new routes in London: new bridges at Battersea and Putney, the
Woolwich steam ferry, and Northumberland Avenue.

9.3 A new world of politics

This may seem a long way from the world of politics, but in fact the entire process was
political, and we need to rethink our definition of politics. In so doing, we must move

away from a narrow conception in which parliaments, ministries, elections and powerful individuals predominate to one which involves a much wider sphere of activity, affecting peoples' lives on a daily basis. The political character of reform was particularly demonstrated in the nature of consultation. In essence, expertise ruled and was self-referential. Other interests were slighted. Northumberland Avenue indeed destroyed the town house of the Duke of Northumberland. More generally, working-class communities found their neighbourhoods rebuilt or reorganised without reference to them.

In addition, the decision to tackle public health essentially through engineering directed by adminstrators ensured that alternative responses, such as measures to alleviate poverty, were sidetracked. The focus was on sewerage systems and clean water, not on securing the availability of food and work or income at levels sufficient to lessen the impact of disease. This priority accorded with that of the reforming middle classes, but to underline the existence of an alternative is not to engage in anachronism: there were suggestions from informed contemporaries that different policies should be followed. William Alison, Professor of Physiology at Edinburgh University, linked cholera and poverty and argued, in his *Observations on the Management of the Poor in Scotland, and its Effects on the Health of the Great Towns* (1840), and his *Observations on the Epidemic Fever in Scotland, and its Connection with the Destitute Condition of the Poor* (1844), that poverty had to be addressed. This helped lead to a reform of the Scottish Poor Law system in 1845, but the Public Health Act of 1848 represented a triumph for the focus on drains.

The attempt to transform the urban environment was part of a wider mission to improve and regulate society. Regulation underpinned expertise, professionalisation and a process of establishing or raising standards that excluded others. Thus the 1858 Medical Act which established state registration of qualified doctors could serve as a basis for linking state authority to medical professionalisation.

Public spaces were defined and, if regulated, encouraged. The Recreation Grounds Act of 1859 and the Public Health Act of 1875 supported the laying out of public parks, while the Commons Act of 1876 sought to protect land outside towns that was beneficial to the community from development. This was not simply an imposition on local communities. Parks were regulated and only certain forms of behaviour were judged appropriate. Municipal parks and buildings also testified to the strength of local identity and the desire to improve the local environment. For instance, Wolverhampton, a rapidly growing industrial town, gained a town hall in 1871 and a People's Park in 1881. The East End Public Park in Wolverhampton followed in 1895.

However, alongside a reliance on self-help and the efforts of local communities, there was a stress on institutional provision and national standards, and steadily greater attempts to create a legislative framework for reform. Furthermore, the process of local reform and improvement was very much affected by existing hierarchies and social assumptions. Thus, the People's Park in Halifax opened in 1857 was paid for by Sir Francis Crossley, the MP and the owner of the local carpet mills.

Yet, there was also pressure on these hierarchies. Sefton Park in Liverpool, opened in 1872 by a member of the royal family, the Duke of Connaught, was created on farmland purchased from the Earl of Sefton by Liverpool Corporation. The traditional interests of Church and land were less powerful than in the past. They were also less respected in themselves and having to win support by showing why they deserved it, a process that many in the Church of England endorsed with some energy. The mismanagement of the

Crimean War (1854–6) helped to boost middle-class values of efficiency in politics at the expense of the aristocracy. This was linked to the movement of Whiggism to Liberalism.

In addition, the role of the churches receded. The influence, and, indeed, control of the churches, and the established Church of England in particular, in the fields of education and social welfare, was very significant until the middle of the century, but then declined in the face of the spreading role of the state. This had many consequences in terms of the attitudes influencing political activism and communal intervention.

The growth of middle-class culture and consciousness in the great northern cities, such as Leeds and Newcastle, represented a new world of politics that was not dominated by the traditional interests. The basis of authority in such cities had moved greatly from traditional to innovative. Their newspapers played a major role in orchestrating opinion in favour of reform. The self-confidence of these urban circles was expressed architecturally in their great town halls. Manchester's, for example, was opened in 1877.

9.4 The nature of power within society

As government became more activist and regulatory, so its control by particular political groupings increasingly became a question of the opportunity to push through policy as much as office-holding for personal profit and prestige. The nature of power within society was discussed to a greater extent than a century earlier. The expanding middle class expected power and status, and was dubious of established institutions and practices that did not seem reformist or useful, and of inherited privilege that lacked purpose. Deference was eroded. Middle-class views and wealth stimulated a demand for, and process of, improvement, civic and moral, that was so central to the movement for reform. The demands that this emerging wealthy class made for change were directed at the habits of the poor among them, but it was also aimed at eroding the privilege of the Establishment. Middle-class interests increasingly set the legislative agenda in late nineteenth-century Britain, although aristocratic influences on policy-making remained strong. In this expanding society, existing voting arrangements appeared redundant to many politicians and the decline in anxiety about radicalism in politics, after the collapse of Chartism in 1848, and the avoidance of a European-style revolution, made it easier to consider fresh reforms. Only Ireland had risen up in 1848: but the Young Ireland revolt had been a damp squib, nothing like as dangerous to English control in Ireland as the 1798 rising, and, having orchestrated the collapse of mass-platform Chartism and having ridden out this particular Irish storm, the British political world was perhaps more willing to consider the idea of reform.

Yet it is also necessary to note the strength of conservatism. Tory division over Corn Law repeal had led to Peel's resignation in 1846 and to the formation of a minority Whig ministry under Lord John Russell. However, neither the 1847 nor the 1852 general elections left a firm Whig majority; indeed the Tories marginally improved their position in 1852 to gain a majority in the Commons. Russell depended on the strength of Tory divisions and on the support of the Peelites. This set the pattern for the 1850s, as the Peelites remained able to hold the balance until 1859. The abandonment of protectionism by the Tory leaders in 1852 helped defuse the issue.

Box 9.1

Whigs

Long-established as one of the leading political groupings, the Whigs became increasingly associated with political and religious reform from the 1790s. The Great Reform Act of 1832 was seen as a triumph for Whiggery, but this itself was soon transformed into Liberalism, as the more complex politics of the mid-century combined with the expanding electorate and a shift in political sensibility to reform the character of politics.

The Whigs benefited from the energetic and skilful character of Lord Palmerston, Prime Minister 1855–8 and 1859–65, a charismatic individual able to win widespread popularity not least by his firm, not to say strident, defence of national interests across the world (see Profile Box 9.1, above). It was entirely in character that Palmerston, in 1856, supported the creation of the National Portrait Gallery. Palmerston supported liberal causes abroad but was much more cautious at home. Palmerston's death in 1865 was important because it removed one of the greatest obstacles to further constitutional reform, something Palmerston had refused to countenance.

Whig–Liberal successes in the general elections of 1865 showed that there had been a more general shift towards the political assumptions and beliefs once described as Whig and now increasingly characterised as Liberal. Indeed, the government majority rose considerably in both elections. The Tories, who were developing into a Conservative Party, suffered from poor leadership, organisational weakness, the decline of deference and landed influence, and the revival of the Liberal–Dissenter alliance in the 1850s.

A further extension to the franchise was central in political debate and manoeuvre after the death of Palmerston. Lord John Russell, the Whig Prime Minister in 1865–6, who replaced Palmerston when he died in office, believed, in contrast, that the more affluent workers should be trusted with the vote. Unable, in the face of a Whig split, to convince the Commons, he resigned. The Conservatives, under the sickly Edward, 14th Earl of Derby, took office and pushed through their own Reform Bill. The Second Reform Act, passed by a minority Tory government (1867), nearly doubled the existing electorate and, by offering household suffrage, gave the right to vote to about 60 per cent of adult males in boroughs, although the percentage on the electoral register rose to only 44.7 by 1871. Aside from all rate-paying householders, £12 occupiers in the counties and £10 lodgers in the boroughs were given the vote. (These sums should be seen in the context of the average worker's wage which was probably around £1 per week, even in the Edwardian years.) The percentage of adult males on the electoral registers for county seats rose to 23.8 in 1871.

Benjamin Disraeli was responsible for much of the parliamentary work and roused the suspicions of the Conservative right (including a future Prime Minister, Salisbury), who stirred up popular anger by claiming that the workers were 'unfit' for the vote. Disraeli needed Liberal votes in order to get the Bill through the Commons, and Liberal amendments were responsible for all borough rate-payers gaining the vote, a measure that enfranchised many manual workers. Derby said that in passing the Act, they were 'taking a leap in the dark'.

Box 9.2

Liberals

Whiggery was transformed into Liberalism in the mid-nineteenth century as previously radical ideas came to achieve a greater profile. Furthermore, the disenchantment of many of the party's aristocratic supporters with its increasingly radical stance led these former Whigs to leave the party, many later becoming Liberal Unionists. By the 1890s, the Liberals were offering a social politics which was clearly different from that of the Conservatives.

There was also a redistribution of seats. Less populous boroughs, such as Honiton, lost their seats. New parliamentary boroughs, such as Darlington, Stockton and the Hartlepools in County Durham, reflected population growth. The representation of Greater London rose to 22 MPs. Redistribution was not without controversy. In 1867, Lord John Russell felt it necessary to defend his administration against accusations:

> The district for Stroud was selected for representation for the same reason that the district of Stoke upon Trent was selected, namely on account of its containing a number of manufacturing villages … As for the story that representation was given to Stroud on account of the influence of the late Lord Fitzhardinge … and that the elevation of Lord Fitzhardinge to the Earldom formed part of the consideration, it is merely a stupid and malignant falsehood.

There were still, however, deficiencies in the electoral system and they were to be shown in the 1874 election when the Liberals won a majority of the votes cast, but a minority of the seats.

The Liberal victory in the general election (1868) after the Second Reform Act reflected clear social tension in some constituencies. For example, in the Caernarvonshire county seat, tenants and quarrymen defied landlords and employers to elect a Liberal. Some landlords responded by evicting tenants. A clear social divide could be seen between populous boroughs, the vast majority of which returned Liberals, and rural seats, the majority of which returned Conservatives.

Liberal victory led to the first government of William Gladstone (1868–74). He pushed through a whole series of reforms, including the disestablishment of the Irish Church (1869), and the introduction of open competition in the civil service (1870), and of the secret ballot (1872). This replacement of public voting by the Ballot Act hit landlord control. The institutionalization of Easter, Whitsun and Bank holidays in 1871 provided holidays with pay and thus more leisure-time to the work-force. In 1872, the powers of turnpike trusts were ended and road maintenance was placed totally under public control, an important limitation of the scope of developed governmental power.

The 1870 Education Act divided the country into school districts and required a certain level of educational provision, introducing the school district in cases where existing parish provision was inadequate, and giving School Boards the right to set rates to support non-denominational Board Schools. Under the 1870 Act, attendance was compulsory between the ages of five and 13. Its provisions, however, were resisted, not least because many were opposed to paying rates to support schools. By 1883 there were 3,602 such schools. In Ealing, tenacious efforts by the Church of England to protect voluntary

William Ewart Gladstone (1809–98)

Entering parliament in 1832, as a Tory, Gladstone served under Peel, becoming President of the Board of Trade (1843–5), before leaving the Tory Party with the other Peelites. Chancellor of Exchequer in 1852–5 and 1859–66, Gladstone became leader of the Liberal Party in 1867 and was Prime Minister on four occasions: 1868–74, 1880–5, 1886, and 1892–4. A noted reformer, Gladstone was able to strike a populist note, but not win sufficient support for his dream of Irish home rule. Instead, he split the Liberals in 1886. The 'People's William' was one of the most interesting and important politicians of his age.

Engraving published *c.* 1870

education and resist the introduction of Board Schools, ignoring the implications of rapid population growth, left 500 children unschooled 25 years after the act. The continued success of voluntary schools was such that in 1883 there were 11,589 Anglican schools and at the end of the century they still educated the majority of children. More generally, the end of long-established distinctions, variations and privileges played a major role in the reform process. The Endowed Schools Commission, established in 1870, redistributed endowments and reformed governing bodies.

These changes were important in themselves and also had ramifications throughout British society. For example, open competition in the Civil Service was an important step in the move from patronage to merit, although the impact in terms of a changed social composition among office-holders was limited. The Bank Holiday Acts of 1871 and 1875 led to a growth in day-tripping. Southend grew rapidly as a resort for London East Enders. This is a reminder of the need not to see changes in isolation. The impact of the Bank Holiday Acts would have been far less had it not been for the railways.

Other intended measures were less benign. In 1871, Gladstone supported his Chancellor of the Exchequer's proposal for a tax on every box of matches sold. This was seen as a way to make the poor pay taxes. In response match-girls demonstrated outside Parliament, and the government had to withdraw the proposal and double the intended increase in income tax.

9.5 Change and reform

In the early 1870s, Gladstone personified a political world centred on change and reform. Reformist aspirations and interventionist tendencies were shown in responses to what were judged local abuses. For example, a Royal Commission was established in 1869 to investigate allegations of electoral bribery in Beverley, North Yorkshire, and led to the town losing its MP. Gladstone was a formidable and multi-faceted individual of great determination and integrity. He was at once classical scholar and theological contro-versialist, with a library of 20,000 books as well as a hewer of trees and a rescuer of prostitutes. A Tory Treasury minister in the 1830s, Gladstone became the leading Liberal politician of the age, committed to reform at home and a moral stance abroad. Gladstone had a charismatic manner and presidential style. His political skills bridged the worlds of Parliament and of public meetings, for, under his leadership, Liberalism became a movement enjoying mass support. Gladstone appealed from Parliament to the public and sought to gain mass support for his politics of action and reform. Both Victorian Liberalism and the Gladstonian Liberal Party had a strong popular appeal, and it is important to appreciate that there was nothing anachronistic about a widespread non-socialist commitment on the part of the working class who felt that liberalism expressed their ideals and advanced their interests. In particular, the commitment of liberalism to both participatory democracy and free-market economics was not bound to fail. While respectful of established institutions, the constitution and the Church, Gladstone had a strong sympathy for progressive causes, and applied much of his intellect and energy to further them. Gladstone moulded, but could not control, the process by which the diversity of Whiggism became the diversity of Liberalism.

The attempt to woo an expanding electorate required a newly-expanded infrastructure of politics capable of creating links between elite and electorate. Deference and traditional political alignments still played a role, but it was much diminished. The press was particularly important in constructing this new political culture. One of the many ways in which Victorian London was at the centre of political life was that of the provision of the news. Through its press, which lay claim to the title of the 'fourth estate' of the realm, London created the image and idiom of nation and empire and shaped opinions. Aside from this political function, the press also played a central economic, social and cultural role, setting and spreading fashions, whether of company statements or through theatrical criticism. In what was increasingly a commercial society, the press played a pivotal role, inspiring emulation, setting the tone, and fulfilling crucial needs for an anonymous mass-readership.

The press was itself affected by change, by the energising and disturbing forces of commercialization and new technology. Legal reform and technological development freed the Victorian press for major development. Newspapers had become expensive in the eighteenth century, in large part due to successive rises in Stamp Duty. In the mid-nineteenth century these so-called 'taxes on knowledge' were abolished: the Advertisement Duties in 1853, the Newspaper Stamp Duty in 1855 and the Paper Duties in 1861. This opened up the possibility of a cheap press and that opportunity was exploited by means of a technology centred on new printing presses and the continuous rolls or 'webs' of paper that fed them. A steam press was first used, by *The Times*, in 1814. Web rotary presses were introduced in England from the late 1860s. Mechanical typesetting was introduced towards the end of the century.

New technology was expensive, but the mass readership opened up by the lower prices that could be charged after the repeal of the newspaper taxes, justified the cost. The consequence was more titles and lower prices. The number of daily morning papers published in London rose from 8 in 1856 to 21 in 1900, and of evenings from 7 to 11, while there was also a tremendous expansion in the provincial and suburban press. The first provincial dailies in Birmingham, Liverpool, Manchester and Sheffield appeared in 1855, in Newcastle in 1857, in Bristol in 1858, in Plymouth in 1860, in Nottingham in 1861, and in Bradford in 1868. Whereas, in 1868, 14 of the largest English provincial towns had daily newspapers, by 1885, 47 English towns had daily papers.

The repeal of stamp duty permitted the appearance of 'penny dailies'. The *Daily Telegraph*, launched in 1855, led the way and by 1888 had a circulation of 300,000. The penny press was in turn squeezed by the 'halfpenny press', the first halfpenny evening paper, the *Echo*, appearing in 1868, while halfpenny morning papers became important in the 1890s with the *Morning Leader* (1892) and the *Daily Mail* (1896), which was to become extremely successful with its bold and simple style. It testified to the dynamic combination of entrepreneurial capitalism and the market created by the expanding urban working class.

The *Echo* peaked at a circulation of 200,000 in 1870. The papers that best served popular tastes were the Sunday papers, *Lloyd's Weekly News*, the *News of the World* and *Reynolds's Newspaper*. *Lloyd's*, the first English paper with a circulation of over 100,000, was selling over 600,000 copies by 1879, over 900,000 by 1893 and in 1896 rose to over a million. The Sunday papers relied on shock and titillation, drawing extensively on police court reporting.

In comparison an eighteenth-century London newspaper was considered a great success if it sold 10,000 copies a week (most influential papers then were weeklies), and 2,000 weekly was a reasonable sale. Thus an enormous expansion had taken place, one that matched the vitality of an imperial capital, swollen by immigration and increasingly influential as an opinion-setter within the country, not least because of the communications revolution produced by the railway and better roads. The development of the railways allowed London newspapers to increase their dominance of the national

Gladstone and Disraeli: The parliamentary exchanges between William Ewart Gladstone and Benjamin Disraeli, the two most prominent politicians of the Victorian period, were legendary.
Punch in 1869 poked fun at the meekness of one particularly mild confrontation. In an image that shows the two addressing each other with apparent decorum, we should nevertheless notice that each man has a heavier weapon behind his back with which (metaphorically) to beat the other later. Disraeli is on the right, Gladstone on the left.
Source: Punch (Vol. 56, 27 February 1869, p. 81)

Benjamin Disraeli (1804–81)

A novelist-turned-Tory-politician, he criticised Peel's repeal of the Corn Laws, becoming Conservative leader in the Commons, and Chancellor of the Exchequer in Earl Derby's governments. Prime Minister in 1868 and 1874–80, Disraeli was best noted for his energetic imperial policies although his second ministry offered a number of important social reforms. He took a leading role in getting Britain control over the Suez Canal, and oversaw Queen Victoria's recognition as Empress of India (1876).

newspaper scene. Thanks to them, these papers could arrive on provincial doorsteps within hours of publication.

Gladstone's Liberals were not the only party using the press and pushing for reform. Indeed, much of the character of British politics was framed by the absence of a party of reaction. Under Benjamin Disraeli, Conservative Prime Minister in 1868 and 1874–80, Conservatism was effectively redefined as different to and opposed to Liberalism, but not as a creed of reaction. In office, the Conservatives did not reverse the Liberal attempt to legislate for social improvement.

Instead, Disraeli sought to fuse social legislation with a sense of national continuity. He attempted, in the aftermath of the 1867 Reform Act, to create a popular Conservatism. Nevertheless Disraeli was less determined to align Conservatism with the middle or working classes than some of his successors. Initially, his cabinet contained only one member from a middle-class background: R.A. Cross, the Home Secretary; W.H. Smith joined him as First Lord of the Admiralty in 1877. The Conservatives came to power in 1874 by equalling the Liberals in the boroughs and overwhelming them in the county seats.

Disraeli was an opportunistic and skilful political tactician who was also an acute thinker, able to create around the themes of national identity and pride, and social cohesion, an alternative political culture and focus of popular support to Liberal moral certainty. Disraeli sought to preserve what he saw as the traditional strengths of the country. He was keen to maintain the landed order and was a warm, although not uncritical, supporter of Victoria. Disraeli also backed social reform, although less energetically than his Liberal opponents and than was subsequently to be claimed. Some of the legislation was inherited from the Gladstone government, and most of it did not receive Disraeli's full attention. Disraeli presented his first Cabinet meeting with no plan for domestic transformation. Furthermore, most of the legislation was permissive, not compulsory. Indeed, Disraeli declared: 'permissive legislation is the characteristic of a free people'. By leaving decisions about implementation largely to urban and rural magistrates, Disraeli managed a wise mixture of prudence and ideology. He avoided political clashes with supporters and accepted a diversity of regulatory regimes that accorded with the different attitudes of local elites and did not suggest the dictates of big government. Conversely, his legislation brought far less benefit to the bulk of the population than the titles of the acts might have suggested. This can be seen both as looking back to the lessons from Tory disunity over the Corn Laws (which, as an anti-Peelite, Disraeli played a fundamental role in engineering) and also forward to Conservative failure in the 1880 election, for Disraeli presented little to win public support, and, in particular, failed to win sufficient middle- or working-class support. Although some of his government's measures, such as the abolition of sugar duties in 1874 (which helped foster the growth of the jam and chocolate industries), appealed to all sections of the community, others were seen was particularly rewarding for the rural community rather than for urban interests. It is, however, necessary to avoid modern preconceptions about priorities. It is no accident that Disraeli also devoted time in the 1874 session to ecclesiastical legislation, passing both the Public Worship Regulation Act which was designed to prevent Ritualism or Romanism (i.e. the use of Roman Catholic ceremonial practices) in the Church of England, and the patronage Act for the Presbyterian Church of Scotland.

Legislation on factories (1874), and Public Health, Artisans' Dwellings, and Pure Food and Drugs Acts (1875) systematized and extended the regulation of important aspects of public health and social welfare. The Factory Act (1874) limited work hours to 10 per day for women and children in the textile industry; another Factory Act followed in 1878. The Artisans Dwelling Act of 1875 made urban renewal possible, but its actual impact in terms of slum clearance was limited. The Metaliferous Mines Act of 1875 followed that of 1872 in seeking better working conditions by, for example, improving ventilation. The Merchant Shipping Act of the same year allowed the Board of Trade to prevent unseaworthy ships from sailing. It typified the extension of government powers that stemmed both from a sense of greater state responsibility, and from the problems created by a growing economy that burst the bounds of traditional controls. The Prison Act (1877) established state control. These were, however, less important for Disraeli and owed less to his personal attention than his active foreign policy, which involved the purchase of shares in the Suez Canal (1875), the creation of the title of Empress of India for Queen Victoria (1876), the acquisition of Cyprus (1878), and wars with the Afghans and Zulus, which broke out in 1879 and 1878, respectively.

Economic difficulties, particularly a run of bad harvests, and political problems, skilfully exploited by Gladstone in his electioneering Midlothian campaigns (1879–80), led to Conservative defeat in the 1880 election. Imperial and Irish problems, however, affected Gladstone's second government (1880–5), with the First Boer War (1880–1) in South Africa, the occupation of Egypt (1882–3), the massacre of Colonel Gordon and his force at Khartoum in Sudan (1885), the Coercion Act, designed to restore order in Ireland (1881), and the murder of Lord Frederick Cavendish, the Chief Secretary for Ireland, in Phoenix Park, Dublin, by the Invincibles, an Irish secret society (1882).

It proved easier to introduce and implement reform in England than in Ireland. The Corrupt and Illegal Practices Act of 1883 served to put the conduct of election campaigns on a more secure footing. In 1884, the Third Reform Act extended to the counties the household franchise granted to the boroughs in 1867, so that over two-thirds of the adult males in the counties and about 63 per cent of the entire adult male population received the vote. Mass democracy was coming nearer. In County Durham, for example, the electorate expanded greatly as the result of the miners gaining the vote. The national electorate rose from 3.15 to 5.7m, although, of these nearly 750,000 were plural votes. Furthermore, the percentage of adult males who could vote was closer to 40 than 63, because so many people changed address and because a voter needed 18 months' continuous residence before he could vote. Women were still denied the vote.

9.6 Electoral politics after 1885

Political power had slipped from the grasp of the landed elite well before the 1885 general election, which is often seen as crucial in the transition to more public forms of electoral politics. Selection of candidates had become more open to populist pressures. Nevertheless, the extension of democracy posed fresh problems to the existing order. Reform movements had politicised groups that now had electoral power. As in 1868, the Conservatives in 1885 were defeated in the first election held with the new franchise. Many rural electors voted against their landlords. Although registration requirements debarred many, democracy challenged the existing social politics, and, in particular, the rural strongholds of Conservatives. Thus, in East Denbighshire, Sir Watkin Williams Wynn was defeated. But the defeats were not only in the countryside. In the 1885 general election, the Tories were routed in County Durham, only winning the City of Durham, a more conservative constituency. Working-men Liberal–Labour candidates were more successful, two of the Durham Miners' Association agents winning seats, although Labour sympathy was mostly contained within Liberalism.

The Third Reform Act was the first time that the whole of the United Kingdom was brought under the same electoral system. Initially rejected by the Conservative-dominated House of Lords, the Bill was passed in return for an agreement for redistribution. The Redistribution of Seats Act of 1885 led to a move to single-member seats and a major redistribution that included the division of many county seats. The Conservative leader, Robert, 3rd Marquess of Salisbury, supported redistribution because he felt it would increase the representation of middle-class areas, such as suburbs and seaside resorts, taking them out of county seats. He thought this would benefit the Conservatives, not least because he sensed middle-class disaffection with growing Liberal radicalism, an important socio-political shift; Salisbury was correct to discern the possibilities of 'Villa Torydom'.

The larger electorate encouraged developments in organisation as well as policy. Politics was increasingly institutional. Thus, for example, the National Union of Scottish Conservative Associations was founded in 1882. The Conservatives created a system of regional organised constituency agents, although by 1900 only half of the constituencies had such office-holders. The Primrose League, founded in 1883, also helped to develop Conservative activism and 'Tory democracy'. The League provided a popular dimension to the Conservative political machinery, and helped challenge popular Liberalism. While, at the working-class fringes of the party, marginal conservative societies, such as the Orange Order, also tended to pledge support for Conservative candidates in parliamentary elections and organised their members around key Conservative principles, such as empire, the established church and union with Ireland.

The changing political world was captured in Anthony Trollope's novel *The Duke's Children* (1879–80). The constituents of the fictional Silverbridge were now less under the control of the Liberal Duke of Omnium, although the influence of the family still played a role:

Robert Cecil, 3rd Marquess of Salisbury (1830-1903)

The leading Conservative of the closing decades of the century. MP from 1853, he became Marquess in 1868. Having served as Indian Secretary and Foreign Secretary, he was Prime Minister in 1885–6, 1886–92 and 1895–1902, also acting as Foreign Secretary for much of the time. Keen on the Church of England, the free market and traditional social norms, Salisbury recognised the importance of winning middle-class votes from what were dubbed the 'Villa Tories'. In this light, Salisbury helped to make the party sensitive to suburban attitudes.

They had loyally returned the Duke himself while he was a commoner, but they had returned him as being part and parcel of the Omnium appendages. That was all over now ... they ... thought that a Conservative would suit them best. That being so, and as they had been told that the Duke's son was a Conservative, they fancied that by electing him they would by no means displease the Duke.

The Duke wanted to maintain the family's liberalism, but his heir, Lord Silverbridge, had his 'own ideas. We've got to protect our position as well as we can against the Radicals and Communists'. The Duke replied, 'I cannot admit that at all, Silverbridge. There is no great political party in this country anxious either for Communism or for revolution'. Silverbridge, however, saw politics in terms of class not 'the public ... The people will look after themselves, and we must look after ourselves'.

The process of reform, both political and social, continued with the Local Government Act (1888), creating directly elected county councils and county boroughs and the London County Council (LCC), and thus a new representation of the community; the first elections were held the following year. The Workmen's Compensation Act (1897), obliged employers to provide compensation for industrial accidents. A welfare state was developing. State intervention in education helped in the decline of illiteracy. The directly elected London County Council was the world's largest municipal authority. It took an activist role in trying to improve London life based on a strong sense of mission and a capacity to produce information on which policy could be based.

The political situation was complicated by the long-standing malaise over the Irish question, which interacted with tensions within both liberalism and the Liberal Party. Fenian terrorism in Ireland, England and Canada led to casualties, and there was both pressure for land reform and agitation for home rule for Ireland (the creation of an Irish parliament able to tackle domestic issues). Gladstone correctly identified Ireland as a major problem of and for British politics. His support for home rule seems especially prescient from the perspective of 2003 as the British state, Catholic republicanism and Protestant unionism continues to wrangle over the future of the island.

Liberal proposals for home rule were defeated in 1886 and 1893 at Westminster, where they helped to divide politicians. Conservatives led the resistance, but the defeat of the First Home Rule Bill in 1886 was due to the defection of 'Liberal Unionists' from

Gladstone's third government. This more than outweighed a degree of popular support within Britain. Gladstone's policies also helped win the support of Parnellite MPs for a co-operation with the Liberals that was to be important in the years before the First World War. Thus, it helped prepare for the constitutional nationalism that was to dominate Irish politics until 1916.

Nevertheless, the political hegemony of the divided Liberals was destroyed in 1886 as the Conservatives, under Salisbury, won the general election. Though the Liberals won the 1892 election, the Conservatives regained power in 1895 and dominated the period 1886–1905, winning elections in 1886, 1895 and 1900. They benefited from the long-term expansion of the middle classes and from their growing urban strength following the 1885 redistribution of constituencies. The Conservatives increasingly became an urban- and suburban-based party. The transformation of the Tory Party was one of the great success stories of nineteenth-century politics. Given the divisions following the controversial repeal of the Corn Laws and the defection of the Peelites, there was a very real chance that the Tories would become little more than a landed rump on the margins of politics. The transformation into a national party representing significant elements of the new urban middle classes was to be very important for twentieth-century politics. The Conservatives benefited from the perceived radicalism of Gladstonian Liberalism which drove the satiated and newly anxious middle-classes (the beneficiaries of the meritocratic reforms of the first Gladstone ministry) into the Conservative camp. Its openness to social trends was shown by a keeness to recruit Catholics and to mobilise female support. The Conservatives put considerable emphasis on imperialism abroad and at home (in Ireland), but downplayed their earlier identification with the Church of England. In part, the Conservatives benefited, like their nationalist counterparts in Europe, from the greater ability of the right to tap populist themes and define itself in nationalist terms after the mid-century crisis. They were also helped by middle-class concern about taxation. The spread in the power and activity of government, particularly local government, led to new commitments, not least by school boards. These pushed up municipal rates. Rising tax demands pressed on a society that was less buoyant and, crucially, less confident economically than that of the middle decades of the century, and this decreased support for the Liberals. In 1882, Salisbury wrote of the rise of 'a great Villa Toryism which requires organisation'.

Salisbury (Prime Minister 1885–6, 1886–92, 1895–1902) himself, however, was not best placed to create a Tory populism. Two-thirds of his cabinet were peers, although it did nothing to advance the landed interest other than not passing budgets like the Liberal one of 1894 which had greatly increased death duties. The Local Government Act of 1888 alienated Conservative landowners, but was pushed through by Salisbury in an attempt to pre-empt something more radical from a future Liberal government. He had shown earlier interest in more powerful local government, writing in 1876 about vesting 'decision in the Local Government Board. No doubt that is the doctrinal situation of all our social difficulties'. Whereas the 1888 Act had replaced the traditional system of local government, which had been dominated by Justices of the Peace (JPs), by elected county councils, the 1894 Act added a system of elected councils for towns and rural districts. These Acts amounted to a revolution in local government which destroyed the socio-political power of the gentry (Box 9.2). Under Salisbury, tariffs (customs duties) were not imposed on imports of food, for fear of affecting the living standards of urban workers. Free trade remained British policy and the centrepiece of British economic ideology.

Box 9.3

Popularity and public politics

The pressure of public demands on politicians can be glimpsed in a letter written by Gladstone to John Jackson, Bishop of London (8 June 1876).

from the number and nature of demands made upon me, and the impossibility, as I find it, of

selection, I have been obliged to form a determination to decline attending all public meetings and celebrations except in cases with which I have some personal relation.

Maggs Catalogue, 1285 (2000), item 124

Imports hit agriculture hard. The price of both wheat and wool fell greatly; and there was, where possible, a switch to milk, fruit and vegetables as there was no competition from imports. There was also a transition in rural political culture and structures: 'Falling rents increasingly took the capital of landlords elsewhere and culture seems to have followed this capital, leaving a "poor vacuum" in many villages' (J. Thirsk (ed.), *The Agrarian History of England and Wales*, Vol. 7, *1850–1914* Cambridge, 2000, p.1506). This created a more volatile situation with farmers, labourers and the local agencies of the state all competing to influence or establish a new order. These problems affected rural interests badly, not least by encouraging migration from the land.

Salisbury and his successor and nephew, Arthur Balfour (Prime Minister, 1902–5), followed a cautious policy on domestic reform. Salisbury, a Marquess and owner of Hatfield House, one of the palaces the English domesticate as 'stately homes', as well as a high Anglican intellectual, derived most of his disposable income from urban property, including London slums. He brought the Conservatives considerable success, but his government came to seem tired in the early 1900s. The Boer War proved far more difficult and costly than he had anticipated, and Salisbury also failed to keep the step ahead of the game that is so important to political success (albeit frequently risky). Thus, Salisbury cannot escape responsibility for the divisions over protectionism that were to affect the government from 1903, nor for the failure to maintain sufficient middle-class support to avoid a sweeping electoral defeat in 1906.

Imperial preference

Until the divisive issue of protectionism and imperial preference developed, imperial expansion helped the Conservatives by making them the undisputed party of empire in British politics. However, like the Liberals, they found it difficult to respond coherently to the pressures of a society in which various groups were defining different demands. Growing pressure for more radical political and social policies encouraged political opinion increasingly to coalesce and polarise along social and class lines, although revolutionary sentiment was limited. Revolutionary Marxism was effectively checked and marginalised in the 1880s. The Social Democratic Federation (SDF) was the nearest thing to a revolutionary Marxist organisation in England. Its impact was peripheral for a variety of reasons, including poor leadership, the unwillingness and failure of the SDF to court and win trade union support, the widespread commitment to reformism (to be seen in the craft unions of the time as well as among the Fabians), based on the belief that the

Karl Marx (1818-83)

Social theorist and founder of modern socialism (often called Marxism). He was influenced by German philosophy, particularly aspects of Hegelianism, French socialism, and the products of the Scots Enlightenment, notably Adam Smith. He wrote important works of history, such as *The Eighteenth Brumaire of Louise Napoleon*. His canon of works is large, including books, essays, journalism, letters, etc. His most notable work, a critique of the very essence of modern society, was *Das Kapital* (*Capital*). He envisaged the continuing crystallisation of modern society into two competing classes from whose struggle would eventually emerge a socialist utopia. His life-long collaborator and fellow German, Friedrich Engels, exerted a considerable influence and his importance is often overlooked.

parliamentary system could be made more democratic and therefore more responsive to working-class needs, and a belief that violence was inappropriate and unnecessary in England.

Instead, change was pursued through the political process. Politics itself was increasingly affected by class issues and alignments, not least as a consequence of the developing problem of labour relations. There was growing pressure for more radical political and social policies. Joseph Chamberlain's 'Unauthorized' Liberal Programme of 1885 called for land reform, and was followed, in 1891 by Gladstone's Newcastle programme which also called for home rule, disestablishment of the Church of England in Wales, free education, a reduction in factory work-hours, electoral reform and the reform or abolition of the House of Lords. That year, the Scottish Liberals called for land reform in the Highlands, an eight-hour day for miners, and an extension of the franchise.

In 1890, the election of the 27-year-old David Lloyd George for Caernarfon Boroughs symbolised the social revolution of the period. A solicitor from a modest background, Lloyd George defeated the Conservative candidate, H.J.E. Nanney, who was the squire of Llanystumdwy. He was keen to present this as a victory for a new Wales and democracy. Lloyd George's background was as a populist. In 1888, he had won much publicity when he fought the Llanfrothen burial case, arguing the right of a quarryman to be buried with Nonconformist rites in an Anglican churchyard in accordance with the Burial Act of 1880. Once elected, Lloyd George criticised the privileges of the aristocracy, landowners, and royalty, although he was far less critical of manufacturing wealth.

Radical policies divided the Liberals, making them appear to some as a threat to stability. The landed interest broke from the Liberals, and there was a coalescence of opinion in defence of property and order under the Conservatives, but one with only a fragile basis among the working class. The latter was still largely Liberal, although Socialist organisations were founded: the Fabian Society in 1884, the SDF in 1883, and the Independent Labour Party in 1893. Salisbury sought to reconcile 'Tory Democracy' with traditional Conservative beliefs, while, at the same time, responding to new problems in a class-based society. This worked better in some areas than others. The West Midlands and Scotland, for example, became more Conservative than Wales, Lancashire more Conservative than north-east England.

Activism was not simply expressed through political bodies. For example, the Co-operative Women's Guild, founded in 1884, had a hundred branches with 6,000 members by 1889. It campaigned not only for women employees, but also for educational and political ends.

While politics was developing towards its class-orientated character in the twentieth century, the social order could be harsh as well as inegalitarian. In London, a campaign against street prostitution launched in 1883 came to an end in 1887 amid public complaints and parliamentary questions about the blackmailing of poor prostitutes, bribery, and harassment through arrests. On 'Bloody Sunday', 13 November 1887, at Trafalgar Square, the symbolic centre of Empire, a meeting called by the Metropolitan Radical Association in protest against the government's failure to tackle unemployment was banned, leading to a violent demonstration involving over 400 arrests and about 200 casualties, including one death. In 1891, Tom Masters, a 13-year-old Northamptonshire farm labourer, was whipped by his employer for insolence.

Pressures from within the Liberal party were supplemented by the creation of more explicitly working-class movements, both political and industrial. The development of trade unions reflected the growing industrialisation and unification of the economy, the growth of larger concerns employing more people, and, by the end of the century, a new, more adversarial and combative working-class consciousness. The Trades Unions Congress (TUC), a federation of trade unions, began in 1868, unionism spread from the skilled craft section to semi-skilled and unskilled workers, and there were major strikes in the London gasworks and docks in 1888–9. James Keir Hardie, Secretary of the Scottish Miners' Federation, founded the Scottish Labour Party (1888) and the Independent Labour Party (1893). The latter pressed for an eight-hour day and 'collective ownership of means of production, distribution and exchange'. Six years later, the TUC advocated an independent working-class political organization, which led, in 1900, to the formation of the Labour Representation Committee, the basis of the Labour Party.

These developments contributed to a situation of sustained doubt, if not a crisis of confidence, in late Victorian society. The earlier process of reform had encouraged an expectation that the state could and should confront and even solve problems. In turn, this helped drive the extension of government organisation and pretensions, and created a new and more intrusive ethos of governance. For example, requirements for state-supported public welfare had been extended thanks to the New Poor Law of 1834 and this *helped* to lead towards the welfare state that was to be pushed by the Liberal government elected in 1906 and 1910. Old-age pensions, for example, were introduced in 1908. The theme of such legislation was that it was national, seeking common standards, and employing authorities as agents of central government. Thus the Poor Law Commission, the Lunacy Commission, the General Board of Health, and the Local Government Board all intervened in the local provision of welfare and health. This matched the role of nationally organised companies in the economy, and was part of a more general erosion of regional and local autonomy. Looked at differently, local autonomy was lost as a result of a transfer of authority and power to the national, not the regional, scale.

Furthermore, thanks to the General Register Office founded in 1837, the government had statistics in order to help plan its policies and interventions. Thus, the 1848 Public

Health Act compelled local authorities to implement local sanitary reform if their annual mortality rates were measured by the Office as above 23 per 1000. This was a world of policy and politics very different to that of the eighteenth century.

9.7 Conclusion

The nineteenth century was marked by the slow erosion of the idea of *laissez-faire* as governments became increasing involved in the lives of the people they represented. As the state grew, so too did expectation as to its further expansion. People looked increasingly for reform to improve their lives.

It is important to recognise that the Conservative Party which emerged from the old Tory groupings at Westminster did very well in an age of increasing populist politics. As the electorate grew – particularly with the changes of 1884 – we might reasonably have expected the party associated with reaction and privilege to have disappeared as new configurations emerged. However, like the Liberals, who grew from the Whigs, the Conservatives were able to tap into reservoirs of support. Working-class Tories like middle-class 'Villa Tories' helped to bolster the power-base of the Conservative tradition. Similarly, the Liberals enjoyed support from many factory owners, nonconformists and Catholics (often of Irish stock). It is long after our period that the Labour Party became one of the key power-holding blocs (not until 1945, in fact). Between 1874 and 1992, the Conservatives were easily the most successful party when it came to winning elections. The essence of British politics during the nineteenth century was that a dynamic, changing, evolving system emerged, tapping into peoples' desires and engaging in debate about future directions. Whilst middle-class powerbrokers came on to the scene, and working-class voters became more important than ever before, the fact is that the traditional elite – the landed magnates – continued to have a strong position in cabinets and the House of Commons. They also had a near-total stranglehold on the House of Lords. As for women; it would be 1918 and 1928 before their quest for political equality began to bear fruit and was won.

▮ Summary

◆ A commitment to reform remained strong in British politics, but it continued to have very different meanings.

◆ Gladstone benefited from the transformation of Whiggery into Liberalism.

◆ The Conservatives responded to changing social patterns and were not a party of reactionaries.

▮ Points to discuss

◆ What did Disraeli and Gladstone stand for?

◆ How far did politics have a class character?

◆ What were the consequences of the extension of the male franchise?

◼ References and further reading

W. Alison, *Observations on the Management of the Poor in Scotland and its Effects on the Health of the Great Towns* (1840).

W. Alison, *Observations on the Epidemic Fever in Scotland, and its Connection with the Destitute Condition of the Poor* (1844).

J. Belchem, *Class, Party and the Political System in Britain, 1867–1914* (Oxford, 1990).

M. Bentley, *The Climax of Liberal Politics: British Liberalism in Theory and Practice, 1868–1918* (1987).

E.F. Biagini, *Gladstone* (Basingstoke, 2000.)

E.F. Biagini, *Liberty, Retrenchment and Reform: Popular Liberalism in the Age of Gladstone, 1860–1880* (Cambridge, 1992).

R. Blake, *Disraeli* (1966).

J.L. Bronstein, *Land Reform and Working-Class Experience in Britain and the United States, 1800–1862* (Stanford, Cal., 1999).

K. Burgess, *The Challenge of Labour: Shaping British Society, 1850–1930* (1980).

P.F. Clarke, *Lancashire and the New Liberalism* (Cambridge, 1971).

E.J. Feuchtwanger, *Disraeli, Democracy and the Conservative Party* (1965).

H.J. Hanham, *Elections and Party Management: Politics in the Time of Gladstone and Disraeli* (Hassocks, 1959).

R. Jenkins, *Gladstone* (Basingstoke, 1996)

H.C.G. Matthew, *Gladstone, 1809–1898* (1907).

J. Parry, *The Rise and Fall of Liberal Government in Victorian Britain* (New Haven, Conn., 1993).

R. Shannon, *The Age of Disraeli, 1868–1881: The Rise of Tory Democracy* (1992).

K. Singlehurst *et al.*, *Aspects of Darlington* (Darlington, 1999).

E.D. Steele, *Palmerston and Liberalism, 1855–1881* (Cambridge, 1991)

J. Thirsk (ed.), *The Agrarian History of England and Wales, Vol 7, 1850–1914* (Cambridge, 2000).

J. Vincent, *Disraeli* (1992).

J. Vincent, *The Formation of the Liberal Party* (Cambridge, 1966)

Ireland and the Irish

Question

CHAPTER 10

Contents

■ Introduction

Even when British politicians were not dealing expressly with the Irish Question, they found themselves very often dealing with Irish questions. Between 1800, when the Act of Union was passed, and 1922, when the Union collapsed, and Ireland was divided into the Free State and Northern Ireland, Irish issues increasingly exercised British governments. By the later century, Ireland was occupying more parliamentary time than most other issues.

Ireland and Britain were different in 1801, but they were far more different by 1922. Differing historical paths – divergent religious, social and economic histories – made the Irish problem progressively more difficult to address. Despite repeated efforts – a combination of oppression and reform – Britain could not convince the majority of Irish men and women that their futures lay in a harmonious union with Britain. But republicanism and militancy were not the recourse of a majority of Irish people; Ireland could have been won over to some sort of federal system at any point in the 19th century, and indeed, even in 1916. But Britain failed to deliver quickly enough what Ireland wanted; time and again, *reform was too little, too late.*

KEY ISSUES

► How do we account for the social and economic problems of Ireland in the period?
► Why was emigration such a significant feature of Irish life?
► What was the relationship between Britain and Ireland under the Act of Union (1800)?
► Why did British politicians fail to answer the 'Irish Question'?
► What was the balance between violent and constitutional methods in Anglo-Irish politics?

Box 10.1

Chronology of the Irish question in the nineteenth century

The key events are listed below.

1801 Act of Union becomes law.

1823 Foundation of O'Connell's Repeal Association, dedicated to winning Catholic Emancipation

1829 Catholic Emancipation Act
O'Connell sits as MP

1830 Reform Acts in Britain and Ireland
Irish Temporalities Act; First debate on repeal of the Act of Union

1835 Lichfield House Compact between Whigs, Radicals and Irish

1837 Irish Poor Law (modelled on the Poor Law Amendment Act, 1834)
Tithe Rent Act

1840 Establishment of the National Association by O'Connell (name later changed to the Loyal National Repeal Association)
Irish Municipal Reform Act

1843 'Monster Meetings' of O'Connell's repeal movement
Maynooth College Act which provided for an annual grant to the Roman Catholic priest-training seminary
Revival of the Orange Order

1845 Outbreak of the 'Potato Blight', a fungal infection that precipitated the Great Irish Famine

1846 Repeal of the Corn Laws; Young Irelanders split from O'Connell's moderate repeal association over the issue of using physical force

1848 Irish Rising

1858 Fenian Brotherhood founded in America

1867 Fenian Rising in Ireland

1868 Amnesty Association founded to fight to free Fenian prisoners

1869 Irish Church Act – disestablishment and disendowment of the Church of Ireland;
Home Government Association (HGA) founded by Isaac Butt

1870 first in a series of Land Acts; Party Processions Acts (1850 and 1860) repealed

1873 Home Rule Confederation of Great Britain founded
Home Rule League founded in Dublin

10.1 Economy and society

Ireland, of all the countries of the United Kingdom, failed to enjoy the fruits of the Industrial Revolution. None of the other three countries enjoyed a blanket success in this regard, but England, Wales and Scotland each saw far greater developments, and far wider benefits, than were apparent in what the Victorians dubbed 'the sister isle'. In terms of population, urbanisation, industrial growth, and standards of living, Ireland's experience was behind that of the others countries of the United Kingdom.

Although the question of population growth has been addressed in another part of this book (see Chapter 5), it is worth stressing here divergences in the population history of the various parts of the British Isles. In 1821, Ireland's population was far larger than Scotland's. Eighty years later, after a period of sustained population decline in Ireland,

Box 10.1 continued

1874 60 Home Rule MPs returned

Obstruction campaign begins (whereby Irish MPs filibustered Commons business until time ran out)

1875 Charles Stewart Parnell enters the Commons as MP for Meath

1876 Irish Republican Brotherhood withdraws support from home-rule movement

Society for the Preservation of the Irish language formed.

1877 Parnell becomes president of the Home Rule Confederation of Great Britain (HRCGB).

1878 John Devoy of the American Irish-nationalist Clan na Gael movement proposes 'New Departure' – a linking of constitutional and Fenian nationalism – to the Parnellites

1879 Land War – a series of protracted violent rural episodes – begins in Irishtown, Co. Mayo

Death of Butt

Irish Land League formed

Boycott system of non-payment against landlords who resisted the Land League

1881 Second Land Act – aimed to guarantee 3 'Fs': fixity of tenure, fair rent and freedom of sale

Parnell imprisoned

1882 Parnell freed from prison after striking a deal (Kilmainham Treaty) with Gladstone

Phoenix Park Murders (6 May) – death of the Irish Secretary, Lord Frederick Cavendish and his Under-Secretary T.H. Burke; Land League dissolved and Irish National League founded

1884 Gaelic Athletic Association founded

1885 Ashbourne Act passed to increase land purchases

1886 First Home Rule Bill defeated

1887 Arthur 'Bloody' Balfour appointed Irish Secretary

Forged letter, linking Parnell to the Phoenix Park Murders, is published in *The Times*.

1890 O'Shea divorce scandal

1891 Congested Districts Boards established under the Land Purchase Act

Parnell dies

Irish Literary Society formed

1893 Second Home Rule Bill rejected by the Lords

1896 Land Act

1898 Formation of the United Irish League

1900 John Redmond elected leader of the Irish Party

Cumann na nGaedheal, the precursor of the modern Fine Gael party, founded by Arthur Griffith.

Scotland had caught up. The contrast with England and Wales's population history is even more striking. In 1821, the population of England and Wales was just over 40 per cent larger than Ireland's; by 1901, this had grown to 700 per cent (Table 10.1). Ireland's population history time was unique in a European context. No other country experienced such decline, most saw only growth – growth, moreover, of a very high order.

Ireland's population was affected by a number of economic factors. Ireland did not experience industrialisation to anything like the extent of England, Wales or Scotland. Ireland remained overwhelmingly rural throughout this period; only eastern Ulster, specifically, Belfast, developed an industrial base worthy of comparison with the centres of British economic development in Lancashire, the Midlands, the north-east, central Scotland or south Wales. The rise of Belfast failed to offset failings in other parts of the economy. Belfast first grew to prominence with the development of factory textile production that had precipitated a decline in domestic, cottage textile production, which,

Table 10.1 Population in England and Wales, Scotland and Ireland, 1801–1901 (m)

	1801	1811	1821	1831	1841	1851	1861	1871	1881	1891	1901
England and Wales	8.9	10.1	12.0	13.9	15.1	17.9	20.1	22.7	26.0	29.0	32.5
Scotland	1.6	1.8	2.9	2.4	2.6	2.9	3.1	3.4	3.7	4.0	4.5
Ireland	6.8	7.8	8.2	6.6	5.8	5.4	5.2	4.7	5.1	4.7	4.5

Source: Census of England and Wales, Reports, 1951.

in the eighteenth century, thrived throughout Ireland and not just in Ulster. Domestic spinning and weaving had provided a vital supplementary income for small-holders in Ireland, but pressure was placed upon this way of life by the development of Lancashire cotton. Irish weavers began to leave Ireland, often going to Scotland, from the 1780s. As cheaper cotton began to pressurise producers of Irish linen, and as the industry became increasingly focused in the towns of eastern Ulster, the Irish rural dweller was left with two primary options: potato-based subsistence agriculture or emigration. The situation became bleaker for domestic cloth producers as the nineteenth century progressed.

While similar experiences were affecting handloom weavers in England, the key difference was that England offered them options. With urban and industrial growth in the 1820s and 1830s of an unknown order, the excess labour, driven out of traditional forms of work, could find labouring work in other sectors. This was much less the case in Ireland, where rural under-employment remained a deep-seated problem throughout the century. In the sphere of urban growth, for example, we can note that in 1901 Dublin and Belfast together contained fewer people than Liverpool alone. Cork, Ireland's third-placed town, was smaller than one of any major textile towns of Lancashire, for example, Preston.

If Ireland's economic problems were obviously tied to the performance of agriculture and the nature of its population, where does this leave industry in the country? While it is correct to characterise Ireland as predominantly rural and in many places economically backward, this is far from the whole story. In the early part of the nineteenth century, 40 per cent of Irishmen and women were employed in trades and handicrafts: many of them were of course based in the countryside or the small towns, and depended solely on the fortunes of agriculture, but it is enough to make us think again if we were to imagine Ireland as a nation of 'peasants' alone. Cotton was produced in Ireland from the mid-eighteenth century and was relatively highly technological, with the same innovations as affected Lancashire and Yorkshire – such as the spinning jenny – coming in to Ireland. As a result, imports of raw cotton, wool and yarn increased ten-fold between the 1780s and the 1820s. Linen and wool were Irish specialities from the early-modern period: coarse linens for the home market were matched by fine products for export. In the mid-nineteenth century, Ireland was engaged in a vigorous two-way trade in linen and flax with Scotland, which was the British Isles' other great producer of these particular types of cloth, with Dundee particularly prominent.

Ireland did not experience an Industrial Revolution to match that in Britain. Belfast was Ireland's industrial beacon, developing, as we seen, sizeable textile mills and a particular reputation, as Ireland more generally already had, for high-quality linen. Belfast's advantage, in terms of textile development, was its closeness to the most industrial parts of Britain: central-belt Scotland and Lancashire. But Belfast's advantage was gained at the cost of other places. In this sense, the wider eastern Ulster area was a beneficiary of the relentless regional specialisation that characterised Industrial Revolutions. Population grew more quickly in Belfast than in any other town in Ireland; while Dublin remained the administrative and intellectual capital of Ireland, Belfast was its industrial bedrock. Rates of pay, levels of skill and concentrations of cutting-edge technologies, for example in engineering and shipbuilding, were greater in Belfast than elsewhere. Whilst Ireland had once had a general spread of domestically-based textile production, factory-based production was almost entirely to Belfast's benefit. Ship-building – most famous on the Clyde and the Tyne – was nevertheless handsomely represented in the Belfast company of Harland and Wolff, which built big ships, such as the magnificent, if ill-fated, *Titanic* (launched in 1912). Yet, for a long time, Belfast was not the centre of Ireland's ship-building industry; then again, Ireland was not noted for ships at all. In the 1840s, Cork was the main place for Irish ships and a paltry 2,000 tons per annum (p.a.) was her output. Sixty years later, Harland and Wolff (along with the less well-known Workman Clark) were turning out 150,000 tons p.a. This remarkable development was not helped by the town's position, 12 miles from the sea, on a narrow river. Other problems, which exemplified further gaps in Ireland's opportunity for industrial development, was the lack of raw material to build ships: coal had to be brought in from Ardossan and steel from Britain, while the timber came from Scandinavia and North America.

Ireland – poor, agricultural, rural with a significant emphasis on subsistence production – could not generate the natural demand that was needed to fire entrepreneurial adventures into industrial and commercial development. The country did not lack a sophisticated banking sector and its industries could not be considered to have been universally under-capitalised: the mills of Belfast were a match, in this respect, for their British counterparts. But Ireland, despite its large (if shrinking, emigrating) population simply did not have the capital in common flow to consume industrial goods. The case of theodolites in Dublin helps to explain this point. In the 1890s, it was uneconomical to produce these expensive (£100 or so) precision instruments in batches of less than 50; yet such a number would, it has been said, supply Ireland's needs for 25 years. In seeking out British and overseas markets, Irish manufacturers of things such as theodolites founds themselves up against British and other competitors. The need to seek out international markets was not unique to Ireland by any means: Britain's economy, when compared to America's, paid lower wages, which decreased the domestic market, relied heavily on high-skill rather than technological elements, and promoted international free trade in the hope of securing and holding on to markets for its goods. America, by contrast, suffered perpetual skills' shortages, thus investing in high levels of technology, and benefiting from a huge domestic market which was protected by tariffs.

Most of Ireland's industries were traditional ones – those which were one step removed from the agricultural sector: brewing, shoe-making, distilling, food production, etc. Other elements, such as engineering, textiles, and ship-building (as opposed to boat-building) were much less widespread. Irish industry tended to have a lower ratio of horsepower per plant than was the case in England (distilling and flax manufacture were exceptions), and often employed more hands per factory: this was true of cotton, for example, where employees were 30 per cent more numerous than in England but horsepower ran at one-tenth.

It is for all these reasons – notably the fatal balance of low levels of urban growth and industrial opportunity – that Ireland developed a culture of emigration far greater than that of any other European nation. In 1860, the US emigration commissioner noted that for every Irish immigrant in America, only five remained in Ireland – the corresponding ratios for Germany and England were 1:33 and 1:42, respectively. Irish women were just as likely to leave as men: by the later century, they were more so. Even prior to the Great Famine (1845–51), more than 1m people had left Ireland; during the famine itself, hunger, disease and the hopelessness of the economic situation prompted around 1m to leave in just a decade. They were the lucky ones, for something like 1.5 million people perished due to the effects of famine and disease (see Box 10.2, p. 173).

The Great Famine broke out in the Autumn of 1845. All but one-sixth of the potato crop was ruined, although some areas escaped altogether. The infection of the potato crop was caused by a new and virulent fungus (*phytophtora infestans*) which spread with alarming speed in moist conditions, reducing the crop to a putrid mass of decaying pulp. Matters were worsened by the fact that the harvests of 1846 and 1848 were total failures; 1847 was a good year, but a shortage of seed potatoes reduced the acreage; 1849 was a partial failure, but acted disastrously when following the previous two years' shortfalls. The cottiers and farm labourers relied upon their potatoes; in the worst instances it was the sole food. This of course sharpened the problem. Moreover, unlike cereal crops, potatoes could not be stored for more than a year: hence, there was little chance of staving off three or four wiped-out harvests, even in the unlikely event that enough surplus could be grown.

Many historians have echoed the contemporary view that because of the weakness of the Irish economy, its over-population, and the poverty of its people, some kind of natural disaster was inevitable. However, despite the pessimism of contemporaries, no one could have foreseen such disaster for the potato crop. This was a new fungus – it ravaged Europe, from Silesia, in Prussia, to Ireland and the Scottish Highlands. Successive British government has been criticised by historians of all political persuasions for their failure to deal adequately with the needs of a starving population.

From 1845, things went from bad to worse. People despairingly ate their seed potatoes – ensuring survival in only the short term, and enforcing the problems associated with total failure in 1846 and 1847. Not until after 1850 did things improve. Moreover, the dislocation of people from their land, and mass emigration, reached a peak in 1851, but continued for several years after.

For political administrators in England, the true test of the Famine was the same test as Ireland always presented – a seemingly intractable political problem. *Punch*, for example, realised from bitter experience the link between Irish economic distress and her political instability. Indeed, one of the longest legacies of the Famine was to be an increasing radical dimension to Irish politics, with groups like the Young Irelanders feeding off its real and symbolic implications. With an appreciation of the problems facing Ireland and other places reliant upon the potato, *Punch*, pronounced on 1845. 'The New Year has a dejected look: for he hears the voices of millions bewailing the potato blight.'

Whatever the cause of Famine, whatever its outcomes, however hideous its extent, both Tory and Whig administrations faced assaults from both sides of the Irish Sea over failures to deal adequately with the problem (Box 10.2). The Irish expected large-scale relief; the governing classes of Britain thought this impracticable. And the reliably savage *Punch* spared no blushes in excoriating the inactivity of groups like the Privy Council. In one sharp

Box 10.2

Great Irish Famine (1845–51)

Caused when a 'potato blight' ruined year after year of the crop that was the staple foodstuff of the Irish poor. Causing hunger, disease and emigration, the famine sent Ireland's population into a spiralling decline. A figure of 8.2 m (1841) became 6.5 m in 1861. By 1901, Ireland's population, just more than 4 m, had receded to its 1780 level. The famine had a deep impact on Ireland in economic, political and cultural terms. Successive governments' failure to deal adequately with the need for poor relief caused widespread criticism, even from the traditionally conservative Catholic Church. Nationalists, such as John Mitchel, took the famine to be a sign of England's harsh colonial rule, and such an evaluation remains powerful in certain quarters. The scale of migration, and the poverty of those emigrants, created social repercussions from Toronto and New York to Newcastle.

satire, these councillors were portrayed as defining Irish hunger as 'a vulgar habit – a wretched prejudice of the common people. Nothing more.' To so many in Britain, the Irish, spared English levels of income tax, were perceived as spongers. And in various localities around the country, sympathy for the plight of the Irish was conspicuous by its absence. Witness this damning leader comment, of 12 December 1846, in the *Whitehaven Herald*:

> The Irish are by nature and habit, dirty, proud, lazy beggars, and so they shall remain till this country sees the expediency of making them shift for themselves, as do the 'thrifty sons of Scotland'.

In Ireland, too, *Punch* deduced, there were men who seemed not to serve the best interests of the country. Daniel O'Connell, for example, was upbraided regularly for his continued campaigns for repeal of the Act of Union. His continued collection of repeal rents (funds from the Irish peasantry to finance his political campaign, at home and abroad) was the source of much mileage for the terrier-like *Punch* (Box 10.4). His idea of relieving his country's distress, the paper argued, was to relieve it of £22,000 per annum. In what Foster calls 'one terrible cartoon' the potato-like O'Connell is portrayed as 'The Real Potato Blight'. Indeed, as Irish political extremism mounted a challenge, as Young Ireland gathered support for the hard line, and republican noises were heard, so *Punch's* sympathy for the Irish cause began to wane. Cartoons reduced their assaults on the English and Irish ruling class and instead turned towards the Irish threat. One such character-isation, 'The Height of Impudence', shows a poor Irishman asking John Bull, 'Spare a thrifle yer honour, for a poor Irish lad to buy ... a blunderbuss with'.

The climax of this tasteless and extreme campaign coincided with the miserable failure of the Irish Rebellion of 1848. This was *Punch's* damning critique:

> Ireland strikes us as being the Prodigal Son of England, always going astray, then coming back, repenting and being forgiven. JOHN BULL may occasionally have been a harsh parent, but we are sure the old fellow means well. It is too bad to see father and son at daggers drawn in this way. When will Ireland be a good boy, and learn to remain quiet at home?

All this, we must remember, and the Irish were dying in their thousands. Indeed, 150 years on, we are left with an image of the famine as an almost total disaster, striking all and everywhere. And it easy to be lost in the horror, in the awfulness of it all. It is easier to

Box 10.3

The condition of Ireland

Between 5 October 1846 and 7 January 1847, John Stuart Mill contributed a series of forty-three leader articles, all entitled `The Condition of Ireland', to the *Morning Chronicle*. The harsh necessities of the famine, Mill believed, offered a chance to combine the relief of destitution with a permanent improvement to economic and social conditions in Ireland. The views expressed in these writings are ones which he went on to develop more fully in his *Principles of Political Economy*. Much of this writing castigated the English ruling class and induced gasps of horror; however, in his own words: 'the profound ignorance of English politicians and the English public concerning all [Irish] social phenomena not generally met with in England (however common elsewhere) made my endeavours an entire failure.'

THE ALPHA AND OMEGA of the schemes for the relief of Ireland – the quintessence of all the propositions we hear is, give, give, give. The points on which there is diversity are only, who is to give, and whom it is to be given to. While some people are for giving themselves, some are only for making others give, and some would have no objection to make the crisis an opportunity for receiving. The cry of some persons is, let England give; and give to the peasantry, to those who are really in want. There is charity in this proposal, if not wisdom, when it comes from this side of the Irish Channel; when from the other side, it is something else; it is the conduct of him who begs for charity, which, if rarely meritorious or dignified, is excusable when there is nothing to be done. But the Irish landlords next present themselves, and exclaim, give to *us*. Lend to us below the market rate of interest, that we may pay off our mortgages; we shall then have a large income for our own use, with part of which we will employ the poor.

Source: *Morning Chronicle*, 7 October, 1846

THAT THE WASTE LANDS OF IRELAND are her best resource for the present temporary emergency – that the large and liberal relief which in a times of famine *must* be given to the peasantry in payment for labour than for idleness, and for productive labour than for unproductive, and that the reclaiming of the waste is chief, not to say the only, field which Ireland affords for employment so productive as to be remunerative – all this is agreed to by everybody, and is so obvious as to be assented to as soon as stated. Six million acres of land, of which let us even suppose that only four million are improveable – here is a mine of wealth which, by a remarkable anomaly, still remains to be worked. The rich, we have been told, could not do it, because they had not the money, or the enterprise, or for some equally good reason; the poor, because they had not the legal right.

Source: *Morning Chronicle*, 17 October 1846.

make blanket statements than it is to try and analyze. To analyze seems too cold; it seems too hard and unjust. Yet we must consider certain things. The Famine struck selectively, not everywhere; not at all times was it a story of ceaseless misery. The more prosperous in the North and Leinster avoided its worst ravages. It is often said that not many large landowners in County Cavan died during the Famine; but against such jests should be set the reality that all were fair game for disease. Those who came into close contact with the dying and diseased, particularly priests, were especially susceptible. In areas where subsistence farming was greatest, people were poorest, and least likely to survive. As a general rule, only those who farmed over 20 acres survived relatively unscathed. That meant a lot of people below that level were affected. Moreover, in these areas they relied on the potato as nowhere else. In Skibbereen, Cork, the situation was as bad as anywhere. One eye witness, a magistrate, travelled there in December 1846, carrying with him as much bread as five men could carry. When he got there he found the town deserted and entered some of the hovels:

Box 10.4

Punch and the Irish

Punch, 15 November 1845: '"Rint" v. Potatoes'. In this image, Daniel O'Connell is attacked for his decision to continue to collect 'repeal rent' (i.e. monies to support his home rule campaign) while the country was in a state of privation due to the Great Famine (1845–51).

The message is offensive to O'Connell but the physical representation is not as bad as would come later, when the Irish were increasingly represented as half-crazed apes. In 'The Irish Devil-Fish' (*Punch*, 18 June 1881), for example, Gladstone wrestles manfully with a demonic monkey-headed octopus. In the age after Darwin's *Origin of Species* (1859), and its shock revelations about the relationship between Man and monkey, simian images became key symbols by which alleged Irish barbarity was portrayed.

"RINT" *v.* POTATOES.—THE IRISH JEREMY DIDDLER.

" You haven't got such a thing as Twelve-pence about you ?—A Farthing a week—a Penny a month—a Shilling a year ? "

In the first, six famished and ghastly skeletons, to all appearances dead, were huddled in a corner on some filthy straw... their wretched legs hanging about, naked above the knees. I approached with horror, and found by low moaning they were alive ... in a few minutes I was surrounded by at least 200 such phantoms, such frightful spectres as no words can describe, either from famine or from fever. Their demoniac yells are still ringing in my ears, and their horrible images are fixed upon my brain ... The same morning the police opened a house on adjoining lands ... and two frozen corpses were found lying upon the mud floor, half devoured by rats.

In Caheragh, County Cork:

A woman and her two children were found dead and half-eaten by dogs; in a neighbouring cottage five more corpses, which had been dead several days, were lying; and Father John O'Sullivan, parish priest of Kenmare, found 'a room full of dead people'; a man, still living, was lying in bed with a dead wife and two dead children, while a starving cat was eating another dead infant.

Even in places where the Famine was not supposed to be so bad, local dignitaries and landowners were constantly visited by streams of sick and hungry women and children.

There is more to Famine than a social disaster. For a number of reasons, many British observers saw the Famine as the inevitable fate of a poor, over-populated country where seven-tenths of the population were tied to the land, and where a large proportion of those people – especially in Western Connaught and Northern Munster – lived at levels which were barely enough to subsist.

For the Irish, however, the Famine meant something else altogether. Although some nationalist leaders, like William Smith O'Brien, advocated emigration as an answer to population problems, these population problems were not seen in a Malthusian way as being solely about numbers. The Irish population problem, for the Irish was a land question – a question to which the British seemingly had all the answers. For Irishmen, then, the poverty of the Irish peasant, small farmer or landless labourer was enforced not by the notion that too many people were chasing too little land, but by the idea that the land was unfairly distributed. This is where the negative image of the absentee landlord came into its own. For many Irish imaginations Ireland's ruling elite – the landowning class – was Anglo-Irish. It was dominated by Irishmen sympathetic to the Act of Union; and English and Scots aristocrats who cared nothing for their Irish estates, milked their tenants of rents, and never visited and never improved the land.

In the 1850s, the famine came to symbolise the acutely unfair nature of Anglo-Irish relations. It was the famine years, and the turmoil of 1848, the years of revolutions which threw up the Young Irelanders, the Fenians, the constitutional home rule movement. The destruction of the Act of Union may have had its seeds in earlier times, but it was in the 1840s that an unwillingness to accept the British began to blossom. The Famine enforced the nationalist view that the system of government in Ireland, and land ownership too, was simply unfair. Moreover, the fact that, whilst the famine raged, Ireland still exported corn and livestock, really rankled the Irish. And this passed into legend – Ireland was starved. A few lines from George Bernard Shaw's play *Man and Superman* sums this up:

Malone: ... me father died of starvation in the Black '47. Maybe you heard of it?

Violet: The Famine?

Malone: (*with smouldering passion*): No, the starvation. When a country is full of food and exporting it, there can be no famine.

This view, has become the received wisdom in the nationalist romantic view of things. And, of course, this image is powerful and there is truth in it. Because of its importance, in both socio-economic and political terms, the famine has taken on mythical status.

Prior to the Famine, emigration had been a movement primarily of the more robust part of the population (emigration to America was expensive at this time). Thereafter, the movement overseas, particularly to United States, became socially pervasive, taking out poor agricultural labourers as well as tradesmen, small farmers and those of means. By 1890, 40 per cent of all the world's Irish-born *were not* living in Ireland. Britain, America, Canada and Australia and New Zealand were the most obvious destinations; all parts of the British Empire, South Africa, mainland Europe, Argentina and Brazil were among the less well-known destinations for Irish emigrants.

10.2 From Union to Famine: Britain and Ireland

The Act of Union was intended by Pitt the Younger to deliver peace and prosperity to Ireland; but its true aim was to make Britain secure in a time of war. It was a direct response to the United Irishmen's rising of 1798, a rebellion, in which 30,000 died, suppressed by the British army and Irish yeomanry. But Pitt intended the act to be accompanied by legislation to ameliorate the grievances of Irish Catholics and Dissenters. The terms of the Act also protected the Irish economy against the potential damage that might be caused by the superior power of British manufacturing. If you like, Ireland was granted special economic status until the 1820s. The Act, then, was not just the design of an oppressive regime; it had its good points and it had its progressive elements.

It is also wrong to imagine that every Irish man and woman was a nationalist and that Britain was 'bad' in all Irish eyes. The fact is that on many levels of society, Ireland and Britain were closely linked, not least through political culture, economies and migration. Before the Famine, the republican element in Irish life was tiny, and the home rule element was small. (Republicans demanded complete severance whereas home rulers were happy for Britain to maintain control of defence and imperial issues; home rulers were really federalists.)

But if the Union was better than nationalist writers have argued, we could ask: what went wrong? It might be suggested that the sequence of events goes like this: if Pitt had been able to deliver Catholic Emancipation before his death in 1806, as he had intended, then more positive issues could have been addressed in the subsequent decades. Moreover, if this had happened, the Famine would have descended on a country more able to deal with it. While most people accepted that organised religion was a positive influence on working-class people, there was a strand of anti-Catholicism running through British society which lessened sympathies for Ireland's plight.

The combination of history and culture which shapes one country's view of another certainly presented challenges to Anglo-Irish relations. While political society was, on the whole, in favour of Catholic emancipation, the King (George III), the popular press, and the mood outside Westminster, did suggest a degree of hostility to the idea of equality between Catholics and Protestants. The context for such an attitude is historical insofar as British institutional traditions were seen to be Protestant and liberal, whereas those of traditional enemies, such as France, were considered despotic and Catholic. Protestantism was a part of the national broadcloth in Britain; Catholicism came increasing to be seen as symbol of Ireland's identity (even though 20 per cent of the Irish were not Catholic). But attitudes to Ireland were shaped by the political realities of the day. Daniel O'Connell's campaign for Catholic emancipation was followed swiftly with a movement for modest home rule. Resistance to evictions, and expressions of popular protest in Ireland were far more frequently violent than in Britain. As some Irish came to articulate a vision of a country free from British rule, Britons correspondingly challenged that position, questioned the tactics of the Irish, alighted on Catholicism as a cultural problem (in terms of integration), and expressed abhorrence at a degree of social violence in the Irish countryside that was so extensive, at times, that even Karl Marx stressed its novelty (in a British context).

The Act of Union did present problems for the balance between nations in the United Kingdom. The Act brought together a country of 6.5 million (80 per cent of whom were Catholics) and three other nations, totalling 11.5 million people, who were mostly Protestant. The demographic proportions are much closer at the beginning of our period because Ireland's population is similar to that of Britain. 100 years later, Ireland population has fallen to 4 million and Britain's has more than tripled to more than 37 million. So, these Irish Catholics mattered very much in 1801. Irish immigration to Britain also increased public awareness both of Ireland and of Catholicism. By the mid-1850s, British Catholicism was enjoying a lease of life not known since the days of Henry VIII – that this was the case, was entirely due to a huge influx of Irish Catholic immigrants into the big industrial towns. So, our narrative is multi-layered.

It took the emergence of Daniel O'Connell (1775–1847) to show English administrators just what a problem Ireland was going to be. What O'Connell did, as no one had done before, was to mobilise ordinary Irish folk – peasants, as they said then – behind his massive, moral-force campaigns, first, for Catholic Emancipation, and, secondly, for home rule. O'Connell was himself a brilliant lawyer – a talent who was denied King's Counsel status because of his religion. He came from a family of prosperous Kerry landlords and was in no sense an ordinary Catholic.

One of the many things brought home in Alvin Jackson's book, *Ireland, 1798–1998* (1998), is that Ireland had an 'Orange Party' – an anti-Catholic and initially anti-democratic party – dedicated first and foremost to its own vested interest long before Edward Carson, the Edwardian Unionist, came along. It was only later that the Orange tradition saw Union with Britain as its salvation. Thus, the Orange Party of O'Connell's time – which O'Connell despised – cannot be equated precisely with the later Unionist tradition because it was not necessarily Unionist. Orange traditions in 1830 were in some respects far more anti-British than O'Connell. What the Orange Party based on Dublin Castle wanted was their own ascendancy, and if the British threatened it by being soft on Catholics, then they might well have to rule their own country. This sort of logic certainly was not absent. So be careful about imagining that all Orangemen in nineteenth-century Ireland were just like the more recent figure of Ian Paisley.

O'Connell's Catholic Association (1824), and later the New Catholic Association, represented a breakthrough to test both British and Orange resolve. It was well organised, financed by levies paid by ordinary folk, and above all developed into Britain and Ireland's first ever genuinely mass political-type movement. Monster demonstrations were held that shook the British establishment. With O'Connell deified by ordinary Catholics, but also working closely with British radicals, and with his enormous energy and terrific powers of oratory, Catholic Emancipation proved to be an unarguable case. The final moments, in the late 1820s, saw O'Connell returned for several parliamentary seats – he wasn't supposed to be, he wasn't supposed to stand; they tried to declare it illegal; but still he was swept home by Catholic Ireland. Even Wellington reluctantly talked to the King of 'this so-called emancipation'; once even the sworn enemies were using the language of anti-slavery to describe Catholics, it was only a matter of time until the case won. The Catholic Emancipation Act (1829) was a great victory for O'Connellism – that mixture of peaceable pressure and what the authorities feared was the enormous, brooding malevolent potential of the masses who supported O'Connell. But it came at a cost. O'Connellism would in the next 10 years prove the weakness of the Union and the weakness of moral-force approaches to reform.

In the 1830s, O'Connell enjoyed a brief dalliance with the British establishment. He supported Melbourne's Whigs, who dominated the decade, a move capped by the Lichfield House Compact of 1835, where this support was formalised. But Melbourne, who did little for Ireland, tested O'Connell's patience. Although there were reforms, 'Justice for Ireland', a cry uttered by many English radicals in this period, was not forthcoming. Ireland remained poor and backward; the main religion, Catholicism, did not enjoy equality with the established church (indeed the idea of an established Church of Ireland appalled Irish Catholics). But O'Connellism itself proved incapable of delivering much of what it campaigned for. O'Connell essentially had two strategies: eloquent speechifying in the House of Commons, and mass oratory on the moors and in the town squares of Ireland. Because of each of these passions and skills, O'Connell developed enemies. He also alienated the radicals who might have delivered revolution to Britain and Ireland – for revolution was anathema to O'Connell, a man who was, in fact, deeply, socially conservative. His one-time collaborator Fergus O'Connor, leader of Chartism's 'Fustian jackets and unshorn chins', denounced him for supporting the Whig–Liberals' odious Poor Law Amendment Act (1834). O'Connell gradually strayed from his Westminster alliance, launching a bid for home rule in the later 1830s. But he was not able to deliver any degree of autonomy for Ireland, because, so long as his campaign lacked even widespread support in Ireland, there was little hope of anything but minority support from British opinion.

In the 1840s, circumstances first by-passed and then swamped the ageing O'Connell. He had once used 'Monster Meetings', as *The Times* called them, to mobilise support for Catholic Emancipation, but in 1843 he committed what was, for his campaign, a tactical error. Facing pressure from the authorities, he called off a Monster Demonstration at Clontarf, near Dublin. O'Connell, who championed a moral-force approach, reacted because of the government threat to send in the troops. From this point, his influence waned.

The Famine threw Ireland into a phase of profound crisis. The effects of the disaster tested key aspects of the British–Irish relationship. It horrified and it sickened observers to see the extent of the suffering. But it also had a chilling bi-product in that it helped to modernise Irish society. Because the effects of the famine – hunger and death – impacted most heavily on the poorest of Ireland's peasantry, it swept away a large part of the Gaelic-speaking population. To this day, genocide and English culpability are key frames of references for those who align with the Sinn Fein tradition. Building on the writings of the political radical, John Mitchel, the latter-day 'bad Britain' approach to Irish history equates the Famine with the Holocaust, by claiming that it was part of a deliberate plan to exterminate some portion of Irish society. Moreover, the Famine also led to a political rising – even though this was a pathetic small-scale skirmish, led in 1848 by the literary romantics of Young Ireland, men like William Smith O'Brien.

While the nationalist notion of this phase of Irish history plays up the extent to which the Famine marked the beginning of an inevitable move towards independence, and though this is undoubtedly an exaggeration, it is fair to say that British rule in Ireland did become increasingly problematical thereafter. Moreover, even Irish political society began to develop a home rule wing which, unlike O'Connell's earlier effort, would remain intact until the middle of the First World War. The demand that Irishmen should play an increasing role in their own affairs became more perceptible in the post-1850 period.

The republican spirit of the men of 1848 lived on, and was redeveloped in the 1850s, by a new group, the Irish Republican Brotherhood, or the Fenians. Fenians took the fight to Britain in quite a different way from the previous generation of radical agitators and romantic rebels. The Fenians were professional operators; their organisational skills derived from the recruitment of military men like John Boyle O'Reilly from the British army, and, later, from the inrush of new blood from the ranks of the American Irish who had been battle-hardened in the American Civil War (1861–5). Like army units, like the modern-day Irish Republican Army (IRA), the Fenians were organised into cells, with complex chains of command. They raised money in America and were able to infiltrate Catholic church networks at parish level in towns and cities where the Irish were numerous, not least in the north of England.

By the mid-1860s, Britain was in a state of heightened alarm at the thought that a Fenian army might be about to rise up from the ranks of the Irish population. There was a bombing campaign on what we today refer to as 'the mainland', and various daring raids were made. In 1867–8, a raid on Chester Castle was thwarted, a policeman was killed in a daring rescue of two Fenian leaders from a Manchester prison van, and a number of civilians were blown up in a bungled bomb attack on Clerkenwell prison. The impact of these events was staggering. Like so many things in Irish history, matters went well for the British and then badly. At first, public opinion was outraged. Then, when the decision was made to hang three men who cannot in all conscience be said to have been responsible for firing a single bullet, liberal opinion, and much Irish opinion, turned on the government. John Bright branded the Home Secretary a coward for not commuting the sentence; Irish nationalists, such as the journalist A.M. Sullivan, used the 'Manchester Martyrs', as they became known, as a stick to beat English rule in Ireland.

The true effects of Fenianism are difficult to deduce. Gladstone is said to have been convinced of the need to 'pacify Ireland' following the Fenian excesses. But Irish historians debate whether the Fenians were either democratic or revolutionary; most doubt their military threat. Their rising in Dublin in 1867 was yet another damp squib for the militants. But the Fenians were great publicists and they did win over a significant proportion of young Irish men to the cause. What is more, Isaac Butt's Amnesty Association (1868) – a group formed to campaign to free Irish Fenian prisoners – led directly into a constitutional movement for repeal of the act of Union. Gladstone's first ministry (1868–74) also pushed a Land Act through parliament, disestablished the Church of Ireland, and generally did more for the Irish than any previous administration. But as with previous, as well as later reforms, this concession was not enough. Two striking features of

Charles Stewart Parnell (1846-91)

An Irish Protestant landlord, who, after being elected MP for Meath in 1875, rapidly succeeded to Isaac Butt's position of leader of the Irish Party in the House of Commons. Fabled as the 'Uncrowned King of Ireland', his presence and charisma, as well as his critical perspective upon Britain's role in Ireland, enabled him to win over widespread Catholic support. He pushed Gladstone to land reform, and eventually (1886) to throw the Liberal Party decisively behind the home rule cause.

Dogged by personal controversy, he survived an accusation of complicity in murder when it was revealed the key evidence, a body of letters, had been forged. However, fathering a number of children by Kitty O'Shea, the wife of one his lieutenants, Captain O'Shea, scandalised Victorian morality when Parnell was named in the subsequent divorce case. Abandoned by Gladstone, the Church and half of his party, Parnell quickly fell from grace, dying at a young age.

British policy in Ireland emerge: first, that amelioration was often accompanied by coercion; secondly, that what was delivered usually came 'too little, too late'.

10.3 The constitutional fight for home rule, 1870s–1914

The career of Isaac Butt, Tory-minded lawyer and friend of Disraeli, was important because it facilitated the later exertions of Charles Stewart Parnell (1845–91). When Parnell came to the Commons as a young MP for Meath in 1875, Butt already had in place a more or less coherent party, and an organisation called the Home Government Association (HGA) (1870), dedicated to pulling togther what was a disparate range of home rule supporters. Butt, though, was not an effective leader, and he had none of Parnell's charisma.

Home rule was not independence. Gladstone had intended it to be a final answer to Ireland's political problems, bolstered by reforms to aid her economic malaise. Most Irish people even in the 1900s, would have been happy with home rule – and many, if not Gladstone, saw it as a satisfactory sort of halfway house between complete freedom and unity under the act of 1801. But critics and nationalists alike, for different reasons, saw any such constitutional concession as the first step to independence.

Parnell's rise was rapid. He quickly developed a reputation as a radical. He campaigned to free the Fenian prisoners, as Butt had done, and along with J.C. Biggar, the Cavan MP, indulged in filibustering – a tactic whereby legislation was simply talked out of parliamentary time. (Their success led to the creation of the still operable 'Guillotine Motion' against irrelevant and overly lengthy speechifying.) By 1870, Parnell had ascended to the presidency of the Home Rule Confederation of Great Britain, which had replaced the

HGA. From 1880 he chaired the Irish party at Westminster and was leader of the Land League. As we shall see, this was a prodigious coming together of powers.

Parnell worried British politicians. He was radical and daring; he spoke in threatening terms, maintaining what Conor Cruise O'Brien brilliantly described as 'a vague penumbra of revolution'. He was able, by the end of his career, to hold popular audiences behind him and to negotiate with the Queen's ministers. It was the darker side to him – his black threats and his generally anti-English disposition (a view he inherited from his American mother) – which enabled him to win the support of extreme planks within the nationalist movement, not least some of the old Fenians. But Parnell was a man of wealth, place and history; he was also a Protestant and a landowner. His uncle had sat in Henry Grattan's legendary parliament of the 1780s, and he had attended Cambridge, from where he was sent down in disgrace. This series of social connections gave him *gravitas* in the House of Commons. Yet his extremism, and his willingness, indeed his desire and (for financial reasons) need, to court radical American Irish support, bolstered further his image as a demagogue.

The late 1870s were propitious years for the young Parnell. Two decades of rising prices and agricultural prosperity nose-dived, in 1879, into the worst depression in Ireland since the Great Famine. Land again became a pressing issue (in fact, it always had been). From the unrest, violence and general discontent emerged a movement, the Land League, designed and controlled by John Devoy, an American Fenian. Devoy was impressed with Parnell's pro-Fenian rhetoric. Here, Devoy thought, was a man who might bring together the three crucial blocs of Irish politics: Fenianism, constitutionalism and agrarianism. Devoy proposed the 'New Departure'. Such a coming together, in just this way, did occur under Parnell's increasingly powerful leadership, but it was an alliance with which Parnell himself was uneasy. Parnell knew the problems of courting the extreme wings; but he did admire the Fenian bravery. And he knew land was everything to a country without an Industrial Revolution to speak of. The Land League, under Parnell, brought together a consensus of parliamentarians, radicals and farmers in a way that changed Irish politics. It also brought in money and supporters from the Irish Diaspora.

Against the pseudo-respectability of Parnell sat a background of growing agrarian militancy, dubbed the Land War. Cattle-maiming, rick-burning, attacks and murder were becoming commonplace. Ireland had a reputation as a violent society and at this point it was becoming more so, as people struggled with the crippling effects of agricultural depression. Gladstone's second ministry came to power in 1880, with the Prime Minister himself committed still further to ameliorating Ireland's woes. But, like all Victorian premiers, Gladstone found Ireland a place of conundrums: in order to make legislation work, he needed the people of Ireland to obey the rule of law; but the rule of law in Ireland, at times of trouble, so often seemed to need coercion. Duly, along with another Land Act (1881) – this time guaranteeing the old Young Ireland demand of the 3 'F's (fixity of tenure, fair rent and freedom of sale) – came a measure of coercion. The Irish secretary W.E. Forster impressed coercion with especial alacrity and thus negated the effects of what was an important Land Act.

Meanwhile, Parnell was in a quandary. He needed to appear tough on the English, but he also knew that his best hope for home rule was to carry Gladstone's Liberals with him. By fronting the Land League – an organisation that was complicit in the Land War – Parnell, the noted historian Roy Foster (1988) claims, was 'riding the tiger'. Never was this clearer than in 1881–2, when the tiger nearly savaged him. Gladstone pressured Parnell to support the Land Act; instead, he demanded that Test Cases be put before tribunals. Forster felt Parnell was working against the act and had Parnell thrown into Kilmainham Gaol in October 1881. The next six months would nearly break, but ultimately make, Parnell. Extremists favoured a rent strike; violence grew; conditions deteriorated. In April 1882, Parnell struck a deal with Gladstone – the 'Kilmainham Treaty' as it was known – whereby he agreed to support the act while the act was amended to help tenants in arrears. Forster was sickened by the deal with Parnell and resigned; the Fenian element in the Land League was outraged that Parnell had compromised. He might have been sunk had not events saved him. On 6 May 1882, as the new Irish Secretary, Lord Frederick Cavendish, strolled in Phoenix Park, Dublin, with his under-secretary, T.H. Burke, the two men were attacked and horribly murdered by men wielding surgical knives. After three years of Land War and extremism, the Phoenix Park Murders pushed things back the way of constitutionalists such as Parnell. He dissolved the Land League in October of that year and replaced it with the Irish National League. He then embarked on a period of development that would see Parnellism, and Irish home rule, established in politics.

Parnell continued to strengthen his position, not least by making the Irish Party in Westminster perhaps the first modern political party. Members were tied by a party whip – 'The pledge', as it was called. This agreement to vote *en masse* on Irish issues, or when the party hierarchy said so, gave them a solidity and identity in excess of any other party of the 1880s or before. The Redistribution Act of 1885 also favoured Parnell by giving Ireland more MPs that its population merited. But relations with the Liberals – relations that perhaps Parnell did not yet realise were vital – became strained. The later years of Gladstone's ministry were disastrous, particularly on imperial questions, not least with the death of General Gordon at Khartoum. Parnell, ever anxious to press the Irish cause, courted the Conservatives in the hope that they might do something the Liberals so far had not. At this stage, we must bear in mind, Gladstone had made no public pledge to support home rule. The Conservatives came to power and Salisbury – an imperial Unionist – tried to buy off Parnell with the Ashbourne Act, which furthered the provision of the 1881 Land Act. Lord Canaervon, one of the architects of Federalism in Canada, told Parnell that the Tories would accept a similar solution to Ireland's needs. T.P. O'Connor, one of Parnell's trusted lieutenants, and the only Irish MP to win a mainland British seat, was charged with the job of turning Irish voters in Britain from Liberal to Tory. There is every reason to think that many people simply ignored the ploy. The 1885 election saw the Conservatives with a majority of 96 over the Liberals – exactly the same number as the total of Irish MPs under Parnell. Parnell's dalliance with the Conservatives came to an end when the federal scheme was ditched and when Gladstone's son made public the revelation that his father was now fully converted to Home Rule. This changed the political ground.

Although Parnell did not know it, this marked the end for Parnellism. Parnell was about to be struck by a series of personal body blows, but these did not end his political life as surely as Gladstone's conversion to home rule. Parnellism – it being the finest example yet of Ireland's constitutional wing at work – relied on holding on to the coat-tails of one of the main British parties. Parnell has been described by Alvin Jackson as 'a vicious technician of power whose personal and political sins were for long contained, but in the end combined to ensure his downfall'. Parnell's clearest route to success was through converting the Liberals, or, less likely, the Tories, to the delivery of home rule. By playing a game of political bargains while enjoying a (for the time) sordid personal life, Parnell was taking huge risks.

Once Gladstonian Liberalism had thrown its weight behind home rule, we might ask, what was Parnell and his party's role? While Parnell had been supremely effective in the early 1880s, his position was undermined by the adoption of his only policy by one of the big parties. Thus, while Parnell was known as the 'uncrowned king' of Ireland, and though many of the people loved him as such, his political position was perhaps bound to be as second fiddle. Moreover, in the second half of the decade, following his conversion, the 'People's William' became, if anything, more popular – and certainly more powerful – than any Irish leader of that time. The fact that Gladstone's first home rule bill of 1886 was defeated does not alter this material fact. So long as revolution was out of the question, it was up to Britain to give Ireland back its freedom. Thus, Parnell was a pawn.

In the end, events beyond his control overtook Parnell. His political life and personal reputation was threatened in 1887 when *The Times* published what turned out to be forged letters accusing Parnell of supporting agrarian crime. In 1889, one of Parnell's party, Captain O'Shea, filed for divorce from his wife, Kitty, citing Parnell as co-respondent. O'Shea knew Parnell had been having an affair with her since the 1880s; in fact, he used the knowledge to bribe Parnell and to gain political office. In the meantime, Mrs O'Shea bore Parnell three children in what must be seen, even in our own times, as a very bizarre and bohemian example of cuckolding. The news scandalised the double-standards Victorian morality. In November 1890, Gladstone took a conventional moral tone and let it be known that, in his view, home rule could not be delivered while Parnell led the party. The Catholic Church also denounced him. The party split on the issue, 43 Parnellites breaking away from 27 who remained with the chief. Parnell then embarked on an epic political campaign in Ireland. He sought to have his own men elected to various seats, but they were defeated; he played the Fenian card, appealing to the marginal men, but he failed. On 6 October 1891, exhausted, bitter, broken, defeated, Parnell died. He was 45. In the 1890s, Gladstone tried – and failed – twice more to have home rule put on to the statute books. The in-built Tory majority in the Lords ensured that it did not happen. Gladstone died seven years after Parnell. He also had been defeated by Ireland.

10.4 A long coda to the nineteenth-century 'Irish Question'

Between 1894 and 1914 there were numerous attempts to ameliorate Ireland's ills with progressive Land Legislation. The Wyndham Act of 1903 was the most radical yet, making provision for tenant ownership of much Irish land. The Unionists called this 'killing home rule with kindness'. But it did not work. In the 1900s, the Parnellites and anti-Parnellites, who had split in 1891, came back together under the tutelage of John Redmond. In 1914, the home rule legislation that moderate nationalists craved was finally put on the statute books; but war meant it was held up by the Suspensory Act until hostilities ceased. But by the time the last shells had been fired on the Western front, late in 1918, H.H. Asquith – inheritor of Gladstone's Irish mantle – had been deposed, Catholic Ireland had become more radicalised, and Unionism was in the ascendant with many British politicians on the conservative wing, and was dominant in Ulster.

Gladstone had under-estimated the animosity that Ulster's Protestant population felt for home rule. He was also wrong to believe that home rule could be the final step. The willingness of men such as Edward Saunderson and, later, Sir Edward Carson, to use the language of violence and of civil war in a sense masked the very real willingness of some Ulster people to fight for their rights against the nationalists. The battle over home rule was, for Unionists in Ireland, primarily an argument about maintaining social and economic advantage. In general, Catholics did very badly on all the main socio-economic indices. Orangemen and Unionists and Protestants occupied the best jobs among the working class and dominated the political elite in Dublin, at least till the Edwardian period when there was a 'greening of Dublin Castle' (an increasing degree of support for measures of reform and a weakening of the Orange power bloc). The Tory Party was itself – by inclination – a part of empire and of union. By the 1900s, 'Unionist' was the preferred name of many candidates for that party. In the 1880s, a coherent and sometimes vehemently anti-Catholic Unionism was promulgated not just by Saunderson but also by British politicians, such as Randolph Churchill, father of Winston. Churchill's famous exhortation 'Ulster will fight, and Ulster will be right', echoed long afterwards among those who opposed home rule. In 1885 Irish unionists formed the Irish Loyal and Patriotic Unionist Alliance and in 1886 a more extreme group, the Loyalist Anti-Repeal Union, was founded by Belfast Orangemen.

The 1880s had seen a growing awareness of racial issues, and this is how Ireland's politics increasingly came to be seen. The Gaelic Athletics Association propagated a pride in Irish sports, and the cultural nationalist revolution, which spawned or influenced a wide range of writers such as Lady Gregory, Douglas Hyde, J.M. Synge, W.B. Yeats, James Joyce and Sean O'Casey. These writers emphasised the importance of Celticism, Irish language and Ireland's difference from Britain. By contrast, Unionists affirmed their Scottish heritage or asserted their right to govern because of an Anglo-Saxon superiority. At grass-roots level, this divided Ireland mentality was perhaps best expressed through, on the Unionist side, the Orange Order and Presbyterianism, and, on the other, the Irish Republican Brotherhood, the Ancient Order of Hibernians and Catholicism. A divided Irishness – which would not have been fully appreciated in Daniel O'Connell's day – was taking over Ireland. Ireland was seen increasingly as a Celtic Catholic entity; Britain was the state which Unionists and Orangemen embraced.

Progressive Protestants provided nationalist movements with some of their most important leaders, dating from Wolfe Tone to Parnell; nor should we overlook the fact that Dublin had a Protestant Unionist grouping too. But the polarities of Ireland's religions and of her geography were becoming more apparent. There was also a class dimension, with trades unions and working-men's societies wrapping themselves in flags of convenience. On the nationalist side, Jim Larkin and James Connolly organised unskilled Catholic workers around the twin themes of class war and nationalist uprising, while their Protestant equivalent, William Walker, a Belfast working-class leader, preached Orange socialism in an old Testament language pregnant with dark foreboding.

Irish politics ebbed and flowed at Westminster; but the issues never went away. It came to the fore again when Asquith and Lloyd George's wide-ranging social reform programme was supported by the Irish under Redmond. Asquith won a much-reduced majority in 1910, after the Lords had defeated his 'People's Budget'. Asquith determined to fix the Lords, and this, and the Liberals' weakened parliamentary presence, increased the strength of the Irish Party and improved the prospect of home rule. The war, of course, interrupted the flow. The home-rule legislation, agreed in 1914, lay in suspended animation for the duration of the conflagration. Redmond refused to join the war-time coalition cabinet, while his Unionist enemies, Carson and Andrew Bonar Law, did join, thus providing a formidable Unionist presence at the heart of war-time government.

The war was to be a time of growing radicalisation in Ireland. War delivered, for nationalists, what peace-time could not; and it did so in a very different fashion than had been anticipated by O'Connell, Parnell or Redmond. The formation, in 1905, of Sinn Fein, threatened Redmond's domination of Irish politics. Sinn Fein was a mixed bag: some were opposed to Redmond's home-rule reformism, others were willing to work alongside for a while (on the grounds that Gladstonian home rule was the first step). Arthur Griffith fell into the moderate camp. Griffith argued for a dual Anglo-Irish monarchy such as existed in Austria–Hungary, so the revolutionary line was far from dominant even at this late stage. Sinn Fein was an abstentionist party: just as it has been in recent years. It only contested one general election before 1918.

On the Unionist side, in 1912, Sir Edward Carson led his Unionists in swearing to fight against home rule. 'Ulster's Solemn League and Covenant' declared that if a home rule parliament was thrust upon them, 'we solemnly and mutually pledge ourselves to refuse to recognise its authority'. Ulster was offering, yet again, its conditional loyalty: if it did not get its way, it would refuse to bow to any wider notion of the will of the people. In 1913, the stakes were increased when Lord Roberts, hero of the Boer War, helped Carson to establish the Ulster Volunteer Force (UVF). Soon, General Sir George Robertson, veteran of the Indian Army, had 100,000 men openly drilling. Politics in Ireland was at crisis point when two of the empire's most distinguished soldiers were so opposed to the home rule cause that they would break the law and risk civil war and possible charges of treason. We should not, therefore, underestimate the depths of resolve which Unionists, too, could muster. Carson was behaving in no different a way than the Young Irelanders or the Fenians of earlier years: yet he was getting away with it because the British establishment was not sure what it wanted. It wanted Ireland gone – but what to do with Ulster?

The degree of Ireland's (and Britain's) problems were demonstrated still further when in 1914, in what became known as the 'Curragh Mutiny', the Lieutenant-General of Ireland, Sir Arthur Paget, refused to move troops into Ulster. 'The railway union is Orange to a man', he declared; 'they'll never move my troops'. In reality he feared the Ulster tinder-box and thought deploying troops would guarantee civil war. Winston Churchill, who opposed his father's Unionist position, was appalled; Woodrow Wilson, the US president declared: 'Carson ought to be hanged for treason'; the Prime Minister, Asquith, lamented: 'I have rarely felt more hopeless in a practical affair.' The nationalist reaction to the UVF was to form, in 1913, the Midland Volunteer Force (later the Irish Volunteers); within 10 months 180,000 men had enlisted. With each move, the stakes seemingly spiralled upwards.

The Unionist tendencies of all British governments tended to shine through. Otherwise home rule, indeed independence, would have been granted years before. But during the war, biases became entrenched and conflict in Ireland seemed increasingly likely. The

UVF was allowed to enlist *en masse* as the 36th Ulster division, whereas the Irish Volunteers were barred from a similar privilege. This meant that if the Ulster men came home, they would be better soldiers than their paramilitary nationalist enemies; or so it was in theory. Gun-running also increased during the war as Irish nationalists, such as Michael Collins, recognised the old adage that England's difficulty was Ireland's opportunity. Yet before 1916, nationalism remained the possession of a small minority of Irish Catholics. Home rulers were abundant – but revolutionaries remained hard-core and small in number. Sean O'Casey looked on in horror and disgust that so many Irish men were clamouring to find 'a poppy-mobbed grave in Flanders'. The Irish Republican Brotherhood (IRB), however, remained committed to a rising.

The Dublin Rising of 1916 raised again questions that had long been asked of the Act of Union and of the Anglo-Irish connection. But it also raised yet again the question of how committed Ireland was to the nationalist position. The rising, like many such actions before (1798, 1803, 1848, 1867) exposed the frailty of Irish nationalist support, as well as demonstrating the gallantry of the few. The government, which had direct access to Germany military codes, and could read German messages by this time, knew arms were threatening the security of Ireland. But they knew nothing of a full-scale rising: this was a first in Irish history, for usually British intelligence was ahead of the insurrectionists. The IRB duped Eoin MacNeill, the leader of the Volunteers, into believing their arms were to be confiscated. MacNeill opposed a general rising and, as a supporter of the suspended home rule act, said he would not participate in a general rising. However, he was tricked by a forged document; by the time he realised it, it was too late. The Rising was doomed before it started. News got out that Sir Roger Casement, the gun-runner for the IRB, had been captured along with the arms.

James Connolly and Patrick Pearse went ahead, marching their Volunteers and the Citizens Army through Dublin to the Post Office where they holed up for five days. Connolly told his men that they were no longer a Citizens Army but members of the Army of the Irish Republic. Eamon De Valera's troops fought some of the most determined campaigns of the short rising, killing and wounding more than 230 British troops. Patrick Pearse read a declaration of Irish freedom to the people on Dublin's streets, but the republic was short-lived. British troops assembled around the GPO building and shelled it. Little fighting occurred outside Dublin, thus demonstrating, as on previous occasions, that support for such actions tended to be localised and did not act as a trigger for general revolution. When the Rising was over, and Pearse, Connolly, De Valera and others were arrested, the reaction in Ireland was one of outrage against their mission. Irishmen died on both sides, but Irish public opinion was incensed that the rising had occurred when so many Irish were giving of their lives in France.

Within a few weeks, however, attitudes changed. As with the Manchester Martyrs, the state, in pursuing a hard line (however normal or understandable that might be under wartime conditions), alienated public opinion which had previously been on its side. More than 100 people were tried and 90 were sentenced to death, first among whom was Pearse. On Wednesday 3 May, Pearse, Tom Clarke and Thomas MacDonagh went to their deaths at Kilmainham Gaol. Four others died the next day, including Pearse's younger brother. On Friday, John MacBride, husband of the suffragette, Maud Gonne, was despatched. What really changed opinion to favour of these martyrs was what has been viewed as the excessive bloodthirstiness of Sir John Maxwell, who had arrived in Ireland as the new Commander-in-Chief on Easter Friday. James Connolly had to be strapped to a chair to face his firing squad, because his foot had been shattered in the fighting at the GPO. His companion, Sean McDermott, who went to his death the same way on the same day, wrote a final letter stating: 'You ought to envy me. The cause for which I die has this week been rebaptized during the past week by the blood of as good men as ever trod God's earth.'

Death is relative; but small numbers can sometimes seem much larger. Fifteen men were shot after the Rising. Perhaps we can appreciate Maxwell's position better when we consider the context in which the Easter Rising was set. In February the same year, thousands had died at Verdun in a battle that raged for a year; and on 1 July a battle began on the River Somme on the Western front that would eventually kill or wound 600,000. But Irish opinion turned on the government. There were also noises of dissent from America, where there was a strong Irish lobby, and transatlantic fears hardened, in some circles, into anti-Englishness. This presented potential problems considering that the British were attempting to persuade the Americans to join the war: indeed, this American hostility may be what saved Eamon De Valera from execution, for he was American-born. It certainly led to the release of men such as Michael Collins, who had been involved on the periphery of 1916, but would be a leader in the Anglo-Irish War of 1919–21.

War with Britain, and division between the two Irelands was perhaps inevitable. There could be no turning back from 1916. Some still hoped that the home rule act would become law once the war was over; but Carson and the one-time Conservative Prime Minister, Andrew Bonar Law, were ensuring that this would never be. And the end of Redmond, who, like his party, died in 1918, added to the likelihood that radicals and the Unionists would both win a victory. The Anglo-Irish War was to ensure that southern Catholic nationalists got what they perceived as the first taste of genuine political freedom since 1801. A Civil War was meant to ensure that Carson's Ulster remained part of Britain – but, in a somewhat ironic twist, given Carson's opposition to the idea, Ulster actually gained effective home rule from Britain.

10.5 Conclusion

Historians are always likely to ask counterfactual – what if? – questions. Could things have been handled differently? Undoubtedly, the absence of war would have resulted in home rule for Ireland – what Ireland got, a Free State, cost them dear in terms of lives. But Ulster would have fought against inclusion in that Free State. Perhaps, then, a divided Ireland was inevitable? Redmond and others liked to believe that if they persuaded London of the efficacy of home rule then Ulster would come on side – in other words, they believed Carson's bluff could be called. This was wrong.

The problems of England and Ireland were increased by their close proximity. Ireland was strategic. Lord Spencer, the Lord Lieutenant of Ireland in 1887, pointed out: 'The geographical position of Ireland, the social and commercial connections between the two renders such a thing [home rule] impossible.' Besides, there was always the risk that Ireland would want more freedoms than had been granted to a mere former colony such as South Africa.

But a certain portion of Irish society can argue with some justification that Britain has blood on her hands; generation after generation of administrators, many of them well-meaning, had failed Ireland. Even within an imperial context – and we cannot judge Salisbury or 'Bloody' Balfour by our standards – Britons were just too mean-spirited with the Irish. Roger Casement, who was executed for high treason, was castigated in the press when entries from his diary, which exposed his homosexuality, were photographed and circulated by British authorities. John Redmond, leader of the Irish Party in the Commons, refused to campaign on Casement's behalf because of it.

The paradoxes of Anglo-Irish relations are captured in attitudes towards Casement. Casement had fallen in with the Germans who violated Belgian neutrality, thus causing the series of events that spiralled into the First World War. By law, he was a traitor and was dealt with accordingly. To an Irish nationalist, however, he was a martyr to the cause of Irish independence. Thus, his final speech is regarded, from this latter position, as a pronunciation to compare with the great final flurries of any Irish leader since Robert Emmet, who was executed in 1803 for leading a rebellion. Casement captured the Anglo-Irish problem, from one perspective, in telling fashion:

> If true religion rests on love, it is equally true that loyalty rests on love. The law I am charged under has no parentage in love, and claims the allegiance of today on the ignorance and blindness of the past … Loyalty is a sentiment not a law. It rests on love, not restraint. The government of Ireland by England rests on restraint, and not on law; and since it demands no love, it can evoke no loyalty.

◼ Summary

◆ Britain and Ireland had a troubled relationship during this period.

◆ Ireland followed a divergent economic path, with low levels of industrial and urban growth and a falling population, which contrasted with the experiences of England, Wales and Scotland.

◆ The Famine of the 1840s was a pivotal moment in Irish history, but it exacerbated, rather than created, the social, economic and political problems with which it is associated.

◆ The Irish experienced the highest levels of emigration in Europe.

◆ Irish political issues – most expressly the battle over Home Rule – came to dominate later Victorian politics.

◆ The First World War (1914–18) finally tipped the balance in favour of Home Rule, but the century before hand had seen a growing pressure for degrees of reform and independence.

◼ Points to discuss

◆ Why was Ireland's relationship with Britain so troubled in this period?

◆ What was the importance of Daniel O'Connell?

◆ What effect did the Great Famine have on Irish society?

◆ What was Parnellism and how effective was it?

◆ Why was Gladstone so interested in Ireland?
◆ What was the importance of Ireland's revolutionary tradition?
◆ How does Ireland compare with the UK's other Celtic countries? (see also chapter 11)

▉ References and further reading

J.C. Beckett, *The Making of Modern Ireland, 1603–1923* (1966).

R.F. Foster, *Modern Ireland, 1603–1972* (1988).

K.T. Hoppen, *Ireland Since 1800: Conflict and Conformity* (2nd edn, 1999).

Alvin Jackson, *Ireland, 1798–1998* (1998).

Donal A. Kerr, '*A Nation of Beggars': Priests, People and Politics in Famine Ireland, 1846–1852* (Oxford, 1994).

F.S.L. Lyons, *Ireland since the Famine* (1972).

C. Ó Gráda, *Ireland Before the Famine and After* (Manchester, 1988).

C. Ó Gráda, *Ireland: A New Economic History 1780–1930* (Oxford, 1994).

Wales and Scotland

 Introduction

People today talk of *Britain* as a country, forgetting that Scotland, England, Wales and Northern Ireland are countries, and that today, the United Kingdom of Great Britain and Ireland is an amalgam of them. Britain is a little less than the United Kingdom (Northern Ireland *less*, to be precise), but its simplest logic is no less than that of the United Kingdom – a series of acts of parliament that confer political union on the peoples of its constituent countries.

The relationship between the various countries of the United Kingdom is currently under political review. Devolution in Scotland, an assembly for Wales, and progress since the 'Good Friday Agreement' in Northern Ireland, have questioned the immutability of the United Kingdom and Britain, both as a nation (that is, a people) and as a state (that is, a political entity). These four nations have a long and complex history. It is hard to raise Scottish or Welsh issues separately in books on nineteenth-century Britain because, with one notable exception, the master narrative of singular, national unity seems unchallenged. Where it was challenged – and challenged with great ferocity – in Ireland, then both the heat and light were sufficient to deafen and blind us to happenings elsewhere in what the English patronisingly referred to as the 'Celtic Fringe'.

This chapter is not a study of Welsh and Scottish nationalism. Although these issues are addressed, the purpose of the chapter is to look more broadly at the histories of Wales and Scotland in the context of British history; in effect, to try to see Britain's history from the Welsh or Scottish perspectives. To this end, the chapter considers social and economic factors as well as the cultural and political elements of life. However, Ireland's history and the political 'Irish Question' is so turbulent in our period, and so important to the wider story of British history, that it is dealt with separately in Chapter 10.

Key issues

▶ How did traditional society in Wales and Scotland fare in this period?

▶ How strong were Scottish and Welsh identities in this period?

▶ What parts of Scotland and Wales shared British economic prosperity in this period?

11.1 Contexts

In 1801, when Ireland was drawn by Act of Parliament into the union known as the United Kingdom, Scotland and Wales had the lowest populations of the four countries. Wales, the first of the home nations to lose its independent status, has always been counted along with England for the purposes of population censuses. Scotland, in 1801, was considerably smaller than Ireland. Levels of urbanisation in Scotland and Ireland were similar, and, though Irish society was more traditional and pastoral than Scotland's, the two countries both had large populations of poor, marginal cultivators. Whereas Ireland's cottier population was spread throughout the country, however, Scotland's cottar or crofter populace was mainly to be found in the north, and particularly on the west coast and in the Hebrides. During the course of the nineteenth century, parts of Wales and Scotland would maintain the sort of traditional rural societies that were comparable to Ireland's.

But other regions of Wales and Scotland also experienced levels of industrialisation and urbanisation that were unheard of outside the Belfast area of eastern Ulster. By 1861, a majority of the Scottish population was found in towns. Indeed, one of the most remarkable features of the comparative history of these countries is the way in which Ireland's population fell while those of England and Wales and Scotland grew. Indeed, the populations of Scotland and Wales came purposefully to reflect the demands of industrial society. Despite the vagaries of economic life in parts of the north, Scotland's population increased dramatically in the nineteenth century, nearly doubling from 2.37m in 1801 to 4.47m a century later. The West of Scotland, especially Strathclyde, sucked in a still larger share of the nation's populace: up from 628,528 (26.6 per cent) in 1831 to 1,976,640 (44.2 per cent) in 1901. Equally, other parts of rural western Scotland were de-populated in similar fashion to other country areas.

In Wales, growth was even more dramatic, if from a more modest base, and finishing with a smaller total than Scotland. In 1801, the population of Wales was 587,000; by 1921, the figure was five times larger at 2.66m. Like Scotland, Wales's population explosion was regional: Glamorgan and Monmouthshire, as key industrial counties, experienced the greatest population growth: they had just 116,000 people in total in 1801, and 1.52m in 1911. At the beginning these two accounted for 20 per cent of the Welsh population; by the later date, this proportion stood at 60 per cent. Other counties, in the north and west (Cardiganshire, Anglesey, Camarthen and Flintshire) also experienced absolute growth. While Swansea, Cardiff, Edinburgh, Aberdeen and Dundee became important commercial and industrial centres in the Celtic and wider British world, it was Glasgow that stood out. Placed at the centre of one of the most highly industrialised regions in the world, it grew by 1914 to more than 1m inhabitants – a size equalled (outside London) by Liverpool alone. These two great ports also shared a less praiseworthy distinction: they were the unhealthiest places in Britain in 1891. Even with high death-rates, however, Glasgow had become the empire's second city by the eve of war in 1914.

While British identity was to some degree shaped by perceptions of the 'Celtic Fringe' as outsider or apart from the nation, not all of Wales, Scotland or Ireland fitted this model. While the Catholic poor of Ireland or the cottar class in the Hebrides, with their own linguistic and cultural heritage, were indeed conceived of as different, Ulster Protestants, the Dublin ruling elite, central and lowland Scots, and the Welsh of the southern industrial belt, were very much part of a wider British identity. Vessels built on the Clyde were fired by Welsh coal supplied as they were being despatched to defend the world's largest empire. This chapter is as much concerned with economic and social inter-connections within the British Isles as with the cultural varieties of the Celtic countries of these isles.

11.2 Culture and society

Wales

Despite being the first of the Celtic countries to be drawn into formal political relations with England, Wales certainly maintained as many levels of distinctive cultural and national identity as did any of the Celtic countries. Wales' language remained (and remains) strong, particularly in the north and west, but, in the nineteenth century, not exclusively so. The emergence of a vigorous, evangelical, dissenting religious tradition also marked Welsh history in this period to an even greater degree than the same influences would mark religious life in northern Scotland or the north-east of England, where, respectively, indigenous Catholicism, Free Presbyterianism and Primitive Methodism took a strong hold. Perhaps only Ireland, with its deeply scored sectarian divide between the Catholic majority and an Ulster Scots Protestant minority surpasses Wales in this regard.

At the same time, South Wales was very much part of a wider British project of industrial development and urban growth. Though distinctive national characteristics and cultural traits could of course survive the homogenising effects of migration, market economics and urban development, Wales, like Scotland, did develop at least two different economies. In each case, we must give adequate cognisance to this fact.

A relative decline in the importance of the countryside occurred in Wales as well as England, and this led to a re-orientation in standard images of 'Welshness'. While Wales maintained a strong pastoral identity, and continued to conjure images of rolling green hills and valleys, it also came to be associated with notions of (then) advanced modernity: coal-mines, iron-works and towns. Nonconformity came to occupy a vital place in the concept of being Welsh: more than 80 per cent of the country was recorded in the 1851 religious census as being outside the established church. Anglicanism had been under assault in Wales since the eighteenth century but, in the nineteenth century, reactions against Anglican privilege consumed much public energy and became a burning issue of the day. The position of the established church was weakened by Welsh pressures but also by those of Irish immigrants who overwhelmingly were Roman Catholic. These immigrants faced considerable hostility from the Welsh, notwithstanding a shared disregard for Anglicanism.

Like the Irish and Scots, the Welsh also played a crucial part in the building of the British Empire, as soldiers, civil servants and adventurers. The Celtic regiments who fought bravely against overwhelming odds at Rourke's Drift (1879) in the Zulu Wars, and now romanticised in the 1964 film *Zulu*, like their Scots counterparts at the battle of Inkerman (1854) in the Crimean War (1854–6), lionised in Robert Gribb's painting, 'The Thin Red Line' (1881), are a vital part of the British master narrative of empire. Perhaps as importantly, and even more revered in his time, was Henry Morton Stanley. Born as John Rowlands in Denbigh in 1841 in dubious circumstances, Stanley was the most famous explorer of his day. He was instrumental in charting the terrain which became King Leopold of Belgium's brutally managed personal fiefdom, the Congo Free State. Stanley, a cold man, whose acts drew criticism from some of his contemporaries, symbolised at once the bold and intrepid spirit with which Europeans went about carving up Africa and other parts of the world, and the acts of great brutality that they were willing to commit in order to achieve their goals.

Wales also played a part in the migrant stream from Europe to the Americas. The nationalist, Michael D. Jones, established an ill-fated Welsh community in Patagonia in 1865. Earlier than this, Welsh miners had played an important part in opening up new mining areas in America's Mid-West and West. Whereas American miners initially lacked the skills to maximise the output from mines and often abandoned seams that still held plentiful supplies, Welsh, Cornish and other miners from Britain were able to re-tap such resources, as well as to provide the skill and labour to tap rich new deposits. Welsh miners were responsible for great improvements in the American coal industry during the mid-nineteenth century. Upper Mississippi, Illinois, Iowa, Wisconsin and Lake Superior were just some of states and regions that by 1850 relied heavily on these miners.

If Wales was characterised as a distinct country, with a particular culture and its own language, this same series of images was at heart something of a paradox. There is very clear room to debate the degree to which Wales is even a nation. Wales had never been a separate country; in this sense it was different from both Scotland and Ireland. But these latter two Celtic nations were different from Wales in other ways. In fact, in many ways, once we get beyond the generalities of a shared Celticism, or of the existence of a native (non-English) tongue, we might consider that there is little else to link the three. Wales did not have a distinct legal system; it was not subjugated or bought as Scotland was prior to the Act of Union of 1707. It did not suffer an overtly colonial model of government, masked by the pretence of equality, as Ireland formally did under the terms of the union between Britain and Ireland (the act coming into force on 1 January 1801), or as she had done previously in more informal ways.

Language, above all other things, set Wales apart. Throughout the seventeenth and eighteenth centuries, the Welsh people maintained a very high usage of the Welsh language. As Wales entered the industrial age, more than fourth-fifths of her people used Welsh in their daily lives. By the end of our period, the figure had fallen back considerably (this despite the fact that, thanks to the rise in population, the total number of Welsh speakers increased throughout the nineteenth century). As industrial and urban society progressed, the proportionately much enlarged Welsh population that spoke Welsh had fallen to around one-half. This fall was partly because many people, particularly in south Wales, were not even Welsh. In 1861, 11 per cent of Swansea's population had been born in the south-west of England.

The language continued to represent Welshness in a way that stressed its importance to the culture of Wales. The language issue was at the forefront of debates about education, for example; it was also used as a battering ram against Conservatism and the Anglican church, two bodies widely, and correctly, associated with England. Liberalism and Nonconformity were presented as genuinely Welsh. The Liberal MP for Merioneth, elected in 1886, T.E. Ellis, declared in his election address his support for home rule for Ireland and Wales, the disestablishment of the Church of England in Wales, land reform, and better educational facilities that were under the control of public, not Anglican, bodies. Welsh language also played a role in many schools established under the terms of the Welsh Intermediate and Technical Education Act of 1889, a state education system different to that in England.

At the same time, there was a growing interest in other aspects of Welsh linguistic culture: poetry, choral singing and a 'revival' of the national eisteddfod, and a re-emphasis on the bardic craft by Edward Williams were all emblems of this. Then there was the influence of Iolo Morganwg (1747–1826), a stonemason, shopkeeper, forger of ancient manuscripts, charlatan and genius, who concocted much of the basis for the modern eisteddfod movement, including its druidical ceremonies. His successful attempt at inventing tradition undoubtedly played an important role in giving the Welsh people a sense of their own national identity and distinctiveness. Ironically, however, it was due to the patronage of the wealthy, anglicised landlords that the eisteddfod developed as an institution between 1815 and 1860. There was also altogether starchier (and perhaps more influential) exponents of Welshness who appeared later in the century. These included Sir Owen Edwards and Sir John Morris Jones. There was a huge and vibrant Welsh-language press. For example, on Anglesey, the press of Lewis Jones at Holyhead produced *Llais y Wlad*, the first newspaper on the island; while David Jones at Amlwch and another Lewis Jones at Llannerch-y-medd also published extensively in Welsh. The Welsh national anthem was composed in 1856.

A range of new institutions sprang up to endorse and develop Welsh identity. University College Aberystwyth, opened in 1872, provided an important plank of Welsh identity in the west. University colleges were also founded in Cardiff (1883) and Bangor (1884). The University of Wales, encompassing these three colleges, received its Royal Charter in 1893. Swansea became the fourth constituent college of the federal University of Wales in 1920. The first university college in Wales had been founded as a church college in 1822 in the town of Lampeter. Both the National Library and National Museum were given royal authorisation in 1907, the library opening in 1909 and the museum in 1920.

The mixture of nonconformity and industrial development would also cement in Welsh life a particular sort of political culture. Whereas Anglicanism was associated with the Tory and, later, Conservative parties, Wales's nonconformity pushed the Liberal party far ahead of its opponent, especially between 1868 and 1918. In political terms, then, Welsh identity proffered a heady mix of influences. Welshness in the nineteenth century was underpinned by religious and political radicalism, economic strength at the heart of an imperial trade economy, and the self-confidence of a people whose language was maintained through high literacy rates and a strong sense of desired identity.

Politically, Wales was Liberal. In 1874, 19 of 30 Welsh seats were held by Gladstone's party; in 1880, the figure had increased to 28 from 30. Gladstone himself had a Welsh country estate, at Hawarden, and was married to a Welsh woman. There were signs, too, that Welsh Liberalism was becoming suffused with wider questions of nationhood. Henry Richards won Merthyr Tydfil for the Liberals in 1868 with a vibrantly nationalist ticket in which Liberalism, Nonconformity and the 'Welsh Nation' were dovetailed in a way that came to characterise one strand of Welsh politics. By the 1880s, Conservative control had been swept from Wales.

Socialism was another political ideology that, while apparent in many parts of Britain, albeit on a small scale, achieved particular prominence in parts of Wales. While advocates of socialism were present, working men – particularly miners – remained resolutely Liberal in our period. Later, however, Wales also became one of the most important recruiting grounds for the emerging Labour Party – but not really till after our period. Keir Hardie won Merthyr Tydfil in 1906 for Labour but the other 29 Welsh seats all went to the Liberals. Yet, socialism and Communism found greater sympathy in Wales than in any other part of Britain, save perhaps for Clydeside. Labour militancy was also more common in South Wales than in most other comparable industrial areas. This was also shown in the hard line adopted by Welsh union leaders, such as A.J. Cooke of the miners' union. Some on the fringes of the Welsh labour movement were regarded as too extreme to achieve high political office with their unions. This was the case with Noah Ablett (1883–1935), the militant South Wales miners' leader, who was a syndicalist, Plebs League organiser and brilliant orator. Ablett went to Ruskin College, Oxford, on a miner's scholarship, and, in the true pit activists' tradition, honed his skills as a checkweighman and miners' agent. He served on the Executive Committee of the Miners Federation of Great Britain (1921–6) but never broke into the union's mainstream, twice being beaten in elections for the post of secretary by what were seen as less militant candidates, including his fellow Welshman, A.J. Cook.

A mixture of Welsh and British developments indicates the complexities of national identity. As with Scotland, one of the most salient themes of nineteenth-century Welsh life was the development of a vibrant, advanced industrial economy in the south – in Cardiff and the valleys to the north, where iron and coal created vast new possibilities, and around Swansea, where these and other minerals helped the fast-growing town become a thriving regional, national and then international centre.

Scotland

Much of Europe was inspired by nationalism, or, depending on one's perspective, suffered from it in the nineteenth century. Multi-national empires, particularly Austro-Hungary and Russia, were challenged by the rise of nationalist politics, and the same was true for Britain in Ireland, and, later, India. Yet in Scotland this was less the case, largely because of Scottish identification with the idea of Britain, the benefits of the British Empire, and close involvement with the Industrial Revolution. Furthermore, Scotland was in effect self-governing, as the central state with its permissive rather than prescriptive attitudes and policies, left much to locally responsible governmental and voluntary agencies.

The nineteenth century saw the development of a sense of national identity centring on a re-emergent cultural identity that did not involve any widespread demand for independence: kilts, bag-pipes, and rich literary consciousness, but no powerful home-rule party. The religious dimension, so obvious in Ireland, was lacking. The National Association for the Vindication of Scottish Rights was launched in 1853: 3,000 people came to the first meeting in Edinburgh, 5,000 in Glasgow. It strongly urged Scottish rights, but was not *explicitly* nationalist. Later, some Scottish nationalists, such as Theodore Napier, identified with the Boers of South Africa.

The Scottish Home Rule Association regarded the exerting of pressure on the most sympathetic political party as the best political strategy. In place of the notion of North Britain, which was rejected by the late nineteenth century, that of Scotland returned, although it was an increasingly Anglicised Scotland. The Secretaryship for Scotland was restored in 1885.

The division between an Anglicised, English-speaking south and a traditional, linguistically distinct society in the north was even more apparent in Scotland than in Wales. The Highlands and Islands region of Scotland was home to several hundred thousand members of what is known as the *Gaidhealtachd* ('land of the Gael', Gaelic-speaking region).

Scottish landed society was even more divided than that of England. Its rich were enormously so, its poor often found in abject squalor. The heads of such houses as Argyll, Bute, Atholl, Buccleuch, and Sutherland were magnates with land and political power to dwarf even some of the big landlords of England. Scotland was, and remains, the property of a disproportionately small number of lairds. When Dr Johnson and James Boswell took their tour of Scotland in the 1770s they were impressed by the extent of some of the nobles' lands: a man like the Duke of Argyll, as in times much earlier, was pretty much a regional princeling. His power over his own land was absolute; no one questioned his authority, custom or manners.

As the nineteenth century progressed, Scottish rural society was the site of growing unease. Reforming landlords had cleared much of their land for sheep – and these 'Highland Clearances' spelt the end of the traditional peasants' way of life in many areas. As cottars (the name for small-holding peasants) and black cattle were pushed towards marginal land beside the sea lochs, where they survived on fishing and kelp (seaweed) farming, or else emigrated, questions began to be asked also by small tenant farmers whose incomes were nowhere near as secure as the rents which fed the landed magnates. But the pressure to leave was not something done with care or charm. The Clearances entered Highlands folk-lore as an act of brutality during a period of harshness. The sheep became a thing of hatred, too, captured in folk literature. A poem of the 1860s mixes the hatred of these four-legged interlopers with respect for Irish nationalist resistance:

> I saw while I was sleeping...
> The Fenians coming over the sea
> To take the heads of the sheep;
> Not one skull will be left attached to a body...
> They will be exterminated from shore to hill;
> Then peace will come to the world
>
> ('Satire on Kenneth of Gesto', Anon. *c.* 1860s)

The Clearances created anti-heroes in two-legged form, apparatchiks who did the landlords' bidding. None was remembered with more ire than Patrick Sellars, the man responsible for overseeing extensive removals in Sutherlandshire, who was attacked in the writings of Donald MacLeod, who himself left Sutherland. MacLeod remembered Sellars' actions in 1814, 'The Year of the Burnings'. Evictions in the Strathnaver region were accompanied by physical and psychological distress: 'Some old men took to the woods and precipices, wandering about in a state approaching to, or of, absolute insanity ... Pregnant women were taken with premature labour and several children died' (see Box 11.1).

The famines of the 1820s and 1840s also prompted harsh actions by landlords. While Edinburgh society raised charitable donations and wrote of relieving Highland distress by establishing Scottish colonies in Canada and Australasia, some landlords initiated their own emigration schemes. Some were ordered; humane as possible. Some others were less so. Between 1848 and 1851 Gordon of Cluny despatched more than 2,700 of his tenants from Benbecula and Barra to Canada. Reluctant emigrants, men who refused to go, were hunted with dogs, bound, gagged and thrown aboard waiting vessels. Perhaps it is little wonder that a romanticised and heroic memory developed and that stories of the heroic futility of resistance (rather than any appreciation of the economic necessity of land modernisation), featured most prominently in Highlanders' own reminiscences of these tragic events. Donald Ross, a prolific contemporary commentator, described with particularly piquancy the despatch of 830 individuals who sailed for Adelaide, Australia, in the *Hercules*:

> The Collen [Cuillin] mountains were in sight for several hours of the passage; but when we rounded Ardnamurchan Point, the emigrants saw the sun for the last time glitter on their splintered peaks, and one prolonged and dismal wail rose from all parts of the vessel; the fathers and mother held up their infant children to take a last view of the mountains of their Fatherland which in a few minutes had faded from their view forever.

It is one of the great ironies of Scottish society in the nineteenth century, that the period witnessed the destruction of a way of life which many people were coming romantically to associate as pure or proper Scottish. Within the primitive black houses of the Gaels of northern Scotland and the Hebridean islands could be found the remnants of a clan way of life which, in the early eighteenth century, had been seen as a symbol of treachery and disloyalty to the British crown. Gaelic and Highland culture enjoyed a renaissance in the nineteenth century, having been outcast following the clansmen's support for the Jacobite pretenders to the throne in 1715 and 1745. Queen Victoria endorsed the new approval of Scottish and Highland culture by choosing to buy a long lease on Balmoral castle. 'Balmorality' and the celebration of Scottishness as Gaelic-ness occurred at just the time when Lowland and central-belt Scotland was being fully incorporated into an industrial and imperial Britishness and when the viability of the unique Highland way of life was being compromised by clearance, landlordism and the difficulties of making ends meet.

While Queen Victoria and her consort, Prince Albert, enjoyed Scotland for its Highland games, salmon fishing and rural quiet, others went about the task of defining Scottishness through Highland and *Gaidhealtachd* culture, too. James MacPherson's (1736–96) rediscovery and publicising of the Ossian myth had an enormous impact on romantic images of the Highlands. The Highlands, like Wordsworth's Lake District, became a precious and spiritual symbol of a world that was otherwise slipping under the

Box 11.1

The Highland Clearances

Donald Macleod's criticism of the clearances and landlordism in the Highlands of Scotland (1840). Donald Macleod (c.1814–1857), was born at Rossal, Strathnaver, in Sutherland, and witnessed clearances there first hand. His account first appeared in the *Edinburgh Weekly Chronicle*, between 1840 and 1841. MacLeod eventually emigrated to Canada.

THE FIRST SUTHERLANDSHIRE EVICTIONS

Previous to 1807, partial removals had taken place, on the estates of Lord Reay, Mr Honeyman of Armidale, and others. But these removals were under ordinary and comparatively favourable circumstances. Those who were ejected from their farms were accommodated with smaller portions of land, and those who chose to emigrate had means in their power to do so, by the sale of their cattle, which then fetched an extraordinary high price.

But in 1807, the system commenced on the property of Lord and Lady Stafford ... – about 90 families were removed from the parishes of Farr and Larg.

These people were, however, in some degree provided for, giving them smaller lots of land – but many of these lots were at a distance of 10 to 17 miles, so that the people had to move their cattle and furniture, leaving the crops on the ground behind. There was much personal suffering, from their having to pull down their houses and carry away the timber of them to erect houses on their new possessions. They had to begin to build new houses immediately, and in the meantime lived and slept in the open air, except for a few, who might be fortunate enough to get an unoccupied barn or shed from some of their charitable new neighbours.

THE EVICTIONS OF 1814

In the month of March 1814, a great number of the inhabitants of the parishes of Farr and Kildonan were summoned to give up their farms at the May term following. In order to ensure and hasten their removal with their cattle, a few days after the summons was given, the greatest part of the heath pasture was set fire to and burnt, by orders of Mr Patrick Sellar [writer and land agent, known as a 'factor'], who had taken these lands for himself.

It is necessary to explain the effects of this: in the spring ... the Highland cattle depend almost solely on heather. Then, as soon as the grass begins to sprout about the roots of the heather bushes, the animals get a good bite and are thus kept in a tolerable condition. Deprived of this resource by the burning, the cattle were generally left without food ... [and] roamed about over their burnt pasture till a great part of them were lost or sold for a mere trifle.

---

wheels of industrial and urban progress. While modernists worshipped the power and vitality of the city and of industry, a romantic sentiment developed among academics, poets and novelists, with the rural world depicted as superior and deeper. Interest in the preservation of Celtic culture, and of the Gaelic language, became pronounced.

Unlike in Wales, however, the number of Gaelic speakers in Scotland declined absolutely and proportionately in the nineteenth century. This is because the language rested, and, indeed, solely existed as a day-to-day tool of communication, within the *Gaidhealtachd* of the north-west and islands. But it was these very areas which suffered most in terms of depopulation and economic stagnation in this period. Nevertheless, with publicists such as Sir Walter Scott (1771–1832) and the monarch herself, and romantic paintings such as Sir Edwin Landseer's *Monarch of the Glen*, adding to the image of the north of Scotland, tourists, travellers, poets, writers and painters continued to be captivated by the region.

Scott's role in advancing the image of the Highlands cannot be exaggerated. Poems such as *The Lord of the Isles* (1815), his travel writings, and novels such as *Waverley* (1814), which preached reconciliation for the two Scotlands, north and south, helped immeasurably. As well, Scott was instrumental in helping to make George IV's visit to Edinburgh in 1822 a most magnificent spectacle. This great occasion was a symbol that Scotland was fully established as a British nation. Correspondingly, the tartanry and music of the Gaels became increasingly seen as defining Scottishness, and, in turn, underpinning Britishness. Scott and Burns served to help to present Scotland as equal to England, and to encourage separatism.

Scotland's native-speaking population never matched the Welsh example in this period. Towards the end of the century, perhaps 5 or 6 per cent of Scots' residents spoke Gaelic. Proportions were much higher in the crofting counties, particularly Ross-shire, Sutherlandshire and Argyllshire, where upwards of 65 per cent in 1881 had the Gaelic tongue. Caithness, Orkney and Shetland, however, were beyond the *Gaidhealtachd* and below the national average with under 10 per cent in the former and less than 4 per cent in the others.

While Scottish society in the south industrialised to a degree remarkable even in a British context, traditional rural culture in the north remained in a state of crisis. The Gaelic language declined, people emigrated (both to the Lowlands and overseas), and land reform, as in Ireland, became a crucial issue. Between 1886 and 1919, there were four important legislative initiatives – The Crofters' Holdings (Scotland) Act, 1886, the Congested Districts (Scotland) Act, 1897, the Small Landholders (Scotland) Act, 1911, and the Land Settlement (Scotland) Act, 1919. Like their numerous counterparts in Ireland (dating from 1870), these Acts, accompanied by reportage, commissions and inquiries, were meant to ameliorate crises and to provide lasting answers. While Liberal administrations echoed their Irish policy by trying to provide security of tenure for smallholders and to ease relations between lairds and tenants, Conservative admini- strations tended to favour enhancement of land purchase of small-holder proprietorship (again, this echoed Irish initiatives, such as the Wyndham Act of 1903). Yet the integrity and viability of Gaelic culture remains, to this day, a key issue in Scottish society. As a forerunner to the legislation of the 1880s, and as a more general theme in nineteenth- century Highlands' history, there was the agitation of small farmers and crofters. Their actions, while regularly compared with those of Ireland, were neither as intense nor as widespread. Levels of organisation were also more impressive in Ireland, where, by the 1880s, following the Land War (1879–81) and with the Plan of Campaign after 1886, the interests of the rural poor were far more integrated with what was in any case a far larger nationalist movement in Ireland. The needs of rural Ireland were never far from the mainstream of Irish politics; the same cannot be said of the Highlands and Islands of Scotland.

11.3 Industry and empire

We have already seen in Chapters 2 and 3 that industrialism was an intensely regional affair: some English counties, such as Buckinghamshire or Westmorland, were relatively untouched by industrial progress, though each had major railways built through them. But, in a UK context, the same variegated experience also had a national impact. Parts of Wales and Scotland were as industrial – indeed more industrial – than almost any other areas of the United Kingdom. Equally, rural hardship in traditional society, was even more apparent in the Highlands of Scotland and northern and central Wales than in any part of Britain, save, perhaps for the mountainous areas of the Lake Counties or north Northumberland.

The case of Scottish industry highlights the intense regionalism of economic growth *within* Scotland. For, as central Scotland grew to industrial maturity, the rural north-west struggled to maintain its unique economic and cultural identity. That is not to say that the Highlands and Islands wanted or deserved their own 'Industrial Revolution'. But there is no doubt that this period witnessed increased divisions between the two Scotlands. Thus, in the 1880s, when the workers of the Clyde were switching from iron to steel ships, the small farmers of Glendale, Skye, were announcing their desperation to the world in the Crofters' War. Wales also developed an impressive industrial base. Coal, metals and related forms of industrial transformed southern Wales as they did central and southern Scotland.

The transformation in population was matched by a change in wealth, as Scotland narrowed the gap with England throughout these years. Scottish wages also increased: having been lower for much of the century, the pay received by the average Scot reached equivalence with the English worker in the 1880s. At the same time, the central belt of Scotland had become one of Britain's wealthiest regions. An official inquiry reported in the 1890s that Scotland covered its own costs in terms of tax revenues and even produced surplus revenue.

So great was central Scotland's industrial prowess that even advanced industrial regions in England paled in relative terms. This was the period when Scotland's reputation as one of the world's leading industrial economy, was made. Its reliance upon heavy engineering and metal manufacture and ship-building – what has in recent times been viewed as an Achilles' heel – was then a positive boon: these were dynamic industries and Scotland stood at the cutting edge. Capital investment, new technology and economies of scale – the sorts of advanced industrial thinking we usually associate with Andrew Carnegie's America – were very much in evidence in Scotland.

In the period 1880–1914, Britain's capital prowess was concentrated in Scotland to a much greater extent than at any other time. Scotland was able to draw on a uniquely rich combination of assets as it sought to develop an industrial base. Mineral resources were plentiful, with both coal and iron-ore available in copious seams around the main centres of industry. Scotland's 145,000 colliers produced 14.5 per cent of all British coal in 1914, with the Lanarkshire and Ayrshire coal-fields rising up alongside the traditional centre of Scottish coal, West Fife. Welsh coal production was yet more impressive, falling behind only the 'Great Northern Coalfield' of Durham and Northumberland in terms of output. In 1870, South Wales coal amounted to some 14m tons; at its peak, in 1913, Wales was accountable for one-fifth of British coal capacity. More coal was exported from the valleys of Wales than for any other coal-field in Britain. Some 70 per cent of production went overseas from Cardiff, the 'coal metropolis'.

Scotland's iron-ore production actually fell in the second half of the century from its peak of 2.5m tons in 1854. However, new sources of the mineral were found in parts of England such as west Cumberland and Teesside, with Scots iron-masters paying for improved rail access in the case of the former. With these ores, and others imported from Spain and elsewhere, Scots iron and steel production held steady between the 1860s and 1914 (notwithstanding periods of decline) at more than 1m tons per annum. Welsh iron-ore production did not reach as high as the Scots peak, but it lasted longer as a natural resource. However, given the relative population sizes, Wales' actual pig iron production was even more remarkable than Scotland's. In 1840, Wales was producing 550,000 tons of pig iron, or 36 per cent of the British total; in 1860, the total had grown to 969,000 tons, or 25 per cent. Although the proportion had dropped to 12 per cent in 1880, this still came close to the Scots figure, with around 900,000 tons per annum being smelted. Much of this production, moreover, was concentrated in Merthyr Tydfil and Dowlais. The Dowlais iron works employed a massive 7,000 workers in the 1840s, and Philip Jenkins (1992) calculates that 150,000 people in the town and region were dependent on the works for their livelihoods.

Rail, too, was a vital part of the Scots and Welsh success stories. It is no coincidence that South Wales iron production reached its height in the 1840s and 1850s when rail opened up massive commercial possibilities for moving bulk goods around the country and also to the port of Cardiff for despatch to the four corners of the globe. By 1900 more than £150m had been invested in this form of transport. Industrialisation also prospered because of natural phenomena: Scotland is blessed with big rivers and these acted as arteries in supplying towns and industries with the access they needed to markets and labour. Glasgow was linked by the Clyde to the sea and then the world. East-coast Scotland had long maintained links with Scandinavia and the Baltic, which were exploited commercially in these years. Dundee, via the Tay, had a direct route to India, which provided the raw materials for her famous textile manufacture. Even then, the limitations of nature were not allowed to stand in the way of what was seen as natural human progress. When the Clydeside ship-building firm of John Brown and Co. in 1913 built the 47,500 ton transatlantic steamer, the *Aquitania*, it paid £10,000 to widen and deepen the Clyde before the vessel could be launched.

Ship-building was at once Scots, transatlantic and global. The capacity of the Clydeside yards put the region at the centre of an increasingly international economic universe. Cunard, a shipping firm which originated in Canada, relied to a remarkable degree on Scots ingenuity and industry. Its ships were among the most reliable, thanks to its engines designed by Robert Napier, 'the prince of marine engineers'. Cunard, and thus Scotland, dominated the Atlantic. Whether the ships ran from the Clyde or the Mersey, they were mostly Clydeside-built. In the 1890s, when steel and steam ships finally eclipsed all competing vessel types, Britain built around 80 per cent of the world's ships. In 1914, on the eve of war, the proportion was still 60 per cent. In 1881, workers on the Clyde built more tons of ships than both the Tyne and Wear put together (341,000 tons against 308,000). In 1914, the superiority remained similar with 757,000 tons launched on the Clyde as against 666,000 on the Tyne and Wear combined. If industrial Britain was a constellation of stars, Clydeside was the brightest.

In this period, ships required iron and then steel. Therefore, ships had a knock-on effect for the production of other metal products. Precision engine parts, plate-work, boilers, mounting blocks, piping, railway lines, girders, nails, screws, rivets, washers – all these required metals of varying grades: iron, steel, brass and copper. Scotsmen dug the ore, smelted the metal and made all the component parts.

Scotland's economic might undoubtedly rested on the ship-building and engineering industries, but there were other spheres of enormous energy. Textiles provided Scotland with an important industry and a significant source of employment, but this has gone relatively unheralded by historians because of the the overwhelming prowess of Lancashire cotton and Yorkshire wool. But Glasgow had long been an important textile centre, importing cotton bales, as did Liverpool, from the southern states of America, and transforming them into cheap garments for the working class. Gradually, though, this market was lost to Lancashire and new and specialised niches were sought. Dundee's involvement in the flax and jute industry is legendary; its sky-line of mills and tenements were once ample testimony to the degree of connection between Scotland and the empire, as jute came from India. Dunfermline produced high-quality linen, and lace-making was notable in Ayrshire. In the 1880s, Scottish textiles employed more than 100,000 workers, two-thirds of whom were women. With specialisation, Scotland settled on an utterly dominant position in three markets: cotton thread, jute and linoleum. With textiles also came the spur for other industries. Chemical production was but one example, with the need for dyes, detergents, and other treatments promoting growth.

The fact may embarrass Scots today, but, in the high age of industrialisation, Scotland's enormous energy underpinned the British imperial endeavour. Scots soldiers were an obvious presence in India and Africa, many of them transported on vessels made on the Clyde. Much of the commercial traffic that gave the empire its economic rationale was carried in Scottish merchant ships. A subtler and far more pervasive influence was at work in the shape of Scots capital penetration. Banks, merchant houses and commercial adventurers from Scotland made notable strides in the partition of the world's economic potential. Miller Bros were deeply ensconced in the otherwise Liverpool-dominated palm olive trade that brought to Britain, from the Niger region of Africa, a vital ingredient of soap. The company later became the hub of the Royal Niger Co., formed in 1886. Another company, Jardine Matheson and Co., established its Indian and Chinese presence following involvement with the murky trade in opium, and it later developed into the largest banking and bill brokers in India and China. All manner of Scots' bankers and financiers developed careers in the Far East, working up through the ranks of companies such as the Hong Kong and Shanghai Bank. This was the case with the Edinburgh-born Charles Addis (1861–1945), who became an important financier and a Foreign Office advisor in China.

While Scots' commercial and banking prowess was being demonstrated on an international stage, smaller-scale industrial acumen was also being tapped elsewhere. Cumbrian iron-smelting businesses were for the most part capitalised and dominated by Scots' companies such as Bairds of Gartsherrie and the famous Carron concern. Industrialists were followed by specialist labour, too, so that many of the skilled men in the shipyards of Tyneside, Wearside and Belfast had been trained on the Clyde. The engineering, steel-making and ship-building works of Barrow-in-Furness attracted so many Scots that, by 1911, the borough was home to proportionately more Scots-born workers than any other in England.

For a variety of reasons, it was in Scotland, based upon Scottish industrial traditions, that class-conscious workers first came *en masse* to express a common heritage through radical politics and militant trades unionism. The great Scottish Labour tradition, whose hegemony has only recently been challenged, developed in the shipyards and the steel mills; it rose from the mines; it was heard above the din of the textile factories. James Keir Hardie, who came from Scots' mining stock, remains the emblematic figure of the British Labour Party in its embryonic years. James Wheatley and Pete Curran were products of Glasgow's Scots–Irish Catholic tradition. James Connolly came from Edinburgh of Irish parents to take the message of class beyond the sectarianism of organised religions.

11.4 Conclusion

In their hey-day, central Scotland and southern Wales were cacophonies of industrial noise and a furnace of industrial heat. Swinging cranes and hooting ships signified the activity of the Clyde; steam pistons and the clang of metal on metal were audible in every small town and village; the blackened faces of emerging miners are emblematic of life in the Rhondda and other Welsh valleys. Engine-shops and rope-works, flour mills and saw mills, tanneries and canneries, chemical factories and dye-works – all of these emitted their own contribution to the sound and smell of an industrial and urban world. In the south and central parts of Scotland, and in south Wales, feats of industrial might demonstrated the successful integration of a different sort of Wales and Scotland into the wider design of a modern, imperial and global Britain.

The idea that Scotland and Wales became more integrated into a wider British identity by virtue of their enjoyment of the benefits of industry and empire, provides one important way of viewing the British experience in our period; there is, however, another perspective. It is one of the most noteworthy images of these years that while Celtic capitalists flexed their muscles on an international stage and became wealthier by large degrees, many of their workers – like their English counterparts – developed a deep-seated, and some might say bridling, sense of 'them and us'. The social consequences of industrialisation were severe. Both Wales and Scotland experienced overcrowding and insanitary conditions in their towns; in Merthyr, in the 1820s, infant mortality was as much as 40 per cent higher than an already fearful average. In both countries, where work was heavy and dangerous, industrial accidents were a daily risk. Pit explosions, falling building materials, burns from molten metals, misfiring rivets, and a plethora of other things could kill a worker or put him out of action for long periods.

Welsh culture thrived during the nineteenth century. The language, while spoken by a smaller proportion of residents of Wales in 1900 than had been the case in 1800, was nevertheless still spoken by a larger actual body of people. Outside of Ireland, we must look to the Highlands and Islands for examples of a failure of government and society to protect and integrate precious vestiges of traditional culture. Language use in the Highlands and Islands declined, just as the population itself fell.

It is one of Britain's deepest ironies that at the very point when the kilt-wearing bag-pipe playing 'noble savage' of romantic depiction became a symbol of Scottish identity and British military prowess, his Highland, Gaelic and clan-centred culture was under most pressure. The independence of the Highland way of life was lost; the uniqueness of the culture remained, though, and became more widely enjoyed through travel writings, guide books, histories, folk-lore and other forms of social reportage.

Summary

◆ Despite having unique cultures, large parts of industrial Wales and Scotland were 'partners in Empire', beneficiaries from Britain's economic and geo-political power in this period.

◆ Economic and social change also brought problems to Scotland and Wales which were not unique.

◆ Traditional society in both countries was put under pressure by social change.

◆ The Gaelic-speaking Highlands fared worse than its Welsh counterpart, where linguistic survival was noticeable.

◆ Highland culture was expropriated in this period, not least by Lowland Scots, with tartans, bag-pipes and the military culture of the clans all being knitted into a wider sense of Britishness.

◆ Wales, but especially Scotland, fitted into the Victorians' general approval for the countryside: painters, writers, folklorists and others contributed to the myths of a unique way of life.

◆ In both countries, nationalist movements were far weaker than in Ireland.

Points to discuss

◆ Where do Wales and Scotland fit into the master narrative of British history in this period?

◆ To what extent are the two countries Anglicised in these years?

◆ Why did neither Wales nor Scotland develop home-rule or nationalist movements to compare with that of Ireland?

◆ Explain how the benefits of industrial wealth were enjoyed only on a regional basis in the two countries.

◆ Compare the fortunes of linguistic, literary and cultural heritage in Wales and Scotland.

References and further reading

Scotland

E. Cameron, *Land for the People? The British Government and the Scottish Highlands, c. 1880–1925* (Edinburgh, 1996).

S.G. Checkland, *Industry and Ethos: Scotland, 1832–1914* (Edinburgh, 1989 edn).

T.M. Devine, *The Scottish Nation, 1700–2000* (1999).

I.C.G. Hutchinson, *A Political History of Scotland, 1832–1924* (Edinburgh, 1986).

B. Lenman, *An Economic History of Modern Scotland* (1977).

G. Morton, *Unionist Nationalism: Governing Urban Scotland, 1830–60* (East Linton, 1999).

T.C. Smout, *A Century of the Scottish People, 1830–1950* (1986).

Wales

John Davis, *A History of Wales* (1993 edn.).

Ieuan Gwynedd Jones, *Mid-Victorian Wales: The Observers and the Observed* (Cardiff, 1992).

Philip Jenkins, *A History of Modern Wales, 1539–1990* (1992).

Kenneth O. Morgan, *Wales in British Politics, 1868–1922* (Cardiff, 1980).

Kenneth O. Morgan, *Rebirth of a Nation: Wales, 1880–1980* (Oxford, 1981).

Britain and the Wider World: 1

Contents

■ Introduction

The relationship between Britain and the wider world is one that would have always attracted attention in a study of this period. This was the age of Britain as *the* world power. Imperialism has to be seen not only as the spread of British power but also in terms of its consequences, such as trade and migration, which are probed in Chapters 2, 3 and 5. In addition, it is necessary to look under the heading of 'Britain and the wider world' at comparisons and contrasts between Britain and other states, in order to provide an important perspective on British history in this period.

Key issues

► Why did Britain become the foremost imperial power?

► What were the consequences of Britain's imperial strength?

► How effective were the British armed forces?

► What comparisons can be drawn between Britain and other states?

► How far was Britain culturally linked to the Continent?

12.1 Eighteenth-century parallels

As discussed in the introductory Chapter 1, Britain was a European power and a world presence from the outset. From 1714 until 1837, the king was also Elector of Hanover. For much of the period 1689–1815, Britain was at war with other European powers. From 1689, she operated very much as part of the Continental political system. War and foreign policy contributed powerfully to the character of the British state. This state was less different from its counterparts on the Continent than is sometimes appreciated. After the protracted (and varied but inter-related) divisions of the period 1638–1716 in Britain, there had been a re-creation of stable government by means of a new consensus. In this consensus, which incorporated much, but not all, of the political nation, patronage and the avoidance of radical changes were dominant, and thus the path of government was smoothed by practices that lessened the chance of unpredictable developments, practices that in short neutered political activity. Therefore, despite the role of a permanent and quite effective Parliament, the Old Corps (ministerial) Whigs could be seen as having created during the reigns of Georges I (1714–27) and II (1727–60) a state that bore comparison with both strong Continental monarchies and with that attempted by the Stuarts, and such comparisons were to be pressed home in the 1760s and early 1770s when George III (1760–1820) broke with the tutelage of the Old Corps Whigs and found himself accused of hankering for absolute monarchy. Contemporaries searched for parallels in the Maupeou Revolution in France (1771) and in Gustavus III's *coup* in Sweden (1772), both seen as measures designed to subordinate 'intermediate institutions' to Crown authority, and in the Swedish case a *coup d'etat* for the monarchy. Throughout our period, British government and policies were judged in comparison with those on the Continent.

The apparent degree of difference between Britain and the Continent was also eroded by the widespread process of public politicisation on the Continent. In France that led to and, to a greater extent, was first stimulated by the mid-century controversies centring on Jansenism and later by those arising from the Maupeou Revolution. Hence by the 1780s there was a considerable measure of convergence between aspects of the public politics of Britain and France. In Parliament, Britain had a more effective 'hinge' or means of achieving, eliciting, sustaining and legitimating co-operation between the crown and a widespread political nation for the achievement of common action than existed in other European states of comparable size. After 1688 both institutions and, more importantly, a political culture embodying genuine modes of representation had developed in Britain. In the 1770s and 1780s, French ministries sought to create a similar consensus and to ground French government in institutions that were more representative of public opinion, by planning provincial assemblies and then summoning first an Assembly of Notables (1787), and subsequently the Estates General (1789). Had the French succeeded in a programme of peaceful constitutional reform then it would be possible to emphasise a degree of convergence, and, initially, that indeed was the theme of British commentators who in 1789 enthusiastically noted the opening stages of what appeared to be a popular and successful revolution that could be compared with the events of 1688–9 in Britain.

12.2 Xenophobia and cosmopolitanism

In the eighteenth century, the British elite became culturally very attuned to Continental developments. This was also linked to a degree of cosmopolitanism in British intellectual life, as shown for example by the quest for impartiality by prominent historians such as Edward Gibbon and William Robertson, both of whom were writers with a Europe-wide reputation. Throughout Europe, the cosmopolitan aspects of eighteenth-century culture were matched by more parochial worlds, the two generally co-existing with little difficulty as they reflected the experiences and preoccupations of different social milieus. In Britain, the relationship was less easy because of a strong discourse, if not polemic, of cultural nationalism which was a marked feature in sections of the world of print throughout the century. This was felt most urgently in London, a metropolitan forcing-house of political, social and cultural tension. The vigorous xenophobia of London newspapers was matched by hostility to foreigners, most obviously in riots against French actors, as in 1738, 1739, 1743, 1749 and 1755. There is clear evidence of tension over cultural borrowing from the Continent, hostility towards being 'a ridiculous Ape of French Manners', and this was to continue into the nineteenth century and powerfully affect popular attitudes towards the Continent. Criticism of this encompassed a certain amount of not so much class conflict, for a fully articulated class system did not exist, but rather of social tension. A sense of cultural betrayal was brilliantly symbolised by food imagery, the claim that, in place of the 'roast beef of Old England', the aristocracy and the royal court preferred continental food and, in particular, French cuisine, with its alleged insubstantiality: sauce not meat.

Much of the expression of xenophobia was clearly an aspect of propaganda by opposition groups, but such propaganda was efficacious only because it played an established and accepted theme. Behind it can be discerned not only national pride and self-confidence, but also a sense of social betrayal and cultural fear: a sense that cosmopolitanism was a threat, both as a situation and as a tendency. It appeared to encapsulate unwelcome forces. Similarly, the homophobia of the period, with its emphasis on the alleged foreign origin of sodomy, has been held to demonstrate the powerful alliance between sexism and national chauvinism.

The cultural nationalism of so much of British public culture offered a definite challenge to cosmopolitanism and there is little sign that in doing so it challenged traditional beliefs. Far from the press expressing novel cultural attitudes, it was giving new force to the politico-cultural inheritance from the sixteenth and seventeenth centuries, especially anti-Catholicism and national self-sufficiency. One of the characteristic features of the British press from the outset was that it was a national press overwhelmingly printed in English. French-language papers were distinctly marginal. The same was true of book and pamphlet publication. The situation was very different across most of the Continent, where publication in a language different to that of the native population encouraged cosmopolitanism, and its identification with the world of learning, opinion, politics and fashion. In that sense the position in Britain prefigured the consequences of linguistic nationalism in other countries during the nineteenth century.

The position in Britain altered under George III (1760–1820) for both political and cultural reasons. George never visited Hanover and took care to associate himself with Britain to a degree that both his predecessors had conspicuously neglected. Until the *Fürstenbund* (League of Princes) of 1785, in which George took a role as Elector of Hanover, Hanoverian issues played little role in British foreign policy and indeed, more generally, there was a shift from concern in Continental affairs to a political and governmental agenda dominated by domestic and imperial issues, a process that culminated in the War of American Independence (1775–83). Victory in the Seven Years' War (1756–63) had left Britain as the world's leading naval power, and this had brought her extensive colonial gains: Canada, Senegal, Grenada, Tobago, Dominica, St Vincent, Florida.

Culturally, there was more self-confidence, and less concern about cultural borrowing. The Royal Academy, founded in 1768, and its long-serving first president Sir Joshua Reynolds, advanced the dignity of British art.

The British view of the Continent in the 1760s, 1770s and 1780s was more distant than it had been over the previous century, but also less aggressive. This can be seen in the move away from an often automatically hostile approach to foreign countries on the part of travellers, to a more varied response. Among the elite, hostility to Catholicism diminished. Catholics had maintained their own religious, cultural, educational and social links with the Continent, and in the late eighteenth century, as attitudes towards Catholicism became less hostile, they found this a less difficult process. Popular hostility, however, remained strong, as the Scottish agitation of 1778–82 against a proposal for Catholic relief, and the Gordon Riots of 1780 in England both amply demonstrated.

12.3 Britain and the challenge of the French Revolution

A self-contained and somewhat distant political attitude towards the Continent was advocated by the MP and experienced diplomat, William, Lord Auckland, who wrote to the Prime Minister, William Pitt the Younger in February 1790:

> Whatever may be the course of circumstances, my political creed turns on the expediency of avoiding wars abroad and innovations at home: nothing else is wanting to confirm for a long period the elevated point on which we stand above all the nations of the world either in present times or in history.

The situation was to change dramatically as a result of the French Revolution, which broke out in 1789. Although many of the revolutionaries looked to British institutions for inspiration, and Britain did not join Austria and Prussia in attacking Revolutionary France in 1792, war broke out the following February.

The Revolution both accentuated and then ruptured the convergence between aspects of the public politics of Britain and France that had been noticeable in the second half of the century. The French Estates General, which had last met in 1614, was not so much revived in 1789 as created anew, and this forum of national politics developed rapidly into a body before which, in comparison with Britain, the government was crippled. In France, political, rather than institutional, reform came to the fore, despite the effort of the royal government to centre on the latter. The pace of this political reform, the urgent desire to create a new constitution, and, crucially, the opposition of powerful domestic elements to the process of reform and bitter divisions among those who sought change, ensured that it soon became better described as revolution, both by its supporters and by its opponents. There was no time to establish widely acceptable constitutional conventions and the elite was fatally fractured, helping to lead to a spiral of disunity and civil violence.

As a result of the revolutionary crisis, a similar process occurred in Britain and in France in the early 1790s: the definition of a political perspective in which foreign and domestic challenges were closely linked, and in which it seemed crucial to mobilise mass support for a struggle with an insidious, but also all too apparent enemy – an obvious foreign rival supporting domestic conspiracy and insurrection. A language of nationalism,

Box 12.1

French revolution (1789–1799)

Breaking out in 1789, this led to the creation of a French Republic (1792) and the execution of the king (1793). War broke out in 1792, and Britain joined her European allies against France in 1793.

The radicalism of the French Revolution, and its at times anti-clerical and irreligious tenets, led it to be seen in Britain as a potential threat to social and political order.

to which paranoia contributed, therefore developed. In France, however, revolution was the cause and consequence of this process of struggle, whereas in Britain the challenge of domestic radicalism and revolutionary France led to a widespread rallying to Country, Crown and Church. This paralleled similar movements elsewhere in Europe, while Britain was also involved more closely with the Continent thanks to her major role in the struggle with Revolutionary, and then Napoleonic France. This process culminated in the major roles taken by Britain at the Congress of Vienna (1814–15) and on the battlefield of Waterloo (1815). The Revolution thus both focused British political concern on the Continent and introduced a marked ideological slant to British political culture, one in which domestic cultural and political preferences were clearly matched to, and given opposing force by, differing responses to the situation on the Continent.

The political shift was readily apparent. In 1739, Britain had gone to war with Spain as a consequence of competing views over Caribbean trade and the following year James Thomson composed *Rule Britannia* with its maritime theme:

> Rule Britannia, rule the waves
> Britons never will be slaves.

In 1754, hostilities had begun with France over control of the Ohio River basin in North America. In 1778 Britain had gone to war with France as a result of Louis XVI's support for the American revolutionaries. Similarly, in 1770 Britain had nearly gone to war with the Bourbon powers (France and Spain) over the Falkland Islands, and in 1790 over Nootka Sound. Yet in 1793 Britain began her longest period of continuous warfare since the Elizabethan war with Spain, not over the fate of empire, but over the control of the United Provinces. Indeed, in imperial terms there was no reason to go to war with revolutionary France. France's navy was in a poor state, her energies were devoted to a Continental war for survival. However, the British government felt it crucial to fight to prevent the French from dominating the Low Countries, particularly the Netherlands. The Continental focus of British foreign policy was rarely so clear as in her repeated attempts to limit French power in 1793–1815.

These attempts had considerable impact on Britain, irrespective of the ideological challenge of Revolution. British society was mobilised for war, not on a scale to compare with revolutionary France, still less with modern 'total war', but, nevertheless, to an extent that was far greater than in recent conflicts. The unprecedented strains on public finance led to income tax. The revived role of political economy produced the first national census. The country was mapped by the Ordnance Survey. In his essay 'Of publick Debts', printed in his *Inquiry into the Nature and Causes of the Wealth of Nations* (1776), Adam Smith had claimed that:

In great empires the people who live in the capital, and in provinces remote from the scene of action, feel many of them scarce any inconveniency from the war; but enjoy, at their ease, the amusement of reading in the newspapers the exploits of their own fleets and armies. To them this amusement compensates the small difference between the taxes which they pay on account of the war, and those which they had been accustomed to pay in time of peace.

Such an interpretation might seem to be given literary backing by the world depicted in the novels of Jane Austen, but it is not one that a close reading of the period would support. The precarious world of credit and debt that many urban artisans were trapped in was dependent on international developments. The urban economy relied on trade, its rural counterpart was affected by high taxation. Privateering, impressment and recruitment affected the national economy and bore down upon the economies of individual families.

Irrespective of their ideological position, the fate of the Continent therefore engaged the attention of the British during the Revolutionary and Napoleonic Wars; indeed more so than in recent wars. After 1741 French advances into central Europe during the War of the Austrian Succession (1740–8) had been held and they had taken several years to conquer the Austrian Netherlands; in the Seven Years' War the French had been less than successful in their German operations; and in the War of American Independence there had been no campaigns on the Continent, except for the unsuccessful siege of Gibraltar. In contrast, the French over-ran much of Europe in the years from 1792, their rapid con-quest of Belgium in November 1792 being but the first of their dramatic advances. The frontiers of Italy, the Rhineland and the Low Countries had been stable for the half-century after 1748; now Europe was being remoulded, new political spaces being created, frontiers redrawn, all in the interests of France. France became an Empire; the Holy Roman Empire came to an end in 1806. Neutrality and non-intervention was not a plaus-ible policy for Britain, no more than a lack of concern and interest was sensible for the British. Whether with the French intervention in Ireland in 1798 or with the Continental System – the Napoleonic attempt of 1806–13 to exclude British trade from the Continent – it was clear that French power affected many aspects of British life.

The ideological challenge was also a potent one that obliged commentators to rethink the nature of Britain's relations with the Continent. A combination of the potential universal mission of the new Republic, the real or feared aspirations of British radicals, and the response of British conservatives ensured that the French Revolution came to play a major role in British politics. Edmund Burke's determined insistence that what happened in France was of direct relevance to Britain appeared somewhat implausible when he published his *Reflection on the Revolution in France, and on the Proceedings in certain Societies in London relative to that event* on 1 November 1790, for France was then very weak. Burke's views soon, however, seemed vindicated by events, because as the Revolution became more radical it nevertheless continued to attract a measure of domestic British support, culminating in the feared insurrection of December 1792. The radicals who appealed to the French National Convention for support sending, for example, petitions and other messages, played into Burke's hands, but, at the same time, their activities reflected a perception that they shared with Burke, namely that events in France were of direct relevance to Britain and that Britain was necessarily involved in a wider European struggle between the supporters and opponents of revolution.

This analysis had been resisted by the Pitt ministry in the spring, summer and early autumn of 1792 when it had insisted on neutrality despite the outbreak of the French

Revolutionary war, but the entry of Britain into the conflict the following year changed the situation. The Revolutionary and Napoleonic Wars reshaped British patriotism, strengthening its association with conservatism in place of its earlier eighteenth-century identification with reforming traditions. As an example of this conservatism, in 1797, the Reverend Edward Nares (1762–1841), Fellow of Merton College Oxford (1788–97) and Regius Professor of Modern History at Oxford (1813–41), preached a sermon on a day of public thanksgiving for a series of British naval victories. Published in 1798 it was dedicated to Elizabeth, Viscountess Bateman, the wife of one of his patrons, the combination of links reflecting the nature of what has been recently termed the English 'church-state'. Just as Burke had stressed the 'moral lessons' to be drawn from history, which he saw as involving the will of God, so Nares proclaimed history of value because it displayed the Providential plan, and, in terms that reflected the assessment of the current situation in Europe, he contrasted the historical perspective with the destructive secular philosophy of present-mindedness with its sense of the end of history:

> the enemy begin their operations on the pretended principle of giving perfect freedom to the mind of man. I call it a pretended principle, not only because their subsequent actions have been entirely in contradiction to it, but because, in fact no principle, as the world at present stands, could be found more inimical to the real interests of human nature. For it is plain, that the first step to be taken in vindication of such a principle, is to discard all ancient opinions as prejudices; every form of government, however matured by age, is to be submitted afresh to the judgment and choice of the passing generation, and the Almighty to be worshipped (if at all) not according to the light vouchsafed to our fore-fathers, but as every short-lived inhabitant of the earth shall, in his wisdom, think proper and sufficient ... when the calamities of war befall us, we are not irrational in considering these also as under the direction of God ... The great point is to discover the heavenly purposes.

Nares came to the reassuring conclusion that British victories proved divine support. The perception of Britain's imperial destiny as having both a Providential purpose and Providential endorsement was a central plan in the Church of England's public theology. The French Revolution gave new energy to the defence of established Christianity. In 1805, Nares gave the Bampton lectures at Oxford, defending Christianity against 'modern infidels', and in 1808 and 1809 was a select preacher at the university. The dedication to George III of the *Supplement* to the third edition of the *Encyclopaedia Britannica* which was published in 1801, declared that it was designed to counteract the French *Encyclopédie*, then seen as a precipitant of revolution. In the face of the new challenge from Revolutionary France, there was much charity and sympathy for French refugees, including clerics. The Jesuit school for English Catholics originally founded at St Omer in 1593 moved to Stonyhurst in Lancashire in 1794. Once atheistic France had been identified with Anti-christ, Catholics could appear as allies.

The Revolutionary and Napoleonic period witnessed both a renewal of the ideological themes of the British *ancien régime* and the birth of modern British conservatism with its scepticism about the possibilities of secular improvement and its stress on historical continuity and national values, rather than present-mindedness and internationalism, or the alternative modern impetus behind British conservatism, the furtherance of capitalism and the concomitant defence of certain sectional interests. This Burkean conservatism was not necessarily restricted to Britain: Burke himself treated pre-Revolutionary Europe as a community and a commonwealth, was very concerned about

Napoleon (1769–1821)

Rose from a modest background in Corsica through military service to sieze power in France in 1799 from the unpopular government of the Directory. First Consul and, from 1804, Emperor of France, he held power until forced to abdicate in 1814. An attempt to regain his power led to military defeat at Waterloo in 1815, after which this bitter opponent of the British was sent as a prisoner to the remote, British-held Atlantic island of St Helena.

the situation in France and was averse to any peace with her that did not entail a counter-revolution. However, a stress on continuity and therefore the value of specific constitutional and political inheritances did not readily lend itself to serving as the basis of an international ideology. Despite Burke's polemic about a European community being assaulted by the French Revolution, the appeal to history against reason was inherently nationalist. Indeed one of the major intellectual problems facing the forces of conservatism or, as they later became, the 'right' in Europe, during the Revolutionary–Napoleonic period and subsequently, was the difficulty in formulating and sustaining an international ideology. The variegated nature of the *ancien régime*, its latent ideology of specific privileges, did not lend itself to this task, no more than did the xenophobic, provincial, proto-nationalist and nationalist responses to French power in 1792–1815. The continued failure of British conservatism to establish Continental links was to culminate in its isolation within the European Economic Community (EEC, later EU) in the late twentieth century.

As with much of Europe, 'Patriotism' in Britain in this period and thereafter, was heavily and increasingly associated with anti-French, and thus, from the early 1790s, to a considerable extent conservative, sentiments. Correspondingly, conservatism was increasingly nationalistic in tone and content, and this was to remain the case throughout the nineteenth century. The experience of the Napoleonic Wars in particular underscored a patriotic discourse on British distinctiveness while simultaneously creating a new iconography of national military heroes. Thus Robert Southey (1774–1843), who became Poet Laureate in 1813, developed the language of patriotism. War with France was justified on moral grounds. Southey also wrote patriotic accounts of Nelson, Wellington and the Duke of Marlborough. In the 1800s, *God Save the King*, which had first been sung publicly during the Jacobite crisis in 1745, came to be called the 'national anthem'.

Britain played a major role in the rallying to Church and Crown that proved such a distinct feature of the 1790s and 1800s across much of Europe, and played a potent role in the definition of nationhood. Nationalism was not only a matter of long-term trends. The short-term crisis of the French Revolutionary period was also crucial. In Britain, Auckland called for a programme of indoctrination in order to achieve an acceptable politicisation of the country:

every possible form of Proclamations to the People, orders for Fast Days, Speeches from the Throne, Discourses from the Pulpit, Discussions in Parliament etc. I am sure that we should gain ground by this. The prosperity and opulence of England are such, that except the lowest and most destitute class, and men of undone fortunes and desperate pursuits, there are none who would not suffer essentially in their fortunes, occupations, comfort, in the glory, strength and well-being of their country, but above all in that sense of security which forms the sole happiness of life, by this new species of French disease which is spreading its contagion among us ... the abandoning of religion is a certain step towards anarchy.

This mixture of national identity, economic interest, religious conviction and a 'sense of security' was to prove very potent. Loyalism was a genuine mass movement, especially in England; even if it proved difficult to sustain the level of engagement, there were many not comprehended within it, and the relationship between government and Loyalism could be ambiguous.

Furthermore, there was in place from the 1770s onwards an alternative and more egalitarian model of political order which posed a substantial threat to the ideological smugness of both Whig and, later, Tory elements in British politics and looked forward towards nineteenth-century radicalism. This alternative model was deployed with great effectiveness in the 1790s by the radicals, particularly Tom Paine, in a way that potentially undercut the attempt to tar radicalism with the slur of advocating pro-French principles. Thus the attempt to associate radicalism with Revolutionary France was a carefully orchestrated polemical move, rather than a wholly obvious and uncontentious one.

12.4 Imperial Britain

The establishment of the British imperial position also owed much to contingent circumstances, principally success in war. The nature of the British empire and of the European world altered dramatically in 1775–1835. In 1775 all English-speakers were subjects of the British crown, while the majority of such subjects outside Britain were white, Christian, of British, or at least European, origin, and ruled with an element of local self-government, albeit not to the satisfaction of many in the Thirteen Colonies. Furthermore, predominantly Catholic populations posed problems in Quebec and Minorca.

The American Revolution brought a permanent schism to the English-speaking world, although it ensured that aspects of British culture, society and ideology, albeit in greatly refracted forms, were to enjoy great influence, outside and after the span of British empire. The modern role of the English language owes more to America than to modern Britain. The settlements and conquests of the period 1783–1815 also changed the character of the empire, not least by bringing numerous non-white and non-Christian people under British control. Some of these gains, such as Ceylon, the Seychelles, Mauritius, Trinidad, Tobago, St Lucia and the 'land-islands' of Cape Colony, Essequibo and Demerara (British Guyana), were achieved at the expense of other European powers. Others, such as much of southern India annexed as a result of the Second and Third Mysore wars (1790–2, 1799), or the protectorate over Oudh established in 1801, were gains at the expense of non-European rulers.

Naval power permitted Britain to dominate the European transoceanic world during the French Revolutionary and Napoleonic wars, during which Britain was at war with

France in 1793–1802, 1803–14 and 1815. French naval power and that of her allies was crippled as a result of British victories, principally Copenhagen (1801 and 1807) over the Danes, Camperdown (1797) over the Dutch, and Cape St Vincent (1797), the Nile (1798) and Trafalgar (1805) over the French and/or Spaniards. As a result, Britain was left free to execute amphibious attacks against the now-isolated centres of other European empires. British naval power helped to make French control of Louisiana redundant, and Napoleon's sale of it to the United States in 1803 was an apt symbol of the Eurocentricism that was such a characteristic feature of French policy after the failure of the Egyptian expedition as a result of Nelson's victory at the battle of the Nile. As British naval strength was crucial not only in Britain's ability to resist France but also in her subsequent international position during the nineteenth century, and was thus central to Britain's expanding imperial interests, it is important to consider its basis. This included a large fleet, drawing on the manpower resources of a substantial merchant marine (although there were never enough sailors to man it), a sophisticated and well-financed administrative structure, and an ability to win engagements that reflected widely diffused qualities of seamanship and gunnery, a skilled and determined corps of captains, and able leadership. This was true not only of command at sea, as with Admiral Horatio Nelson's innovative tactics and ability to inspire his captains, but also of effective leadership of the navy as an institution. Earl St Vincent, a former admiral, was an energetic First Lord of the Admiralty, in 1801–4, although his hostility to naval contractors and his campaign for economy in the naval dockyards limited the rate of construction and repair, placing the navy in a difficult position in 1804. The reversal of this policy when St Vincent resigned that year, ensured that by the end of 1808 the commissioned fleet totalled 113 of the line and 596 other ships. Admiral Charles Middleton, created Lord Barham in 1805, was effective as First Lord (1805–6) and played an important role in developing organisational efficiency and in providing able leadership during the Trafalgar campaign. Other able administrators were legion: Samuel Bentham and John Payne, for example, did much to develop the navy's bureaucracy and land-based infrastructure. New naval facilities were developed both in Britain and abroad, for example at Malta, where Nelson established a ropeworks. Cape Town, Madras, Bermuda, Barbados, Trincomalee and Bombay were all developed as naval bases. Resources permitted, and administrative systems supported, the maintenance both of the largest fleet in the world and a crucially large number of smaller warships.

British success owed much to her naval power, but more to her insular status. Of the islands lying off the European mainland, only Britain was both independent and a major power. This allowed, indeed required, her to concentrate on her naval forces, unlike her Continental counterparts which, even if also maritime powers, as most obviously with France and Spain, devoted major resources to their armies. This concentration was crucial to Britain's success in defeating the Bourbons in the struggle for oceanic mastery in 1739–63: War of Jenkins' Ear with Spain, 1739–48; War of Austrian Succession with France, hostilities, 1743–8; Seven Years War with France, 1756–63 (hostilities begun 1754); and war with Spain 1762–3. It was also crucial to Britain's ability first to survive the attempt to reverse the verdict during the War of American Independence, and secondly to resist Revolutionary France and Napoleon. As, however, in the case of conflict with Germany in 1940–4, political will, insular status and sea (and in 1940 air) defences, were sufficient to maintain national independence, and would probably have led to the defeat of invasion attempts, but they were insufficient to defeat the rival state. For that, it was necessary to have powerful allies. Audiences cheered George Colman's *The Surrender of Calais* when it was first performed in July 1791. It was a perfect war-time piece:

> Rear, rear our English banner high
> In token proud of victory!
> Where'er our god of battle strides
> Loud sound the trump of fame!
> Where'er the English warrior rides,
> May laurelled conquest grace his name.

Despite Britain's naval power, the Revolutionary and Napoleonic wars with France were an extremely difficult struggle, and it was by no means clear that French domination of western Europe would be shortlived. The failure of the First and Second Coalitions against France left Britain isolated, and, by the Treaty of Amiens (1802), she had to accept French dominance of Western Europe and to return all her overseas gains from France, Spain and the Dutch (except Trinidad and the Dutch bases in Ceylon, modern-day Sri Lanka). These terms were bitterly criticised in parliament, but were also viewed by the Addington government as little more than a truce. Provocative French steps in Europe and further afield, including French attempts to acquire Florida and to build up their navy, aroused concern and led to the refusal to evacuate Malta, already seen as a crucial Mediterranean base, despite having agreed to do so. In May 1803, war resumed.

The conflict broadened out in 1805 when the Third Coalition was assembled against France, but in 1805–7 Napoleon defeated Austria, Prussia and Russia, returning to defeat Austria again in 1809. However, Napoleon made no serious effort to settle differences with Britain, foolishly so, as the resources of world-wide British trade financed opposition to France. Negotiations in 1806 were designed by Napoleon only to isolate Britain, preparatory to an eventual new French attack. The British were prepared to accept French hegemony in West and Central Europe, but Napoleon was not ready to made such hegemony even vaguely palatable.

Instead, he launched an assault on British trade, his Continental System, which began with the Berlin Decree of 1806. This amounted to a blockade of Britain, the confiscation of all British goods and the arrest of all Britons. Portugal was invaded in 1807 to break off British trade. The following year, Napoleon tried to take over Spain, which began the Peninsula War. British troops were sent to Portugal in 1808 and eventually overcame the French in Spain in 1813. Although the French failure to subjugate Portugal and Spain was important, the crucial failures were those in Russia in 1812 and Germany in 1813. Napoleon's invasion of Russia was a disaster – a calamity he was unable to contain and which eventually led to his loss of control of Germany. Then, with the 1814 allied invasion of France, Napoleon abdicated to Elba.

However, the following year, he returned from exile, seized power in France anew and invaded Belgium. There on 18 June 1815 he was defeated by a British–Dutch–German army under the Duke of Wellington at Waterloo (Box 12.1). Defensive firepower beat off successive frontal attacks by the French, and the arrival of Prussian forces on the French right spelled the end for Napoleon. France was thereafter invaded. Then, Napoleon, on 15 July 1815, surrendered himself into the hands of an astonished Captain Frederick Maitland of *HMS Bellerophon*. The British naval blockade made it impossible for him to flee. Instead, Napoleon was taken to the British island of St Helena in the South Atlantic,

Box 12.2

Celebrating national greatness

National greatness was celebrated on many occasions especially anniversaries of victories such as Trafalgar and Waterloo. The state funeral of the Duke of Wellington provided an opportunity to link the nation, state and church.

The *Illustrated London News* of 20 November 1852 declared as follows.

The grave has closed over the mortal remains of the greatest man of our age, and one of the purest-minded men recorded in history. Wellington and Nelson sleep side by side under the dome of St Paul's, and the national mausoleum of our isles has received the most illustrious of its dead. With a pomp and circumstance, a fervour of popular respect, a solemnity and a grandeur never to be surpassed in the obsequies of any other hero hereafter to be born to become the benefactor of this country, the sacred relics of Arthur Duke of Wellington have been deposited in the place long since set apart for them by the unanimous decision of his countrymen. All that ingenuity could suggest in the funeral trappings, and that imagination and fancy could devise to surround the ceremonial with the accessories that most forcible

impress the minds of a multitude, all the grace that Royalty could lend, all the aid that the state could afford in every one of its departments, all the imposing circumstances derivable from the assemblage of great masses of men arrayed with military splendour and in military mourning, together with the less dramatic but even more affecting grief expressed by the sober trappings of respectful and sympathetic crowds, all the dignity that could be conferred by the presence of the civil and legislative power of the great and ancient kingdom; and lastly, all the sanctity and awe inspired by the grandest of religious services performed in the grandest Protestant temple in the world, were combined to render the scene, inside and outside of St Paul's Cathedral on Thursday last, the most memorable in our annals … To the mind of the people, and to the superstition of thousands who would be loth to confess, although they would find it impossible to deny, the hold of such feelings upon their imagination, 'the signs and portents of nature' were added to the commemorative deeds of men, to render the last scene in the history of the hero more awe-inspiring than it might otherwise have been!

where he died in 1821. On land, but more particularly at sea, as Napoleon's incarceration showed, British power was clear.

Napoleon was not only defeated in Europe; France had also lost the struggle for oceanic mastery and colonial predominance. Thanks to repeated naval victories from the Glorious First of June in 1794 on, the British had been left free to execute amphibious attacks on the isolated colonial centres of non-European powers, and also to make gains at the expense of non-European peoples. The route to India was secured: Cape Town was captured from the Dutch in 1795 and, after it had been restored in 1802, again in 1806. In the Indian Ocean, the Seychelles were taken in 1794, Réunion and Mauritius in 1810. The British were also able to consolidate their position in India. In 1798, the Nizam of Hyderabad was obliged under British pressure to disband his French-officered unit. Seringapatam, the capital of the Sultanate of Mysore, which had been a serious foe since the 1760s, was stormed in 1799. The booty included a pair of bronze cannon which now flank the stairway at Powis Castle. In 1803, Wellington defeated the Marathas. In 1815, the kingdom of Kandy in Sri Lanka was conquered. India became the basis of British power and influence around the Indian Ocean. It also proved possible to expand the colony that had been founded at Botany Bay in Australia in 1788. Batavia, the leading British base on Java, was captured in 1811. The Pacific became a sphere for British, rather than Spanish, expansion.

The Congress of Vienna that sought in 1814–15 to settle the problems of the European world, left Britain with a dramatically stronger position. Her control of Cape Colony, the

Seychelles, Mauritius, Trinidad, Tobago, St Lucia, Malta, Surinam, and Ceylon (Sri Lanka), were all recognised. Britannia ruled far more than just the waves.

The British played a major role in drawing up the new territorial settlement after 1815 at Vienna. The Congress established a principle designed both to reward allied powers and to limit France. The Austrian Netherlands (Belgium) and the United Provinces (modern Netherlands) were joined as the kingdom of the United Netherlands under the pro-British house of Orange. Prussia gained much of the Lower Rhineland, including Cologne, closing a potential avenue for French advance, and the same end was achieved in northern Italy with the strengthening of Piedmont. By the Quadruple Alliance of 20 November 1815, the four great powers – Austria, Britain, Prussia and Russia – renewed their anti-French *entente* for twenty years.

London also was the capital of a growing empire. Turning away from Europe's conflicts gave Britain the opportunity to expand elsewhere. Equilibrium in Europe provided opportunity abroad, and a sense of Britain as naturally a major military power followed the Napoleonic Wars. Wellington was Prime Minister in 1828–30, while Trafalgar Square, begun in the 1820s, soared with Nelson's column, which was topped by Edward Bailey's eighteen-foot-high statue. The bronze lions followed in 1867. Nelson monuments were also erected in Dublin and Edinburgh, while his victorious death at Trafalgar was commemorated in paintings, engravings and dinners of celebration.

The distinctive feature of the post-medieval European empires was their desire and ability to project their power across the globe: by the late eighteenth and early nineteenth centuries, Britain was clearly most successful in doing so. There was an interesting parallel with Russia. Both powers were in a way outside Europe, able to a considerable extent to protect their home base or centres of power from other European states, yet also able to play a major role in European politics. Their geo-political isolation should not be exaggerated. With reason, British governments feared invasion on a number of occasions from 1690 to 1813, and again thereafter from the mid-nineteenth century on. Russia was invaded, as by Sweden in 1708–9 and by Napoleon in 1812, attacked, as by Sweden in 1741 and 1788, or threatened, as by Prussia in 1791. Nevertheless, their strategic position was different to that of other European states: just as they had avoided the ravages of the Thirty Years' War (1618–48), so they were to see off Napoleon and thus thwart the last attempt before the age of nationalism to remodel the European political space.

In almost every other respect – social, economic, religious, political – the differences between Britain and Russia were vast. The histories of the two countries before and since the early nineteenth century have been utterly dissimilar. Thus, their geo-political similarity at this juncture, in marked contrast to the rest of Europe, is a caution against assuming that on all criteria Britain was closest to nearby parts of Europe and against too great a stress on consistent parallel developments of different states as opposed to more short-term convergences and divergences.

12.5 Conclusion

Victory over Napoleon, command of the high seas, and the protection of its growing empire strengthened Britain's role in the world. The naval power upon which this was built would last for more than a century. In that time, the loss of the American colonies would become a distant memory as India became the jewel in what was a large, complex and ornate crown. The French Revolutionary and Napoleonic wars provided an opportunity for the British to advance at the expense of her one-time great naval rival, France. Consolidation, containment and further expansion would mark the nineteenth century for Britain and her empire. Trade would become the essential of the British economy; London's role as a great financial centre, the hub of empire, would create wealth far greater in extent and depth than that which came from the manufacturing centres in the north. Industry was important, but invisible earnings – stocks, shares and bonds – were more important still. The complexity of Britain's imperial network should not, however, deflect us from its importance.

Summary

◆ The crisis of 1793–1815 was formative for the British state and empire.
◆ Nineteenth-century British history rests on the political trajectory and military achievements of this period.
◆ British imperial possessions, and the ability to take more, rested to some extent upon the outcome of the French Wars.
◆ Britain became a great imperial power in the nineteenth century, but the basis of that empire was laid long before.

Points to discuss

◆ What was the impact of the French Revolution on Britain?
◆ What opportunties, in global terms, did the defeat of France create after 1815?

References and further reading

C. Bayly, *Imperial Meridian: The British Empire and the World, 1780–1830* (Harlow, 1989).

J.M. Black, *Britain as a Military Power, 1688–1815* (1999).

(See Chapter 13 for further references.)

Britain and the Wider World: 2

CHAPTER **13**

Contents

▌ Introduction

The nineteenth century was Britain's century, not only because of her imperial and economic power but also because, although Britain experienced fundamental socio-economic changes, which brought considerable dislocation and hardship, she did so *without revolution or sustained social disorder*. Although the failure to integrate Ireland successfully into Britain and its future were serious problems, the nineteenth century was the first in which 'the British problem' did not lead to war or insurrection. The economic advantages of Union were too apparent for many Scots to doubt its advantage.

Many of the special assets which Britain enjoyed or developed were subsequently to dwindle, disappear or become liabilities. Her insular position and imperial role; early, comparatively labour-intensive, industrialisation; the dominance of London; and rule by Crown-in-Parliament, have all proved mixed blessings. To some contemporaries, Britain's success appeared challenged, threatened, even precarious and it may now appear to have been short-lived. But while it lasted it was real, even if flawed. Nineteenth-century Britain had much in common with her neighbours, but, for a while, she followed a path as distinctive as sixteenth-century Spain or the United Provinces (Netherlands) in the seventeenth century.

Key issues

▶ What was distinctive about Britain?

▶ How far was Britain culturally linked to the Continent?

13.1 Empire and free trade

1851 saw a great celebration of Britain's success. The Great Exhibition was an impressive tribute to the majestic products of manufacturing skill and prowess. Planned by Prince Albert in 1849, it was seen by him as a demonstration of British achievement and as reflecting 'England's mission, duty, and interest, to put herself at the head of the diffusion of civilisation and the attainment of liberty'. The Exhibition revealed some of the results both of the Industrial Revolution and of the territorial revolution created by the rise of the British empire. At the time of the Great Exhibition, James Wyld built a large model of the globe. 'Wyld's Great Globe' was exhibited in a large circular building in Leicester Square in 1851–62. Gas-lit, it was sixty feet high, about forty feet in diameter, and the largest hitherto constructed. No eccentric, Wyld was an active parliamentarian, Master of the Clothworkers' Company, and a leading promoter of technical education. He reflected a widespread British confidence in their superiority and rule. In the *Notes to Accompany* his globe, dedicated to Prince Albert, Wyld wrote:

> What comparisons suggest themselves between the condition of the Pacific region in the time of Cook and now? What was then held by illiterate savages now constitutes the rising communities of New South Wales ... the civilizing sway of the English crown ... an empire more extended than is governed by any other sceptre.

Empire was not simply a matter of power politics, military interests, élite careers and an ideology of mission that appealed to the propertied and proselytizing. The Protestant churches of Britain devoted their resources to missionary activity outside Europe, particularly, though not only, within the Empire, and not to proselytism on the Continent. A sense of mission, often linked to or expressed in racial and cultural arrogance, was a characteristic also of the imperialism of other European states, as well as of the Americans in the United States, and subsequently in the Pacific, and of expatriate Europeans, such as the Australians in their interior and in the south-west Pacific. For long, most British scholars treated British imperialism as different in type from its Continental counterparts – more hesitant, commercial, moral and defensive – but this approach is increasingly questioned.

Most clearly in the final decades of the century, Empire had relevance and meaning throughout British society, as was reflected in the jingoistic strains of popular culture: adventure stories, the ballads of the music hall and the images depicted on advertisements for mass-produced goods. Empire reflected and sustained the widespread racist assertions and assumptions of the period, both of which were amply demonstrated in its literature. Launching the Boy Scout movement in 1908, Baden-Powell exploited his own reputation as a war hero in the Boer War (1899–1902), celebrated by the press, and the model of masculinity allegedly provided by the self-sufficiency and vigour of life on the frontiers of empire. Newspapers spent substantial sums on the telegraphy that brought news of imperial conflict. The sieges of the Indian Mutiny (1857–9) and the Boer War offered drama for the entire country, although that did not imply that imperialism was popular with all the working class. Many workers appear to have been pretty apathetic. The crowds that applauded the relief of Mafeking in 1900 were mainly clerks and medical students, rather than labourers.

If Empire was a crucial component of British nationalism, especially towards the end of the century, it was also of great economic importance, both for exports and for imports.

The difficulty of competing in Europe and the United States and of expanding sales in traditional colonial markets in Canada and the West Indies, ensured that the bulk of the rise in exports in 1816–42 was obtained from markets in Africa, Asia and Latin America, areas of formal (territorial control) and informal empire (economically subordinated but not territorially controlled). As a result of the end of protection for British agriculture with the repeal of the Corn Laws in 1846, and of the technological changes, including steam-ships, refrigerated shipholds (in the 1880s), barbed wire and long-distance railways, that led to the development of agricultural production for the European market in other temperate climates and to the ability of move products rapidly without spoilage, Britain in the 1870s and 1880s became part of a global agrarian system. Britain had been agricul-turally self-sufficient in 1815, but from the 1860s cheap grain imports greatly affected British agriculture. For food imports, Britain looked to empire, both formal and informal – New Zealand , Canada and Argentina – rather than to the Continent of Europe. Grain from Germany, Poland and the Ukraine, the latter two both ruled by Russia, was only purchased in significant quantities in some years. Some Continental agricultural products were important in Britain, most obviously fruit and vegetables, German sugar-beet, and by the end of the century Danish bacon and eggs were the staple of the British breakfast. Nevertheless, it was North American grain, Argentine beef and Australasian wool and mutton that were crucial. In addition, Britain became a vital market for these producers. About half of all Canadian exports by value in 1891–1915 were wheat and flour for Britain, and timber was also important.

English became the *lingua franca* of business, the language of profit, across most of the world, a development that owed much to expatriate communities and to the role of British finance and shipping. By 1835, the *British Packet and Argentine News* was an established weekly in Buenos Aires, the capital of Argentina, with a strong mercantile emphasis. It regularly reported the movement of foreign ships and the current prices of such commodities as skins, wool and salt. The rival as a *lingua franca* was French which in many respects was more important on the Continent until at least 1917.

A major difference between Britain and Continental countries, especially in the mid-nineteenth century, was that Britain traded abroad far more than they did, and far more widely. Her leading industrial sectors, textiles and metal products, were dependent on exports. Continental economies were more self-sufficient; what foreign trade they did was mainly with other European countries (including Britain). As a result, Britain was dependent on foreign trade, and on the wider world outside Europe, in a way that they were not. This was related to other aspects of Britain's distinctiveness: her outward-lookingness and internationalism; her interest in peace, which was believed to create the best conditions for trade; and her opposition to a large and expensive army. Vulnerable foreign powers were persuaded or forced into accepting free -trade agreements that opened markets to British goods: Turkey in 1838, Egypt and Persia in 1841 and China in 1842. Thailand (1857), Japan (1860) and Morocco followed.

Empire and Free Trade were later to co-exist with difficulty but in the third quarter of the nineteenth century they were both part of the official ideology of the strongest political and economic power in the world. The successful imperialism of free trade reflected the triumph of domestic interests committed to open markets, as well as the dynamics of imperial expansion, although during the heyday of free trade the formal empire played a relatively small role in the British export/import economy. Those who pushed free trade hardest, for example Richard Cobden and John Bright, were most hostile to the formal empire as it was and opposed to its expansion.

The role of free trade as a popular creed and as a commitment to low indirect taxation on the necessities of life was then peculiar to Britain: as the United States was later to show in the 1940s, free trade held attractions for the leading trading and financial power. Sterling, on the gold standard from the 1820s, was the major currency used in international trade and finance. Sterling was the reserve currency and medium of exchange. From the 1820s, Britain exported vast quantities of investment capital, and this played a crucial role in the rise of the City of London as the leading world financial centre. Britain's position as the leading exporter of manufactured goods to non-European primary producers, aided by the interest from her foreign investments, funded economic growth and investment.

In Britain, free trade furthered a major transfer of power away from agricultural interests and regions. A similar shift of power and influence from land to industrial, commercial and particularly urban wealth and ideas occurred on the Continent; although, as in Britain, this process was resisted in aristocratic, landed and military spheres. The attempt by the Conservative-dominated British House of Lords in 1909 to thwart the 'People's' Budget, with its 'super-tax' on the wealthy and its taxation measures on land-ownership, was eventually overcome by the Liberals. There were similar political and social tensions on the Continent.

Empire and crucial global economic links scarcely suggest that Britain had much to do with the Continent. The dynastic link with Hanover was broken in 1837, on the death of William IV, as succession there could only be made to the male heirs (unlike in Britain), while Prince Albert's early death in 1861 cut short his influence. Thereafter, the reign of Victoria was the longest period since that of Elizabeth without a foreign-born royal consort. Albert was a friend of the Prussian royal family and took a closer interest in European power politics than Victoria. Nevertheless, Victoria still took a very close interest in Continental power politics, in which she had a family role. She married her relatives into the Continental royal families and became the matriarch of the European monarchies: Kaiser Wilhelm II of Germany was her grandson. Victoria turned for advice to her uncle, King Leopold I of Belgium and felt close to his wife Louise. They often met in the late 1830s and 1840s.

Britain was, in relative terms, militarily stronger than she had ever been before, although her naval forces were under considerable pressure because of rising commitments and concern about the actions and plans of other powers. Nevertheless, from Trafalgar (1805) Britain was supreme at sea. Demonstrations of naval strength, such as the Spithead Review of 1853, greatly impressed contemporaries. Thanks to her naval strength, Britain was able to a considerable extent to feel insulated from Continental developments and to be free to intervene elsewhere in the world. Distinctive because of her naval strength, Britain can also be seen as unusual in her military power: India can be seen as the basis for a British land empire, so that Britain was indeed a 'dual monarchy'.

Between 1815 and 1851, while other European states made only modest colonial gains, the British empire expanded across several continents. This largely reflected the already far-flung character of her imperial possessions in 1815, and of the challenges and opportunities that arose from them. For example, Britain's position in Bengal led to concern about Burmese expansion. The aggressive, expansionist kingdom of Burma, keen to consolidate its frontiers and end disorder in neighbouring principalities, stirred up the East

India Company's fears and its defensive determination to support protectorates in north-east India. India was the most important area of expansion, and the British showed that they were capable of conceiving and sustaining strategies and logistics that spanned all of India. Although the British lost an entire Anglo-Indian division in a poorly conducted winter-time evacuation of Afghanistan in 1842, they acquired the Maratha dominions in Western India in 1818, Arakan and Tenasserim from Burma in 1826, Mysore in Southern India in 1831, Sind in 1843, and the Punjab in 1849. Kashmir became a vassal state in 1848. Lower Burma was to follow in 1852, Nagpur, Jhansi and Berar in 1853, and Awadh (Oudh) in 1856.

The British also expanded in Malaya, gaining Malacca and Singapore; and annexed Aden in 1839, the first time it had been captured by a European power. British warships moved into the Persian Gulf, while Argentinian and American interest in the Falkland Islands was countered by their occupation by the British in 1832–3. Success against China in the Opium War (1839–42) led to the acquisition of Hong Kong in 1842. This conflict arose from the Chinese attempt to enforce their prohibition on the import of opium. The seizure of opium held by British merchants and their expulsion from Canton led to pressure within Britain for a response. The demand for compensation was backed up by force. By the Treay of Nanking of 1842, which ended the wars, freedom of trade was enforced at the expense of China's right to regulate its economy and society. The Opium War was the first time a West European state had waged war on China, the first European victory over the Chinese, and one achieved in China itself.

In addition to this, this time further east, the British also enhanced their presence in Australia and New Zealand. In Australia, the Aborigines were hit hard by Western diseases, especially smallpox and influenza. These not only killed many, but also hit social patterns and morale. Aborigine resistance was also affected by the very fragmented nature of the Aboriginal peoples, which greatly lessened the possibility of joint resistance to colonial oppression. Also in the southern hemisphere, in South Africa, the British expanded outwards from Cape Colony. Natal was annexed in 1845. British success owed something to the new-found potential of steampower at sea: warships were now able to manoeuvre in calms and make headway against contrary winds. In the First Burmese War of 1824–5 the 60 horsepower engine of the British East India Company's steamer *Diana* allowed her to operate on the swiftly flowing Irrawaddy, and was crucial to the British advance 400 miles upriver.

Territorial expansion provided raw materials, markets and employment, and, combined with evangelism, encouraged a sense of Britain as at the cutting edge of civilisation. The economic value of colonies increased as steamships and railways aided continental and global economic integration. Cultural and ideological factors focused on the attraction of empire. Imperialism became normative. This drew on a sense of mission, as well as triumphalism, racialism and cultural arrogance, all supporting a belief that the West was unbeatable and was bringing civilization to a benighted world. The net result was a commitment that encouraged persistence in the face of adversity.

The country's destiny increasingly seemed imperial and oceanic. The varied consequences included the ability to send plant-hunters all over the world, enriching British gardens with plants never seen before in Britain, and encouraging the creation of arboreta, such as that at Westonbirt, to display trees from far-flung places. At Killerton, the country seat of the Aclands, these included the Californian Giant Redwood, named Wellingtonia after the Duke because it stood so high above its fellows. British capital and expertise played a major role in many parts of the world. Economic growth greatly increased the available investment capital for the world outside. Banking houses such as Barings provided the credit for the development of railways abroad, as with America's first railroad, the Baltimore and Ohio. The British also exported to the world. Coal from ports such as Cardiff, Seaham, Hartlepool and Sunderland powered locomotives and forges elsewhere.

13.2 Continental links

Yet it would be misleading both to overlook nineteenth-century Britain's links with the Continent and to treat her in isolation. If Britain's global responsibilities meant that she took a view of the world in which 'Europe' was simply one element, it was nevertheless a very important one. The concepts of the 'Balance of Power' from the eighteenth century and the 'Concert of Europe' in the nineteenth indicate how central the Continent was in the conduct of British foreign policy. British ministers had played a crucial role in the peace settlement of 1814–15 agreed at the Congress of Vienna. As after the Peace of Utrecht (1713), ministers were, thereafter, concerned about the fate of the settlement and about other international developments. Thus, the unravelling in 1830 of the attempt in 1815 to create a strong and stable Low Countries in the form of a greater Netherlands led to British diplomatic action, designed, in particular, to deter an increase in French influence. There was also concern about Portugal, a traditional ally, and in 1827 British troops were sent to Lisbon when the government was threatened by a Spanish-supported insurrection. Canning and Palmerston followed Continental developments closely, and crises in Spain and Greece led to particular interest. British ministers were very worried about what they saw as French aggression – in Spain in the 1820s and 1830s, in the Near East in 1840–1, and in Italy and on the Rhine in the 1850s and 1860s. Canning protested without success in 1823 when French troops helped suppress a liberal revolution in Spain. Prussian strength then seemed far less of a threat, not least because Prussia was neither a maritime nor a colonial power.

In addition, imperial issues could have a European dimension, most obviously with 'the Eastern Question', created by Turkish weakness and Russian ambitions in the Balkans and the Near East. British opposition to Russian expansion led to the Crimean War and later to threats of conflict in the 1870s. The terms 'Jingoes' and 'Jingoism' were coined in 1878 as a result of a music hall song by 'The Great Macdermott', the chorus of which stated, 'We don't want to fight, but by jingo if we do, we've got the ships, we've got the men, we've got the money too'.

Britain was no more insulated economically than politically. Economic growth did not mean that there were no fears of Continental economic competition. British commentators were aware of the benefits and drawbacks of reliance on Continental grain. There was a dangerous Continental grain mountain until the 1830s, and then an even more worrying general shortage, and this change was one of the major reasons for the repeal of the corn laws in 1846. Concern about German commercial competition was also a significant factor. In the parliamentary debates of February–March 1839 on the corn laws, in response to the depression, almost every speaker was aware of the threat from foreign manufacturing, especially because of the Prussian-led German *Zollverein* (Customs Union). The *Zollverein*'s tariffs against British manufactured imports led to frequent protests from British manufacturers and merchants.

The Continent was not only a source of competition. Free trade was always the real British interest because she traded so much not only with her empire, but also with the whole world, including the Continent, which for much of the nineteenth century was Britain's best market. In mid-century, British notions of economic liberalism were influential in much of Europe, although anxiety about British dominance of international trade encouraged protectionism.

For Britain, reliance on Empire alone for trade was never feasible, as most commentators were aware. Instead, Britain exported to the Continent large quantities of finished goods, particularly machinery, woollens and metal products, as well as semi-finished manufactures, such as yarn. Prohibitions on the export of machinery were repealed in 1843, and machinery exports were accompanied by technical information and advice, managers and large numbers of British workers to operate the machines. In the third quarter of the century, British exports to the most rapidly industrializing parts of Europe rose further than overall export growth, although this was reversed during the following quarter. In the Edwardian period, Britain's second most important export market (after India) was Germany.

Technological change had brought the outer world closer, enabling the more rapid and predictable movement of messages, people and goods. In 1821, the Dover–Calais packet service was converted to steam. Thirty years later, the first messages were sent through the new submarine cable between Dover and Calais.

13.3 Cultural links

Links were not only of the type of exports of British locomotives. More generally, educated Victorians were acutely aware of what they shared with other European peoples as a result of a common culture based upon Christianity and the legacy of ancient Greece and Rome. Gladstone published three books on Homer. Edward, 14th Earl of Derby, Prime Minister in 1852, 1858–9 and 1866–8, was a classical scholar of note. He delivered part of his inaugural speech as Chancellor of Oxford in 1853 in Latin and translated Homer's *Iliad*. Sir John Herschel (1792–1866), a leading scientist, translated the *Iliad*, as well as Dante and Schiller. The British elite idealized their perception of ancient Greece. The growing number of public schools made the classics the centre of their teaching. Those who could afford to do so performed and listened to German music, read French novels and visited the art galleries of Italy. Continental works were also available and influential in translation. Thus, the Scottish writer James Thomson (1834–82), published important translations of Heine and Leopardi, both of whom influenced his work. His poem *The City of Dreadful Night* (1874), the leading work of Victorian pessimism, took its motto from Leopardi.

These links were also apparent at the popular end of the market. Victorian melodrama drew heavily on Continental sources. The plot of *London by Night* (1843), a work attributed to Charles Selby, was based on Eugène Sue's *Les Mystères de Paris* (1842–3), while *The Corsican Brothers*, the London success of 1852, was based on Alexandre Dumas

Liverpool waterfront 1874: The bustle of a great imperial port

the elder's novel *Les Frères Corses* (1845). Melodrama, however, also testified to the resonance of hostile images. Thus, in William Travers' *London by Night* (1868) a wicked French madame inveigled unsuspecting British virgins into her brothel. The villainous Rigaud in Dickens' novel *Little Dorrit* (1855–7) was a 'cosmoplitan gentleman' of Swiss and French parentage, born in Belgium, 'a citizen of the world'.

Travel abroad was not just exhilarating: it was also regarded as a crucial aspect of a civilized upbringing. George III had never gone abroad, but Victoria visited Louis-Philippe in 1843, and in 1845 accompanied Albert revisiting the scenes of his youth at Coburg, Gotha and Bonn, and meeting the rulers of Belgium and France. In her later years, Victoria travelled to the Continent, particularly France, almost every year; she even held a 'summit meeting' with the leading German minister Bismarck in 1888. Her son Edward VII was a frequent traveller. Encounters abroad were often of lasting effect. Mass foreign tourism, developed in part thanks to the pioneering development of the tourist industry by Thomas Cook, even though his operations began more modestly with trips within the British Isles.

Foreign travel helped to create or strengthen images of other places and countries. Venice inspired Byron, Browning and Ruskin. Wordsworth was greatly influenced by the *idea* of Italy, a fusion of Classical civilisation and landscape and hopes of modern regeneration, and engaged with Italian poets, moralists and historians; while Dickens, a keen supporter of Italian independence, devoted much space in the journals he edited to Continental topics. Spain became familiar to British artists and the British public only after the painter David Roberts' travels in the 1830s. In mid-century the notion of Spain as colourful and exotic was popularised by the artists John Phillip and John Burgess. A growing number of tourists arrived in Britain, although their numbers never approached those of Britons going abroad. Reasons for travel varied. Empress Elizabeth of Austria twice visited Northamptonshire to hunt with the Pytchley, and in 1879 accepted Earl Spencer's suggestion that she hunt in Ireland.

Britain was open to Continental influences in many fields, not least music. Haydn had been a great success on his visits in 1791–2 and 1794–5, and Spohr was invited over in 1819 by the Philharmonic Society, which also commissioned Beethoven's Ninth Symphony. Rossini had mixed success, but made much money in 1824, and Weber composed his opera *Oberon* for Covent Garden in 1826 only to die of tuberculosis in London soon after the successful opening. Johann Strauss the Elder and his orchestra came over for Victoria's coronation in 1838 and were extremely successful, and in 1847 Verdi produced his new opera *I Masnadieri* at Covent Garden with great success. Continental pianists, such as Franz Liszt in 1827, Henri Herz and Sigismund Thalberg, were very popular in London. In 1840–1 Liszt returned and toured Britain, playing in Dublin, Edinburgh and the English provinces, as part of an ad hoc cosmopolitan tour that included a British musical comedian and a French *prima donna*. Mendelssohn and, later, Dvorak were especially popular in Britain. Mendelssohn's *Elijah* was written for the 1846 Birmingham Festival. Offenbach's operettas reached London in the 1860s, Strauss' *Die Fledermaus* in 1875.

Edward Dannreuther introduced the concertos of Chopin, Grieg, Liszt and Tchaikovsky to London audiences and organized Wagner programmes. Charles Hallé, a German conductor who had studied and worked in Paris, came to Britain as a result of the 1848 revolution and in 1858 founded what was to become a famous orchestra in Manchester. The Hallé's fame rose under the conductorship of Hans Richter (1897–1911), a Hungarian conductor who had trained in Vienna and been a conductor at Munich, Budapest and Vienna as well as giving a series of annual concerts in London from 1879 until 1897.

Before interest in foreign music is uncritically regarded as a sign of cosmopolitanism, it is important to note that the British celebrated their own nationality in this praise of the foreign music. Composers who were willing to pander to British taste, such as Mendelssohn and his oratorios, were cultivated. Verdi was popular in large part because he was seen as a liberal nationalist defying autocracy and the papacy. His operas could be seen to offer a model in which Britain was superior. This process did not only occur in the area of high culture. Pedro V of Portugal (1853–61) pleased Queen Victoria when he visited her at Osborne because, although he went to mass, he criticised the ignorance and immorality of Portuguese society and praised Britain.

British composers were also influenced by their Continental counterparts. Mendelssohn's oratorios spawned a host of imitations. Composers thought of as quintessentially English, were open to foreign influences. Parry, the son of a Gloucestershire landowner who collected Italian Primitives, was trained by Dannreuther and greatly influenced by Brahms and Wagner, writing an *Elegy for Brahms* and attending the 1876 Bayreuth *Ring* cycle in company with Bruckner, Saint-Saëns and Tchaikovsky. Sir Arthur Sullivan studied music at Leipzig. Elgar was greatly influenced by Brahms and Wagner, Delius by the writings on art of the German philosopher Nietzsche. Brahms and Wagner were most influential from about 1880 until 1914. Wagner's development of the vocabulary of music to the ultimate point of tonality and his exploration of chromaticism were of importance for British music, while his belief in the need for reconciling art and the community was very influential among intellectuals from about 1880 until 1914.

Wagner's exploration of mythology and psychology in his musical dramas anticipated Freud and Jung and influenced D.H. Lawrence, T.S. Eliot and James Joyce. George Bernard Shaw used Wagner's *Ring* in order to support his critique of capitalism.

British culture had less influence on the Continent. Dickens, for example, was read more in America. British art and music did not set the tone abroad. Nevertheless, there were influences, often in unexpected fields. Thus, new English bookbinding styles were adopted in France in the first half of the century, while the work of T.J. Cobden-Sanderson was admired in Germany. Shakespeare was very influential in the development of Russian realism and Chekhov, Dostoevsky and Turgenev were greatly influenced by him and more generally by British culture. Chekhov was impressed by British liberalism and technology, while Turgenev visited London frequently, was impressed by Byron, Scott and Dickens, stayed with Tennyson, knew George Eliot and received an honorary DCL at Oxford. British interest in Russian culture, for example the popularity of Chekhov, Dostoevsky and Turgenev, did not extend to support for the policies of the Russian state, which were often condemned as cruel and aggressive, as in Swinburne's *Ballad of Bulgarie*.

13.4 Political concern

The British people were also involved in what was happening politically on the Continent. This was obviously true of the Napoleonic and Crimean Wars, but, in addition, the Greek War of Independence and the *Risorgimento* (Italian unification) aroused enormous interest – more so than many of the minor British colonial wars and acquisitions of colonial territory. The Tory *Morning Post* referred critically in 1829 to 'the spurious sentimentality so prevalent both in England and France on the subject of Greece'. The local newspaper in William Bell Scott's painting *The Nineteenth Century, Iron and Coal*, finished in 1861, carries an advertisement for a 'Grand Panorama!!! Garibaldi in Italy. Struggles for Freedom...', a show that ran in Newcastle that March. The painting also included a poster advertising 'prime Rotterdam hay'. Great attention to foreign affairs was displayed throughout the century.

The manner in which the Italian hero Garibaldi was applauded by English working-class crowds – though reviled by Irish Catholics, fearful for the pope – when he visited England in 1864 testified to the way in which Victorians of most social classes were able to relate many of the events taking place on the Continent to their own struggles and aspirations. This was especially so in the case of radicals, many of whom had strong inter-nationalist views. London workers in 1850 were angered by the visit of Julius Haynau, an Austrian general who had played an allegedly cruel role in the suppression of the 1848–9 Hungarian revolution. He was mobbed by a crowd of London draymen. The failure to relieve General Gordon at Khartoum in the Sudan in 1885, a colonial cause célèbre, caused outrage and was a major blow to the popularity of Gladstone's second government, but in 1876 Gladstone had been able to embarrass Disraeli's ministry seriously over the massacre of Bulgarians by the Turks. The atrocities had a considerable impact on diplomatic, religious and intellectual relations with the Continent. Yet interest in Continental affairs was also patchy. This was especially true of eastern Europe. Violent events, such as the Polish risings against Russian rule in 1830 and 1863 or the Bulgarian massacres, could arouse concern, but it was generally occasional, and little was known about much of the Balkans or the Ukraine.

Nevertheless, Continental news remained very important in the British press, although more attention was devoted to imperial questions from the 1870s. The war correspondent and popular author of adventure stories for boys, George Alfred Henty (1832–1902), covered the Austro-Italian and Franco-Prussian wars, the Paris Commune and the Carlist revolt in Spain, but he also followed such heroes of empire as Napier and Wolseley on their African campaigns. Several of Henty's earlier stories dealt with themes from European history, but in the preface of his *With Wolfe in Canada. The Winning of a Continent* (1887), he stressed Britain's transoceanic destiny, adding, 'Never was the short-sightedness of human beings shown more distinctly than when France wasted her strength and treasure in a sterile contest on the continent of Europe, and permitted, with scarce an effort, her North American colonies to be torn from her.' Henty's stories, such as *Under Drake's Flag* (1883), *With Clive in India: or the Beginnings of an Empire* (1884), *St. George for England: a tale of Cressy [Crécy] and Poitiers* (1885), *Held Fast for England. A tale of the Siege of Gibraltar* (1892), *Under Wellington's Command* (1899) and *With Kitchener in the Soudan* (1903) enjoyed substantial sales. They contained some upright foreigners, for example French partisans during the Franco-Prussian war, but the British were best. This was generally the case in popular fiction. In Anthony Hope's novel, *The Prisoner of Zenda*, the publishing sensation of 1894, the British hero, Rudolf Rassendyll, was an exemplary foil to the villains Black Michael and Rupert of Hentzau.

13.5 Nationalism and xenophobia

Interest in the Continent was not incompatible with a sense of British superiority. The perfectibility or perfection of the British constitution were asserted. As reform legislation was passed within Britain, so British imperial power spread (not that there was a causal relationship), and the two processes were fused as first internal self-government, and later dominion status, were granted to some British colonies. New Zealand achieved self-government in 1852; Newfoundland, New South Wales, Victoria, Tasmania and South Australia in 1855; Queensland in 1859; the dominion of Canada in 1867.

It is scarcely surprising that an optimistic conception of British history was the dominant account in academic and popular circles. This was helped by the generally pacific character of the Chartist reform movement in the late 1830s and 1840s and the failure of its attempt to use extra-parliamentary agitation to put pressure on Parliament; and by the relatively peaceful nature of the 'Year of Revolutions' – 1848 – in Britain, compared to the widespread, violent disturbances and numerous changes of government on the Continent. A progressive move towards liberty was discerned in Britain past and present, a seamless web that stretched back to Magna Carta in 1215 and other episodes which could be presented as the constitutional struggles of the baronage in medieval England, and forward to the extensions of the franchise in 1832, 1867 and 1884. These were seen as arising naturally from the country's development. The historian and politician, Macaulay (1800–59), played a major role in renewing the Whig interpretation of history. He had a world readership and helped to focus attention on the 'Glorious Revolution' of 1688 as a crucial episode in the development of Britain.

This public myth, the Whig interpretation of history, offered a comforting and glorious account that seemed appropriate for a state which ruled much of the globe, which was exporting its constitutional arrangements to other parts of the world, and which could watch convulsions on the Continent as evidence of the political backwardness of its states and of the superiority of Britain. The leading British role in the abolition of the slave trade encouraged other states to follow the Abolition Acts of 1807 and 1833, which emancipated slaves in Britain and, with the second act, her colonies. The emancipation of the slaves also led to self-righteousness, while Evangelicalism further encouraged a sense of national distinctiveness and mission. The peaceful experience of Dissent in nineteenth-century Britain was also distinctive. Protestant Dissenters had a major impact on the whole fabric of society: disestablished religion contributed significantly to the 'progressive' ethos of eighteenth- and nineteenth-century Britain.

Religious toleration was seen as a major aspect of the Whig inheritance. Indeed the Whig government of Viscount Melbourne (1835–41) in part depended on the support of Irish Catholic MPs: in the 1830s there were at least 40 Catholic MPs, all bar one sitting for Irish constituencies. Although a devout Anglican, Queen Victoria was ready to attend Presbyterian services in Scotland and Lutheran services in Germany and she saw herself equally as the monarch of all her subjects, whether Hindu, Jewish or of any other faith. Her Proclamation to the People of India of 1858 repudiated any right or desire to impose on the faith of her subjects and promised all, irrespective of religion, the rights of law. In 1868 Victoria visited a Catholic mass in Switzerland and in 1887 Pope Leo XIII was allowed to send an envoy to congratulate Victoria on her Golden Jubilee: the Queen was conspicuously gracious to him. On her state visits to Ireland in 1861 and 1900, Victoria met the heads of the Catholic hierarchy, and Lord Salisbury's second government had in the Home Secretary, Henry Mathews, the first Catholic cabinet minister since the seventeenth century.

The peaceful situation in England, Scotland and Wales, but not Ireland, contrasted with the bitter divisions in French, German, Italian and Spanish society and their recent histories of internal conflict and revolution, that made it far harder to imagine a convincing account of long-term and unitary national development.

Victorian Britain displayed a sense of national uniqueness, nationalistic self-confidence and a xenophobic contempt for foreigners, especially Catholics. This xenophobia can, however, be seen in terms not of a hostility to foreignness *per se* but rather as one to what was seen as backward and illiberal. The latter were defined in accordance with British criteria, but these criteria were also seen as of wider applicability. Thus, hostility was based on a system of values, not on racialism. It was the lack of 'liberty' on the Continent that was most criticised. Thus, as with the earlier use of Protestantism to define values and nationhood, the criteria applied to judge Continental societies in the Victorian period could also be used to criticise aspects of British society. Conversely, if they adopted or shared British values, foreigners and foreign ideas could be acceptable. The rejection of foreigners and foreignness was deep-rooted, but it did not prevent Benjamin Disraeli, whose paternal grandfather was an Italian Jewish immigrant, from becoming Prime Minister. Sir John Seeley, Regius Professor of Modern History at Cambridge, both emphasised the role of imperial expansion in modern British history in his *Expansion of England* (1883) and reflected his interest in German culture and history in his *The Life and Times of Stein* (1878).

As so often, however, national confidence was tempered by concern. Confidence was most developed in the 1850s and 1860s, which were abnormally prosperous decades, and even then it was not unqualified. Concern arose from a number of causes, each of which was of varying effect: strategic, political, economic, cultural and religious. It is easiest to place an explanation and a date on the first two because they left clear markers in governmental, parliamentary and newspaper records. A more active France was a source of anxiety, and invasion by her, thanks to a 'steam[ship] bridge' from Cherbourg to Portsmouth or through a planned Channel tunnel, was feared in 1847–8, 1851–2 and 1859–60.

Yet it was in alliance with France, as well as with Sardinia and Turkey, that Britain fought Russia in the Crimean War (1854–6), the last war that she waged with a European power until the First World War broke out in 1914, a length of time unprecedented since the Norman Conquest. Britain lacked the large European army necessary to compete effectively in European power politics, and, as in the early-modern period, the eighteenth century, 1793–1815, 1914–18 and 1939–45, required a powerful ally to help were she to seek to do so. While the British navy displayed its strength in its wideranging attacks on Russia during the Crimean War, the army's weakness was demonstrated and its prestige lessened, not least when Sebastopol fell to the French rather than the British. Britain had earlier co-operated with France and Russia in supporting Greek independence under the Treaty of London of 1827. Such co-operation, however, proved short-lived. The Anglo-French alliance broke down before the Crimean war ended, and British suspicion of Napoleon III revived markedly.

A sense of religious challenge reflected concern about the position of Catholics in Britain, and Church–State struggles on the Continent were followed closely. Anti-Catholicism was given fresh impetus by the growing strength of the Catholic Church in Ireland, and, in particular, by developments in the United Kingdom: Irish immigration, the Oxford movement (see below), and the re-establishment of a Catholic hierarchy and the revival of papal dignities in 1850. Pius IX's bull restoring the Roman Catholic hierarchy in England was issued without consultation with the government and the situation was exacerbated by the triumphalist note struck by the new archbishop of Westminster, Cardinal Wiseman. Prominent 'old Catholics', such as the Duke of Norfolk, disapproved of his new zeal for public activity. Anti-Catholic sermons, publications, petitions and rallies were matched by renewed vigour in the celebration of the fifth of November, Guy Fawkes' night. The Ecclesiastical Titles Act, passed in the Commons by 433 votes to 95, banned the new hierarchy in 1851. Public tensions over religious questions increased appreciably. A Catholic street procession was attacked in Stockport in 1852 and in 1867 the army was called in to deal with disturbances following anti-Catholic public meetings in Birmingham.

The Oxford Movement, a High Church movement launched in 1833 that affirmed Catholic liturgy and doctrine within the limits of Anglicanism and opposed secular power, led to the Church of England becoming fearful of a fifth column. This was strengthened when two of the leaders, John Newman in 1845 and Henry Manning in 1851, converted to Roman Catholicism. Thereafter those who remained within the Church of England and sought to transform it from within – Anglo-Catholics and Puseyites – were even more urgently seen as possible traitors. Victoria was unhappy with the views and ceremonial innovations of the Puseyites and hostile to appointing them bishops. The situation in the early 1850s led to a shift in the Queen's position towards Catholics. In her early years she had been conciliatory and in 1850 Victoria declared that she could not bear to hear violent abuse of Catholics. She told her children not to share in the 'vulgar prejudice' against Catholics. In 1848 the British government had offered Pope Pius IX asylum on Malta when he was faced by serious disturbances in Rome. From the early 1850s, however, Victoria's position hardened and by the early 1870s her private attitude was somewhat like that of a Protestant crusader; she strongly disapproved of conversions to Catholicism, for example those of the 3rd Marquess of Bute in 1868 and of the Marquess of Ripon in 1874. In her final years there was a second dramatic transformation and Victoria became in some respects a philo-Catholic.

Anti-Catholicism was also heightened by developments abroad. Pope Pius IX (1846–78) stated the doctrine of the Immaculate Conception (1854), issued the bull *Syllabus Errarum* [*Syllabus of Errors*] (1864), which criticised liberalism, and convoked the First Vatican Council (1869–70) which issued the declaration of Papal Infallibility. All these moves appeared to vindicate traditional views of the reactionary nature of Catholicism and served to increase suspicion about the intentions of the Catholic Church and the loyalties of Catholics. In Germany, this led to the *Kulturkampf* (culture struggle) of 1873–87 as the government attacked the position of the Catholic Church: the Falk Laws of 1873 subjected the church to state regulation. There was nothing comparable in Britain, but it was clear that Catholic Emancipation – the repeal of civil disabilities to which Catholics were subject – in 1829 had not ended religious tension. Indeed in 1837 the Duke of Newcastle introduced into the Lords a bill to repeal Catholic Emancipation. It was defeated but it testified to concern about religious questions and a continuing sense among many Protestants that national identity was synonymous with British Protestantism.

There was also a degree of intellectual rivalry between Britain and the Continent. The leading French composer Hector Berlioz might adore Shakespeare, but influential nineteenth-century Romantic and nationalist Continental philosophers, such as Hegel and Nietzsche, looked down on the pedestrian and unphilosophical English. Lord Byron, who did make a positive impact, had left Britain in disgrace. Nevertheless, Walter Scott was a renowned figure on the Continent. Furthermore, British liberal thinkers were influential. This was especially true of Scottish Enlightenment thinkers, particularly Adam Smith, but also Ferguson, Robertson and Miller, while Jeremy Bentham had a major European reputation. His works were published in French, German, Portuguese and Spanish and he was involved in the Greek politics of the 1820s. A provisional count of references to major European political thinkers in the debates of the Second Greek National Assembly in 1862–4 has revealed that three of the top four cited were British: Bentham, Macaulay and Mill; the French liberal Benjamin Constant was the fourth. Mill's liberalism was widely influential. Britain was an attractive model to nineteenth-century Germans, not least because her constitution and development could be interpreted in different ways and her example thus appropriated by different political tendencies.

The British in turn were affected by Continental intellectual developments. German literature, philosophy, theology, and classical and philological studies were followed with great attention. Coleridge introduced both Kantian ideas and German critical theory. He visited Germany in 1798 and 1828, and on the former occasion attended lectures at the University of Göttingen. Greatly influenced by Kant, Schiller, Schelling and both August Wilhelm and Karl Wilhelm Schlegel, Coleridge was an important exponent of the principles of German Romanticism. Other writers were also greatly influenced by German

Romanticism. The Scottish historian, philospher and critic Thomas Carlyle produced a *Life of Schiller* (1823–4) and a translation of Goethe's *Wilhelm Meister's Apprenticeship* (1824). He later offered a heroic view of the famous King of Prussia in his most ambitious work, *The History of Frederick the Great* (1858–65). Ranke, and German historical scholarship in general, had a major impact on British historians. Hegel was influential from the 1880s. Nietzsche's thesis that art could enable man to live in a world without God, his justification of the artist and his idea of the 'superman', were influential from about 1900 and affected D.H. Lawrence and other young writers.

Liberal German biblical scholarship was more influential than Nietzsche. It affected British intellectuals from the 1850s and, in particular, the 1870s. Higher Criticism, the study of the Bible as literature, challenged the literal inspiration of scripture. David Friedrich Strauss (1808–74) contradicted the historicity of supernatural elements in the Gospels in his *Das Leben Jesu* (1835–6). This was translated by the English novelist George Eliot as *The Life of Jesus, Critically Examined by Dr David Strauss* (1846) and led to the loss of her faith. She also translated *Das Wesen des Christentums* (1841) of Ludwig Feuerbach (1804–72), as the *Essence of Christianity* (1854). Feuerbach saw religion as the product of self-alienation and the projection of ideal qualities onto an invented 'other'.

German biblical scholarship affected Anglican christology, as well as their doctrine of the atonement and view of human nature. It also led English Presbyterianism and Congregationalism to move away from orthodox Calvinism. By 1910 their theology was more liberal and less Calvinistic than it had been in the 1860s. These changes were controversial and resisted by traditional thinkers, but by 1914 even Anglo-Catholics were equivocating on such earlier staples as the Fall, original sin and the doctrine of the atonement. Protestantism was loosened up as the traditional authority of the Bible was challenged, while the right of private judgement in religious matters was increasingly stressed by Protestants. These shifts also reflected the inroads on conventional religious beliefs made by scientific developments and, in particular, Darwin's theory of evolution, as well as the impact of a more optimistic view of human nature.

Nationalism played a major role in a sense of distance from the Continent, not simply because of British attitudes, but also because of the development of a consciousness of national identity, politically, economically, culturally, and ethnically, in the Continental states of the period. The reign of Victoria was the age of the unification of Germany (1871) and Italy (1870). Furthermore, under the Third Republic many of the debilitating domestic divisions that had challenged French political stability since the 1780s were eased. Political reform on the Continent ensured that by 1865 some European states had more extensive franchises than those of Britain. Despite the absence in England of a paramilitary police force, there was probably little difference in policing strategies between London and Paris, while any notion of a specifically more benevolent model has to take note of Ireland. Whether they had a 'democratic' facet or not, Continental states increasingly seemed better able to challenge British interests.

Irish nationalism was a major problem for the British state, one that posed serious problems of civil order in Ireland and of political management at Westminster. As a result, Britain faced problems that bore some relation to those of other 'multiple states' affected by internal nationalist pressures, most obviously, Austria-Hungary and Russia and thus contrasted with states that did not face similar problems of diversity and where nationalism could more easily serve to reflect and unite the country, for example France.

13.6 The challenge of European rivals, 1870–1914

The process of late Victorian imperial expansion and economic growth took place in a context of European competition that was far more serious, and gave rise to far more concern, than the position in 1815–70, worrying as that had been at times. The international context was less comforting than in the third quarter of the nineteenth century. This was due to the greater economic strength of the major Continental powers, their determination to make colonial gains in pursuit of their own 'place in the sun', and the relative decline in British power. These factors combined and interacted to produce a strong sense of disquiet in British governmental circles, as well as an increase in popular hostility to foreign countries and peoples.

At the close of the nineteenth century, there was less confidence that British institutions and practices were best, and a sense that reform was necessary. There was, for example, much interest in the German educational system in the 1890s and early 1900s, and the national efficiency movement looked to German models. In 1890, Spenser Wilkinson, then a leader writer for the *Manchester Guardian* and later the first Professor of the History of Warfare at Oxford, published *The Brain of an Army*: a call for the formation of a general staff on the German model. The Marquess of Salisbury, Conservative Prime Minister 1885–6, 1886–92, 1895–1902, was not alone in being pessimistic about the future of the empire.

The tremendous growth in German power, and an accompanying increase in her international ambitions towards the end of the century, posed a challenge to Britain, in whose governing circles there had been widespread support for German unification and a failure to appreciate its possible consequences. The philosopher and historian David Hume, travelling through Germany in 1748, had written to his brother, 'Germany is undoubtedly a very fine Country, full of industrious, honest People, and were it united it would be the greatest Power that ever was in the World'. There had, however, then seemed little prospect of this, not least because of Austro-Prussian rivalry. By the 1870s the situation was very different.

More established political rivals, France and Russia, were also developing as major economic powers, while American strength was ever more apparent in the New World and, increasingly, the Pacific. The leading imperial challenges to Britain of *c.*1870–*c.*1902 were French and Russian. The Continent was from *c.*1885 to *c.*1903 locked in an effective balance of power or diplomatic stalemate: Germany and Austro-Hungary v. France and Russia. Hence there was the impetus and opportunity for Britain to turn to extra-European expansion.

The major powers competed in part by expanding their influence and power in non-European parts of the globe, a sphere where rivalries could be pursued with a measure of safety and without too substantial a deployment of resources. As a result, and given the importance of imperial considerations in British governmental, political, and popular thinking, it is not surprising that British relations with and concern about the Continental powers registered not so much in disputes arising from European issues, as in differences and clashes centring on distant, but no longer obscure, points on the globe, ranging from

Fashoda in the forests of the Upper Nile – a flash-point for rivalry with France throughout the century – to the islands of the western Pacific.

The background to imperial expansion in the second half of the century was a major crisis in the leading British colony, India, in the 1850s. The Indian Mutiny of 1857–9 was triggered by the British demand that their Indian soldiers use a new cartridge greased in animal tallow for their new Enfield rifles, a measure that was widely unacceptable for religious reasons. The rising was violently suppressed by British and loyal Indian troops, especially Gurkhas and Sikhs, in the largest deployment of British forces since the Napoleonic Wars and before the Boer War of 1899–1902. At the end of the 1850s, however, the British army took on a bold challenge when it attacked the centre of Chinese power. After initial checks, an Anglo-French force advanced to and occupied Beijing in 1860.

In the 1860s and 1870s, the pace of British expansion increased. Native resistance was overcome in New Zealand, although the Maoris used well-sited trench and *pa* (fort) systems that were difficult to bombard or storm, and inflicted serious defeats on the British. In Africa, Lagos was annexed in 1861, and, although an expedition against one of the more powerful African people, the Asante, was wrecked by disease in 1864, in 1873–4 a fresh expedition under Garnet Wolseley was more successful. Wolseley benefited from the assistance of other African peoples, especially the Fante, but his superior fire-power – Gatling machine guns, breech-loading rifles and seven-pounder artillery – was crucial. Ethiopia had been successfully invaded in 1867, although no attempt was made to annex it.

By 1900 the British had an empire covering a fifth of the world's land surface and including 400m people. There were defeats on the way. At Isandlwana in 1879 a 20,000-strong Zulu army defeated a British force of 1,800, by enveloping the British flanks and benefiting from the British running out of ammunition. In 1880, at Maiwand, an Afghan army armed with British cannon and Enfield rifles defeated an outgunned and smaller British force.

Elsewhere, the British were more successful in battle. At Gingindlovu, Khambula and Ulundi in 1879, heavy defensive infantry fire from prepared positions, supported by artillery, stopped Zulu attacks before the Zulus could reach the British lines. Wolseley stormed the Egyptian earthworks at Tel el Kebir in 1882. Egypt and the Sudan became protectorates that year. In 1885, Mandalay in Burma was captured, and in 1895–6 the Asante, Matabele and Mashona defeated in Africa. The fate of Sudan was settled at Omdurman in 1898 when British artillery, machine-guns and rifles devastated the attacking Mahdists, with 31,000 casualties for the latter and only 430 for the Anglo-Egyptian force. Technology and resources were not only at stake on the battlefield. In 1896, the British invading force built a railway straight across the desert from Wadi Halfa to Abu Hamed. Extended to Atbara in 1898, it played a major role in the supply of the British forces. By 1900, the British had constructed 20,000 miles of railways in India.

Britain's most difficult transoceanic conflict was, as earlier with the War of American Independence, with people of European descent, the Afrikaner republics of the Orange Free State and the Transvaal in Southern Africa. In the First Boer War, the British were defeated at Majuba Hill in 1881 and forced to accept Boer independence. A lengthier struggle in 1899–1902 initially found the British outnumbered and poorly led, while the Boers' superior marksmanship with smokeless, long-range Mauser magazine rifles, and their effective combination of the strategic offensive and a successful use of defensive positions, inflicted heavy casualties in the winter of 1899–1900.

More effective generalship changed the situation in 1900, and the ability of Britain to allocate about £200 m and deploy 400,000 troops was a testimony to the strength of both her economic and imperial systems, although the dispatch of so much of the regular army left it far below normal strength in the British Isles. Other colonies, such as Australia and New Zealand, also sent troops. Once the Boer republics had been over-run in 1900, their mounted infantry challenged British control, leading to a blockhouse system with barbed-wire fences, scorched earth policies and reprisals. This led to the 1902 Treaty of Vereeniging, a bitter but conditional Boer surrender. Income tax had had to be doubled in Britain to pay for the war, and it also greatly pushed up government borrowing. The Conservative policy of low taxation, especially low income tax, and financial retrenchment, had to be abandoned under the pressure of imperial expansion.

Much British imperial expansion in 1880–1914 arose directly from the response to the real or apparent plans of other powers, although the search for markets was also important. Thus both economic and political security were at stake and the 'imperialist phase' has been seen as marking the beginning of the long decline from the zenith of British power. Sovereignty and territorial control became crucial goals, rather than influence and island and port possessions, the characteristic features of much, although by no means all, British expansion earlier in the century. Thus, suspicion of Russian designs on the Turkish Empire and French schemes in North Africa led the British to move into Cyprus and Egypt; concern about French ambitions led to the conquest of Mandalay (1885) and the annexation of Upper Burma (1886); while Russia's advance across Central Asia led to attempts to strengthen and move forward the 'north-west frontier' of British India and also the development of British influence in southern Iran and the Persian Gulf, through which the British laid the telegraph route from London to India. French and German expansion in Africa led Britain to take counter measures, in Gambia, Sierra Leone, the Gold Coast, Nigeria and Uganda.

Specific clashes of colonial influence interacted with a more general sense of imperial insecurity. In 1884, there was concern about British naval weakness and the increase in the French navy. In 1889, public pressure and the need to give credibility to Mediterranean policies obliged the government to pass the Naval Defence Act, which sought a two-power standard – superiority over the next two largest naval powers combined. Expenditure of £21.5m over five years was authorized. The importance of naval dominance was taken for granted. It was a pre-requisite of an ideal of national self-sufficiency that peaked in the late nineteenth century.

By the turn of the century, it was Germany, with its great economic strength and its search for a 'place in the sun', that was increasingly seen as the principal threat. Carlyle had received the Order of Merit of Prussia as a result of writing to *The Times* on behalf of Prussia in the Franco-Prussian War of 1870–1; but in 1871, the collapse of the French Second Empire had inspired *The Commune in London*, a pamphlet that foresaw a successful Prussian invasion of Britain and the establishment of a republican commune in London. Many British commentators were then more concerned about France and, in particular, Russia; but the situation was to change. In 1897, Wilhelm II and his government gave a new thrust to German colonial expansion in their *Weltpolitik*. In December 1899, the rising journalist J.L. Garvin decided that Germany and not, as he had previously thought, France and Russia, was the greatest threat to Britain. Rejecting the view of Joseph Chamberlain, Secretary of State for the Colonies, that Britain and Germany were natural allies, their peoples of a similar racial 'character', Garvin saw 'the Anglo-Saxons' as the obstacle to Germany's naval and commercial policy.

British resources and political will were subsequently tested in a major naval race between the two powers, in which the British launched *HMS Dreadnought*, the first of a new class of battleships, in 1906. A projected German invasion was central to *The Riddle of the Sands* (1903), a novel by Erskine Childers, which was first planned in 1897, a year in which the Germans indeed discussed such a project. Frederick, 16th Earl of Derby, who in 1904 had become President of the British Empire League, agreed in 1907 to preside over the Franco-British Exhibition in London. The Anglo-French *entente* of 1904 was followed by military talks with her aimed at dealing with a German threat. Their consequences were to play a major role in leading Britain towards the First World War (1914–18). Russian defeat in the Russo-Japanese war of 1904–5 weakened Russia as a balancing element within Europe, thereby exposing France to German diplomatic pressure, and creating British alarm about German intentions, as in the First Moroccan Crisis of 1905–6. This crisis, provoked by Germany, was followed by Anglo-French staff talks aimed at dealing with a German threat. In 1907 British military manoeuvres were conducted for the first time on the basis that Germany, not France, was the enemy. That year, fears of Germany contributed to an Anglo-Russian entente.

Yet, as was customary, political opinion was divided. Alongside hostility to Germany in political and official circles, there were politicians, such as the 5th Marquess of Lansdowne, Foreign Secretary 1900–5, and his fellow-Liberal-Unionist, the Earl of Selborne, First Lord of the Admiralty, and Lord Sanderson, Undersecretary at the Foreign Office, who sought to maintain good relations, although Lansdowne also negotiated the *entente* with France. Wilhelm II was given an honorary degree by Oxford. The *ententes* with France and Russia were not alliances and Britain failed to make her position clear, thus encouraging Germany to hope that she would not act in the event of war.

13.7 Britain and the Continent before the First World War

The states that were vying for position at the turn of the century were also changing rapidly. Britain in the late nineteenth and early twentieth centuries experienced social changes similar to those of the Continent. Although the Church of England still played a major role in society and had not suffered heavily from involvement in contentious politics, as the Church had done in France (where it was disestablished in 1905), Germany and Italy, its political, religious, intellectual and educational authority had been challenged. Britain shared in a more general disestablishment and secularization.

Similarly, as on the Continent, a hierarchical society and its values co-existed with rapid social change. Throughout Europe there were significant transformations, both cause and consequence of societies with spreading education and political rights, and widespread urbanization and industrialization. These brought social dislocation, instability and anxiety, expressed, in part, in Britain, as on the Continent, by hostility to immigrants.

Deference and traditional social patterns ebbed. Privilege co-existed with meritocratic notions, and greatly expanded institutions that, within limits, reflected the latter – the civil service, the professions, the public schools, the universities, and the armed forces – played a role in the creation of a new social and cultural establishment different to the traditional aristocracy.

Working-class political consciousness and activism developed markedly in Britain as on the Continent. It was also characterised by a sense of international solidarity that drew on a tradition in British radicalism from the 1790s. As then, with the favourable and hostile responses to the French Revolution, there was a sense of parallels and links in domestic political developments throughout Europe, although there were relatively more working-class leaders who were 'international' in outlook in France and Germany. Nevertheless, the British Labour and Socialist movements, and, in particular, leaders such as James Keir Hardie and Ramsay MacDonald, had genuine links with Continental counterparts. These were stronger than the links between 1918 and 1939 and even more than post-1945 co-operation. Yet, there were also major differences. British Liberalism could and can be seen as a mass movement similar to Continental republicanism or socialism, but it was hardly republican or Socialist and even as a mass movement it needs qualification, given its leadership from within the governing elite. In addition, the British Labour/Socialist movement was very much on the periphery of the Second International: Marxism was decidedly weak in Britain compared with most Continental countries. By Continental standards, the Liberal party was particularly popular and its Conservative rival notably liberal.

Notions of similar development challenged any sense of British uniqueness, although, as already mentioned, such a sense had been challenged before, most obviously by the awareness of common Protestantism from the sixteenth century, so that England, or Scotland, was only one of the elect nations. Similarly, in Victorian and Edwardian Liberal or, even more, Socialist eyes, British disputes had an international dimension. If the conservative notion of an organic British, or at least English, system was to be contested, it was necessary to resort to universal principles and reasonable to look abroad for examples. The direction of such a search was confined. Whereas in the 1980s it was to be considered appropriate to turn to Japan for examples of labour relations and industrial organisation, in the late nineteenth and early twentieth centuries the only other developed industrial states were in Europe and North America.

The British attitude towards America was ambivalent. Thanks to the steamship, the Atlantic shrank: crossings became faster, more comfortable, safer and more predictable. In 1914 it took only a week to cross between Britain and the United States, as compared to six weeks in the 1850s. Many Victorians wrote about this new land. Independence had been followed by a considerable measure of divergence as a separate national American culture was established, although there were significant regional differences. Dickens, Trollope and the historian James Bryce were all taken by America's energy and drive, yet often shocked by its populist politics which were seen as vulgar and dangerous. A standard means of criticizing a politician was to accuse him of the 'Americanization' of British politics, and Gladstone and Joseph Chamberlain both suffered accordingly.

It is possible to stress both convergence and divergence between Britain and the Continent when discussing the period 1815–1914. Similar social and economic trends impacted upon different cultures. Industrialization in the Donbass was not the same as industrialization in Silesia or Lancashire. Yet the overall impression is one of converging experiences, not least in terms of demography. Similar transformations were planned and executed in the major European cities, including the construction of underground railways and major road systems. Throughout western and central Europe, public education and later low-rent housing programmes were designed to cope with the disruption of urbanisation and social change.

In addition, the functional similarity in domestic power relationships between Britain and the Continent in the eighteenth century (government co-operation with the social elite), was, in some respects, increasingly matched in the field of political thought and governmental ideology; for example, Utilitarianism was not an attitude constrained by particular constitutional traditions. It is necessary, however, to be cautious before assuming any general, smooth and gradual increase. Furthermore, it is similarly important to be cautious about assuming progressively greater British interest in Continental developments. Instead, for example, British interest in French domestic politics has been seen as becoming less apparent, so that the constitutional innovations of 1875 aroused little response. Nevertheless, even if political, legal and institutional traditions separated Britain from Continental states, they had problems in common. Comparisons became more pertinent. Thus, Sir John Acton Bt, then a Liberal MP close to Gladstone, later the distinguished historian Lord Acton, wrote in an essay on nationality in the *Home and Foreign Review* of July 1862: 'If we take the establishment of liberty for the realisation of moral duties to be the end of civil society, we must conclude that those states are substantially the most perfect which, like the British and Austrian Empires, include various distinct nationalities without oppressing them.'

Thus, in this case, alongside a stress on British excellence there was a readiness to search for a Continental comparison. As Acton was a Catholic with a German mother and a German–Italian wife, who had been educated at the University of Munich, he was especially open to Continental influences. Acton, however, was not alone in looking abroad. Edwin Chadwick (1800–90) looked to French practice when urging changes in the policing of Britain. The Royal Commission established in 1839 on which he served proposed a national police force, responsive to local authorities but managed nationally. Chadwick, who was the architect of the Poor Law Amendment Act of 1834 and was later appointed one of the commissioners of the new Board of Health set up under the Public Health Act of 1848, was criticised for his interest in professional administration from the centre and for drawing on foreign methods, a criticism also made of Prince Albert, but the willingness of 'progressive' thinkers to look abroad was instructive. Specifically Prussian administrative practice held a strong appeal in the mid-century, as can be seen in the work of Thomas Carlyle; and even Dickens was attracted by Prussian centralism in the 1850s and 1860s. It is indeed possible to discern a common framework in administrative developments, for example in policing in England, France, Prussia and the United States, although distinct 'national traditions and experience' were also crucial. The 1839 and 1856 Constabulary Acts did not institute a national police or even a national system of management.

A willingness to look abroad was not restricted to administrative principles and practices, but was true, more generally, of education. Military thinking was dominated not by Britain's experience of colonial warfare, but by discussion of Napoleon's campaigns in Italy and in 1813–14, and the Wars of German unification in 1866 and 1870. Continental work in science, especially in chemistry, a field in which the Germans made considerable advances, attracted British attention. The intellectual world of the eighteenth and early nineteenth centuries had not been closed to Continental influences, especially in Scotland, and even Oxford, so often derided, had a justified European-wide reputation. Nevertheless, in the second half of the nineteenth century Continental influences increased, in philosophy, political and economic theory and science. Hegel's work had an impact on Oxford, while in the 1880s Marx's views were disseminated in English. In 1883, H.M. Hyndman's *The Historical Basis of Socialism in England* appeared, offering a view of class development that drew heavily on Marx. In 1885, the group variously termed the 'Hampstead Marx Circle' or 'Hampstead Historic Society', which included George Bernard Shaw and Sidney Webb, began meeting to discuss Marx's work which they approached through the French translation. Two years later, an English translation of *Das Kapital* appeared in London.

Britain also shared in the artistic movements of the late nineteenth and early twentieth centuries. Just as the French Impressionists reacted against the particular conventions of academic painting, so their British counterparts, such as the 'Glasgow Boys', James Guthrie, E.A. Walton and W.Y. MacGregor, adopted a new and vigorous style, that in their case drew on the French Barbizon School and the French naturalist artist Bastien-Lepage. Thanks to the dealer Alexander Reid, who was painted by his friend Van Gogh, the Glasgow artists acquired international sales and reputation, while Degas and the Impressionaists were introduced to Scotland.

At the same time, British writers played a role in the European *fin de siècle* movement. The Irish writer Oscar Wilde wrote his play *Salomé* in French in 1891. An English translation with illustrations by Aubrey Beardsley first appeared in 1894, but as the play was banned by the Lord Chamberlain it was first performed in Paris in 1896. *Salome* inspired Richard Strauss' opera, first performed in 1905. At a distance from the *avant-garde*, other arts were influenced by Continental developments and practitioners. Franz Winterhalter and Jacques Tissot were key figures in Victorian fashionable portraiture, although John Everett Millais was also important.

13.8 Conclusion

There were many links between Britain and the Continent in this period. In many respects, they were stronger than the situation today, as the United States had not yet developed as the powerful alternative model it was to become. Instead, however, Britain was greatly affected by the pull of Empire, and, thus, of a transoceanic world of trades and empires. Europe may have provided a great cultural attraction to Britain, and its industries – particularly later in the century – may have offered competition as well as models to this country, but Europe was also the political sphere that most concerned the British. Whilst defending and maintaining its empire created many potential sites of conflict with European and non-European people, the balance of power on the Continent itself was also of interest to Britain, just as it had been in previous periods. The wider world – whether empire-building, European wars, military service or world-wide migration – affected Britain as a nation and Britons as people. These wider roles were vital layers in the complex political history of Britain at this time.

▨ Summary

◆ Relations with Europe were not a central issue, either to British identity or to British politics.

◆ The development of Britain as a great imperial power provided a new set of interests and identities that built on an already strong sense of British exceptionalism.

◆ By the 1890s there was growing concern about Britain's position with regard to the Continent.

▨ Points to discuss

◆ How far should Britain be seen as a European country?

◆ What did national identity mean in this period?

◆ What was the impact of anti-Catholicism?

▨ References and further reading

C. Bourne, *The Foreign Policy of Victorian England, 1830–1902* (Oxford, 1970).

R. Bullen, Palmerston, *Guizot and the Collapse of the Entente Cordiale* (1974).

M. Chamberlain, *'Pax Britannica': British Foreign Policy, 1789–1914* (1988).

C.C. Eldridge, *England's Mission: The Imperial Idea in the Age of Gladstone and Disraeli, 1868–1880* (1973).

M. Swartz, *The Politics of British Foreign Policy in the Era of Disraeli and Gladstone* (1985).

14 | Women

Contents

Introduction

Many of the rights which women today take for granted have been achieved in the years since their nineteenth-century antecedents first began to raise murmurs of discontent at the gender inequalities that fenced their daily lives. Yet, despite the work of such leading figures as Mary Wollstencraft, John Stuart Mill or the Pankhursts, the desire of a growing number of women to be emancipated, and to enjoy fuller, and then equal, relations with men did not bear ripe fruit until the twentieth century. When the First World War broke out in 1914, many of the most basic measurements of equal citizenship had not been achieved. Single women over 30 years of age, for example, gained the vote in 1918; universal suffrage – that is, equal voting rights for men *and* women – was not achieved until 1928. Until this latter date, notwithstanding what were enormous gains in the social and economic spheres, British women remained second-class citizens.

Women in the nineteenth century were affected by a common assumption – one accepted by many feminists as well as most men – that they were *different from men*. This not only affected women's daily lives but also influenced the thinking of the women's movement. Thus, when women appeared in social reform movements it was to add a feminine touch: a caring side (so it was argued). Because women were considered to be naturally more caring and less violent than men it was assumed that they would be attracted by the prospect of relieving the sufferings of the brutish inmates of Newgate and other prisons or the plantation slaves of Alabama. Those who believed their Bible and feared God – which was most people at this time – found it easy to accommodate the idea that women and men had been born to fulfil different roles in life: men were hunters and leaders, women were made for a supportive, nurturing role. This sense of division between men and women – and a commensurate division of their spheres of activity – was an obstacle to female emancipation and its supporters throughout the century in question.

Rights and obligations are measured by a greater number of indices. It is not enough to adduce a sense of the individual's or group's worth in society simply by referring to their right to vote in elections. The experiences of women in the nineteenth century, as at any other time, were prescribed by questions of class and ethnicity as well as by gender. Proscriptions upon women's activities included the masculine dominance of the social relations of daily life, as well as the absence of legislative equality. Like men, women had to earn a living or contribute in some way to the well-being of the family. In some ways, middle-class women enjoyed far greater freedom than did the wives of coal miners or young female factory hands. Yet what linked them together was the fact that they were perceived as different because of their sexuality, an accident of birth and biology. The latter certainly had consequences. Women suffered from the limited and primitive nature of contraceptive practices. Frequent child-birth was distressing; and many women died during child-birth, ensuring that many children were raised by stepmothers. Female pelvises were often distorted by rickets due to childhood malnourishment, while there was no adequate training in midwifery. To most men in nineteenth-century society, the primary functions of women were domestic: to bear and raise children; to feed, clothe and clean for the family; and to support the men and older male offspring in their masculine pursuit of waged work outside the home.

Key issues

▶ What were the different roles of women in the nineteenth century?

▶ Did that position change noticeably over the century in question?

▶ What types of work did women do?

▶ What were the main features of the campaign for female emancipation in this period?

14.1 Working-class women and their 'communities'

Women occupied a vital role in the working-class communities of nineteenth-century Britain. Although a world that stressed hard work and gainful employment was in a sense bound to the pursuits which men traditionally held to be their own, there was a positive emphasis, too, on the role that women performed in producing the next generation of good subjects. Where women did work, their economic roles were regarded as subordinate to those of men. Yet women were charged with the task of making ends meet: they were the ones who had to barter with the grocer or pawn furniture to supplement the family's budget.

The notion of 'separate spheres' dominated women's lives. The idea that the domestic world of the hearth and stove belonged to women was juxtaposed with the equally rigid idea that the world of work was manly and dangerous. The reality was less clearcut than this notion might suggest. If men and women were divided into these 'separate spheres' in classic mining communities such as the north-east of England, this was much less true of, for examples, mill towns, such as Preston, where women found work as mill-hands, thus leading to a blurring of the two spheres in question. The crudeness of the 'separate spheres' idea should be apparent to anyone who thinks hard about it, for life is rarely so easily placed in distinct boxes. But its true utility was not in its description of an objective reality so much as its explication of a mind-set, a moral value system. Besides, even if women toiled for nine hours per day in the cotton mill, they were still expected to look after the home. With lodgers, extended family residents, and generally larger families than we know today, women were pressed into action very vigorously on the domestic front, and it fell to the daughters to ensure that the mother's work could be done by helping out with domestic chores.

Women helped to provide their families' survival strategies for everyday life in the working-class neighbourhood. Women created ties between families and households; in doing so, women added life and meaning to the communities in which they raised their families. It was they who created a shared idea of what were working-class values and identities. Like men, who were bonded together in the common experience of paid employment outside the home, women were similarly linked with those outside the home, as they bought goods, shared experiences and pooled skills. It was the activities of women that made the inanimate house into a home, and made the bricks and mortar of the street into a vibrant neighbourhood.

Where women had a unique social or cultural function it was at the level of street or home. Building upon the biological fact that she alone could bear children, it was thus seen as a truism that the woman alone could bear responsibility for raising children. Mothers prepared the boys for work as much as they trained the girls to become the next generation of obedient wives and good mothers. The male-dominated boarding schools of the elite were very different. Here it was common to separate family members in a far more drastic way than was apparent in working-class communities. Sending a young boy away to school at the age of five or six inevitably weakened bonds that were still firm in the households of the poorer.

The role of the mother also carried with it the guardianship of the community's moral behaviour as it affected life on the street, day after day. Important research by Melanie

Table 14.1   The following table indicates the major employment patterns for women in this period

Five major occupational categores of women in England and Wales, 1841–1901 (000s)

	1841	1851	1861	1871	1881	1891
Domestic service	989	1135	1407	1678	1750	2036
Textiles	358	635	675	726	745	795
Clothing	200	491	596	594	667	759
Professional occupations	49	103	126	152	203	264
Agriculture, etc	81	229	163	135	116	80

Source: Census of England and Wales, 1911

Tebbutt has shown the importance of women's street conversation – their gossip – as an enabling feature of the working-class community. Gossip – despite the fact that the term is commonly used as an insult these days – was always far more than idle chat. It served a social function that facilitated the passage of information between individuals, families and groups. Such communication provided just one of the ways in which women passed their values around the community.

As is the case today, gossip also carried, for some members of the community, a negative connotation. Those whom the majority chose to snub were often the same people whose moral conduct did not meet with the wider approval of the neighbourhood matrons. Gossip was a network for communicating ideas and viewpoints, the result of which could sometimes be the passing of judgements on others' sexual behaviour. Gossip led to remarks on individuals' drunkenness or led to the denigration of their ethnic origins, for example their Jewishness. This could also lead to conflict between families or groups within working-class communities.

In performing their public function within the community, women's roles were competitive as well as co-operative. Women sometimes would fight each other over perceived slights to their families, or if their children were threatened. Women also competed with others to maintain the best house in the street. It was a sign of respectability and of pride-values passed down from mothers to daughters – to be seen scrubbing the front step or maintaining a window box. Women were taught to have pride in their men: it was seen as one's duty to ensure that the children and menfolk were as well turned out as their meagre budgets might allow. Thus, a brilliant white and well-starched collar or a tidy, pressed suit, without holes and seeming not in need of repair, was perceived to be a measure of what kind of woman was behind the man wearing the clothes. Such competitiveness masked the fact that women were raised from a very early age to allocate themselves a second-class position in society. Mothers taught their daughters to sew, knit and crochet; working-class autobiographies and diaries repeatedly capture this essential characteristic of the woman's role.

There is no question that, in Victorian society, men were put first, and this obviously affected most aspects of life. For the celebration of Queen Victoria's Golden Jubilee in 1887 the women and children of Ashby de la Zouch sat down to a tea of sandwiches, bread and butter, and cake in the marketplace, while the men earlier had had a meal of roast beef, mutton, potatoes, plum pudding and beer. Kate Taylor, who was born in 1891, the fourteenth of fifteen children to an agricultural labourer and his wife, at Pakenham Surrey, remembers her father's generosity as 'foolish' because of the way it impacted on the family's life by draining their resources. Taylor's father, who played in a band, invited his fellow players back to his house for dinner. In an act that combined face-saving and the foolishness which angered Taylor, her mother ushered the children out of the house while her father and his friends consumed the meal that had been meant for them. 'After they had gone', Taylor remembered, 'we would scavenge for any crumbs they may have left from dinner' (John Burnett, *Destiny Obscure*, 1992, p.305).

Women were viewed by the authorities as managers of a civil, proper and orderly working-class community. Educators and clerics targeted women as the likeliest purveyors of respectful and well-mannered children. While both Catholic and Protestant churches were concerned about mixed marriages, they all exerted considerable pressure to convert the man and to make sure the children were brought up in the mother's faith.

Experience taught the Irish Catholic priest that if the woman could be 'saved' by the church, then her children would attend its Sunday school and thus follow the true path. In the Catholic faith, in particular, motherhood was idealised, with the Virgin Mary set up as a role model of the value of female suffering and of the importance of raising children close to God. While Methodists or Baptists would have balked at the iconic nature of such Catholic representations of the women's role, they too stressed the human salvation that rested in the hands of the community's wives and mothers.

We must not over-state the extent to which women fulfilled such a near-divine and virtuous role. Women and men might be found lying drunk outside a pub on a Saturday night. Nevertheless, it is important to stress that the pure and saintly woman was part of the perceived order of things in Victorian society insofar as there was a well-defined moral code by which social superiors would have working-class women conduct their lives. In practice, the female role was as precarious as life itself. Family budgets were almost universally tight for working people; they were also uneven: a man's or a woman's income varied from week to week, depending upon brisk or slack trade. Lodgers were plentiful in towns with dynamic economies, when work was plentiful and well-paid; but the end of a big contract could see thousands flocking off to pastures new. Women were generally not blamed for family poverty in their children's reminiscences. A good mother worked hard; if she could not pay the bills, if she had to pawn clothes, jewellery or furniture, if she could not feed her children, most seem to agree that it was not through want of trying. 'My mother's life was one long life of loving sacrifice', wrote Mrs Burrows of her life in the 1850s and 1860s; 'No woman ever strove more earnestly for her children's welfare than my mother did' (Burnett, *Destiny Obscure*, p.235). Women, both single and married, suffered from the generally limited and primitive nature of contraceptive practices. Many single women resorted to abortion, which was both treated as a crime and hazardous to health. Frequent childbirth was exhausting; and many women died giving birth, ensuring that many children were brought up by stepmothers. It was not until the introduction of sulphonamides after 1936 that mortality figures fell substantially. Physically, as well as mentally, women ran risks through child-birth and the ever-present fear of illness. Couples rarely raised all the children that they produced; sometimes several infant deaths, still-birth and miscarriages all helped to ensure that the performance of the woman's function mixed anxiety with danger.

The housewife's ability to dispense the family's budget depended almost entirely upon the male's willingness to hand over his pay packet. Many men failed to do this; by so doing, they undermined the woman's role and severely limited her opportunity to make ends meet. Drunkenness among breadwinners was a terrible burden for families, women and children alike. Doris Ponton born in Southwark, London, in 1909, claimed that her relationship with her father was 'one of love when he wasn't drunk, the worse for drink, which he was every weekend when he was on leave'. John James Bezer, a Chartist writing of his childhood in the early part of the nineteenth century, was more barbed: 'Father was a drunkard, a great spendthrift, an awful reprobate... "Quarter Days" ... were the days mother and I always dreaded most; instead of receiving little extra comforts we received extra big thumps, for the drink maddened him (Burnett, *Destiny Obscure*, p.245).

Incidents of wife-beating were common, although neighbours and the like were less likely to intervene, and the authorities did not have the heightened sensitivities towards such events that they have today. Neglect and abandonment were also commonplace:

again, such travails testify to the precariousness of the life of the working-class woman. Violence against women and children was essentially a daily occurrence. In the North Devon lace factories, children were beaten with wooden and iron bars, punched and kicked. But we must remember, too, that nineteenth-century society was much more pervasively violent – certainly in terms of casual assaults on individuals – than in later periods. The law was also less protective of people than now. Victorians experienced public executions until the 1860s. Men who had served in the armed forces would have witnessed military floggings until later. Institutionalised, legal violence against prisoners was an accepted part of the prison regime; sentences of hard labour were common enough and meant exactly what the term implied: gruelling, back-breaking, soul-destroying toil, sewing heavy sacks, breaking stones or crushing bones. Those who read newspapers were also treated to daily accounts of the violence committed under the influence of alcohol. Assaults on the police happened with striking regularity; prize-fighting, between men stripped to the waist, occurred on open ground and street corners in order to settled disputes in what was perceived to be a manly fashion. Moralists and reformers, however, expressed outrage at these aspects of working-class life.

While single women, career women, and working-class girls who had jobs, were in a position of relative independence, the most important determinant of a married woman's life was the requirements of her husband's work. This especially meant shaping life according to the man's work rhythms. For example, oral testimony and autobiography suggests that the wives of miners were only able to grab snatches of sleep because of the shifts worked by their husbands, sons or lodgers. If a woman had to care for four or five working miners, she would find that there always someone coming home covered in grime, each of the returning men hungry, thirsty and tired. A miner's wife offered testimony to the Sankey Commission in 1919 which explained a situation that we can consider to have been commonplace in an earlier period: 'my husband and three sons are all on different shifts, and one or other of them is leaving or entering the house and requiring a meal every three hours in the 24.' Jack Lawson, a former miner and one-time Labour MP, remembered his mother's routine at home as a most remorseless mixture of snatched sleep and hard work. Lawson claimed that she rose at three in the morning to see his father off to work at Boldon colliery, between Jarrow and Sunderland. Two hours later, at five in the morning, she had to do the same for her sons. Lawson obviously asked his mother what she thought of this gruelling regime, and why she did it. Her answer expressed the kinds of anxieties associated with being a miner's wife: 'it might be the last time she would see us.' For the miner's wife, it was 'unthinkable that we should go to work while she was in bed' (J. Lawson, *A Man's Life*, 1932).

To this sort of toil must be added the general – if not universal – lack of help which a woman could expect from her male family members. It was rare for men to engage in what they viewed as unmanly household tasks. Husbands simply were not accustomed to performing domestic work; nor did they think it befitted their station in life. Catherine Cookson, the famous north-east of England historical novelist, captured this fact in her autobiography, *Our Kate* (1974). '[I]n those days' she wrote, 'a man went out to work and that, to his mind, was enough… [I]t lowered a man's prestige if he as much as lifted a cup.' Their wives were, by contrast, raised to see just such things, not so much as chores, but as a matter of duty.

14.2 Women at work

The concept of 'separate spheres' derives partly from Marxist scholarship on the changing nature of the family in modern society. It is sometimes claimed that the family was transformed by capitalism, industrialisation and urban growth from a unit of both production and consumption to one primarily of consumption. Thus, work was emphasised as being separate from the home; and with this separation, men's and women's roles were also divided. In effect, if this model is accurate, men brought in the money while women kept up the home. Such an attitude (while not expressed in Marxist terms, necessarily) was commonplace among Victorian men. Because their role brought in money, without which the family or household could not survive, it is easy to see why they saw it as more important than the contribution made by women.

Why, then, would women work? It would be entirely fallacious to argue that the woman's participation in the economy withered away in these years. As with so many 'Victorian values', the role of the woman as a supposedly mute or decorative support for her husband is partly mythical. Women, after all, outnumbered men and so the domestic norm of hiding behind the man, trapped in a purely domestic sphere, was unattainable for a significant proportion of women. Within working-class communities, few men brought in enough money to support a family in anything approaching comfort. With illness, infirmity and enforced idleness so common among working-class communities, there were additional reasons why women might seek gainful employment.

The absence of an effective social welfare system and the low wages paid to most women ensured that prostitution was the fate of many. Part-time prostitution was related to economic conditions. Sexual harassment of women in the work-place and on the streets was a problem, as was the sexual abuse of children.

As Table 14.1 and Table 14.2 illustrate, the majority of women in this period had no employment; or, rather, they had no form of work that was recorded the census. While the proportion of women who worked never really took off in these years (rising from a low of one-quarter in 1841 to a peak of 36.6 per cent in 1871), the minority category – those who worked – was not an insignificant total. Britain's widows, spinsters, unmarried girls of working age, and married women who needed to work were sufficiently numerous to ensure that the following proportions of women were in employment between 1841 and 1911.

By far the most significant category of paid female work outside the family home was domestic service. Between 1841 and 1911, this type of occupation accounted for between 989,000 and 2.1m women (the peak year was 1911). This growth in absolute numbers,

Table 14.2 Proportion of women recorded as employed in the censuses of Great Britain, 1841–1911 (m)

	1841	%	1851	%	1861	%	1871	%	1881	%	1891	%	1901	%	1911	%
Occupied	1.8	25.0	2.8	34.6	3.3	36.3	3.7	36.6	3.9	33.9	4.5	34.6	4.8	32.0	5.4	31.0
Unoccup.	5.4		5.3		5.8		6.4		7.6		8.5		10.2		12.0	

Source: Census of England and Wales, 1911: Census of Scotland, 1911

however, concealed a marked decline in the percentage share of employed women who worked 'in service'. In 1841, the figure was 55 per cent, and by 1911 this had fallen to 39 per cent, although in the meantime there had been a marked rise in the number of servants in the 1850s and 1860s, with the 1871 census commenting: 'Wives and daughters at home do now less domestic work than their predecessors: hence the excessive demands for female servants.' The role of service in female employment was less important in areas where industry played a major role, but it helped to provide the setting for much female employment and social subordination in more rural areas. In 1901, 43 per cent of all women declaring an occupation in Oxfordshire were servants: in 1861 nearly 40 per cent of Oxfordshire maids were 19 or under and 8.6 per cent were younger than 15 (Horn, 2001, p.67).

The next largest category was textiles which provided work for 358,000 in 1841, 635,000 in 1851, and a peak of 825,000 in 1911, after which date the total declined. Throughout our period, around 15–20 per cent of women were employed in these industries. Interestingly, the numbers of men employed in textiles did not grow as swiftly, and by 1901 there were 40 per cent more women working in these industries than men. Clothing accounted for 200,000 in 1841 and 491,000 in 1851, rising steadily thereafter to a peak of 825,000 in 1911. The peak year for women employed in agriculture and related work was 1851, when nearly a quarter of a million were thus engaged; this figure had fallen back to 80,000 by 1881, reflecting migration from the countryside, but grew again to more than 100,000 in 1911. Other important trades occupying women included metal manufacture (jobs such as buffing and polishing cutlery in Sheffield and Birmingham), chemicals, stationary and books, skin and leather work, which together accounted for more than 250,000 in 1911. By the later nineteenth century, the general food and drink industry provided 308,000 jobs for women.

There were entire towns and regions where women's work was almost as common as men's. Mill towns, for example, offered a ready supply of women's work beyond the domestic arena. In heavy engineering towns and in mining districts female work was much less common. This, it has been argued, was partly because men's wages were higher in such industries, which, in turn, led to a culture of snobbery among well-paid working men whereby the companionship of a house-maker rather than a a fellow worker was supposed to reflect well on the man. Similar snobberies also afflicted women in these situations; domestic matters, such as home-baking and well-scrubbed children, became an even greater source of public pride where women did not work. In contrast, mill girls were among the first to buy convenience foods, such as mass-produced bread and fish and chips – the sort of activity regarded with horror by the wife of a miner or a ship's engineer.

Despite such impressions, employers in traditional male arenas were aware that women's work added stability to the communities they were trying to build. In the 1870s, when James Ramsden, W.H. Schneider and the Duke of Devonshire, were building up the metal and ship-building boom-town of Barrow-in-Furness, they deliberately established a flax and jute mill precisely because they hoped it would staunch the flow of labour migrants out of the town. Though wages in Barrow were high, and skilled work was plentiful, Ramsden and his colleagues were convinced that the want of women's work prevented young men from putting down roots.

Conditions of employment for women were often, but by no means always, worse than for men. Rates of pay for women were universally lower. Women worked shifts, as did their menfolk, but there was much less regulation of women's work and unionisation levels were very low for women. A seamstress employed in an urban sweatshop might have to labour through the night if the opportunity arose because a lull in trade could easily mean a month of slack time to follow. Even where women performed similar tasks to men, their pay tended to be lower. Where women and men worked side by side, such as in the cotton mills of Lancashire, the men tended to get the better jobs and, thus, higher pay. Although, with piece-rates being the same for men and women, wage differentials in textiles were less than in other industries, the story is still not one of equality, with women earning only about three-fifths of a man's wage for doing similar work.

Part-time employment also occupied far more women than we are aware of, and many women worked at home for wages. Sewing, washing, doll-making and all kinds of stitching work could be carried out in the worker's own home, but statistical evidence for this is elusive. Work such as street-selling and hawking also occupied space between the public and private spheres in that it could be conducted relatively close to the home and impinged less on women's family roles than factory work where contracts of employment required inflexible absences from the home.

Because men were the majority of householders they were charged with providing census enumerators with details of their households' income. Many chose to ignore the fact that their wives took in other people's laundry, and even women who were classified as 'at home' or as 'housewife' might have had two or three lodgers living under their roofs, with all the additional work – washing, cleaning and cooking – that this implies. All of this, then, raised problems inherent in official sources. The absence of true measurements of women's work does not only affect our understanding of the working class. Middle-class women also took on voluntary work of the sort that was not (and still is not) recorded in census returns. Thus, for example, the Congregational Christian Instructional Society in 1835 was able to provide 2,000 volunteers to visit 40,000 families. Although these pursuits were charitable – that is, without payment – and represented an extension of the woman's 'caring' domestic role, it is arguable that they had an effect on the levels of women's consciousness at the time, offering them a different perspective on the world around.

But if we move beyond aggregate figures to ask about the social impact of work, the image becomes hazier. We must deduce, even though measurement is impossible, that all work types influenced the cultural lives and social roles of women. Women undoubtedly played a major part in the 'Industrial Revolution'. Their role in Britain's great factory system of Lancashire and Yorkshire textiles deemed that it could not be seen any other way. Yet the Victorian world stressed more their domestic role alongside their peformance of jobs that attracted low esteem. Many women were also poorly educated before compulsory education was introduced. In 1871, an overall 27 per cent of brides in England and Wales were unable to sign their names on the register.

The failure of women to achieve equality of pay, or of occupational opportunity, must be seen as features of these years. The *Observer* and *Sunday Times* had female editors by the 1890s, but in each case this was Rachel Beer, whose husband owned the titles. Women performed surgery from 1871 and qualified in dentistry in 1895. These new women, as the press depicted them, were important; not just for their novelty factor but because they were opening doors for other women. Professional and commercial occupations accounted for 530,000 women in 1911, but we must bear in mind that this figure was nearly to double in the 10 years to 1921. Thus, though women's employment patterns were changing, and evolving, the higher grades of work were attained much more frequently after our period than during it. There were, too, famous women whose successes in public life lent their sex certain kudos, but not enough to turn the male establishment from chauvinism to enlightenment. Arguably, great Victorian women such as Florence Nightingale, Harriet Martineau, or Queen Victoria herself, were too few and far between to represent a new trend.

14.3 Women, citizenship and the struggle for political equality

As we noted at the beginning of this chapter, equal voting rights for men and women did not come about until after our period. That is not to say that a number of women, and some men, did not campaign for emancipation. There were other ways in which women began to make inroads into the male world of Victorian Britain, but the struggle was long and hard.

Women's demands for reform were intimately connected with appeals for even wider types of reform. At each stage of our period, we can identify particular impulses for change that had a gender dimension. The French Revolution contained a strong element of reflection about the roles of men and women, as well as of rich and poor. Chartism and the quest for radical constitutional change in the late 1830s and 1840s involved both men and women. The vogue philosophies such as liberalism and positivism threw up male as well as female reformers, both men and women who challenged the subjugation of women. As the campaigns of the militant Suffragettes (a movement for votes and rights for women) took shape towards the end of our period, they must be contextualised with calls for social intervention to improve the lives of ordinary people. Thus it is no coincidence that it was in the post-war years, when the dominant Victorian idea of *laissez-faire* had been smashed, that women finally came politically of age.

Although the campaign for political emancipation developed most clearly later in the century, there were important forerunners. Mary Wollstencraft in many ways set the scene with an important piece of enlightenment thinking, *A Vindication of the Rights of Women* (1792). However, Wollstencraft's writings were in many ways ahead of their time, and hostility to radicalism in the period of the French Revolution affected the response to them. It was many years before such ideas gained significant support.

There undoubtedly was an awakening feminist conscious in Britain and America in the 1830s. The ultra-radical supporters of Robert Owen, the socialist and co-operator, were espousing a spirited support for women's rights at about this time. The model communities which Owen's supporters formed evinced no gender inequality but were more numerous in America where women (apart from blacks) generally enjoyed greater freedom than in Britain. It has been argued, however, that the radicalism of Owenism put many women off the movement.

The new and increasing public roles of women – seen especially in charitable work and in social reform movements – clearly had an important effect on women's consciousness. It is interesting to note the important role of Quaker women, such as Elizabeth Fry (1780–1845), in the campaign for penal reform, the abolition of slavery and temperance.

Moral reform was more generally an area in which women sought to exercise influence, though American women were more to the fore at this time. The most important event in the reform movement at this time, and intimately connected to the abolition of slavery issue, was the feminist rally at Seneca Falls in 1848. While drawing deliberately on the language of the American constitution to demand equal rights for women, the Seneca convention only narrowly endorsed the right to vote, and there was no equivalent organisation in Britain.

British radical organisations were muted in their support for female suffrage. The London Workingmen's Association, one of the seedbeds for the later Chartist movement, had, like other movements, called for 'universal' suffrage – but this did not in practice mean men's *and* women's votes. The Chartist movement, formed in the winter of 1837–8, demanded numerous political reforms (see Chapter 8), and counted on the support of many women, but, again, the rights of women were not a central plank. Although there were around 80 Female Political Unions and Chartist Associations, Chartism demanded (as one of its six points) 'universal manhood suffrage', with no equal demand for women's voting rights. The women who supported Chartism were effectively campaigning for their husbands' votes.

A link had been made between feminism and the campaign to abolish slavery in the 1830s so it is not surprising that many radicals drew analogies between the experiences of women and blacks. The Owenites were to do so in the 1830s and John Stuart Mill continued the theme in the 1860s. The Female Political Union, formed in Newcastle in 1839, made a cogent case:

> When told of the oppression exercised upon the enslaved negroes of our colonies, we raised our voices in denunciation of their tyrants and never rested until the dealers in human blood were compelled to abandon their hell-born traffic; but we have learned by bitter experience that slavery is not confined to colour or clime.

Other intellectual impulses continued to attack the weak foundations of claims that women were somehow inferior to men. This was true of Barbara Bodichon's *A Brief Summary of the Most Important Laws Concerning Women* (1855). Yet, it would be misleading to suggest that new ideas were necessarily favourable to feminist positions. Gender relations were affected by the declining influence of religion and the rise of scientists to become the new authorities. Other ideas of the intellectual superiority of men over women were given new authority by claims that the greater brain size of men proved the point. Medicine presented women as hormonally unstable. The natural differences between men and women were stressed in order to make women appear unsuitable for public positions. Seen as potentially hysterical, women appeared to some commentators as incapable of being entrusted with the vote. Furthermore, ideologies of race and empire helped shape the dominant constructions of masculinity, and these ideologies did not award women a commanding role.

Men, too, were sometimes supporters of the women's movement, such as it was at this time. William Thompson, the socialist, offered such thoughts in his *Appeal on One Half of the Human Race* (1825), the title itself going some way to explain the insidious nature of discrimination against women. The most famous male supporter of the rights of women was John Stuart Mill (1806–73). Mill had taught his sister to read and write Greek when she was a child and remained a life-long supporter of sexual equality. His *Subjection of*

Women (1869) remains a masterpiece of liberal philosophy from that period. Like others, Mill compared women with slaves, although he was careful to choose his words precisely. 'I am far from pretending that wives are in general no better treated than slaves; but no slave is a slave to the same lengths, and in so full a sense of the word, as a wife is.' More pertinently, perhaps, Mill also captured the artificiality of the woman's allotted role: 'What is called the nature of woman is essentially an artificial thing – the result of forced repression in some directions, unnatural stimulation in others.'

If working-class women were more likely to empathise with the men of their class than with the women of higher classes, then it should come as no surprise that the earliest campaigns for women's rights were inherently bourgeois in their composition. It was, in its first manifestations, a drawing-room movement. In the mid-Victorian years the women's movement emerged as part of a wider reformism that was liberal and non-conformist in origins and membership. Under women such as Barbara Leigh Smith (founder of the *English Women's Journal*, 1858) and through the Society for Promoting the Employment of Women (founded 1859), women's movements at first publicised a range of social–moral issues with concerted pressure for votes emerging but much later. The Married Women's Property Act (1882) marked a breakthrough for this sort of pressure-group campaigning. Whereas previously women had lost all independent property rights on marriage, this Act granted married women the same legal status as single women. Although this act was of particular interest to middle-class women, and demonstrates the perhaps bourgeois feel of the movement, some of its campaign issues nevertheless connected women of all classes. This was the case with Josephine Butler's campaign against the Contagious Diseases Acts (1864, 1866, 1869). The Acts were meant to prevent the spread of venereal disease among members of the armed forces. Legislation was passed giving police in ports and garrison towns the power to arrest any women whom they suspected of being a prostitute. The Acts also enabled police to have the women medically examined and placed in a secure hospital for treatment. These Acts outraged women's groups and liberals alike; the philosophy that underpinned them was clearly that women were to blame for men's sexual conduct and health! When it was mooted that the legislation should be extended to the civilian population, Butler and the Ladies National Association mounted a vigorous campaign. The Acts remained in place until 1886, but activism against them clearly helped to bring some women together.

The quest for the vote essentially began, according to Martin Pugh, during the second reform crisis (1866–7) when J.S. Mill put the subject to Parliament. The emergence of the National Society for Women's Suffrage and its successor, from 1897, the National Union of Women's Suffrage Societies (NUWSS), under the leadership of Lydia Becker and then Millicent Fawcett, were criticised for their gradualist approach. Yet their exertions did tell. By 1869, women had the vote in municipal (local) elections; similar rights for county council elections came nineteen years later. By the 1890s most MPs had come to accept the idea of women voting in general elections – even if the legislation was slower in coming.

The women's movement was always split between militants and moderates. The latter, with their emphasis upon duty and family loyalty, tended to dominate the movement, although the Edwardian years saw a significant development with the formation of the Pankhursts' Women's Social and Political Union (WSPO, 1903). In so doing, Mrs Pankhurst and her two daughters, Sylvia and Christabel, moved the campaign up a gear. Women were now pushing much harder for political reform than had previously been the case. The WSPU employed militant tactics: this was a vocal organisation, which moved beyond the usual boundaries of political protest at that time. Women chained themselves to railings, they broke high-street windows with toffee hammers; and, when imprisoned, they went on hunger strikes, prompting the government to force 'Cat and Mouse' measures through Parliament. This gave the authorities the power to release hunger strikers and to re-arrest them once they had reached full fitness again.

There was, then, a spate of activity in the period 1903–14, which demonstrated an intense commitment by a small minority of women. There is no doubt that this campaigning helped to convince some of those around them, including men, that women's roles needed to be reconsidered, albeit not a wholesale way. The Labour Party officially endorsed women's suffrage in 1912. While some, such as Emily Davison, who threw herself under the King's horse at the Derby in 1912, were willing to martyr themselves the legislation they demanded – the right to vote – did not come until 1918. It is arguable, moreover, that it was the experience of the First World War, where women were mobilised to work in factories and fields, and to support the nation's war effort to a previously unimaginable degree, that finally led politicians to support the cause of women's citizenship.

14.4 Conclusion

It is important to notice nuances and shifts in the way women were, the way they were perceived, and the position they occupied in society. Many of our current views about Victorian society are misleadingly two-dimensional. Women were clearly affected by the processes of social and economic change. But, by modern standards, equality remained a long way off even at the end of our period. The general notion of equality then was one of respect for separate functions and development. The woman's special role was defined as that of home and family, and was used to justify their exclusion from other spheres. Nevertheless, the role they played in the home and in the community was a vital part of working-class life – without that role, other members of the community would not have been able to function easily in their roles.

Recent scholarship has re-evaluated notions of Victorian sexuality in order to suggest that the image of universal repression was misleading. Sexual pleasure was generally given discreet approval within marriage, but, in the case of *women*, was harshly treated outside it. At a more mundane level, women ate less well, and placed themselves, and often their children, behind men in the pecking order. In general terms, the world of work was also biased against women. Industrialisation ensured that more, predominantly single, women worked in factories, although it reduced rural opportunities, such as spinning. Women mostly moved into the low-skill, low-pay 'sweated' sector, and were generally worse treated than men, a practice in which the trade unions co-operated with the management.

The extensions of the franchise in the nineteenth century had brought no benefit to women, and in the 1900s a vociferous suffragette movement demanded the vote for them. The militant tactics of the WSPU were designed to force public attention. We must conclude that the situation was very different to that a century earlier. Although the strains and consequences of the First World War dissolved much of the old order, it was already fast eroding before the pressures of change and the sense of inexorable development.

Summary

◆ Women's roles changed in this period but equality remained a distant dream.

◆ Women continued to be defined in terms of their home roles.

◆ Women performed a greater range of paid employment in this period, but, despite shifting patterns and new opportunities, domestic service remained dominant.

◆ Women tended to work for lower wages than men, even where they did similar work.

◆ Women's sexual experiences were not universally repressive or repressive, although Victorian moral conventions placed enormous burdens on women to behave in a particular restrained way.

◆ Political emancipation was won in the twentieth century, but the seeds for this change were planted in the Victorian age.

Points to discuss

◆ How did Victorian (male) society characterise women?

◆ How useful is the concept of 'separate spheres' for women and men?

◆ How did women's occupational roles change over time?

◆ What is the link between social reform and the quest for emancipation?

◆ Did women's political situation change in this period?

References and further reading

B. Bodichon, *A Brief Summary of the Most Important Laws Concerning Women* (1855).

J. Burnett, *Destiny Obscure: Autobiographies of Childhood, Education and Family from the 1820s to the 1920s* (London, 1982; 1992 edn).

C. Chinn, *They Worked all their Lives: Women of the Urban Poor in England, 1880–1939* (Manchester, 1988).

L.A. Hall, *Sex, Gender and Social Change in Britain since 1880* (2000).

M. Hilton and P. Hirsch (eds), *Practical Visionaries: Women, Education and Social Progress, 1790–1920* (Edinburgh, 2000)

P. Levine, *Victorian Feminism* (London, 1987).

J. Lewis, *Women in England, 1870–1950* (Brighton, 1984).

J. Lewis (ed.), *Labour and Love: Women's Experience of Home and Family, 1850–1940* (Oxford, 1986).

I. Pinchbeck, *Women Workers in the Industrial Revolution, 1750–1850* (London, 1930; 1969 edn).

M. Pugh, *Votes for Women in Britain, 1867–1928* (London, 1994).

E. Roberts, *A Woman's Place: An Oral History of Working-Class Women, 1890–1940* (1984).

E. Ross, *Love and Toil: Motherhood in Outcast London, 1870–1918* (Oxford, 1993).

S. Rowbotham, *Hidden From History* (1974).

J. Saville, 'Aspects of the social economy of working-class women in nineteenth-century Britain', in C. Holmes and A. Booth (eds), *Economy and Society: European Industrialisation and its Social Consequences: Essays Presented to Sidney Pollard* (Leicester, 1991)

R.B. Shoemaker, *Gender in English Society, 1650–1850: The Emergence of Separate Spheres?* (Basingstoke, 1998).

M.J. Tebbut, *Women's Talk: a Social History of 'Gossip' in Working-Class Neighbourhoods, 1880–1960* (Aldershot, 1995).

Morality, Sexuality and 'Victorian Values'

 ## Introduction

'*Victorian values*' is in common usage today, but mainly as a term of abuse. This is partly because of Margaret Thatcher's attempt in the 1980s to seize some sort of moral high ground by harking back to a time when family, good manners and public decency were supposedly guiding principles of individuals' behaviour. Criticisms of 'Victorian values' have come from a broad spectrum of interests and are derived partly from the attempts of sections of the political Right to gain advantage from associating with it. The most vituperative attacks have come from the Left, from where 'Victorian values' have been denigrated as patriarchal, racist, cruel, starchy and aloof.

These perspectives tell us something about our response to the Victorian past. Whereas the Victorian era saw Britain reach its apogee as an economic superpower and as governor of the world's largest empire, today's Britain is uncertain about its future position in the world. The competition over the Victorian past, from both Left and Right, is an acknowledgement of the importance of the Victorian period of our recent history. Any appreciation of where Britain lies now must be shaped by the lessons of that particularly colourful age.

In this chapter, we seek to understand more of the moral value-system of the nineteenth century, for it was, on the surface at least, markedly different from today's much more publicly permissive society. Yet, at the same time, morality was both a private and a public endeavour, and what people preached was often very different from what they practised. Double standards in personal and societal morality are nothing new. In this respect, the Victorians cannot be singled out as different. In assessing the developing morality of the Victorian world we will notice a growing uniformity, the emergence almost of a national code of behaviour. It is this homogenising influence (an aspect of wider conformity facilitated by improved communications and literacy, etc) which shapes our image of the Victorian world as a place of particularly acute moral hypocrisy. For, by stressing public conformity to what amounted to a code of practice, the Victorians threw greater light on the supposed non-conformers – prostitutes, homosexuals, bohemians, drunkards, brawlers, and so on. Moral reformers in the nineteenth century made attacks upon, and thus attempted to reform, a whole swathe of working-class leisure activities (see Chapter 7). But here, we discuss, in more general terms, the development of a Victorian moral philosophy and what were its major traits.

It would be easy to ignore the issues arising from Victorian morality, and to present an apparently unproblematic narrative of an age of progress and success for Britain. This is how eminent Victorians would have wanted us to remember them. Yet this would be unhelpful, because it does a disservice to wider questions about how we respond to the past. In many ways, the Victorian age is taken today as the epitome of how the recent past was somehow superior, better organised and, equally, more moral than our own time. In our efforts to understand the doldrums through which Britain has passed in recent times, we inevitably find ourselves drawn to making comparisons with the last great high-point in British life. The cost of welfare programmes, the problem of drug abuse among the young, the supposed immorality of teenage pregnancy, and so on, led the self-appointed keepers of contemporary morality to draw repeated comparisons with the supposedly superior attitudes and patterns of behaviour among the men and women of Victorian Britain. Much of this moralising draws upon crisis; but the Victorian world was far from perfect, and also had its crises of morality, faith and enterprise. Victorians themselves, it might be argued, reinvented morality because they were unhappy with the state of their own world. In questions of morality, then, history repeats itself.

Key issues

▶ To what extent can we talk about a code of 'Victorian values'?

▶ Was Victorian society more 'moral' than those which preceded or followed it?

▶ How did Victorian morality affect women?

▶ What are the main features of Victorian sexual morality?

15.1 Society and the individual

Public opinion may be said to be, that sentiment on any given subject which is entertained by the best informed, most intelligent, and most moral person in the community, which is gradually spread and adopted by nearly all persons of any education or proper feeling in a civilised state. It may be also said, that this feeling exists in a community, and becomes powerful in proportion as communications are to be found. As most of these requisites are to be found in the middle class of society as well as the upper, it follows that the power of public opinion depends in a great measure on the proportion that the upper and middle class of society bear to the lower, or on the quantity of intelligence and wealth that exists in the community.

William Mackinnon's assertion of a socially-specific public opinion in his *On the Rise, Progress and Present State of Public Opinion in Great Britain and Other Parts of the World* (1828) captured the moral dimension to public consciousness that was so powerful in the period. A call for moral policing and improvement can be seen as an aspect of a wider secular evangelicalism that complemented the religious variety. The virtuous had to unite to convert or compel the reprobate. The resulting social politics was very much that of a moral politeness which drew on the major cultural themes of the middling orders in this period, especially Christian conduct, polite behaviour and moral improvement, and was important to the shaping of that body of society. The shaping of the middle orders in terms of a set of practices and opinions required their agreement and thus entailed the striking of resonances to elicit a process of identification.

This required criticism of those who were not comprehended, and a call for the moralising of a supposedly dissolute population. In the *Birmingham Chronicle* of 19 June 1823, 'Mercator' attacked the profanity of 'the lewd rabble which daily infest a gateway fronting the Bull-ring'. A letter in the *Taunton Courier* of 16 January 1828 condemned drunkenness in the streets and obscenity to women, and referred to 'the morals of that portion of the population which is commonly called the lower class, but among which, in other places (and I would fain hope in this), may be found men much respected for information, such as, till lately, was expected from the educated classes only', but also 'to the extreme laxity of morals now pervading the bulk of the lower class'. The issue of 19 March 1828 commented on the conviction of three prostitutes:

> By the praiseworthy efforts of some respectable individuals, the inhabitants of this town are likely to be protected, for the future, from the audacious profligacy which has so flagrantly been exhibited in our streets. The insults and revolting behaviour of the most vicious of the lower classes, especially of the females, have been for some time past of a nature to demand some corrective interference, and the present example, which our Guildhall report supplies, will, it is hoped, operate as a timely warning among those who are only to be restrained from daring infamy by the severity of public justice.

Paternalism grounded in moral behaviour and religious attitudes rather than economic dominance was the justification of the social policy required for the well-ordered society that was presented as a necessary moral good.

This paternalism was to influence legislative programmes and their discussion in the press. The *Leeds Mercury*, for example, explicitly pressed the values of the 'middle class', opposed universal suffrage, supported factory legislation designed to proscribe or limit children's employment, and defined reform in a way that enhanced order and capitalism. Christian welfare rather than egalitarianism was advanced. The *Birmingham Commercial Herald* of 3 January 1818 declared:

> We have beheld the sufferings of the labouring classes, destitute of employment, met by the Christian liberality of their wealthier neighbours; we have seen resistance to constitutional authorities quelled by the timely interference of legal power.

The paper called for patience over poverty and the economy, a remedy in line with its New Year editorialising about a 'righteous Providence' (3 January 1814) and 'the Supreme Disposer of events' (2 January 1815).

Victorians stressed the idea of civic virtue, a general thesis which could imply many different things. Drawing from classical civilisations – Greece and Rome – which the

Victorians admired greatly, civic-mindedness was meant to demonstrate an individual's willingness to support the institutional life of society at all levels. The nineteenth century was an age of increasing awareness of local and regional as well as of national pride. To be a good subject, a Victorian was supposed to uphold the monarch, Parliament, church and the law. Responsible membership of society was stressed at this time. Critics, however, might point out that this emphasis upon society and its legitimacy was a product of a fear that precisely the opposite might be true – that society might in fact be dissolving amid the stresses of industrial and urban growth.

The early years of the development of urban society – particular the 1830s and 1840s, what the writer Thomas Carlyle somewhat narrowly termed the 'Condition of England' period – saw many ancient bonds break down. This, at least, was how critics of modern society – Tory patricians as much as Chartist radicals – saw their world. Whereas rural society had derived its legitimacy from the closeness of each stratum of society, with squires passing frequently among their yeoman farmers, modern urban society was more impersonal. The cramming together of thousands of working people in the tight confines of towns and cities – where policing was limited at first and social conditions were abject – created new scope for crime and unrest. Victorian commentators feared moral atrophy and social decay; thus the emphasis upon the civic ethos was an ameliorative measure.

Victorian morality placed people within a hierarchy. With society becoming more impersonal, moral values came increasingly to be stressed in terms of what individuals could do for society through their own personal morality. Thus it was that there developed in the nineteenth century an unshakeable faith in the nostrum of self-help; and this lay at the heart of the Victorian idea of progress. In the earlier part of the century, social thinkers and legislators came increasingly to view liberal individualism as a powerful virtue.

The idea of self-help was closely linked to the economic doctrine of *laissez-faire*. These two creeds were part of a dominant ideology which viewed state intervention as having a deleterious effect on the capacity of individuals to realise their full potential. An over-weening, interventionist state was thought likely to stifle the entrepreneurial energies of individuals. On this basis, state activity in the social sphere – such as the Poor Law (regularly refined and rethought since Elizabethan times) – was criticised because it supposedly encouraged a culture of dependency. The cornerstone of the *laissez-faire* and self-help ideal was Adam Smith's *Inquiry into the Nature and causes of the Wealth of Nations* (1776), a book which provided a devastating critique of the excessive regulation of the mercantile system of the eighteenth century. Writers such as Edmund Burke (in his *Essay on Scarcity* published in 1800) expressed the self-help idea because it spurred the labouring classes to work hard to look to themselves, not the state, for their living. Self-help and *laissez-faire* were popularised and distilled by later political economists and social reformers, finding their most famous expression in the harsh regime of the New Poor Law, introduced by the Poor Law Amendment Act, 1834 (see Chapter 8). The Act was meant to reaffirm the common view that poverty was the individual's responsibility; and that a fear of its effects was a crucial impetus to self-improvement. Self-help implied thrift, and the two attributes together were the foundation of independence.

The idea that the individual could succeed, and so make society a better place, by his (rarely did Victorians use 'her' except when talking about queens or ships) efforts was clearly the view of Samuel Smiles (1812–1904), the prophet of liberal-individualism. The bible of Smilesian values was *Self-Help* (1859), an enormously popular book of good

Box 15.1

"Self-help'

Extract from Samuel Smiles, *Self-Help* (1859).

'HEAVEN helps those who help themselves' is a well-tried maxim, embodying in a small compass the results of vast human experience. The spirit of self-help is the root of all genuine growth in the individual; and, exhibited in the lives of many, it constitutes the true source of national vigour and strength. Help from without is often enfeebling in its effects, but help from within invariably invigorates. Whatever is done *for* men or classes, to a certain extent takes away the stimulus and necessity of doing for themselves; and where men are subjected to over-guidance and over-government, the inevitable tendency is to render them comparatively helpless...

The spirit of self-help, as exhibited in the energetic action of individuals, has in all times been a marked feature in the English character, and furnishes the true measure of our power as a nation ... Even the humblest person, who sets before his fellows an example of industry, sobriety, and upright honesty of purpose in life, has a present as well as a future influence upon the well-being of his country; for his life and character pass unconsciously into the lives of others, and propagate good examples for all time to come.

Daily experience shows that it is energetic individualism which produces the most powerful effects upon the life and actions of others, and really constitutes the best practical education. Schools, academies, and colleges, give but the merest beginnings of culture in comparison with it. Far more influential is the life-education daily given in our homes, in the streets, behind counters, in workshops, at the loom and the plough, in counting-houses and manufactories, and in busy haunts of men.

Source: Samuel Smiles, Self-Help (London, John Murray, 1886 edn), pp. 1–3

examples which enjoyed huge sales and numerous print-runs, and was translated into many languages (see Box 15.1). Smiles sought to articulate a view that men of humble origins could go on to great things if they avoided immoral or dissolute temptation and worked hard to improve themselves. Smiles's *Self-Help* is a compilation of biographies, or hagiographies, of great men who advanced beyond the relatively low circumstances of their birth. Whereas previous stories of this sort had focused on classical heroes, generals and kings, Smiles stressed the contribution of once ordinary men in ordinary spheres of life, although stress was laid upon 'work', so that even Joshua Reynolds and David Wilkie were included in a chapter entitled 'workers in art'. All the great Victorians were included in later editions of Smiles; alongside Beethoven and Chaucer we can find Sir Robert Peel and the then famous explorer of Africa, Dr Livingstone.

Smiles opened his account with the religious maxim 'Heaven helps those who help themselves'. He considered that 'The spirit of self-help is the root of all genuine growth in the individual'; by this measure, society and the nation would benefit, for self-help also 'constitutes the true source of national vigour and strength'. If Smiles embodied a near-religious vision of the way human society might be improved and protected, there was a less than saintly aspect to his vision, articulated in a later book, *Thrift* (1875). In *Thrift*, perhaps more than in *Self-Help*, Smiles captured the spirit of the age. The Victorians feared the sort of jealously that led to resentment of another's success. The old British pastime of criticising the successful was already known in Smiles' time, and, because of continuing inequalities in the distribution of wealth, it was important that a credo was developed to deflect criticism of this fact. It was in this light that Smiles argued: 'When workmen, by their industry and frugality, have secured their own independence, they will cease to regard the sight of others' well-being as a wrong inflicted on themselves.' As the

Manchester doctor, educationist and social reformer, JP Kay Shuttleworth, commented in his *The Moral and Physical Condition of the Working Class in … Manchester* (1833), the prospect for self-improvement made the 'success of the middle classes less a subject of envy than of emulation'. In general terms, self-help provided a powerful corrective to the rigorous rankings of the class system.

The creed of self-help was closely linked to another quality which the Victorians were wont to stress: that the individual had a duty to work for the greater good of society. Indeed, other titles in Smiles's formidable canon included *Character* (1871) and *Duty* (1887). First among the Victorian duties was the need to work. The bible could be drawn into service as a reminder to people that work was the requirement for those who wished to eat ('By the sweat of thy brow halt thou eat bread'). As Helen Ekin Skerrett wrote in *Letters to a Daughter* (1887):

> Certain self-evident duties are imposed upon every rational begin. One of the first of these is the duty of being employed a large proportion of our time. It is probable that nearly all young people have a certain dislike for work, and self-control must come in to help them do the work that belongs to them to do.

Work was perceived to be both a responsibility and a duty. This did not simply mean paid employment, however. After all, two-thirds of women were recorded in the census as not being in paid employment, while members of the wealthy elite could hardly justify their existences if work had been so narrowly defined. In Victorian moral ordinances, work was also a 'calling' or a 'mission'; it was much more than simple remunerative toil. Manual labour, paid for in hard-earned shillings, was fine for navvies and dock-workers, but for the middle classes, the aristocracy, and for women and children, there were other duties that needed to be attended to. Leadership – in the community or of the nation – was stressed as the natural work of those born in the right class. Those lucky enough to be born wealthy were expected to do their duty to the poor. This meant spending some of their abundant free time working for charities. For women, a cult of domesticity built up around the useful pursuit of home-making and child-rearing. For children, great stress was placed upon the training of the mind and the body – in schools, at home, at their father or mother's knee, and on the sports field – in order to be useful and hardworking adults in the future.

Work, duty, good moral character – all these things stressed the respectability of the individual and its benefits to society. To be respectable covered a gamut of situations and types of behaviour. As an essentially time-bound, changeable and subjective term, it defies concrete definition. There is no doubt, however, that 'respectability' was meant to be a way of emphasising appropriate behaviour across class boundaries. Victorians were conscious of the dichotomy of riches and poverty. They saw examples of both on a daily basis on their streets, and it was important that values were found which could weld people who, in class terms, were markedly different. At the same time, although all were expected to conform to social norms, particular obligations were placed on the affluent. They were expected to set and maintain the tone. Thus, on 6 November 1823, an editorial in the *Birmingham Chronicle* discussed the notorious recent 'Gill's Hill Murder' of William Weare, a solicitor and card-cheat:

> The most horrible circumstance in this murder is the condition of life and worldly circumstances of the parties principally accused. Thurtell, the person principally implicated, was a man of good property, and of very respectable family connections.

Respectability, on one level, was the public obedience to cherished moral norms. Cleanliness was next to Godliness for Victorians and so a respectable family, however poor that family might be, would always have the outward appearance of tidiness, for this demonstrated pride of appearance. Public drunkenness was much frowned upon, even though heavy drinking was commonplace. Violence against the family, while common enough behind closed doors, was greeted with opprobrious denunciation if it occurred on the street. Chastity (as we will see later) was important, especially among girls. Any outward sense that an individual or family had loose sexual morals would evoke outrage from the conformist majority, whatever their own hypocrisies. Equally, an earnest approach to life was valued above frivolity or levity.

It is important that the modern-day audience remembers that the idea of teenagers as a separate group was a product of the late 1950s. Till that point, people were perceived to be either children or adults. Consequently, in its search for dignified and moral behaviour, Victorian society stressed the need to draw out the adult in the child; thus small boys of wealthy families were dressed as 'adults in miniature' and the girls as china dolls. Children were required to be 'seen and not heard'. And 'street urchins' and 'whippersnappers' – young children who ran wild on the streets, making a living as best they could – were viewed as a nuisance. Classical characterisation, such as Dickens's 'Artful Dodger','Toby Crackit' and 'Charley Bates' (immortalised in *Oliver Twist*, 1837), fixed in peoples' minds the depths to which children could sink without the guidance of good parents or a decent orphanage. This fear about the morality of children continued to exercise commentators at the end of the century. Arnold Freeman noted in *Boy Life and Labour: The Manufacture of Inefficiency* (1914), that society frowned upon the boy who 'spends a large part of his spare time in loafing' around the streets, 'playing games, singing, exchanging witticisms, and generally making himself obnoxious to the police and the public'. Bad language, excessive noisiness or cheek to adults might easily result in a cuff round the ear. It was not uncommon for magistrates to instruct policemen to administer a sound thrashing to errant young boys. This was an age without our heightened fears over physical abuse of children, and so on.

Whereas thrift helped the poor labourer to save money, charity – a biblical virtue – helped the rich to justify their wealth. In an age before a mass welfare state, when the limited provision of the Poor Law was the safety net of the poor, private charity assumed an unrivalled position in society. Charitable giving saw more mouths fed, more feet shod, and more sickness treated, than poor law guardians could ever have coped with. Even at the beginning of the century, private donations to charity totalled a little under £5m per annum. Sampson Low's summary of London charities (1862) provides us with a clear idea of the degree to which charity penetrated even society's darker recesses. He found a total of 640 institutions, a fifth of which had been established in the previous 10 years:

> 124 colleges, hospitals, almshouses and other institutions for the aged
> 80 hospitals and infirmaries
> 72 trade, provident and benevolent funds
> 56 bible and home missionary societies and funds
> 16 charities for the deaf, dumb, blind and crippled
> 14 orphanages.

Over the next 20 years, London's charities continued to grow both in absolute number and in levels of income and expenditure. Some charities were set up on an ad hoc basis to deal with particular crises, such as Whitehaven's 'Ladies' Irish Clothing Society' which established to collect and to send garments to the needy of Ireland during the terrible years of the Great Famine (1845–51). Whatever their meaning, and however short their lives, charities such as these provided the middle classes – and commonly women – with what they saw as a very serious role in life.

15.2 Men, women and morality

We have already seen in Chapter 14 on women's lives that gender divisions were even more significant in nineteenth-century society than they are today. Few women were able to acquire highly paid professional jobs until the end of our period, women could not vote in parliamentary elections, and ordinary women would have been justified in believing that their class and their gender represented a double burden.

Attitudes towards women were shaped by a wider moral concern for society's well-being. Although our own society is far from perfect in respect of gender politics or sexual discrimination, the Victorian world was noted for even greater divisions between the sexes. While it is important that we do not judge the Victorians' attitudes to women in light of our own undoubtedly more liberal standpoint, we can nevertheless sketch very real contrasts. These differences between men and women, moreover, lie at the heart of all Victorian social relations.

As women struggled to break free of their traditional roles, there developed a contrary viewpoint stressing the different character of women. Victorian periodicals were filled with essays and short sketches of the (mythical) ideal of womanhood. While feminists writers have dismissed such writings as nonsensical ruminations in the face of a growing agitation for women's rights (which objectively speaking is quite true) there is also no doubt that the female model influenced women's lives to some degree. This was particularly true of working-class women who were most vulnerable to the criticisms of moralists and who had little alternative to the lives they led. Few men at that time would have questioned the words found in Alfred Lord Tennyson's poem *The Princess* (1847):

> Man for the field and woman for the hearth;
> Man for the sword, and for the needle she;
> Man with the head, and women with the heart;
> Man to command, and woman to obey;
> All else is confusion.

John Ruskin's 'Of Queen's Gardens' (1865) announced the idea of separate spheres in rather more prosaic terms:

> The man's power is active, progressive, defensive. He is eminently the doer, the creator, the discoverer, the defender. His intellect is for speculation and invention; his energy is for adventure, war, and conquest whenever war is just, whenever conquest is necessary. But the woman's power is for rule, not for battle, – and her intellect is not for invention or creation, but for sweet ordering, arrangement and decision … The man in his rough work in the open world, must encounter all peril and trial.

We might question the validity of the views of a man whose wife, Effie, ran off with the painter John Everett Millais during the 1850s, because he (Ruskin) found pubic hair so repellent that he could not consummate the marriage. Nevertheless, this type of portrayal of women did become common. According to Victorian moral values, women were ascribed a natural role, the result of nature's gifts, just like men. Moralists armed with brushes as well as pens, probed public morality and reminded their audiences of the dangers that lurked in the world. William Holman Hunt, a deeply religious man, and a leading figure in the serious-minded Pre-Raphaelite movement of the 1850s, was one of Victorian Britain's leading producers of paintings with a moral ethic (see also Chapter 17). Almost everything he produced was suffused with philosophical or theological rumin-ations on the moral side of life. As well as producing deeply spiritual biblical allegories, such as *The Scapegoat* (1854), which represents Christ suffering in the form of a goat in the desert, he also addressed directly moral–religious issues that confronted Victorians. His painting, *Hireling Shepherd* (1851) in which a shepherd woos a young girl whilst his untended sheep 'blow' their stomachs on rich green grass and corn, was an allegorical representation of slackness among Anglican ministers who similarly neglected *their* flocks. Perhaps the most didactic of his paintings was *The Awakening Conscience*, in which a young woman's honour is about to be saved as she experiences some sort of moral conversion and starts up from the knee of her song-singing companion. The detail of the painting is over-loaded with meaning: the cat and the dead bird under the table, the painting of *Woman Taken in Adultery* hovering over a cheap rosewood piano. Even the wallpaper shows fruits and vines at the peril of thieving birds because the surrounding cupids are asleep. Such moralising was common both on canvas and on paper.

Marriage was perceived as the summit of the female achievement and the site of their most profitable work. Women required protection from the brutish outside world. Women were denied the vote because they were not men's equals; the argument went that they had no mind for politics. And when some demanded the vote, irrespective of these male views, they were told that a vote for a woman would be like giving two votes to the husband. In other words, women had no minds of their own. If men dealt with the dangers of the outside world while bringing home the bread, women were viewed as the real rock upon which the family fortune's rested. Women were to nurture the children and to prepare them for later life; the husband's desires were to be placed to the fore of the wife's; her own ambitions and desires were to be suppressed in the name of the vocation to which she was born. Once women had been raised this way, it seemed to stand to reason that these icons of domestic probity might be naïve and thus could easily fall prey to unscrupulous men.

Many of the moral codes by which women were supposed to live their lives were formulated and enforced by male priests. Poor women, in particular, were pressured into ideal behaviour by their churches. Daily tours of the towns and cities of Victorian Britain gave priests an insight into working-class life which few others in their social situation could muster. Some even committed their thoughts to paper, writing instruction manuals of womanly behaviour that were akin to Samuel Smiles' outpourings on thrift, self-help and duty. One such cleric, the Reverend Bernard O'Reilly, penned an influential book, *The Mirror of True Womanhood: A Book of Instruction for Women* (1883). Running into 13 editions, this manual typified the thrust of Catholic self-improvement at this time. O'Reilly exhorted women to follow the cherished example of Christ's mother, Mary. Working-class women needed to be taught 'what royalty of spirit can and ought to be theirs' if they were to follow the example of 'that great Mother who knew how to make the poor home of Joseph so rich'. The emphasis, typically, was placed upon the domestic arena and the important role which women must play in securing the moral and spiritual welfare of the family:

> What every Christian country needs most are these great-souled wives, mothers, and sisters, in the dwellings of our over-burdened labourers; women for whom the roof above them and the four walls which enclose them are the only world they care to know, the little paradise which they set their hearts on making pleasant, sunny and fragrant for the husband.

Many women writers, reformers and activists refuted the pathetic dignity of Victorian notions of femininity. They wanted a less protected position in the world. Census enumerators (almost definitely inadvertently) added value to the working women when in 1851 they developed an elaborate system of occupational classification consisting of 17 classes, and numerous sub-classes. 'At the head of the FIRST CLASS', it was asserted, 'stands HER MAJESTY THE QUEEN.' The portrayal of the queen as a working woman might seem fanciful to us, but it asserted a view echoed later. As Dinah Mulak Craik argued in an essay of 1886 (published in *Good Words*), 'working women in all ranks, from our Queen downwards, are, and ought to be, objects of respect to the entire community'.

Increasing levels of political campaigning marked the women's movement as the century progressed, accompanied by new levels of public activity among women. The freedoms which women enjoyed during the First World War and after were not a feature of nineteenth-century life, but inroads were beginning to be made, not least, as we have seen, in the arena of work (Chapter 14). By the 1890s popular journals and magazines such as *Punch* were beginning to write of the 'New Woman' – a physically imposing character who wore her hair down, rode a bike, and looked down on men. Such independent-minded women needed no chaperoning and were quite happy speaking up for themselves in public. They also tended to be single, choosing to be so because they had a decent white-collar job and did not want to be in thrall to some domineering male nor to lose their previous independence. The new woman may have been partially a creation of necessity as well as a reflection of her time, because male employment in the colonial service and the armed forces, as well as imprisonment, and dangerous jobs ensured that women of marriageable age out-numbered men throughout the century.

Men's roles changed, too, but not as noticeably as women's, nor in the same way. Whereas once a gentleman had been solely a man of high birth, in the eighteenth century, the term came to be an acceptable tag for all manner of professional men. A barrister or a clergyman might be a gentleman by trade. This was a well-established convention by 1800. But in the nineteenth century, in yet another attempt to chip away at the rigid social distinctions of class, 'gentleman' or 'gentlemanly' became an adjective to describe conduct as well as a noun to account for a particular social station. Thus, by the mid-Victorian period, it was quite apt to describe a working-man as 'gentlemanly' if his conduct suggested as much. In 1865, Cardinal Newman wrote in the *Cornhill Magazine* of the gentleman as a man of many virtues: 'he is patient, forbearing, and resigned, on philosophical principles.'

Foppishness, vanity and pride in a man were denigrated, for these were not gentlemanly virtues. The eighteenth-century dandy would have been quite out of place in a nineteenth-century setting of grey morning suits, black ties and serious contemplation. The Prime Minister, Benjamin Disraeli, was noted for his flamboyant clothes and the

THE LADIES OF THE CREATION!

No. I.

THE PARLIAMENTARY FEMALE.

Father of the Family. "COME, DEAR; WE SO SELDOM GO OUT TOGETHER NOW—CAN'T YOU TAKE US ALL TO THE PLAY TO-NIGHT?"

Mistress of the House and M.P. "HOW YOU TALK, CHARLES! DON'T YOU SEE THAT I AM TOO BUSY. I HAVE A COMMITTEE TO-MORROW MORNING, AND I HAVE MY SPEECH ON THE GREAT CROCHET QUESTION TO PREPARE FOR THE EVENING."

An example of the 'New Woman'

ringlets in his hair. Even though he sprang to fame in the 1840s as a novelist and politician, and was Prime Minister in the 1870s, Disraeli was seen as a man of the Romantic period (1790s–1830s). This was because he dressed according to those more flamboyant times, and his attire drew comment and suggestion later on when fashions had become more austere. Terms such as 'ungentlemanly conduct' passed into sporting parlance at this time; just as the phrase, 'it isn't cricket' traversed the other way from sport into daily life.

Despite the emphasis upon gentlemanly conduct, marital desertions were generally a matter of men leaving, with the women bearing the burden of supporting the children: poverty made some men heedless of the Victorian cult of the family and patriarchy. Before an Act of Parliament instituted divorce proceedings in 1857, divorce required a private Act of Parliament, a very difficult process open only to the wealthy, or a separation achieved through the ecclesiastical courts, which did not allow remarriage. Even after the Act, divorce still remained costly, and therefore was not a possibility for the working class. As a result, former practices of 'self-divorce' continued, while cohabitation was another option, though offering most women no economic security.

Violence against women was a major problem in Victorian society. Newspaper reports, for any provincial town will reveal countless stories of women becoming embroiled in the fights of drunken males. Women were at risk from their lodgers, drinkers in pubs, men on the street and, most of all, from their marital partners. This was recognised at the time and there was legislation that attempted to staunch its flow. The Matrimonial Causes Act (1878), which was strengthened periodically thereafter, granted the right of legal separation to beaten wives, with the requirement for former husbands to make maintenance payments. In the 10 years from 1897, magistrates granted nearly 90,000 separation orders under the provision of this act. Great divisions continued to exist between men and women; and no arena showed this more starkly than that of sexuality and love.

15.3 Sexuality and love

It is important that we do not confuse today's language of sex and sexuality with that used in the nineteenth century. Sex was not used to describe a physical act between two people; it described the biological facts of a person's being. When Elizabeth Gaskell referred (as she repeatedly did) to 'lovers' in her descriptions of the relationships of the eponymous heroine in *Mary Barton* (1848), the author was referring to the innocent rituals of courtship not sexual intercourse. While prostitution was rife in urban Britain, and illegitimate births were common, although far less so than in today's society, this does not mean that women or men were granted sexual freedom either before or after marriage. Moral codes concerning sexual behaviour defied the logic of what was going on in the world; then again, this is often the case – after all, why launch a moral crusade against this or that form of behaviour if it is not common? The fact that so many individuals contravened the strict moral codes of Victorian society explains why those codes were so strict in the first place.

Fashions reflected moral codes as surely as any public expression of taste. In times before or since it has been quite common for women to wear clothes which displayed parts of their breasts or legs – but in the high Victorian period moralising attitudes to fashion required women to 'cover up'. An almost puritanical dress code included dresses buttoned up past the nape of the neck and heavy woollen stocking and ankle boots covered by layers of near-floor-length petticoats and skirt or dress. Arms were often covered (although later photos of Queen Victoria display forearms, if no more). It is noticeable that, whatever else changed in the nineteenth century, these stifling forms of female fashion remained the convention. The rise of the seaside holiday and the bathing machine saw women emerging in swimsuits and the like, but these included more yards of cloth than most 21st century women would wear on a winter's day! In general, women who wore bright colours during the day, or displayed garters or cleavage, would be labelled as 'loose'. The tap-rooms, gin-palaces and brothels of London may have been reminiscent of eighteenth-century scenes from Henry Fielding's *Tom Jones* (1749), but in respectable society conventions were much less flamboyant, with self-control and solemnity emphasised.

The hypocrisy of Victorian life was never more obvious than in attitudes towards sex. The four-time Prime Minister, W.E. Gladstone claimed his legendary evening walks among the prostitutes of London's East End were akin to missionary work: it is said that he hoped to reform the ladies of the night. Such was Gladstone's standing in Victorian society, and so famous was his religious piety and public morality, that his explanation was largely accepted. Nevertheless, while Gladstone's reputation saved him from the glare of publicity that his conduct might otherwise have merited, there was, more generally, a greater pressure for moral conformity in Victorian society.

A general promotion of the need to stifle sexual urges was not restricted to women: codes of behaviour also became stricter for men. Whereas eighteenth-century noblemen made no secret of their lovers and illegitimate children, Victorian gentlemen faced greater pressures. This is not to say that they did not have affairs; rather, they were required to show a little more care in hiding their tracks. An extramarital affair, for example, would be likely to lose a nineteenth-century MP his parliamentary seat. Charles Stewart Parnell's affair with Kitty O'Shea – the wife of one of his parliamentary lieutenants, Captain O'Shea – which produced several of Parnell's children while the O'Sheas were still married, scandalised conventional morality. Captain O'Shea chose to name Parnell in his divorce case, in 1890, and Parnell never recovered from these events, dying soon afterwards following a frenzied but futile series of political campaigns aimed at rebuilding his shattered political career (see Chapter 10).

While this affair was particularly complicated because it involved three people – and various children – from similar social classes, many affairs went unnoticed, indeed were permitted, so long as the women were plucked from a lower social group. The important point, from the male perspective, was to preserve the man's inheritance; to make sure that no illegitimate children appeared later to lay claim to part of the inheritance and also to preserve male prestige. There were double standards, with one code for men and another for women. Women were required to remain chaste and pure; but it is worth remembering that such pressures were not limited to Victorian society in Britain and Ireland.

Moreover, the responsibility for sexual morality was placed firmly with women. Although men were required to be gentlemanly, they were not held responsible for their own sexual behaviour – that was the role of women. Women were supposed to protect their families from the problems of what the Victorians saw as hereditary diseases, some of them sexually transmitted. Victorian science declared that syphilis led to malformed infants and that gonorrhoea caused blindness in babies. If the ideal woman was one who was virginal and completely innocent until her wedding night, it seems a little much to ask her to enquire about her prospective partner's peccadilloes.

The suggestion that women should be held accountable for society's sexual behaviour was never more obvious than in the legislation passed several times in the 1860s under the generic heading, The Contagious Diseases Acts (1864, 1866, 1869). These Acts initially applied to port towns and urban centres with army garrisons close by. The legislation was the result of growing alarm at the rates of venereal disease among members of the armed services. Rather than penalising the men for availing themselves of the services of prostitutes, the authorities instead targeted the women. Police were given powers to arrest any woman in places such as Liverpool, Portsmouth or Catterick under even the suspicion of being a prostitute. The arrested women were then forced into secure hospitals for medical treatment. Women's groups campaigned against the acts, and opposed their extension to the civilian population throughout the urban north, although they were not repealed until 1886. The Acts themselves may have spurred feminists, but they gave a clear impression of how Victorian society viewed prostitution and what was seen as loose moral conduct.

But most of these women were driven on to the streets by economic hardship or by an unwanted pregnancy which scarred their reputation. Thus many prostitutes were former serving girls who had been 'ruined' by the sexual advances of a son of the household. Among the lowest classes of urban people, fathers were often complicit in the street-walking of their young daughters. Desperate straits required desperate measures and soon such behaviour became normalised among the poor. Drunkenness and alcoholism were other causes of prostitution. Dickens' portrayal of Nancy, the pathetic, doomed heroine of *Oliver Twist*, obliquely, somewhat coyly, suggests how easy it was for a woman to fall prey to professional gangs. And in *Mary Barton*, Elizabeth Gaskell captures the horror that Victorian society felt at the sight of a 'fallen women' in her portrayal of the stunted relationship of John Barton and his sister-in-law.

It is impossible to know how many prostitutes there were in Victorian Britain, but each city certainly had hundreds, if not thousands. Bracebridge Hemyng's study of prostitution suggests that in 1857 London had 8,600 who plied this trade. Importunate behaviour offended the sensibilities of what might be thought of as the decent folk, and visitors to Britain's big cities made note of the extent to which prostitutes touted for trade. London in fact gained the reputation as the 'whoreshop of the world'. White slave traders could pluck poor women from the streets and send them anywhere in the globe. Pornography and erotic literature could be bought on London's streets.

Most Victorians saw prostitution as the end of the road; others chose to ignore it; still others were cynical in their praise of its utility. Few, however, were as sardonic as W.H. Lecky, whose *History of European Morals* (1869) contained the following pronouncement on the prostitute: 'Herself the supreme example of vice, she is ultimately the most efficient guardian of virtue. But for her the unchallenged purity of countless happy homes would be polluted.' There were exceptions to this complacent masculine viewpoint. A relatively enlightened student of prostitution, Dr William Acton, wrote in his book, *Prostitution* (1857), that it was a transitory stage through which many women passed. If poverty was endemic, and if most working-class families passed through it at one point or other, then prostitution similarly was a response, equally temporary but just as real. Like much that offended Victorian moralists, prostitution was largely a result of economic exigencies.

According to the rules of Victorian morality, women were not supposed to enjoy sex. The act of sexual intercourse was not intended for anyone's gratification; it was supposed to be simply the duty that produced the next generation. Acton, cited in the previous paragraph, may have understood the economic necessity of prostitution, but this was partly because he acknowledged it was a rational decision based purely upon economic conditions. He, too, believed that most women were untroubled by the desires of carnal knowledge, and 'know little or nothing of the pleasures of the flesh'. This point was put more forcibly, as late as 1914, by a doctor (and remembered in Sir Lawrence Jones' *An Edwardian Youth*, 1956). He claimed: 'nine out of ten women are indifferent to sex or actively dislike it; the tenth, who enjoys it, will always be a harlot.'

Recent work, however, has re-evaluated notions of Victorian sexuality in order to suggest that the image of universal repression was misleading. However, while sexual pleasure was given generally discreet approval within marriage it was harshly treated, in the case of *women*, outside it. Thus, some workhouses made 'disorderly and profligate women' wear distinctive yellow clothes, though the practice was stopped in the 1840s. The Foundling Hospital in London, founded in 1741 to deal with abandoned babies, accepted in the nineteenth century infants only from mothers who could prove that they had had sex against their will or on a promise of marriage and were otherwise of irreproachable character, a policy designed to exclude prostitutes. Such restrictions and admonitions can be presented as social policing, but the response to it frequently revealed a lack of deference that suggests a society, both rural and urban, male and female, that cannot be presented as deferential if that is intended to imply a degree of conformity that approximated to dominant social norms. Thomas Newcome, Rector of Shenley in Hertfordshire, 1800–48, and a JP, recorded in 1822: 'Two Girls – Sunday Scholars formerly – who came before me without feeling or shame (but such a little measure as I could inject into them) to swear bastards to Ridge parish. I detailed the above, "sign of the times."'

15.4 Art and sexuality

Representations of the body – the penis, the breasts, and so on – was acceptable in art. Perhaps there was a certain prurience in the paintings of Frederick, Lord Leighton of Stretton (1830–96), Lawrence Alma Tadema (1836–1912) or Albert Moore (1841–93), all of whom depicted scenes of extensive nudity in their paintings of classical subject matter? One of the finest examples of this mildly erotic style of painting is the work of John William Waterhouse (1849–1917). His 'Hylas and the Nymphs' offers an overtly sexual painting based on the fate of Hercules' young man-servant Hylas, who, while searching for water during his adventures with Jason and the Argonauts, is lured into a pool by beautiful nymphs and drowned.

From art with sexual imagery there also developed art politics with sex as a central plank. The Aesthetic Movement of the 1870s and 1880s, founded by William Pater, an Oxford don, and involving such luminaries as William Morris (1834–96), Edward Coley Burne-Jones (1833–98), Dante Gabriel Rossetti (1828–82), James Abbott McNeill Whistler (1834–1903) and Aubrey Beardsley (1872–98), propounded Morris' aphorism of 'art for art's sake'. In claiming art unto itself, the Aesthetes were moving away from Ruskin's idea that art should represent life and that its creators should be social reformers. Poets such as Algernon Swinburne (1837–1909) were also noted Aesthetes, although Oscar Wilde (1854–1900) became perhaps the most famous member of the movement. With their long hair and decadent ways, these young men were attempting to throw off the code of moral and social conformity. Critics associated Aestheticism with decadence, and that is how the movement appeared to move as the end of the century approached.

This movement effectively died in 1895 when Oscar Wilde was imprisoned for homosexual practices. The Aesthetic movement attracted many bohemian admirers – cruelly parodied by *Punch* as long-haired men and short-haired women – a proportion of whom were homosexuals. Even artistic movements were at risk from the moral strictures of a conventional society. Wilde died only five years after his term of imprisonment, a term that was poignantly captured in his *Ballad of Reading Gaol* (1898). Throughout the century, homosexuality had been regarded with utter abhorrence by the law-makers, journalists and clergymen who saw themselves as the guardians of public morals. In the main, homosexual practices were kept secret. Furtive behaviour and clandestine meetings were the only option in a society so sure of its narrow moral path. Those who were caught out faced the sort of treatment and public opprobrium heaped upon Wilde, or on William John Bankes (1786–1855), the beautifier of the stately home, Kingston Lacy, who was prosecuted in 1841 for a homosexual act with a soldier. Banks fled to spend the rest of his life in Italy. A little after Wilde's travails, in 1903, another case of exposed homosexuality hit the headlines of the newspapers. The man concerned was a British war hero, the highly-decorated Major General Sir Hector Macdonald. Macdonald was exposed as a homosexual and summoned for court-martial. Before this could happen, however, Macdonald fled to France and committed suicide in a Paris hotel. The news of Macdonald's demise had a powerful effect on another closet homosexual, then a consular official in the Belgian Congo. His name was Roger Casement, and, in less than 10 years, his lurid diary entries recounting furtive liaisons with various men shocked society and helped to swing the pendulum against him when he was branded a traitor for his Irish nationalist activities (see Chapter 10). When Casement was tried for treason and sentenced to death, the diaries helped to seal his reputation if not his fate. The entries were recklessly honest: 'Agostino kissed many times. 4 dollars'; 'Down and oh! Oh! quick, about 18'. This provided the British authorities with just the weapon needed to influence the case and ruin his name and to drive a wedge between him and his American supporter who campaigned for clemency. Casement was hanged on 3 August 1916. He went to the gallows with what was then perceived as a double stain upon his honour: treachery and homosexuality.

15.5 Conclusion

We cannot but conclude that Victorian morality was rigid and stifling. It was particularly hard on women, and offered nothing of comfort to those who did not meet its narrow definitions of 'decent' or 'proper' conduct. It is important to recognise that matters of morality are governed by the conventions ascribed to at given times and are different according to national culture and custom. The context that is generally forgotten is that of the world outside Britain at that time. To criticise social conditions or the treatment of women, as if Britain could have been abstracted from the situation elsewhere, is in some ways unhelpful and, in a profound sense, like much criticism of the Victorian period, ahistorical. Yet we should note that the benefits of society and economy were distributed unequally, in both class and gender terms, and moral codes were strict by our standards. In some respects, the British can be considered more liberal than other major European powers. In Europe, where her prestige owed much to her economic sophistication, Britain was seen as a force for liberalism, in politics, economics, religion and culture.

Summary

◆ Victorian morality has had a long and pervasive influence in later periods.

◆ Morality, particularly sexual morality, was undoubtedly heavily gendered, impacting most profoundly upon women.

◆ Notions of the Victorians as sexually repressed, morally stiff and personally cold need to be reconsidered against the backdrop of a much more complex society than has sometimes been portrayed.

◆ Despite its stifling notion of what as morally acceptable, Britain remained, to some extent, a model society, particularly for countries experiencing, or demanding, significant social change.

◼ Points to discuss

◆ What are 'Victorian values'?
◆ To what extent is nineteenth-century morality 'hypocritical'?
◆ What moral constraints were imposed on women?
◆ Can we talk about a distinctive male morality in this period?
◆ How would you characterise Victorian attitudes towards sex and sexuality?
◆ In what ways does Victorian art reflect, or confound, accepted moral codes?

◼ References and further reading

W. Acton, *Prostitution* (1857).

L.A. Hall, *Sex, Gender and Social Change in Britain since 1880* (2000)

W.H. Lecky, *History of European Morals*, Vol. 2 (1857).

W. Mackinnon, *On the Rise, Progress and Present States of Public Opinion in Great Britain and Other Parts of the World* (1828).

S. Rowbotham, *Hidden From History* (1974)

M. Sweet, *Inventing the Victorians* (2001)

J. Treuherz, *et al.*, *Hard Times: Social Realism in Victorian Art* (Manchester, 1987)

Religion and Belief

Introduction

Today, at the beginning of the third millennium, church attendances in England have fallen to below 1m. As churches are boarded up and sold off, and as other forms of recreational activity apparently come to replace the act of collective worship, it is perhaps difficult for us to understand times in which *religion occupied a central position in the cultural and political life*. The nineteenth century was such a time. In fact, it can be argued that Britons were more religious than at any time since the Reformation. This is probably misleading, insofar as it is difficult to compare populations that were very different in size and distribution. What we can say, however, is that piety played an important role in Victorian society. Religious issues tormented Anglo-Irish relations, but also permeated the daily lives of ordinary people in Scotland, England and Wales as different denominations fought for mastery of the school curriculum, and so on. At the same time, moralists and religious commentators lamented declining church attendances and the decline of public worship. Piety and issues of religious importance may have influenced Victorian politics, but how far did they impact on the lives of an emerging urban mass? Certainly, the picture is a variegated one.

Key issues

▶ What is religion?

▶ How diverse was British religious practice?

► What role did religion play in the people's lives?
► What was the link between religion and politics?

16.1 The nature of religion

When broadly conceived, most religions have a core of similarity between them. That is, they all seem to unite individual and group behaviour. Most types of religious practice seem to have public ceremonies and private requirements. All religions have some doctrinal foundation which provides their *sine qua non*. Few religions are at least partly based upon the notion that they are different from some other form of worship: in many cases, this latter notion – an idea of doctrinal difference – can lead to deep-seated animosities, even hatred and fighting.

The fact that religion is personal, does not mean that it cannot be codified or explained in rational terms. An individual's reason for subscribing to a particular creed of belief may be beyond the intuition of the historian, but the linkages between groups of people who act on similar impulses can be organised and understood in sociological terms.

The Anglican, Roman Catholic, Presbyterian or Methodist churches differ in their approach to religion and worship, and are separated on a doctrinal level, but they are similar, in mechanistic terms, for the way in which they impose a code of ethical behaviour on the adherents of their particular branch of faith. The rituals of these churches are very different, in a number of ways, but each of them requires certain types of behaviour. This is why some sociologists and historians have subscribed to Karl Marx's dictum that 'religion is the opiate of the masses'. For Marx, then, religion deflected human beings from the contradictions in their daily material lives; it masked their oppression by those in power. In other words, religion contributed to the false consciousness of the masses while propagating the hegemony of the ruling elites. For sociologists who follow Emile Durkheim (1858–1917), society is welded by mutual interests, and by collective needs, rather than simply riven by competitive self-serving groups or individuals. For Durkheim, religion was a social cement – one of the many such adhesives that he noted (Box 16.1). At the same time, religion expressed the group's collective or shared mental structures. Difficult to define, and in some ways not unlike the inexplicable shared ideals that link football fans, religion is seen in the Durkheimian analysis as one factor turning a collection of individuals into a society.

Religion certainly served functional needs for nineteenth-century people, providing them with a prop, and an identity, with strength through group action. Not unlike other affinities of associational attachments, religion governed sociability. Its purpose was worldly as well as otherwordly. In times of great social change, and even more in periods of war and upheaval, religiosity can grow and prosper as people cling on to the reliable things in life. In this way, then, major motivations for religious conservatism or radicalism were provided by the world around. Thus, millenarian sects – those which focused their attention on the end of the world and the last battle mentioned in the Bible's Book of Revelations – prospered during and after the Civil War (1642–6) when turmoil replaced stability. During the eighteenth century, reactions against the Church of England, and its

Box 16.1

Morals v. religion 'Maximise morals, minimise religion': George Jacob Holyoake on religion

At present all intentions are tincture, and all endeavours warped, by supernaturalism. The young are trained, and the old are induced, to consider humanity as besides their true interest, and this world of only secondary importance. The question is no less than one of human conduct wrongly directed, and involves the national bowing down at the shrine of error. This fatal mistake demands vigorous and effectual correction. Reason and humanity alike cry aloud for the annihilation of the pernicious delusions.

Religion ... we deem to be 'a broad, blazing, refulgent, meridan fraud' – a libel on human nature – the sink of virtue, and the grave of independence. It has confounded moral distinctions, obscured political rights, and trampled on the tenderest affections. Never was pronounced a precept of higher import, never was taught a duty of greater magnitude than – 'Maximise morals, minimise religion'.

The Movement: Anti-Persecution Gazette, no. 1, 1853

apparent failure to cope with changes to society, fed the need for new, more radical Christian sects. George Whitfield's Calvinist Methodists and John Wesley's Arminian Methodist movement were major parts of the fastest-growing religious development in Britain at this time.

Calvinism and Methodism enjoyed their greatest successes in isolated areas where Anglican roots were shallow. Thus, in nineteenth-century England, the lowest levels of Anglican adherence were found in the north-east of England. Such was the case in particular within the mining districts, where there thrived the most austere (and thus anti-Anglican) version of the Wesleyan message; a similar picture emerged among the labouring poor more generally, though not among agricultural workers at this point.

If Anglicanism was precarious in County Durham and parts of Northumberland, it was even less secure in Wales, Scotland and Ireland. In Wales, Anglican livings were controlled by lay landowners, and parishes tended to be poor and poorly serviced. The church there was badly organised, and foundered on the problems of communication (particularly with Welsh-speakers) and inadequate resources. Here, Howell Harris had led a Calvinist Methodist upsurge in the 1740s.

In Scotland, by the nineteenth century, the Presbyterian tradition had long since triumphed over Episcopalianism: indeed, the Presbyterian Church became the established church after James VI (and I of England) had been driven out by the 'Glorious Revolution' of 1688. The Church of Scotland, unlike the Church of England was thus a church controlled by lay elders (presbyters) rather than by priests (episcopal). Episcopalians were associated with the Jacobite Pretender who had failed to wrest the Scottish crown in 1715 and 1745. While Presbyterianism remained strongest in Scotland, and was the established church north of the border, it, too, was increasingly challenged by the forces of evangelicalism, most notably in the form of demands for greater congregational say in the appointment of ministers. The Church of Ireland was held in a position of completely artificial dominance over the Catholic population, which, on the eve of the Act of Union (1800) comprised around 80 per cent of the population. The church was, in an Irish context, a very obvious instrument of political control: its livings were used to buy support and to reward favour in an even more blatant way than occurred in England. With 2,000 clergymen in the eighteenth century, the church was a huge burden, and over-staffed, given the Catholicism of the majority and the importance of dissenting traditions among the Scots–Irish Presbyterians in Ulster.

Religion was buried deep in the psyche of the British people in the nineteenth century. It influenced them to a great degree and affected the way in which they saw other parts of their lives. Religion was a focal point of community life. The church offered a physical presence – a palpable suggestion of a more metaphysical sense of being. Churches were social as well as religious entities. Thus it was quite possible that the village parson in eighteenth-century England may have ministered to his parishioners on the same day as he sold them church ales. Churches offered a service to people from birth till death; they guided the God-fearing from childhood, punctuating their lives with rituals that confirmed their religiosity, their membership of a community. Churches baptised, married and buried people; at each stage, the rituals of the church sounded a ringing endorsement of the true believer's character. From such earthly commitment to the church's teachings, the individual could hope to aspire to heavenly reward. People then – as now, but in far greater number – believed in God and heaven and so subscribed to the idea that the church represented the linkage between the mortal world and the hereafter.

16.2 Conformity and diversity

Although religion in Britain in our period may have appeared diverse, it was, by modern standards, relatively homogeneous. Despite a long-standing Jewish presence, it was not until the twentieth century, when followers of Islam, Hinduism and other non-Christian faiths began to enter the country, that religious practice in Britain became really varied in what we might call global terms. Britain in 1700 or 1800 and 1900 was Christian – but the Christian faith was shot through with so many divisions of practice and disagreements of interpretation that fragmentation and a challenge to the hegemony of the Church of England must be a major theme of our discussion here. In the eighteenth century there was a myriad of small sects. Nevertheless, three main religious groupings can be noted: the Anglicans, who followed the Church of England, the Church of Ireland or Episcopalianism in Scotland; the Dissenters, a group that included Presbyterians, Methodists, Baptists, Congregationalists; and Roman Catholics.

In 1800, the Anglican church was the established religion in England. Like the Presbyterian Church of Scotland and the Church of Ireland, the Church of England was granted pre-eminent rights in maintaining the spiritual life of the nation. The mechanism for the unity of church and state were also mechanical and secular: government held control of clerical appointments in that church, many of which were made with clear political purposes. Clergymen of the Anglican church usually enjoyed substantial livings from church lands (and their rents), tithes and other benefits. Thus, parish priests and bishops, though spiritual leaders above all else, were also important lay figures in their communities, not least as landlords. Despite the good living that might be got by an efficient parson in a wealthy parish, not all posts were as lucrative. Nor, indeed, were all clergy so efficient as to benefit from the full potential of their livings. Some clergymen were as poor as labouring men, supplementing their religious offices with monies earned in ordinary work. The system was also far from universally efficient in terms of providing good instruction to the faithful. An enquiry of 1812, for example, found that the problem of absenteeism among the clergy was so bad that more than 1,000 parishes in England and Wales had no clerical service. The Anglican Church was bureaucratically inefficient and viewed by some as corrupt; and the loosening of its spiritual and temporal grip in the regions was a vital component of the emergence of Methodism and other sects.

While it has long been asserted that Anglican faith was in decline throughout the eighteenth and early nineteenth centuries, new scholarship challenges such a view. The church certainly lost ground to new faiths, and the historian Alan Gilbert (1976) once described the 60 years after 1740 as 'an era of disaster' for the Anglican church. Toleration of competing sects increased in the years after the Jacobite Rising, and there is no doubting the great inroads made by Wesley. In the nineteenth century, too, increased intra-Christian diversity would continue to be a hallmark of religious change. However, the deep importance of Anglican faith cannot be overlooked; the lay associations with the Church of England should not be ignored either. Nor should the continuing political pre-eminence of the established church. Anglicanism in the nineteenth century (and arguably into the twentieth century) continued to be seen as 'the Tory party at prayer'. Each monarch of England belonged to the established church, and was Defender of the Faith (*the faith* being Anglicanism). Moreover, Tories conceived of the church as a central plank in their ideology; 'church and state' was a common cry among loyalist crowds in the French Revolution period.

The identification of a particular denomination with the state clearly gave a preferential position to believers in that faith. But this was not just an ideological position: the state enforced the collection of church tithes by law. This evoked great fury in Ireland, in particular, where parishes full of Catholics were forced to pay towards the upkeep of an alien church, but it also angered those who followed dissenting sects. It is no surprise, perhaps, that dissenters were prominent among those who emigrated to America in the eighteenth century, nor that they, as J.C.D. Clark has shown in *Languages of Liberty* (1994), played a major part in rejecting British rule during the American Revolution. In Britain, tithes remained a hot political issues until 1838 when the Tithe Commutation Act was pushed through parliament. The political closeness of Anglicanism and Toryism tells a more complex story. While Methodism constituted the most obvious single challenge to the established church, it was only one of a number of challenges. The others may be grouped together under a heading such as 'political and social change', but this does not do their force or diversity a great deal of service. The Anglican church, by its very nature, stood as a bulwark against the forces of change that confronted British society in the generation before the French Revolution. It makes an interesting connection to note Clark's findings that when the two sides in the American War of Independence drew their battle lines, those in favour of British colonial rule were Anglican and stood on one side, while those espousing the theories of the radical thinker John Locke (1632–1704) rather than those of the defender of the old constitution, Sir William Blackstone (1723–80), and demanding independence, were dissenters, often of Scots and Irish stock.

In Britain, too, Anglicanism came to be associated with the forces of reaction. High Tories – Ultras, as they were known – were among the most reactionary members of the ruling political elite. They resisted the French Revolutionary enthusiasm of the 1790s and opposed Catholic emancipation with a Bible in one hand and lurid stories of popish depravity in the other. On most of the big issues of the day – parliamentary reform, trade unions, religious toleration – the Ultras, and with them the hierarchy of the Anglican church, adopted a conservative position. The apogee of this particular view of the world was acted out under Lord Liverpool's first administration (1815–22) at a time when social unrest presented perhaps a unique challenge to Anglican–Tory orthodoxy.

At the same time as social forces pressed upon society at large, reformism also pressurised the Church of England from within. Evangelicalism was not just a force that worked from outside the established church; some Anglican ministers themselves began to take on board a more evangelical notion of faith. During the later eighteenth century the Anglican Church became more structured and better organised. It worked on the premise of conversion but also of improving religious care for those whom it already held as adherents. An important player here was Charles Simeon (1759–1836). Simeon recognised the laxity in Anglican organisation and saw the need to improve the way in which the church executed its mission to the adherents of the faith. Evangelical influences were limited at first: very few adherents of a more radical form of Anglicanism were trusted with bishops' livings. Thus, the movement for reform within the established church tended to be most influential at the grass-roots level of country rural parishes. But evangelical practices did begin to spread widely. The idea of individuals reading their bible at home, rather than having it read to them in church, became more accepted. The communal effect of hymn singing and the spread of devout literature also marked a new age for the Anglican church which had been learned in lessons from movements external to the church, such as Wesleyanism.

The strength of Methodism in the eighteenth and nineteenth centuries, and the responsiveness of people to the wider evangelical revival, was undoubtedly sponsored by social change (see Profile Box 16.2). Wesley looked to the awakening of the Holy Spirit as a reason, while many of the recipients of new systems of worship simply felt sold short by Anglicanism or else feared the rapid changes that were going on around them. Growing towns such as Manchester and Liverpool struggled until well after 1850 to provide enough pew spaces for burgeoning populations; yet, in the increasingly impersonal world of the town, religious communalism offered a response to change. Wesley ministered in the open air to make up for the lack of chapels at his disposal; and other less famous itinerant preachers were just as effective from the back of a cart as they might have been from a pulpit.

Wesley, and other evangelical dissenters, presented members with a strict social code which was not universally popular. Denouncing licentiousness, drinking and ribald rural pursuits, such as animal fights, led to hostility among some rural communities, and rioting sometimes broke out at Wesleyan meetings. On the other hand, such dissenting sects also propounded the view, later associated with the German sociologist Max Weber (1864–1920) that membership of the sect was an endorsement of the individual's good character. This view was popular among those who saw benefit in social improvement and the cementing of group ties. For Weber, this was where Protestantism encouraged a business and work ethic. Wesleyans, like the Quakers and other groups, impressed the need for scrupulous social attitudes and practices upon members. In other words, therefore, dissenting religions also encouraged a mentality in members that suited the economic opportunities of the time. Methodism was popular among small traders and workshop owners because it was good for business.

One of Wesley's most enduring legacies was his anti-Catholicism, although in this he

Box 16.2

Methodism

A form of popular Protestantism which, though varying in nature and scale, is traditionally associated with **John Wesley** (1703-91). At first, it was a movement of societies within the Church of England; later, during the nineteenth century, it became a series of autonomous denominations operating independently from the established church. A sect, or sects, underpinned by an egalitarian ethos in which all could be preachers, while perfectibility could be achieved on earth, Methodists, and their variants, met in small groups and were most powerful where the Church of England was weakest. Some 7.7 per cent of the population of England and Wales was thought to be Methodist in 1851; this aspect of the faith had, however, reached its zenith by then.

was no more than conventional for his time. Many dissenters took the ritualism of the Church of England as their point of departure. Indeed, ritualism – the use of Catholic-style High Church practices in the Anglican service – was to be a long-standing complaint within the evangelical wing of the established church, and among dissenting sects. Catholicism was viewed in British theological and political history as an alien continental system; it was equated with backwardness and the repression of personal development. The 'Whig view of history' (as the historian Herbert Butterfield dubbed it), which articulated a particular view of British history – a history of civil and religious liberty and national improvement – rejected Catholicism as the dark force from which Britons had escaped. Catholicism was equated with enemies of Britain, such as the Jacobites and France. In theological terms, Catholics were scorned because of their reliance upon priests. Most of the dissenting sects saw the bible as the true mediator between Man and God, whereas in Catholic liturgy the pope, and to a lesser extent his priests, were God's representatives on earth and the real mediating force. Protestant evangelicals abhorred aspects of Rome's seven sacraments – particularly transubstantiation (the belief that the communion bread and wine was the body and blood of Christ). In political terms, Anglicans viewed Catholicism as inconsistent with the requirements of all subjects to support church and state as though the two were indivisible; Catholics, on the other hand, were thought to hold a 'dual allegiance': to the country of their domicile and to the pope in Rome. This matter was complicated further in the case of Irish migrants, whose loyalties were thought not to be to England, Wales or Scotland, where they lived, but to Rome and to Ireland.

In the eighteenth century, Catholicism had been a diminishing faith. The number of adherents fell by two-thirds to only 70,000 or so. Although the Penal Laws – which forbade Catholic priests from wearing ceremonial garb, banned Catholic churches and prevented Catholics from holding public office – contributed to this atrophy, they were in fact enforced with much greater celerity in Ireland than in England. In Scotland, a fearsome anti-Catholic tradition, which dated to the mid-seventeenth century, still exists more strongly there today than in any other part of Britain. Catholic numbers were small; landed elites protected small parishes of believers, although membership of the church waned in the eighteenth century. Catholicism was really limited to a couple of per cent of the population in 1800, most of whom were to be found in the Midlands, in rural parts of Lancashire, in parts of Wales, and in the outer Hebrides, particularly on islands such as Benbecula and South Uist.

What changed the profile of English Catholicism was Irish immigration, growing steadily until 1800 and rapidly thereafter. In addition, the Act of Union (1800) between Britain and Ireland acted, overnight, to throw a country of 6.5m (80 per cent of whom were Catholics) into a constitutional broth with three other nations, totalling 11.5m people, who were mostly Protestant. The demographic proportions are much closer at the beginning of our period because Ireland's population is similar to that of Britain. 100 years later, Ireland's population had fallen to 4 million and Britain's has more than tripled to more than 37 million.

Public awareness of Catholicism had always been high. Anti-Catholicism was part of the national fabric of all Britain. There had been a serious riot in London, in 1780, when Lord George Gordon whipped up a fearsome popular backlash against legislation that relaxed the Penal Laws. But the participants in these riots had no Irish connection; nor did they attack Irish residents of the capital. In the nineteenth century, however, Irishness and Catholicism became increasingly synonymous in the eyes of British onlookers: when anti-Catholic riots occurred, there was often an Irish dimension. This is because Ireland presented such a huge political problem for those who had sought to yoke her to the Union; and Ireland's problems were often cast as a matter of Catholics as a benighted and oppressed majority. In Britain, moreover, the great upsurge in Catholic communicants and numbers of chapels and churches was entirely down to the inrush of Irish workers.

16.3 The Victorian crisis of faith?

The 1830s were a crucial time for religion in Britain. The repeal of the Test and Corporations Act (1828) and Catholic emancipation (1829) freed dissenters and Catholics to take a much greater role in public life. In a sense, they were bound to challenge the established churches. Although very much a Christian country, Britain had ceased to be a confessional state. The 1830s was also a decade of great social change. Rates of urban and industrial growth were greater than at any time before, but progress also engendered hardship and turmoil for certain social groups. As groups like the handloom weavers lost out to the competition of the machine, residents across the urban spectrum faced over-crowding, disease and resulting social unrest. That the 1830s saw the wave of evangelical fervour, the spread of the police, violent reaction against the Poor Law, a critical inquiry into the problems of Irish immigration, and indeed numerous other enquiries into the 'Condition of England', speaks clearly of the depth and scale of the problems. Religion, like politics, reflected the mood of the nation – and in the 1830s, the mood was one of fear, trepidation and a lack of certainty about the future.

Nonconformity

The principal challenge to the Church of England came not from atheism, but from Dissent. Its vitality led to many new congregations. Without the authority of an established church it was difficult to prevent splits. Thus, for example, the Primitive Methodists formed in 1811 and the Weslyan Reform Methodists in 1849. Six years earlier, in the Disruption of 1843, the Church of Scotland divided on the issue of lay patronage, with one body of opinion forming the Free Presbyterian church, in which lay elders and elected ministers demonstrated an urge for freedom from hierarchical systems of church government.

Dissent thus became increasingly more focused on new denominational creeds. Whereas Wesley had remained a life-long member of the Church of England, new Methodists were emerging with a different, separatist agenda. Religion was becoming more aggressively competitive because, as social mobility and economic change could threaten orthodoxies in every field, they also created opportunities offering a different vision of how to make sense of the world. Church and State Toryism, the old Anglican elite, came under fire from a new generation of monied industrial and commercial men whose religion was usually dissenting (with Quakerism significantly over-represented) and whose politics was Liberal. Dissenters demanded a break between church and state. The British Anti-State Church Association (1844), later the Society for the Liberation of the Church from State Patronage and Control (1853), was merely a formalisation of deeply-held convictions. As well as pressing for religious equality, this emerging middle class also demanded political reforms that would increase their influence. Much of the legislation of the early 1830s reflected their needs. The Reform Act (1832) increased their electoral power. The Poor Law Amendment Act (1834) responded to their complaints about the burden upon their pockets of the rates. The Municipal Corporations Act (1835) provided them with the political and revenue-raising powers with which they could remodel their towns.

Despite attacks upon it by dissenters, the Church of England did not stand still nor atrophy in the nineteenth century. Anglicanism dominated life in Britain in a way that others could not. It had 26 bishops in the House of Lords, its clergy were of the same class as the elites who governed the country, and acceptance of the church's 39 articles was a pre-requisite for graduating from Oxford and Cambridge. The Church's control of most of the public schools helped to extend its influence. Churchmen also dominated government posts.

However, the Church of England struggled, like other churches, to meet the needs of a mushrooming population and the role of the parish in education and social welfare declined in favour of new governmental agencies. Municipal and county government were better able than the Church to implement the aspirations of society for reform and control, and in many towns prestige and authority held by the vicar passed to an elected Mayor. Furthermore, local government offered a way to incorporate Dissenters, while the local role of the Church was affected by attacks on church rates. The universities of Oxford and Cambridge, hitherto Anglican monopolies, where all the teaching was conducted by clerics, were opened to non-Anglicans by legislation in 1854 and 1856. The Church of Ireland was disestablished by Gladstone in 1869.

Nevertheless, the Church of England still played a major role in a society which was very much Christian in its precepts. There were numerous clergymen who were important figures in all localities. The Church also reformed itself, rationalising its structure and revenues, and improving its pastoral care. There was a powerful state-directed movement of Church reform from the 1830s, but the Church was capable of renovating itself in the first half of the century by reform at diocesan level; it did not have to wait for the Ecclesiastical Commission which in 1835 was made responsible for the Church's estates and revenues. Key office-holders, such as archdeacons and rural deans, began to exercise their supervisory role more systematically and were able to counter factionalism and to engage with a wide range of Anglican sympathies. The responsiveness of the church organisation increased with the growth of diocesan assemblies in the 1860s and the introduction of rural deanery chapters in most sees by the mid-1870s. Clerical education was fostered and the missionary role of the church expanded. In Lincoln Cathedral, for example, there were attempts from the 1860s to improve the frequency of services, the care of the poor and education.

Church-building became more widespread, and buildings more splendid, than at any time. Churches and chapels were also enlarged. West Orchard Chapel, Coventry, a leading centre of congregational evangelicalism, was, when opened in 1777, able to accommodate 300. In 1787 the chapel was increased in size so that it could seat 600 people, and in 1820, when it was rebuilt, its capacity had been further enlarged to 1200. Under the Church-Building Act of 1818, it became easier to build new churches, while £1m was voted by parliament to encourage church-building with another £500,000 following in 1824. Anglican Church interiors were rebuilt in order to replace box pews, which belonged to families, with rows of identical, open pews, most of which were rent-free and open to all. Churches competed to define the culture of the new urban centres; the spires of Anglican churches and cathedrals were occasionally matched but never entirely done down by competing edifices for Roman Catholic or Dissenting worship. Anglicanism could call upon the power and patronage of local elites, whose donations helped to build the churches; whereas Catholicism relied mainly upon the pennies of the Irish poor. In the 1860s and 1870s, in the fast-growing Victorian new town of Barrow-in-Furness, competition between the denominations was fierce. Until the Anglicans opened St James' parish church, St Mary of Furness, a Pugin-designed Catholic church, was the tallest and grandest building in the town. But there were some sorts of religious construction work that Catholics could not compete with. Barrow provided an example of this when on 26 September 1878, the wealthy magnate, the Duke of Devonshire donated half of the required £24,000 so that four Anglican churches – dedicated to Matthew, Mark, Luke and John – could be opened simultaneously. In Cornwall, a diocese was created at Truro in 1877, more than 30 new churches were built in 1830–69 and more than another 50 by the end of the century. The number of Anglican ministers with care of souls in the western half of the Rural Deanery of Kidderminster, an area greatly affected by industrialisation, rose from five in 1818 to 11 in 1904.

Reforming Anglicanism?

Evangelicalism in the Church of England took many forms. Some were concerned as much by the social policing of working-class leisure pursuits; others, as represented by William Wilberforce and the Earl of Shaftesbury, concentrated on social reforms – such as the abolition of slavery and the exclusion of children from mines – which had a distinctly moral-Christian edge. In theological terms, evangelicalism was broad-based and multi-faceted, including John Nelson Darby's Plymouth Brethren, Edward Irving's Catholic Apostolic church, and John Keble's Romantic High Church views, or the 'Oxford Movement' of his disciple, J.H. Newman. The Oxford movement evangelised in what appeared to be a socially conservative way. The name 'Oxford Movement' came from its emergence as a resistor of liberal reforms in the university of that name. Long overdue reforms which had been recommended by the Ecclesiastical Commission (1835–6) were opposed. The

Oxford Movement was labelled 'Tractarian' because of the writings it produced in the 1830s and early 1840s and was also dubbed 'Puseyite' (after Edward B. Pusey, Professor of Hebrew at Oxford Univeristy, who led the movement in the 1840s)

The movement was most important as an Anglo-Catholic influence – an affirmation of High Church principles – in an age where dissent was breaking away from the Roman Catholic model of hierarchical and (from a radical Protestant viewpoint) ritualistic ceremonials. In the final one of the tracts – *Tract 90* – Newman sought to show that the 39 Articles of the Anglican church equated to an expression of true Catholic faith. This resulted in Newman's virtual excommunication: he was eventually to become a Roman Catholic archbishop following the Restoration of the Papal Hierarchy in 1850. Pusey, meanwhile, was mercilessly lampooned in *Punch* as the pope's 'cat's paw', or else as a moth flying too close to the candle's flame (see Box 16.2). Tractarianism drew support from many people, clerical and lay – the most famous of the latter being Glastone, four time Liberal Prime Minister from the 1860s to the 1890s. It also had a magnificent outlet in the medieval churches built by the architect and convert to Catholicism, A.W. Pugin. The lasting effect of the Oxford Movement was to exacerbate division between 'High' and 'Low' church elements within Anglicanism. In social terms, in communities up and down the country, it helped to encourage a bewildering range of differing viewpoints. For the rest of the century, Catholic-style Ritualism was denounced from elements within the church; while the prospect of a Rome-ward movement of the Church of England provided ammunition for dissenters whose precise aim had been (in their eyes) to escape from Rome and Romanisation. Two sorts of Anglo-Catholics emerged in the wake of the Oxford movement: the high profile, often intellectual converts to Rome amidst hysterical denunciations; and those who remained inside the church and sought, against a background of frenzied hostility, to change it. The result, in general terms, was undoubtedly a crisis of faith that tapped into wider anxieties about Catholicism and which found an appropriate context in the changing world of Victorian Britain.

The crisis in the Church of England brought about by the Oxford Movement was outstripped in the autumn of 1850 when the pope re-established the Roman Catholic hierarchy in England and Wales along the lines of the diocesan structure of the Anglican church. (Scotland's needs, in this regard, were not tackled until the 1870s.) The pressure of so many incoming Irish Catholics raised the profile of their religion and made inadequate the system of church government which had existed since 1688, with four Vicars Apostolic presiding over four Vicarates of England and Wales: London, Northern, Midland and Western. Without a system of diocese and parish, archbishop and bishop, the Roman Catholic church in England and Wales could not minister adequately to its growing working-class flock.

The action of the Pope, in re-establishing the church to its pre-Reformation position, prompted a remarkably intense reaction, providing clear evidence of the average Briton's love of Protestantism and hatred of Catholicism. Meetings, often ecumenical, were held in most towns and cities of England and Wales to protest at this perceived incursion by an alien power. *The Times* dubbed the Pope's action the 'Papal Aggression' – a term which entered the imagination of the British people. The hostility was not restricted to clerics and politicians. Numerous petitions flooded Westminster to demand that the government of Lord John Russell take firm action. In a letter to the Bishop of Durham, which was subsequently published in *The Times*, Russell expressed regret at the pope's action: 'My

Box 16.3

'The Pusey-ite Moth and the Roman Candle', *Punch*, vol. 19, 1850, p.217.

E.B. Pusey, Regius Professor of Hebrew at Oxford, was one of the founders of the Oxford or Tractarian movement, and sympathiser with John Henry Newman, later convert to Catholicism. Pusey was mercilessly lampooned by *Punch*, especially at the time of the Restoration of the Roman Catholic Hierarchy ('Papal Aggression'). Here he is shown transfixed by the flame of Rome.

THE PUSEYITE MOTH AND ROMAN CANDLE.

" Fly away *Silly* Moth."

Box 16.4

Reactions to 'the Papal Aggression'

Lord John Russell's letter to the Bishop of Durham is reproduced here. It is striking, today, to imagine a Prime Minister becoming so deeply involved in a debate between varieties of religious opinion. However, in 1850, the then Prime Minister, Lord John Russell, in a sense unleashed what became a storm of indignation among Anglicans and Dissenters about the renaissance of the Roman Catholic Church in England and Wales. Although it was *The Times* which dubbed the episode the 'Papal Aggression', and though Russell's tone is actually moderate by comparison to some, his words – issued first to the Bishop of Durham and then printed in *The Times* – clearly gelled opposition to the re-establishment of a system of Roman Catholic church government (diocese, parishes, Archbishops, bishops, etc.) in England and Wales.

Downing Street, 4 November 1850.

  MY DEAR LORD, – I agree with you in considering 'late aggression of the Pope upon our Protestantism' as 'insolent and insidious', and I therefore feel as indignant as you can do on the subject.

I not only promoted to the utmost of my power the claims of the Roman Catholics to all civil rights, but I thought it right and even desirable that the ecclesiastical system of the Roman Catholics should be the means of giving instruction to the numerous Irish immigrants in London and elsewhere, who without such would have been left in heathen ignorance ...

I have little hope that the propounders and framers of these innovations will desist from their insidious course. But I rely with confidence on the people of England; and I will not bate a jot of heart or hope, so long as the glorious principles and the immortal martyrs of the Reformation shall be held in reverence by the great mass of a nation which looks with contempt on mummeries and superstition, and with scorn at the laborious endeavours which are now making to confine the intellect and enslave the soul. I remain, with great respect, &c.

J. RUSSELL

Dear Lord, I agree with you in considering the "late aggression on our Protestantism" as "insolent and insidious", and I therefore feel as indignant as you do upon the subject' (see Box 16.4) Palmerston also was cool. He was well aware of the role of the Papacy in supporting reactionary governments on the Continent.

Up and down the country, journalists took a lead from their Prime Minster and *The Times*, joined in the denunciation (Box 16.4). In major northern cities, where large Irish populations had already bred resentment because of the Famine influx, responses to the Pope's decision were particularly acute. The *Liverpool Standard*, of 29 October 1850, considered the restoration showed how 'Rome scoffs at the authority of the Protestant Sovereign of the British Empire, and resolves to treat her dominions as if they were a fief under its absolute control' and on the same day the *Cumberland Paquet* explained how every newspaper in the land was filled with details of the 'insidious Popish manoeuvre'. Ordinary Protestants were stirred up by this issue, and the flames of passion were hardly doused when, in a provocative act, the new Catholic Archbishop of Westminster, Cardinal Wiseman, issued a Pastoral Address which boasted of 'Catholic England ... restored to its orbit in the ecclesiastical firmament from which its light had long vanished'. The Catholic Bishop Ullathorne of Birmingham attempted to calm the situation, but Wiseman's talk of 'governing' the counties of his diocese was impolitic to say the least, for it 'reactivated traditional English fears of Romish plots, doubtful Catholic loyalties and foreign influences' (see Box 16.6). If these anxieties were not in themselves enough, the continuing

Box 16.5

The provincial press on the 'Papal Aggression'

While Box 16.2 demonstrates the concern of the upper classes, this extract from The *Carlisle Journal*, of 20 December 1850, shows that anger at the Pope's decision penetrated deep into the consciousness of provincial society. What gave the movement against the re-establishment of the hierarchy its impetus was the enormous breadth and depth of feeling against this move. While riots and violence occurred in some places – notably Liverpool and Stockport – the mood of opposition was one of public, intractable, but peaceable resistance. As in this extract, opponents stressed their 'liberality' in most things.

> Cumberland has spoken out upon the pretensions put forward by the Pope to supreme spiritual jurisdiction in our land. Counties are not easily moved. It requires no little time, under the most favourable circumstances, to set in motion the somewhat cumbrous machinery for testing the opinions of an extensive and scattered population; and the spontaneous appearance of requisition to the High Sheriff, signed by the leading men of all districts, representing wealth, intelligence, and heterogenous [sic] opinions, as well in religious faith as in politics, and calling for an opportunity of publicly expressing their sentiments, always indicates a strong and widespread feeling on some subjects that 'comes home to men's business and bosoms'.

Such an indication was presented by the County Meeting on Wednesday last – a gathering of which in numbers and influence has never been surpassed, and seldom paralleled in Cumberland. If the proceedings were not characterised by entire unanimity the preponderance of opinion, not to speak of weight of argument, was decisively and undeniably on the side of the requisitionists. The Roman Catholics, who were the chief dissentients, will of course differ with us on this point; but there were circumstances connected with the demonstration that might well suggest in their minds that misgivings as to their wisdom in identifying themselves with the policy which was inaugurated by the establishment of a Catholic Church hierarchy, and in raising the cry of persecution against all who condemn it. It is a fact of deep significance that among the most active promoters of that demonstration were men whose liberality of opinions is unimpeachable – who have stood foremost in the fight of freedom, when to engage in it was taboo'd in society – and who, amongst other services, lent their influence and weight to the movement which succeeded in placing Roman Catholics upon civil and religious equality with their fellow subjects [through the Catholic Emancipation Act, 1829].

inflow of Famine Irish sharpened fears. The reaction was not, however, simply inspired by the large numbers of Irish, though their presence increased the prospect for violent reaction from nativist agitators. The hysterical reactions of Victorian Protestants allied vague notions of national identity with more focused political realities. Since the 1830s, *The Times* and the *Quarterly Review* led the way in reasserting the age-old view that Catholicism was backward, disloyal, superstitious, sacerdotal (priest-dominated) and thoroughly out of character with rational, liberal British institutions. The migrants were simply providing physical targets for already existing prejudices.

Popular responses to the 'Papal Aggression'

The issue of the Papal Aggression brought the impartiality of the state into question. This was certainly the case on 27 November 1850 when there was serious trouble in Birkenhead after local magistrates called a meeting at the Town Hall to discuss the Papal Aggression, as Frank Neal has shown in his study, *Sectarian Violence: The Liverpool Experience, 1819–1914* (1988). Irish Catholics were incensed, and their priest, Fr Browne, said he would attend, while appealing for his co-religionists to stay calm. However, allegations of

Box 16.6

'Great Cattle Show: The Roman Bull that didn't get the prize', *Punch*, 1850, vol.19, 257. Here the Pope is cast as a bull (The word 'bull' is used to describe Vactican edicts). This particular bull is the one announcing the restoration of English Catholic Church and drew the opprobrium of English Protestants.

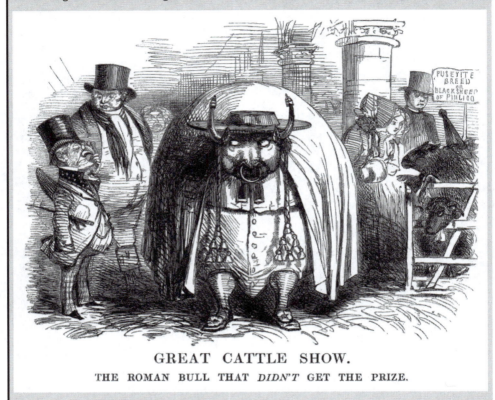

GREAT CATTLE SHOW.
THE ROMAN BULL THAT *DIDN'T* GET THE PRIZE.

insensitive and inadequate policing led to a great disturbance. The Town Hall was stoned by angry Irish Catholics and the Riot Act was read. When Fr Browne appeared at a broken window, and raised his arm, the effect was reportedly magical, with calm suddenly falling over the crowd. The fact that a priest could police whereas the police could not, was seen at the time as an indication of the cultural gulf separating the two sides on the issue of papal authority.

The following summer was also tense, and the Orange Order's marching season in Liverpool in July was marred by the wielding of weapons and the firing of shots, as well as the usual drunken punch-ups. Quite a stir was caused by the death of two men, one of whom was Irish, and the dismissal from the force of PC Green because he was an Orange lodge member. Such intelligence simply confirmed Catholic suspicions – suspicions that were hardly allayed during the turbulent 'no-popery' atmosphere of the election year of 1852, when amid the general turmoil, a pregnant women died after being kicked in the stomach by a policeman. The Orange demonstrations that followed closely after this incident caused unusual exasperation, just as the 'Papal Aggression' raised the ire of staunch Protestants like the Orangemen in such a way as had not been seen since Catholic Emancipation was granted by Parliament in 1829. To these working-class defenders of the Protestant faith, the Pope's action was provocative and annoying. The feelings were such that the Lord Chief Justice banned all processions, Orange or otherwise, within the city's boundaries.

But it was not just in Liverpool – the most sectarian of all Britain's cities at this time – that the 'Papal Aggression' was seen as tantamount to incitement to riot. One of the most infamous incidents of post-1850 violence occurred when the Cheshire town of Stockport was hit on several occasions in June 1852 by violence associated with the restoration. The immediate catalyst was the Tory government's issue of a ban on Catholic processions just three weeks before the general election. The move was intended to prevent trouble, although Liberals dismissed it as electioneering or pandering to sectarian passions. In Stockport, where Catholics had held an annual parade for nearly two decades, Lord Derby's instruction was met with polarised opinions. While Catholics were angered, Orangemen used the ban to publicise their own political views and to air their anti-Catholic rhetoric. Despite Orange protestations, the procession went ahead without incident. The next day, however, saw effigies of Catholic clergy being burned by the local Protestant Association. Thereafter, the situation began to deteriorate, with fighting breaking out around the town. The residents of an Irish enclave called 'Rock Row' were dragged out and beaten, and their homes were ransacked. Although a detachment of troops was mustered and the Riot Act read, the inflamed mob still managed to ransack Stockport's two Catholic chapels as well as the priest's house and nearby vestries. Several days later, 24 Irish families were without homes and one of their countrymen was dead. Although the Irish were clearly the aggrieved party, only two of the 113 arrested were English. This intense outburst of riotous behaviour was promoted by the general 'no-popery' atmosphere pervading the early 1850s, but the activities of a group of local Tory politicians and clerics, who encouraged sectarian animosities for party political ends, were clearly to blame for the scale of the Stockport example. The waning fortunes of the local Tories between 1847 and 1852 had increased their sense of desperation and thus it was that the Orange card was deployed without regard for the town's communal stability.

The pope's action in re-establishing the paper hierarchy of England and Wales also sent Scots Protestants into paroxysms of fear that they might be next. (In fact the same did not happen in Scotland until 1878.) Thousands of hostile meetings were held in isolated villages as well as large towns of Scotland. The fires of sectarianism were kept alive by a thriving trade in trash novels, penny song-sheets, handbills, and in periodicals with apt titles like *The Bulwark, or Reformation Journal*.

Reactions to the Irish immigration of 1840s and 1850s melted into the innate anti-Catholicism of Scots Calvinist traditions. Although the Church of Scotland expended much of its energy battling with the dissenting traditions after the disruption of 1843, anti-Catholicism had a remarkable galvanising effect on ordinary Scots workers who lived cheek by jowl with the Irish. Such men and women became particularly susceptible to the wild and intemperate ranting of 'no-popery' lectures such as John Sayers Orr, the self-styled 'Archangel Gabriel'. Orr had a fancy for dressing up in the style of 'pious woodcuts, letting his hair sweep down over his shoulders and summoning his audiences with blasts of his trumpet', so Handley claims. On 12 July 1851, in response to the 'Papal Aggression', 'the Archangel Gabriel's' demagoguery led to the Greenock's Catholic chapel house being attacked by a mob. As the rioting unfolded, the 'Archangel Gabriel' escaped from the trouble and flew from the town. But he re-appeared in Edinburgh, Dundee, Liverpool and New York, where he addressed crowds of up to 10,000.

Other methods, non-violent but nonetheless offensive, were also put to work against poor Irish Catholics. The Reverend Patrick McMenemy of the Presbyterian Church of Ireland was typical of a breed of maverick Irish clerics who came to known trouble spots in Britain to ply an evangelising trade. McMenemy arrived in Edinburgh in 1848 and established a proselytising mission. His preachers forced their way into the homes of the poor Irish Catholics of Grassmarket, West Port and Cowgate in order to read them scripture in the Irish tongue.

Some element of the violence was wholly imported and enacted by Irish on Irish. The Orange Order remained resolutely an Irish organisation in nineteenth-century Scotland and its marches and meetings, which grew rapidly in the post-famine years, did much to instil a Belfast-style culture of sectarianism into Scottish life. Scottish anti-Catholicism, then, was both Scots and Irish. Such antipathy, fuelled by the famine immigration, was much exacerbated by the Fenian activities of the 1860s. The Fenians were somewhat akin to the modern-day IRA in their willingness to use violence to advance claims for a free Ireland. With bombings and raids on arsenals, prisons and other public official property, the Fenian episodes of 1867–8, culminating in several executions and a failed rising in Ireland, whipped up negative public reactions on both sides of the border.

Even after the initial Fenian threat had subsided, there continued to be ample fuel for the fires of sectarianism. An Orange-versus-Green mentality had become firmly and inextricably enmeshed within Scots culture by the 1850s, and it became stronger for generations thereafter. Riots occurred periodically in the 1870s and 1880s. The most serious occurrence exploded on the citizens of Partick in August 1875, during centenary celebrations for the hero of Catholic Emancipation and the early Irish home rule movement, Daniel O'Connell. A great fight occurred between home rulers and Orangemen, with men and women alike joining the mêlée. It took days for order to prevail.

The Restoration of the Papal Hierarchy in Scotland in 1878 offered further encouragement to Orange and Green protagonists to fight over dead kings and live popes. They were resolutely divided on political issues, most notably home rule for Ireland, and continued to squabble about education and religious practice until long after the Second World War. Indeed, only in Canada and Liverpool would sectarianism scorch ordinary lives as it did in Scotland – but nowhere else, save in Ulster, have the embers glowed so long.

Irreligion, atheism and secularism

Religious bodies had to deal not only with those who fell out of devout behaviour for lack of church provision in the towns, or for reasons of apathy, but also for reason of open or philosophical rejection. Atheism undoubtedly grew in the nineteenth century, but few were active advocates of such an extreme, at least not in the early part of the century. Radical freethought, within which a rejection of standard religion was a part, was closely associated with political radicalism, republicanism and revolution: many of these, moreover, were not just atheistic but were actively anti-religious. They saw the church as more than patrician; indeed, as a prop for the *ancien régime* and their critique of religion owed much to the rational ideas of the later eighteenth century and the actions of revolutionaries in 1790s France. Churches which feared for their existence at the hands of Godless men such as Thomas Paine or William Godwin at least could be comforted by the fact that secular elites feared the same sorts of people, but for rather different reasons. It is no small wonder, however, that the authorities equated religiosity with political contentment and saw, in organised religion, a calming, conservative force.

Much radical freethought was actually religious in the sense that though it rejected 'sacerdotalism' (the priesthood and its influence) it was still founded on a system of belief with deities, and so on. Zetetic (Free Enquiry) demagogues such as Richard Carlile and the Christian mystic, the Reverend Robert Taylor, who was called the 'Devil's Chaplain', offered a mish-mash of alternative religious ideas, drawing on freethought and Eastern mysticism. The most famous freethinker of the century was Robert Owen. His prophesies of a new order were based on the creation of the perfect environment: he believed that human beings were good, and that the threat to salvation came not from the evil of humans but from the imperfections of the world about them. His Association of All the Classes of All Nations (1835) promised a moral restructuring of society by building upon the assault upon economic greed that was being led by his co-operative movement. Like the co-operative, Owen's association appealed to better-off working-men – not labourers but artisans. Owenism was supplanted in the 1840s by the rationalism of Charles Southwell (1814–60) and George Jacob Holyoake (1817–1906). Rationalism was based on the belief that reason and science should shape human life, with a general morality, as opposed to religious morality, granted pre-eminence in life. Holyoake's ideas are well captured in the sub-title to one of his journal publications, *The Movement*, the 'anti-persecution gazette and a register of progress [as well as] a weekly journal of republican politics, anti-theology and utilitarian morals'. The first edition of *The Movement* (1853) made Holyoake's position on religion clear, when he cited Jeremy Bentham: 'Maximise morals, minimise religion.' The phrase was to be carried on the front page of each edition, just below the mast-head (see Box 16.1). Holyoake's secularising crusade grew in size in the 1850s. He engaged actively in lecture and debating campaigns, and published a newspaper, the *Reasoner*, which appeared for 15 years after 1846. He supported radical political causes such as Italian republicanism and the extension of the franchise at home.

Holyoake was not actually that much of a radical figure. He connected with a highbrow London set which included such luminaries as John Stuart Mill and Harriet Martineau. The greatest – or perhaps most publicised – secularist of the century was Charles Bradlaugh (1833–91). Bradlaugh, who quarrelled with Holyoake, led a more radical secularism, focused on his newspaper, the *National Reformer*, which stood against Holyoake's *National Reformer*, which he ran with the spurned former deputy of Bradlaugh, Charles Watts (1836–1906). Bradlaugh supported reform of parliament and was ably supported by one of the most forceful women activists of the period, Annie Besant (1847–1933). Bradlaugh was eventually elected to parliament for the seat of Northampton in 1880, but he caused a sensation, when, following his election, he refused to take the oath of allegiance. A Select Committee ruled that the Affirmations Act (1855) allowed for objections only of a religious nature (i.e. Quakerism); Bradlaugh's irreligion did not count. Bradlaugh offered to take the oath but was told he could not do so, having already declared that it meant nothing to him. The case was a national embarrassment, and Bradlaugh became something of a national celebrity. Time after time the electors of Northampton re-elected him; each time he was faced with the same impasse.

For all that they espoused secularism, societies such as Bradlaugh's National Secular Society effectively mimicked religion with their spiritual and social organisation: lectures, meetings, hymn books, and so forth. It is unlikely that more than 50,000 people were influenced by the movement and less than one-tenth of that figure joined societies affirming their atheism or agnosticism. Nevertheless, the ripples of irreligion spread wide, and, in social and intellectual terms, these various movements were important throughout the century.

16.4 Churches for the urban world

The twin issues of Catholic regeneration and Irish immigration would have exercised British Protestants at any point in their history, but something less collided into the bulwark at about the same time. This was the issue of falling church attendance. The religious census of 1851 demonstrated to Victorians that their society, although deeply concerned with religious issues, was in fact becoming more irreligious. The Census of Religious Worship was the first (and last) attempt by government to record all places where public worship was held, the frequency of their services, the extent of their accommodation, and the number of people in them. The paradox was that while 34,467 places of worship in England and Wales were identified, and millions of religious pamphlets were being distributed by voluntary associations committed to the salvation of the lower classes, more than 5m people stayed away from church on census Sunday, 30 March. The census itself reflected not only Victorian conviction in the value of data, but also concern about the spiritual state of the nation and whether the religious infrastructure was keeping up with population change.

Within the general picture of increasing faithlessness there also a doubly fearsome detail: that while Catholicism was *the* growth denomination, and dissenters were becoming more numerous, it was the Church of England, which had about one-half of all church-goers, which was most affected by downward trends (Box 16.7). The census revealed nearly 11m attendances in England and Wales (60.8 per cent of the population) of which 48.6 per cent were in Anglican churches and 51.4 per cent in others, a return that led to Anglican anger. The urban scene seemed to favour Catholic and dissenting missions; while Anglicanism held firm or grew in the rural south and in small towns, the big cities and the northern towns – vital spots in the industrialisation process – were where nonconformity enjoyed its greatest successes. Irish Catholics were also better attenders than their English equivalents, and this became even more so after the 1850s when the influence of Cardinal Paul Cullen's 'Devolution Revolution', which spread conformity of practice across Ireland, had become embedded in the cultural consciousness of later waves of immigrants. At the same time, a lack of pew space, shortages of personnel and money, the impersonal nature of big towns and cities, and a high turnover of population – all these things made it hard for all denominations to achieve the cohesiveness that marked rural parish life at that time.

The census figures showed quite clearly that, although working-class church attendance was lower than clerics would have liked, a majority of those who went to church

Box 16.7

'The Ritualist conspiracy'

This article, by Lady Wimbourne, was first published in October 1898, in the periodical, *Nineteenth Century*, and subsequently appeared as a popular pamphlet in the same year. It captures the basic fears that many Anglicans had had for decades about the spread of Catholic practices in their church. The language, which seems exaggerated to us, demonstrates how powerfully Victorians felt about their religious institutions, not least the established church. The piece also shows how Christians were torn between the desire to see working people properly and morally ministered to and the desire for the ministering to be of a particular type.

> We in England are awakening to a fact – a fact the importance of which cannot be over-estimated – namely, that our Church [of England] is suffering from a deadly disease which threatens its very existence. This disease is of such an insidious character that it has for years been eating like a canker into the heart of the Church without sufficiently altering its external appearance to attract much attention. We have long known that what is called Ritualism existed in a greater or less degree among us, and for the most part people have viewed it with disfavour.

They have, however, recognised that many of those who practised it were earnest, hard-working men, doing a good work in crowded districts, where the main object appeared to be to win men by any means to Christianity, and they have therefore tolerated what was in the main contrary to their inclination. There has also been a feeling that the English Church [i.e. the Church of England] was intended to be wide enough to contain within its fold men of divergent views on religious matters, so long as those views were consonant with the cardinal doctrines of our Church as expressed by the Prayer Book, which was looked upon as a guarantee of orthodoxy.

Ritualism, therefore, thus tolerated, has grown and developed unobserved into an enormous system, until we find, to our surprise and alarm, that not *Ritualism* but *Romanism* is the danger that is threatening us, and that it has taken such a hold on a large portion of the community that it will require all the wisdom, all the energy, and all the determination of those who guide the destinies of our Church and country to eradicate it. ...

---

were, nevertheless, working class. Their attendance was affected by their circumstances, including work patterns. John Davies, Rector of St Clement's, Worcester, reported in the census:

> The parishioners of St Clement's consist chiefly of the working class (some very poor indeed) many of whom seldom ever attend Sunday Morning Service. The Saturday Market and the late payment of wages on the evening of that day contribute probably in no small degree to produce this result. The same cause operates injuriously also with reference to the attendance of children at school and church on Sunday morning, the parents being up late on Saturday night ... Many parents, well-disposed to attend public worship absent themselves on account of their dress and the same remark is applicable to their children as relating to school and church.

Davies added of the Worcester Episcopal Floating Chapel:

> The opening of this chapel appears to have been productive, through the Divine Blessing of beneficial effects or the boatmen, while collateral benefits have also resulted. But the prevalence of Sunday traffic has an injurious tendency upon the morals of this class of men ... Not only fishermen, but scavengers, sweeps, beggars have occasionally joined the congregation ... I have often noticed people present, who I had reason to believe would have never attended their own parish church or any other on account of their dress, etc. (J. Aitkenhead, *Census of Religious Worship, 1851: Returns for Worcester*, Worcester, 2000).

Women stood out in all denominations as the most reliable attenders. Priests made a great play for female support, knowing that it was the mother rather than the father who would guarantee the devotion of the next generation. Whether it was because of this sort of effort by priests, a greater natural piety among females, or a sense of duty because it was they who had to take children into church, working-class women had a better record of religious devotion than their menfolk. Among Anglicans, according to Charles Booth and Seebohm Rowntree's social investigations into working-class life in London and York, respectively, women comprised two-thirds of church attenders; with Catholics the figure was around 60 per cent. Only among nonconformists were male and female ratios similar.

Later, local censuses confirmed what had been found in 1851: that established churches were in effect the largest of a number of denominations in England and Wales; that Catholicism, now settled and stridently and self-defensively evangelical, along with dissenting chapels, thrived. The success of religious alternatives was demonstrated by the development of Forward Movement in the mid-1880s, designed to conserve and convert the cities with a broad-based evangelical and social message. Perhaps most striking of all the dissenting successes can be seen in the rapid expansion of William and Catherine Booth's Salvation Army (1870). This evangelical movement with its military metaphors and crusading work of conversion, had over 10,000 members in the early 1880s. The band was apparently a means of making an impression amidst the hoots of derision; women were the equals of men; and the social dimension, which we know so well today, soon became a key aspect of Salvationists' work.

There is no doubt, therefore, that providing for the spiritual needs of urban-dwellers was the key challenge for all denominations. Churches were not always attuned to the needs of ordinary people. This was not only true in the towns and cities but also in rural areas. In Hook Norton in Oxfordshire, where more people had attended nonconformist than Anglican service on census Sunday in 1851, the Rector reported to the Bishop in 1875 that at least half the population were habitually absent from church and that over the previous three years matters had deteriorated 'especially since the formation of the Agricultural Labourers' Union'. The Victorian worker and his family shared a rather untheoretical, almost matter-of-fact view of religion in which a basically neighbourly and reasonably clean-living life was enough to guarantee salvation. Organised religion was also regarded with some suspicion. Anglicanism was considered elitist and patrician, or at least this was its historical position, while all denominations tended to pour scorn on the uncivilised and brutish behaviour of urban workers. The churches were of course imbued with the 'Victorian values' that dominated social and economic thought in Britain at this time. Self-help, cleanliness, Sabbatarianism and temperance were all part of the credo of the churches, and these sentiments often clashed with the social philosophy of the poorer working people, even if the upwardly mobile were attracted. Attempts to reform drink culture, for example, drew support from sober-minded artisans, often archetypal chapel-going trade union leaders, as well as from middle-class philanthropists. Whereas, for dock workers, navvies or unskilled labourers, the pub was more of an attraction than the church, and thus, just as likely to be the fulcrum of community. Irish priests did particularly well with the immigrant population, especially after the 1850s when their number increased to match the size of the flock. Irish priests had a particularly revered position in Irish spiritual and social life; although much of their day-to-day endorsement came from a willingness to ignore a bit of drinking and fighting so long as it was not injurious to children or the family. Neverthless, the line between drinking and drunkenness is a fine one, and priests of all creeds were aware that a drunkard would inevitably deny much-needed income from his family. Thus, whatever the toleration of human foibles, clergy were generally at the forefront of drink reform and temperance movements.

The churches did reach out to the lower classes through their charitable works, and millions of young children were enrolled in Sunday Schools. Because they took place on the Sabbath, these schools did not affect what children could do to earn money during what was, even at the end of our period, at least a five-and-a-half day working week. Parents appreciated the need for rudimentary education, although they selected schools, like other commodities, on a 'need' and 'afford' basis. There was competition between denominations to control the working class through Sunday Schools, just as later on, when state education spread, there were fearsome sectarian fights over the contents of curricula. There is no doubt, too, that Sunday schools penetrated the consciousness of working-class communities, with their fairs, parades, day-trips and other social functions.

The social provision of churches extended beyond schools and into most aspects of people's lives. For faithful adherents, religious affiliations were some of the most important threads of their community's fabric. Churches provided spiritual comfort and sociability to those entering the growing towns; this was never more apparent than in the case of the Irish Catholics, whose arrival in the urban centres coincided with the greatest social upheavals in the process of industrialisation. Sometimes, the needs of a desperate Irish flock encouraged the Catholic Church to offer an important social function. Protestants of all nationalities, too, shared this social sense, and all churches concentrated on a comprehensive mixture of religious and social functions, including leisure and sporting activities. An example of this occurred in 1887 when a Catholic priest founded Glasgow Celtic football club. Church involvement in sporting and leisure-time activities derived from a wide notion or moral and physical improvement. Much of this energy for properly nurturing the character of working-class children derived from a fear and loathing of the drink culture which they might otherwise slip into as young adults.

16.5 Conclusion

The number of churches in Britain grew in a bewildering fashion in the nineteenth centuries; the country remained devout in a way, and to an extent that is very different from our own age. A thread of continuity clearly runs across the period as clergy and lay believers struggled to come to terms with inertia, disorganisation, social upheaval and cultural competition from other forms of free-time activity. This is not to suggest that religion, in the round, can be compared with football, except that both might have pressurised the time of the same worker on a weekend afternoon. The churches all recognised that in the urban world, there was competition for people's attention. The people craved symbols of stability that helped them make sense of their new surroundings. This may have been particularly noticeable in the way Irish Catholic zeal – an amorphous or elusive quality – was turned into strict conformity and so many new churches. But artisans, and better placed working men and women, also took the message from religion that a social profile as well as a spiritual provision was the key to a full if not always fulfilled life. Religion was, then, important. It was mentioned in every debate in the House of Commons and hundreds of individual pieces of legislation lie as testament to its continuing and sometimes over-riding impact on the way Victorians saw their world. When missionaries went into Bethnal Green or Borneo it was with a civilising Christian mission.

Yet, crises of faith marked the period, and dogmatic divisions over the nature of faith also lived on. In the Edwardian years, activists were still panicking about Ritualism in the Church of England – so much so, in fact, that they eventually got a Royal Commission which investigated this great threat to the nation's moral fabric. Religion may have been passing from the lives of many thousands of Victorians, not least those who, like G.J. Holyoake, chose alternatives such as secularism and socialism.

Summary

◆ There was an increasing variety in the range of types of religious practice in this period.
◆ Dissenting traditions grew, but Anglicanism remained religiously and political powerful.
◆ Catholicism was one of the main growth denominations, primarily owing to mass Irish immigration.
◆ Secular traditions also became prominent and must be seen alongside traditional religiosity as one aspect of
◆ how people enforced or rejected faith.
◆ Church attendances fell but people remained religious; attending church was not the only way to demonstrate belief in God.
◆ Many of those who did not go to church on a regular basis believed in God and strove to live their lives with a view to some future Judgement Day.

Points to discuss

◆ Why, and in what way, was religion central to Victorian life?
◆ How did the range of religious sects develop in this period?
◆ What factors led to a renaissance of Roman Catholicism in Victorian Britain?
◆ How did churches fare in the urban world?
◆ How important were secular, agnostic or atheist tendencies?

References and further reading

J. Aitkenhead, *Census of Religious Worship, 1851: Returns for Worcester* (Worcester, 2000).

S. Budd, *Varieties of Unbelief: Atheists and Agnostics in English Society, 1850–1860* (1977).

A. Burns, *The Diocesan Revival in the Church of England, c.1800–1870* (Oxford, 1999).

J.C.D. Clark, *Languages of liberty* (Cambridge, 1994).

A.D. Gilbert, *Religion and Society in Industrial England, 1740–1914: Church, Chapel and Social Change* (1976).

S. Gilley and W.J. Shiels (eds), *A History of Religion in Britain: Practice and Belief from Pre-Roman Times to the Present* (Oxford, 1994).

J.E. Handley, *The Irish in Modern Scotland* (Cork, 1947).

D. Hempton, *Religion and Political Culture in Britain and Ireland: From the Glorious Revolution to the Decline of Empire* (Cambridge, 1996).

K.S. Inglis, *Churches and the Working Class in Victorian England* (1965).

G.I.T. Machin, *Politics and the Churches in Great Britain, 1832–1868* (Oxford, 1987).

G.I.T. Machin, *Politics and the Churches in Great Britain, 1869–1921* (Oxford, 1987).

Hugh McLeod, *Religion and Society, 1850–1914* (Basingstoke, 1996).

G. Parsons (ed.), *Religion in Victorian Britain* 4 Vols (Manchester, 1988).

E. Royle, *Victorian Infidels: The Origins of the British Secularist Movement, 1791–1866* (Manchester, 1974).

E. Royle, *Radicals, Secularists and Republicans: Popular Freethought in Britain, 1866–1915* (Manchester, 1980).

H. Schlossberg, *The Silent Revolution and the Making of Victorian England* (Columbus, Oh. 2000).

N. Scotland, *'Good and Proper Men': Lord Palmerston and the Bench of Bishops* (Cambridge, 2000).

W.R. Ward, *Religion and Society in England, 1790–1850* (1972).

17 Cultural Trends

Contents

Introduction

For most readers culture means *high culture*, the world of poets and painters. Yet culture can also be understood in a much broader fashion. This is true not only of its products – popular music to opera – but also of the way in which they are produced, and the contexts of cultural activity. Culture, in other words, can mean both the products of 'high' and 'low', 'elite' and 'popular', culture, and also the way in which these are received, or 'negotiated', as part of a whole way of life. There is a push-pull tension. Styles are important, but so also is the consumption of culture and its impact on the consumers. This wider approach will be the subject of this chapter. As far as examples are concerned, emphasis will be on the culture of print – published material – because it is more accessible, throughout the country and further afield, than, for example, architecture or paintings. A network of school and public libraries holds many of the works and they are also generally available in inexpensive paperback editions.

Key issues

▶ What were the principal changes in popular culture, in the sense of the whole way of life of the community?

▶ How far was culture an expression of identity?

▶ What was the relationship between culture and consumerism?

▶ Why was the novel so important?

17.1 The triumphant marketplace

The triumph of the market is the major theme in nineteenth-century British cultural history. By the 'market', we mean the role of consumers in determining the success of particular art forms and artists. Such a situation was scarcely new. The cultural market-place indeed had come to the fore in Britain in the eighteenth century, as patronage by individual wealthy patrons was largely replaced by the anonymous patronage of the market. This entailed producing works for sale to individuals the artist had not met. It led to a new series of cultural meeting points and places of cultural consumption: art galleries and auctions, concert halls and choral festivals. The crucial links were provided by entrepreneurs: concert organisers, art auctioneers, and, most significantly, publishers. Publishers financed book production and arranged the sale of the finished product. These entrepreneurs treated culture as a commodity, a commodity whose value was set by the market. Furthermore, this was a particularly fluid market, one in which style and novelty were crucial in enhancing value and attracting recognition and sale.

This situation remained the case during the nineteenth century, but the market greatly changed. This was largely owing to the movement of the bulk of the population into a market that had been hitherto defined essentially (although not exclusively) in terms of the middling orders. In the Victorian period, the bulk of the working class, especially the skilled artisans, gained time and money for leisure. Much of this was spent on sport, and, in the Victorian period, football emerged as a very popular spectator sport, while other sports, such as horse-racing, also attracted a large working-class following. Greyhound-racing, a sport closely associated with working-class men, was not introduced to the United Kingdom until 1926. Aside from sport, there was also a marked growth in leisure facilities catering for the urban working class.

Many of these leisure pursuits of course presupposed significant urban populations. Generally, urban pastimes were marked by far greater organisation and had the capacity to be larger and more concentrated than in the shires. There also emerged a much more distinct division between participant and observer, especially in team sport, where spectators were becoming increasingly numerous. Sporting activities became increasing highly organised, competitive and commercialised – changes which derived part of their impetus from the permeation of the public schools' new emphasis on the value of character-building and the manly qualities of team sports. Certain types of leisure facilities needed urban populations to finance and sustain them, for example libraries, reading rooms and bath-houses. The same could be said for music halls, where the entertainment has been seen as epitomising the culture of urban workers. The music hall was escapist on one level, yet it was was also central to working-class life – a real part of the world in which these people lived. Much of this activity focused on the large music halls that were built in this period, such as the Alhambra in Bradford. These places offered both spectator entertain-ment and an opportunity to participate, by singing along or engaging in repartee with the performers. By the end of our period, however, with the advent of 'moving pictures', many music halls were converted into cinemas, which by 1914 numbered some 4,000.

During the same period, *organised* middle-class cultural activity greatly expanded. This owed much to the expansion of the middle class in cities, and their pursuit of culture not only for pleasure, but, also, as a way of defining their purpose and leadership. The middle class patronised a great upsurge in art, poetry, and the performance or production of music, leading to popular art movements such as the Pre-Raphaelites – the most famous of whom were William Holman Hunt (1827–1910), John Everett Millais (1829–96) and Dante Gabriel Rossetti (1828–82) – who enjoyed considerable popularity from the early-1850s. Cities, such as Birmingham, Glasgow, Leeds, Liverpool, Manchester and Newcastle, founded major art collections and musical institutions, such as the Hallé Orchestra in Manchester in 1857. Although the great art collections that can now be found in Manchester's Whitworth Gallery or Liverpool's Walker Gallery were the product of commercial, urban, middle-class wealth, their purpose was somewhat more broad-ranging than these origins. Labouring men and women queued for hours to file past Ford Madox Brown's classic painting *Work* when it was finally finished in 1865. For these people, viewing art was like viewing a movie premiere today. Thus art informed the public as well as the elite.

Interest and self-improvement focused on other activities as well. For example, there were many enthusiasts committed to natural history, astronomy and geology. Such activities were in part institutionalised with, for example, numerous natural history societies and observatories around the country. This process extended to include the study of history itself, especially local history. Societies for local history were founded and their journals helped publicise their proceedings: research thus had a public function and voice.

There was also a boom in middle-class sports, such as golf and lawn tennis, whose rules were systematised in 1874. Sporting institutions and facilities were created across Britain, constituting foci for local sociability. Northumberland Cricket Club, for example, had a ground in Newcastle by the 1850s, while Newcastle Golf Club expanded its activities in the 1890s. Civic organisations played a major role in such expansion, but the essential dynamo was commercial. This was even more obviously the case with individual activity, whether the expansion of private music-making (by individuals and by families) or the great expansion of reading. The purchase of books, magazines and newspapers expanded greatly.

17.2 The novelists' Britain

The nineteenth century was less 'visual' than the modern age. There was no equivalent to the stimulus and excitement of cinema and television, both of which made visual appeal normative in modern culture. Instead, it was the written word that took precedence. This reflected the traditional prestige of print – the medium of the bible and the classics, as well as its power as the language of authority, and the impact of rising literacy. More people were able to enjoy the printed word than ever before, and print culture itself became more normative. Whereas Birmingham had 12 printers in 1799, it had 33 in 1828.

Much of our image of Victorian Britain comes from the famous novels of the period, especially those of Charles Dickens (1812–70) (Profile Box 17.1). Whereas Jane Austen

Charles Dickens (1812-70)

The leading novelist of his period. In his childhood, Dickens experienced certain hardship. His father went to the Marshalsea Debtors' Prison and, at the age of 12, Dickens began menial work in London at Warren's blacking factory, a shocking experience for him. Later, after being employed as an office boy, a court reporter and a journalist, Dickens became a writer; the successful serialisation of his *Pickwick Papers* started in 1836, and thereafter he wrote numerous novels. He was a committed reformer, especially over capital punishment, housing and prostitution.

(1775–1817), now the best-known novelist of Regency England, is noted foremost for her acute observation of provincial propertied society, and Sir Walter Scott (1771–1832), the leading Scottish novelist of the period, for his historical works, Dickens deliberately addressed social conditions and urban society. In his childhood, Dickens had experience of hardship. His father went to the Marshalsea Debtors' Prison and, at the age of 12, Dickens began menial work in London in Warren's blacking factory, a shocking experience for him. Later, after work as an office-boy, a court reporter and a journalist, Dickens began as a writer, the successful serialisation of his *Pickwick Papers* starting in 1836. He was a committed reformer, especially over capital punishment, housing and prostitution.

Dickens' novels presented the inadequacies of existing institutions. In *Nicholas Nickleby*, published in monthly parts in 1838–9, Nicholas, sent to teach at Dotheboys Hall in Yorkshire, is horrified by the headmaster, Wackford Squeers, who, knowing their uncaring parents will not intervene, mistreats and starves the pupils and doses them with brimstone and treacle. Nicholas rebels and thrashes Squeers unconscious. The story also featured Ralph Nickleby as a dishonest and callous financier, and Sir Mulberry Hawk as a selfish and sinister member of society. *Bleak House* (1852–3) is an indictment of the coldness of law and church, the delays of the former and the smugness of the righteous Reverend Chadband. Society, in the persons of Sir Leicester Dedlock – 'his family is as old as the hills and infinitely more respectable' – and his wife, is revealed as haughty and also as concealing a guilty secret. Such secrets are an aspect of the melodramatic character of much of Dickens' work. Such melodrama was very popular with the public. It joined fiction and theatre, not least through the drama of public readings, such as those held, with great success, by Dickens. As with the orphan Smike in *Nicholas Nickleby*, society also fails the poor in *Bleak House*, in this case Jo, a young crossing-sweeper. Both die. In *Hard Times* (1854), Dickens attacked utilitarianism in the person of the fact-obsessed, unloving hardware merchant Thomas Gradgrind. In *Little Dorrit* (1855–7), society worships Merdle, a great but fraudulent financier, 'a new power in the country', while government, in the shape of the Circumlocution Office, is callously inefficient. At dinner at Merdle's 'Treasury hoped he might venture to congratulate one of England's world-famed capitalists and merchant-princes ... To extend the triumphs of such men, was to extend the triumphs and resources of the nation.'

Not only a novelist, Dickens also launched the weekly magazine *Household Words* in 1850. He won great success. *The Old Curiosity Shop* (1840–1) sold 100,000 copies, his weekly magazine from 1859, *All the Year Round*, as many as 300,000. A fine observer of people, Dickens was also a recorder of a changing society. This was captured in his short story 'Dullborough Town', published in *All the Year Round* on 30 June 1860. The story was about a return to childhood haunts:

> Most of us come from Dullborough who come from a country town ... the Station had swallowed up the playing-field. It was gone. The two beautiful hawthorn-trees, the hedge, the turf, and all those buttercups and daisies had given place to the stoniest of jolting roads ... The coach that had carried me away, was melodiously called Timpson's Blue-Eyed Maid, and belonged to Timpson, at the coach-office up-street; the locomotive engine that had brought me back, was called severely No. 97, and belonged to SER [South Eastern Railway], and was spitting ashes and hot-water over the blighted ground.'

In *Dombey and Son* (1846–8), a train runs over the villain Carker 'and licked his stream of life up with its fiery heat'.

Dickens was not alone in his concerns. His one-time collaborator Wilkie Collins (1824–89) dealt with issues such as divorce, vivisection, and the impact of hereditary and environment. In *The Woman in White* (1859–60), Anne Catherick is incarcerated in a mental asylum in order to conceal a secret. Evangelical busybodies are attacked in the person of Miss Clack in *The Moonstone* (1868). *Man and Wife* (1870) castigates the cult of athleticism and criticises the marriage laws. In *The New Magdalen* (1873), Collins condemns sexual hypocrisy. Wracked by gout, Collins took large quantities of laudanum and the drug had a major impact on his work.

Social issues attracted other prominent writers. Elizabeth Gaskell (1810–65) wrote about industrial strife, working-class living standards, and the role of entrepreneurs in *Mary Barton* (1848); she was more positive about entrepreneurs in *North and South* (1855). George Eliot, the pseudonym of Mary Anne Evans (1819–80), depicted a seducing squire in *Adam Bede* (1859), social ostracism in *The Mill on the Floss* (1860), the cruel selfishness of the two sons of the squire in *Silas Marner* (1861), corrupt electioneering in *Felix Holt* (1866), a hypocritical banker in *Middlemarch* (1871–2), and the decadent mores of society in *Daniel Deronda* (1878). Her work also recorded the pressures of social organisation and mores. Social rank is seen as divisive in *Middlemarch*. Both writers exemplified the importance of women in the writing of novels; they were also very important in readership, and increasingly so as female literacy rose.

In novels such as *Far from the Madding Crowd* (1874) and *The Mayor of Casterbridge* (1886), Thomas Hardy (1840–1928) recorded the bleaker side of country life and the corrosive pressure of urban mores on rural ways. Rural society was presented as steeped in folk-lore and customs, and suspicious of new men of business. Hardy's *Jude the Obscure* (1895) dealt with exclusion from scholarship as a result of class. Earlier, the agricultural labourer John Clare had depicted the plight of the rural poor in *Poems Descriptive of Rural Life* (1820) and his long poem *The Village Minstrel* (1821). George Gissing (1857–1903) presented urban poverty and the harsh binds of heredity in *Workers in the Dawn* (1880). In *Demos: A Story of English Socialism* (1886), he was however biting about the motives and integrity of socialist leaders. Other social comment writings included Andrew Mearns' tract, *The Bitter Cry of Outcast London* (1883).

Other novelists were less noted for social criticism; *Vanity Fair* (1847–8), the panoramic masterpiece of William Makepeace Thackeray (1811–63), offered a realistic account of individual drives rather than a prescription for social action. In *The Way We Live Now* (1874–5), Anthony Trollope (1815–82) condemned the corruption of what he saw as 'the commercial profligacy of the age', but much of Trollope's work was far less pointed. Trollope was particularly popular with contemporaries for his Barsetshire sequence (1855–67) which provided a realistic but essentially benign account of middle-class provincial, especially clerical, society. Trollope also wrote a series of political novels, the Palliser novels, which appeared in 1864–80. These, and his other novels, offered a fine and close account of character and an intimate understanding of human action which provided the basis for his sympathetic yet ironic treatment of character. Trollope's productivity – 47 novels and much else including travel books and biography beside an active career in the Post Office – surpassed that of his mother Frances Trollope (1780–1863) who had been driven by family debts to publish 41 books. There was little social criticism in the works of Edward Bulwer Lytton (1803–73), now little known, but, in his prime, frequently seen as the country's foremost man of letters for works such as *The Last Days of Pompeii* (1834). A friend of Dickens who was an active MP before being raised to the peerage, Bulwer Lytton's career indicated the potential profit of authorship and the variety of styles and forms that gifted (and not so gifted) writers could employ. Bulwer Lytton wrote 24 novels, 10 plays, 11 volumes of poetry, translations, essays, and historical and sociological studies, and was also a magazine editor. Among his genres was that of the 'silver-fork novelist', the portrayer of drama or at least events in high society. Bulwer Lytton's *Pelham, or, The Adventures of a Gentleman* (1828) was a successful example, and Disraeli's novels can also be located in this genre.

Scottish fiction tended to abandon confrontational attitudes towards contemporary industrialisation in favour of historical, ruralist and fantasy writing often intended to reinforce a separate identity. This was true of James Hogg (1770–1835), the self-styled 'king of the mountain and fairy school', George MacDonald (1824–1905), an accomplished fantasy writer, and Robert Louis Stevenson (1850–94). Although best known as a writer for children, the author of *Treasure Island* (1883), *Kidnapped* (1886) and *The Black Arrow* (1888), Stevenson tackled many other topics and some of his work has been seen as important in the development of modernism.

The writers of the age sought a wide readership, not only for personal profit but also because they thought it important to write for a mass readership. This was not seen as incompatible with literary excellence, and these attitudes reflected the distance between the literary world of the nineteenth century and that of two centuries earlier.

17.3 Poetry

Novels were not the sole form of printed culture. In terms of what was conventionally seen as such culture, namely literature, this was an age in which poetry made a major impact. In the early decades of the century this was a matter of the Romantic poets, especially William Wordsworth (1770–1850), Samuel Taylor Coleridge (1772–1834), and Robert Southey (1774–1843). The Cumbrian-born Wordsworth was a supporter of Revolutionary France in the 1790s who became the most celebrated of the English Romantics with works such as the *Lyrical Ballads* (1798; 2nd edn, 1800), *The Prelude* (1799; longer form 1805) and *The Excursion* (1814). Wordsworth was very much a poet of elemental forces with a fine eye for landscape. He lived most of his life in the Lake District which he celebrated in poetry and prose.

Coleridge was another early radical who became reconciled to the Establishment. Famous works included *Kubla Khan* (1797) and *The Rime of the Ancient Mariner* (1798). Coleridge was also an important critic. Southey was a less gifted writer, but, like Wordsworth, became both conservative in disposition and politics and Poet Laureate.

Several prominent poets of the period did not follow this political journey. Percy Bysshe Shelley (1792–1822), the author of *Prometheus Unbound*, was a democrat who led what was, by the standards of the age, an irregular personal life. He developed the radical potential of Romanticism in order to attack religion, law, the state and capitalism. For Shelley, politics and literature were not separable. The flavour of his critique can be gauged from some stanzas in his *The Masque of Anarchy* (1819):

> As I lay asleep in Italy
> There came a voice from over the
> Sea,
> And with great force it forth led
> me
> To walk in the visions of Poesy.

> I met Murder on the way –
> He had a mask like Castlereagh [Foreign Secretary] –
> Very smooth he looked, yet grim;
> Seven blood-hounds followed him;

> Next came Fraud and he had on,
> Like Eldon [Lord Chancellor], an ermined gown;
> His big tears, for he wept well,
> Turned to mill-stones as they fell, ...

> Clothed with the Bible, as with
> light,
> And the shadows of the night,
> Like Sidmouth [Home Secretary], next, Hypocrisy
> On a crocodile went by.

He wrote it from Italy, after hearing of the Peterloo Massacre.

George, 6th Lord Byron (1788–1824) was another radical with an irregular personal life, who went to live broad and died there. Byron's satire was less comprehensive in its denunciation of society than that of Shelley, but it could be very pointed. Byron also developed the image of the Byronic hero, a wandering outcast from an unjust society. John Keats (1795–1821) was less melodramatic and political, and developed a more intimate style of Romantic imagination and expression. His prominent works included *Isabella, or, the Pot of Basil*, *Hyperion*, *The Eve of St Agnes*, and *La Belle Dame Sans Merci*.

Wordsworth's successor as Poet Laureate in 1850 was Alfred 1st Lord Tennyson (1809–92). He helped reconcile poetry and the Establishment. A favourite of Queen Victoria, Tennyson was raised to the peerage in 1883. Tennyson was no bluff rhymster, but a neurotic and withdrawn figure who grasped sadness. The self-sacrifice endorsed in poems such as *Enoch Arden* (1864) was very popular. As the protagonist of morality and

Empire, Tennyson was also safe, and he was a master of poetry as understood in the period. It was self-sacrifice, not of the Byronic outcast, but of the servant of a social morality.

Despite the importance of the prolific and talented Robert Browning (1812–89), Tennyson dominated the poetic world even more than Dickens did that of fiction, but there were of course other poets. One of the most prominent was the multi-talented William Morris (1834–96), a member of the Pre-Raphaelite school. Yet none of the poets of the period approached the intensity and quality of the Romantics. The best work of the poets of the next generation, for example the Irish master of language William Butler Yeats (1865–1939), dated from after 1900.

17.4 Drama

The nineteenth century is not generally seen as the highpoint of the British stage. This was certainly true of England, Scotland and Wales, while in Ireland the Irish Literary Theatre did not open until 1899, and the Abbey Theatre until 1904, and John Millington Synge (1871–1909) did not write his first play, *In the Shadow of the Glen* until 1903 or his major work, *The Playboy of the Western World*, until 1907.

British drama of the sixteenth, seventeenth and twentieth century enjoys a considerably higher reputation than that of the nineteenth. Even the eighteenth century can boast playwrights of the quality of John Gay and Richard Brinsley Sheridan. The latter lived until 1816, but *The Critic* (1779) was his last first-rate play, and *Pizaro* (1799) his last really successful work.

The current theatrical repertoire includes very few nineteenth-century works. Plays such as Bulwer Lytton's *Richelieu*, which opened the Theatre Royal Stratford East in 1884, are now forgotten. The Gilbert and Sullivan operettas were as much musical as theatre, and it is not until Oscar Wilde in the 1890s that one finds works still frequently acted today. *Lady Windermere's Fan* (1892), *A Woman of No Importance* (1893), *An Ideal Husband* (1895) and *The Importance of Being Earnest* (1895) were ironic and brilliant portrayals of high society. *Salomé*, which was refused a licence in 1892 and first performed in Paris in 1896, was a very different work – a highly charged account of the relationship between Salome and St John the Baptist. The 1890s also saw the appearance of the first of the plays of George Bernard Shaw (1856–1950). Several – *Widowers' Houses* (1892), *Mrs Warren's Profession* (1893), and *The Philanderer* (1893) – were performed only privately as they were thought unlikely to obtain a licence: the Lord Chamberlain, through the Examiner of Plays, had to give a licence before any public performances on the stage. This, in particular, restricted new and different works.

Widowers' Houses (1892), Shaw's first play, which was produced for the Independent Theatre Club, was far more 'realistic' than those of Wilde, and Shaw emphasised its realism and didacticism. The play dealt openly and harshly with economic power and social relations in a way that was very different to the rest of nineteenth-century drama. It concerns the relationship between the aristocratic Henry Trench and Blanche Sartorius whose father gains his wealth by slum landlordism. Trench is appalled only for Sartorius to point out that Trench's money has come from similar sources. A series of realistic works produced publicly began with Shaw's *Arms and the Man* in 1894. The politically-

Oscar Fingall O'Flahertie Wilde (1854–1900)

Irish writer, wit and aesthete who glorified beauty for its own sake. His comedic wit which stands out in his most noted works, for example *Lady Windermere's Fan* (1892) and *The Importance of Being Earnest* (1895). He produced just one novel, *The Picture of Dorian Gray* (1891). He spent two years in prison for homosexual offences, the experiences of which he captured in print, particularly in his poem, *The Ballad of Reading Gaol* (1898). He died in Paris, after a lonely exile.

committed Shaw pushed the notion of the dramatist as a public figure able to turn a searching light on society.

This was not, however, the staple of the Regency and Victorian stage. In general, there was a preference for far less cerebral work. Leading actors, such as Edmund Kean and Charles Kean, offered Shakespeare or far less distinguished modern works. Melodrama, mocked in Shaw's hilarious send-up *Poison, Passion and Petrification*, was a regular, as was its counterpoint, a somewhat sickly romantic drama that centred on such plot devices as long-lost family members and mistaken identities. These devices were both used and mocked in the Gilbert and Sullivan operettas.

For most of the century, the theatre was dominated by actor-managers such as Henry Irving (1838–1905). This helps explain the nature of the British theatre. A prominent actor, Irving in 1878 became leassee and manager of the Lyceum in London. There, his emphasis was on the opulence and drama of the productions, not the novelty of the play. Thus, for example, Irving shunned the work of Shaw and of the realist Norwegian playright Ibsen. Irving preferred Shakespeare, or plays such as Tennyson's (now forgotten) *Becket* which he put on with great success in 1893. Other now-forgotten plays were also successes. For example, in the 1860s and 1870s Thomas Robertson's comedies such as *Society* (1865), *Ours* (1866), *Caste* (1867), *Play* (1868), *School* (1869) and *M.P.* (1870) were produced with considerable success. Robertson (1829–71) has been seen as offering a detailed account of domestic life that laid the basis for the later revival of serious drama by Shaw. His plays were described as 'cup-and-saucer drama'.

Robertson was seen as introducing a realistic note that changed the theatre by Sir Arthur Wing Pinero (1855–1934) who wrote not only successful farces, such as *The Magistrate* (1885), but also social dramas that focused on the difficult position of women, for example *The Second Mrs Tanqueray* (1893), *The Notorious Mrs Ebbsmith* (1895) and *The Benefit of the Doubt* (1895). In the powerful first of these, Paula Tanqueray commits suicide because of the social stigma created by the engagement of her seducer to her step-daughter and her opposition to the match. Pinero also dealt with seduction in his controversial *The Profligate* (1889).

Irving, who was knighted in 1895, the first actor to be thus honoured, ran the most famous theatrical company of the period. It was also a touring company. The railway made it possible for London companies to take on a national role. This led to a major change in the structure of the theatrical world. Earlier in the century, the London theatre had been complemented by 'stock' companies which were located in one theatre or appeared in several that were joined in a circuit. This ensured a local theatrical life across urban Britain. It also underlay the building of numerous theatres in the provinces. For example, the Duke of Grafton's Servants, based in the Theatre Royal in Norwich, and the Norfolk and Suffolk Company of Comedians toured East Anglia respectively until 1852 and 1844. Such activity encouraged the construction of numerous theatres, such as at Ipswich (1803) and Bury St Edmunds (1819).

The world of the stock company was swept aside by the development of the London-based 'long-run' system. In place of the large cost permanent companies, necessary for a repertory (range) of plays, managers preferred a long run of a single play. This could best be secured by new stars, such as Irving's leading lady Ellen Terry (1847–1928), spectacular productions with an emphasis on scenery and music, familiar plots, and uncontentious approaches. Augustus Harris, manager of the Theatre Royal at Drury Lane from 1879 until 1896, set the tone with spectaculars featuring avalanches, earthquakes, horse-races and snowstorms. Furthermore, the success of the run could be increased either by sending the company on a rail-borne tour or by using second and third companies at the same time as the main company coined the London market and ensured continued favourable publicity. This system scarcely encouraged adventurous drama. It did, however, bring profit to managements, thus encouraging investment in new theatres, particularly in London, for example the new Her Majesty's Theatre built in 1897. Theatre-building was driven by the profitability of the stage. In particular, existing runs financed new construction. The Prince of Wales Theatre built in London in 1884 was financed by the profits of a forgotten work *The Colonel* and then used to stage Charles Hawtrey's farce *The Private Secretary*. The Lyric Theatre which opened in Shaftesbury Avenue in 1888 was the result of the entrepreneurial energy of Henry J. Leslie. He financed it with the profits he had already made with his now forgotten comic opera *Dorothy*, which was transferred to the new theatre. Other works of the 1890s, now all forgotten, included Leslie's *Doris* and *The Red Hussar*, other comic operas – *La Cigale* (1890), *Little Christopher Columbus* (1893) and *Florodora* (1899), and Wilson Barret's then very successful play *The Sign of the Cross* (1896). The Lyric was also the name of a theatre opened in Hammersmith in 1888. There was also investment in ever more spectacular productions. This dynamic theatrical world persisted until the cinema made a major impact from the 1910s, although for the years prior to Shaw and Wilde it did not leave many plays that are still performed today.

17.5 Music-hall

In many respects the emphasis on commercial factors and production values (as opposed to content) seen in the theatre was a counterpoint of the music hall which made such an impact from the 1850s. Music hall was variety – song, music, acrobatics, dance – and emphasised an interaction between performers and audience. Music halls originally sold food and drink, although the latter was increasingly abolished as they were made more respectable. The Star at Bolton, founded in 1832 is seen as the first music hall, although they were most successful in London. Charles Morton, who founded the Canterbury at Lambeth in 1851, is seen as the 'father of the music hall'.

Music hall was performance art; although the songs were printed and sold in large numbers, the printed version could not command the impact of singers such as Dan Leno or Marie Lloyd. They and other singers acted songs such as 'Oh, Mister Porter', or 'The Galloping Major' (who gallops so much his new wife returns to her mother), to suggest a sexuality that was banished from public culture. Indeed, Marie Lloyd (1870–1922), though 'the Queen of the Halls', was not socially acceptable.

17.6 Architecture

New theatres and music halls were an important aspect of the expanding cultural infrastructure. So also were the art galleries and museums that proliferated in every major, and many minor, towns as they sought to proclaim their cultural status and offer improvement.

The civic building is a major part of the cultural heritage of the nineteenth century. In the twentieth century, especially during the post-1945 Modernist vogue, Victorian architecture was much castigated and many buildings were destroyed, or left stranded amid a new world of concrete and cars. Nevertheless, an enormous amount survives in city centres, and this remains an aspect of the culture that can be readily approached.

The early decades of the century witnessed a variety of styles, but neo-classicism played a major role in several of them. Greek Revival was particularly important. Classical porticoes decorated major buildings. Sir John Soane (1753–1837) was one of the most influential exponents of the new style. Having won a competition in 1788 to design a new building, he presided over work at one of the central institutions of national life, the Bank of England. Classical themes also played a role in the work of John Nash (1752–1835) who worked extensively in London for the Prince Regent. Nash's style was more varied than that of Soane, and he was also responsible for the Pavilion at Brighton which was built for the Prince in an ebullient idea of Chinese style.

The neo-classicism of the late eighteenth century drew heavily on Roman models, but that of the early nineteenth was more influenced by that of ancient Greece, for example the Doric and Ionic Orders. Architects such as William Wilkins (1778–1839), Sir Robert Smirke (1780–1867), C.R. Cockerell (1788–1863), and H.W. Inwood (1794–1843) all made lengthy trips to Greece. This inspiration was spread throughout Britain by training, as young architects served as apprentices in London. Thus William Burn took back to Edinburgh what he had learned in Smirke's office. Greek Revival led to works such as Wilkins' Grecian-style buildings at Downing College, Cambridge (1807–20), Thomas Hamilton's monument to Robert Burns at Alloway (1818), and his Royal High School in Edinburgh (1825–9).

Greek Revival did not stand alone. Neo-Gothic was important, especially in ecclesiastical architecture and for country houses, such as James Wyatt's vast Fonthill Abbey for William Beckford and Sir Walter Scott's building of Abbotsford (1816–23). The case for Gothic Revival was pushed hard by Augustus Pugin (1812–52), an architect who felt that the Revival had a mission. Pugin saw Gothic as the quintessentially Christian style. Having made his case for the Gothic in *Contrasts* (1836), Pugin built a series of works including

Alton Towers (1836). His arguments and designs hit home at the right moment as, after a long period in which *relatively* few new churches had been built, there was a period of massive church-building. This was largely due to the expansion of urban Britain as cities grew, not least thanks to movement from the countryside. Furthermore, Catholic emancipation was followed by the building of many Catholic churches. Gothic Revival was thus a counterpoint of religious activism (although far less so for Low Church congregations). It was favoured by the Oxford Movement and by the influential cultural commentator John Ruskin (1819–1900). Ruskin's lectures in Scotland in 1853 had a great impact, not least on the church architect F.T. Pilkington. In place of classical order, Ruskin advocated varied sky-lines and steeply-pitched roofs.

The Scots were also influenced by Scottish baronial style, as architects such as David Bryce searched for ideas and details from the legacy of the sixteenth and seventeenth century. Balmoral Castle (1853–8) helped make this style an ideal.

Influential architects in the Gothic Revival style included Sir George Scott (1811–78), William Butterfield (1814–1900), G.E. Street (1824–81), Norman Shaw (1831–1912) and Alfred Waterhouse. They were active in building and 'restoring' churches. Butterfield's work includes All Saints, Margaret Street (1859) and Keble College, Oxford (1873–6).

There was also much secular building in the Gothic style, especially from the 1850s as this style replaced Greek Revival. Thus, Scott's work included the Midland Hotel at St. Pancras Station (1865–71) and the Albert Memorial (1863), while other prominent buildings included Waterhouse's Manchester Town Hall (1869–77), and G.E. Street's Law Courts in London (1874–82).

Yet Gothic Revival did not enjoy an unchallenged ascendancy. Sir Charles Barry (1795–1860), worked in both Gothic and Greek Revival styles, but also developed a neo-Renaissance style, using Italian *palazzi* as models. This neo-Renaissance style was also employed by other architects, such as Gilbert Scott in his Foreign Office building. Barry indicated the electicism that was, alongside stylistic disputes, a pronounced feature of the period. Thus, his range was from the neo-Gothic Houses of Parliament and to the Greek Revival Manchester Athenaeum. As the century waned the neo-Gothic became increasingly repetitive. The variety of the Arts and Crafts movement associated with William Morris (1834–96) helped, however, to lighten it. Morris popularised an interest in craftsmanship.

Other architectural styles and themes included, at the close of the century, Art Nouveau which drew on Continental developments and was particularly associated with Glasgow architects especially Charles Rennie Mackintosh (1868–1928). Mackintosh stressed functionalism and modernity, and criticised the revival of past styles. His 1896 design for the Glasgow School of Art was a triumph of functionalism, as were the houses he built in the early 1900s.

Mackintosh's functionalism had not of course been absent earlier in the century, although he lent theoretical force to what had been more silent during earlier stylistic debates. Indeed, the railway and other examples of new industrial technology brought a requirement for new buildings and in new forms; while advances in construction techniques and in interior design requirements also encouraged a search for effective designs. The most famous individual work was Paxton's Crystal Palace, but railway stations, and, more generally, iron-fronted commercial and industrial premises recorded and helped popularise new designs.

Artistic styles do not exist and interact in an historical vacuum. Indeed those of the nineteenth century can be discussed in terms of the cultural politics of a society experiencing rapid change. The functional works just referred to can be seen as engineered buildings, built without too much or indeed any theoretical reflection. However, there was also a cultural reaction to industrialisation, the counterpoint to disquiet about urban crowds and conduct. By the 1840s, the horrors of industrialisation encouraged a nostalgic return to medievalism in some quarters. Although there was no strict equivalence, this can be related to the High-Anglican Oxford Movement in the Church of England, and also to the resurgence of British Catholicism.

The most obvious manifestation of this cultural politics was architectural, the very historicist Gothic revival. Pugin was a Catholic stylistic polemicist, responsible for the Catholic cathedrals at Birmingham (1841) and Newcastle (1844). Much, but by no means all, artistic patronage reflected institutional and personal commitments. For example, a magnificent decorated chapel, of High Victorian Gothic Revival type, was built at Clumber Park in 1886–9 by G.F. Bodley for the 7th Duke of Newcastle, a prominent Anglo-Catholic. The stained glass and other contents were in the same style. A similar church was built at Studley Royal by William Burges in 1871–8 for another Anglo-Catholic, the 1st Marquess of Ripon.

17.7 Painting

Modern interest in nineteenth-century painting focuses on J.M.W. Turner (1775–1851) and the Pre-Raphaelites. They were indeed important, and in some circles enjoyed considerable popularity. However, before discussing their work, it is worth noting that neither represented the mainstream. Instead, a far more established figure would be Queen Victoria's (and her subjects') favourite painter, Edwin Landseer (1802–73) who was knighted in 1850 and offered the Presidency of the Royal Academy in 1865. Although he died insane, Landseer was safe. Characteristic of his style was *Windsor Castle in Modern Times*. This showed Victoria and Albert as an idealized family with the gardens of Windsor Castle visible through the open window. Albert has just been shooting, but the dead birds on the carpet do not bleed and have no visible signs of injury. Everyone is appropriate and devoted, including the dogs. Landseer was a specialist in animal paintings and noted for works such as *The Stag at Bay* and *The Monarch of the Glen*. Engravings of these paintings were printed in large number. Landseer was not noted as an explorer of the urban scene, although he left his mark on London when he sculpted the lions at the foot of Nelson's Column (1867). Daniel Maclise (1806–70) was a counterpart of Landseer, although today far less well known. Nevertheless, at the time he was much applauded as a great artist. A close friend of Dickens, and an accomplished draughtsman who painted statuesque forms, Maclise illustrated themes from Shakespeare, for example *Macbeth and the Weird Sisters* (1836), and from British history, such as *Alfred the Great in the Tent of Guthruyn* (1852), painting as well as *Wellington and Blücher at Waterloo* (1861), and *The Death of Nelson* (1864) for the Houses of Parliament. These paintings were regarded as a great triumph and Maclise received £7,000 for the two.

Another prominent figure of the period, now forgotten, was Sir Charles Eastlake (1793–1865), who became President of the Royal Academy in 1850. Eastlake was noted for portraits, historical scenes, and picturesque displays of Mediterranean scenes and people, for example his *Pilgrims in Sight of St. Peter's* (1825), and religious works, especially *Christ blessing little Children* (1839) and *Christ weeping over Jerusalem* (1841).

Animals, sporting pictures and exemplary historical, religious and military scenes were popular, as were scenes of rural bliss. There were of course paintings reflecting the less benign aspects of life, but most of these were tempered in their realism. Thomas Kennington's *The Pinch of Poverty* (1889) did not provide a picture of smiling joy, but poverty was generally far harsher in its consequences than this genteel scene with its charming flower seller and romantically pale mother. The same was true of John Dollman's *The Immigrants' Ship* (1884). Despair and hardship were not emphasised.

Turner offered scenes of commercial life – for example his *Keelmen Heaving in Coals by Moonlight* – but was primarily, as in that painting, interested in light, or rather luminosity, colour and shape. His was Romanticism on canvas and was criticised for its lack of formalism by Sir George Beaumont (1753–1827). Turner moved from landscapes to the more abstract works of the 1840s.

Turner was to inspire the Impressionists and also to push the symbolisation of the elements further than hitherto. His was a different account of landscape to that by John Constable (1776–1837), although, like Turner, Constable departed from what they saw as the mannered interpretation of landscape in the eighteenth century and, instead, sought to present a total vision of nature. This, for example, involved blobs of pure colour to represent sunlight. Landscape painting became less original and more stereotypical in the hands of the successors of Constable and Turner.

After Constable and Turner, British painting in this century is mostly noted for the works of the Pre-Raphaelite Movement. This term was adopted in 1848, the 'year of revolutions', by a group, or, as they called themselves, Brotherhood, of young English painters, the most prominent of whom were John Everett Millais, William Holman Hunt and Dante Gabriel Rosetti. They sought to react against what they saw as the empty formalism of the then fashionable 'subject' painting, for example the Shakespearean and historical works of Daniel Maclise. The phrase 'Pre-Raphaelite' was a reaction against current lodestars of artistic quality and also the notion that beauty was essential to art, which was associated with Raphael. Instead, the Pre-Raphaelites stressed the moral purpose of art. In addition, they offered a primitivism that rested on the suggestion that the medieval period was purer and less artificial. There was thus a parallel to the Gothic Revival in architecture.

This Brotherhood, a coming together of extremely young and idealistic men, spawned some of the most important works of the Victorian period. After Turner and Constable, these painters are perhaps the most important in modern British history. The Pre-Raphaelites came together, it is said, after several of the future members witnessed a Chartist demonstration in 1848, a time marked by fevered speculation about the prospect for riot and rising. Enthused by the political climate, Millais and Hunt in particular sought their own revolution – a revolution in art – thus demonstrated how art and life are so inextricably linked. The central tenet of these young painters was take their art back to a purer time – a time before Raphael (hence the name) – when painting was noted for its boldness of line, clarity of colour and worthiness of subject matter. The Pre-Raphaelites echoed the work of the German Nazarene school, though this had been done before, as can be seen in Ford Madox Brown's strong echoes of the Nazarene style in his *Wycliffe reading his Translation of the Bible to John of Gaunt* (1847–8). Among the Pre-Raphaelites, despite Millais' numerous religious canvases, only Hunt was to remain as tied to religious themes as the German school. Shakespeare, Tennyson and myths and legends provided the pre-Raphaelites with a range of other themes for consideration in paint. Works such as Millais' *Ophelia* (1852), completed when the painter was only 22 years old, and Hunt's *Claudio and Isabella* (1850) and *The Hireling Shepherd* (1851), finished when Hunt was similarly young, stand out as exemplars of the draughtmanship and colour control shown by the two greatest exponents of the Pre-Raphaelite mood. The paintings they produced excited keen interest in the early 1850s, although its members drifted after the mid-1850s. The painters continued their work, but Millais moved into the mainstream, painting frivolous subjects.

The religious paintings of the Pre-Raphaelites elicited a more critical response than those of a more worldly nature, such as Henry Wallis' or John Brett's paintings, both entitled *The Stonebreaker* (1857 and 1858, respectively). Purity was controversial not least when focused on attempts to provide a realistic portrayal of the life of the Holy Family, as in Hunt's *Girlhood of Mary Virgin* (1849) and Millais' *Christ in the House of His Parents* (1850), the latter of which was bitterly criticised, not least by Dickens. Such works exemplified the Pre-Raphaelite claim to focus on nature directly perceived and to show what life must have been like, rather than to be guided by artistic classifications and rules. The Movement, which had been initially constituted as a secret Brotherhood, dissolved by 1855, but its themes remained influential, including among many of those who were not members of the Brotherhood, or indeed of the second Brotherhood founded by Rossetti, Edward Burne-Jones and William Morris. Thus, for example, Ford Madox Brown (1821–93), although never a member, was sufficiently impressed to depart from his earlier Romantic historical painting and, instead, paint in the Pre-Raphaelite manner, most famously *Chaucer at the Court of Edward III* (1851) and *Work* (1863). In many ways, too, Brown pre-empted the Brotherhood, and he resisted their overtures to join, saying he was too old. *Work* dignified labour and was based on navvies whom Brown saw working in Hampstead. As a reminder of the frequent close interaction of art with the wider world, Brown depicted in the painting Thomas Carlyle, whose *Past and Present* (1843) had stressed the disadvantages of unemployment, and F.D. Maurice, the Christian Socialist principal of the Working Men's College where Brown had taught. Although an English movement, the Pre-Raphaelites influenced a number of Scottish painters including William Dyce (1806–1864), the painter of *The Man of Sorrows* (1859), Sir Joseph Noel Paton (1821–1901), Sir William Fettes Douglas (1822–91), and William Bell Scott (1811–90), the painter of *Industry of the Tyne: Iron and Coal* (1861).

Among the Brotherhood, Hunt (1827–1910) remained faithful to its aims. He travelled on several occasions to Egypt and Palestine, in order to ground his paintings of biblical scenes accurately. The popularity of his paintings, such as *The Light of the World*, *The Scapegoat* and *The Hireling Shepherd*, is a reminder of the strong Christian commitment of Victorian society. Millais (1829–96) followed a different course, becoming a fashionable painter and pillar of the artistic establishment. Created a baronet in 1885, Millais was elected President of the Royal Academy in 1896. He found favour with Shakespearean scenes such as *Ophelia* (1852), but, later, with undemanding sentimental portraits, for example *The Blind Girl* (1856), and *Bubbles* (1886).

By the time of Millais' death, the contours of the artistic world were very different to those the Brotherhood had reacted against. A sense of *fin de siècle* affected the mood of the

1890s. Paintings such as *Circe Invidiosa* (1892) by J.W. Waterhouse (1849–1917) illustrated the appeal of the exotic and the erotic, although no painter made as great a success of mixing the exotic with the historical as did Sir Lawrence Alma-Tadema with his vast output of highly detailed studies of Roman, Greek and Egyptian life in classical times. Alma-Tadema's work incensed critics such as Ruskin, who abhored the 'Romans in Togas' approach to history; Ruskin, in fact, rubbished Alma-Tadema's canvas, *The Pyhrric Victory*, which depicts Grecian warriors in a war-dance with their shields raised and backs bent, describing the subjects as resembling a line of beetles. Alma Tadema's paintings also emphasised the female form in as much detail as was permissable in Victorian society, a trait he shared with Waterhouse. The emphasis on the exotic can also be seen in the work of the artificial decorative patterns of Aubrey Beardsley (1872–98), the illustrator of the English version of Wilde's *Salomé*, *The Yellow Book* (1894), and *The Savoy* (1896–8). Other Art Nouveau figures included Arthur Mackmurdo (1851–1942), Charles Ricketts (1866–1931), and Walter Crane (1845–1915). They emphasised ornamentation in their reaction to academic 'historicism'. The aestheticism, self-absorption, and ostentation of some Art Nouveau figures, especially Beardsley, were not akin to the moral purpose of the Pre-Raphaelites, although Crane can be seen as a continuer of the Pre-Raphaelite tradition.

Art Nouveau had less of an impact on British society than the Art and Crafts Movement of the second half of the century. This again can be seen as a reaction against industrialisation. The prime inspiration of the movement was William Morris, an advocate of personal production and hand industry, not of machinisation and standardisation. Morris had a influence on many of the leading craftsmen of the 1880s and 1890s, and the movement led to the foundation of the Guild and School of Arts and Crafts in 1888. Such artistic movements were important, but their influence on public taste should not be exaggerated. Landseer's *The Stag at Bay* remained very popular at the century's close.

17.8 Music

The nineteenth century was intensely musical, although it is today frequently regarded as the dead period between Handel and a twentieth-century revival by Elgar and, even more, Vaughan Williams and Britten. This is misleading. Musical life in Victorian Britain was active to an extent that is very different to the situation today when people primarily *listen* to music systems, the radio and concerts. In the nineteenth century, in contrast, people played and sang. The piano was the centre piece of the Victorian drawing room, and playing it was regarded as an important accomplishment. The singing of songs and ballads was an important family activity.

There was also much communal musical activity. Street balladeers had been driven away as street entertainers were punished under vagrancy legislation, but brass bands became very popular in the 1880s and 1890s. Amateur choral singing had developed in the eighteenth century and remained strong. Major choral societies were founded, such as that at Huddersfield in 1836. Concert halls provided forums for such societies.

Much of the music performed was written by foreign composers, but there were British counterparts, although possibly the most talented in the early decades, Dublin-born John

Sir Edward Elgar (1857–1934)

The leading figure in English music in his lifetime, with music of a powerful and attractive elegaic tone. Famous works include *The Enigma Variations* (1899) and the oratorio *The Dream of Gerontius* (1900). His life and work reflected the strength of provincial culture and its close link to metropolitan circles. Elgar was born close to Worcester and his music reflects strong associations with his native region.

Field (1782–1837), spent most of his career in Russia. Later in the century, Sir Hubert Parry (1848–1918), Charles Villiers Stanford (1852–1924), Sir Edward Elgar (1857–1934), and Sir Arthur Sullivan (1842–1900) were influential in reviving British music. Stanford and Parry played a major role as professors at the Royal College of Music, from its foundation in 1883, in training the next generation of composers.

Victorian composers are generally recalled for their secular music, but they also composed religious works. The various religious groupings were keen to develop church music, and the Oxford Movement was particularly important in encouraging church music. (J Berrow, '"A worse performance"? Aspects of liturgical music in nineteenth-century Worcestershire', *Transactions of the Worcester Archaeological Society*, 3rd series, 17, (2000), pp.223–33). Parry and Stanford both played a major role in the British choral tradition, and Sullivan's output included *Onward Christian Soldiers* (1871) and the oratorio *The Light of the World* (1873). These were popular works. So also were the fruits of Sullivan's collaboration with W.S. Gilbert, a series of comic operettas, famously *HMS Pinafore* (1878), *The Pirates of Penzance* (1879) and *The Mikado* (1885). Gilbert's libretti held up a lighthearted and witty mirror to his audiences. It was what many of them wanted to see and the partnership was successful, sufficiently so for the entrepreneur D'Oyly Carte to build the Savoy Theatre (1881) for the operettas. The partnership, however, dissolved after the relative failure of *The Grand Duke* in 1896. As more generally in an artistic world that largely existed without government subsidy, commercial motives were central.

17.9 Conclusion

As the nineteenth century closed, Britain had a buoyant cultural world by western standards. It rested on mass literacy, a highly urbanised society, and the wealth of one of the leading economies in the world. The metropolitan settings of culture were lavish and expanding in number. The London Coliseum, which opened in 1904, included tea rooms, a cigar bar, and an American bar. The London Palladium, which followed in 1910, included facilities for gentlemen changing into evening dress. The Bechstein Hall, a concert hall now known as the Wigmore Hall, was built in 1901 at the cost of £100,000.

From the 1890s, theatre syndicates from existing music hall managements built new venues such as the 'palaces' for more respectable customers. The prime inequality was class-based, but the working class in jobs still had access to inexpensive forms of culture, such as newspapers and music halls. While not synonymous with mass entertainment, popular culture was well served by it. Furthermore, although the situation was very far from being one of equality, especially as far as the entrepreneurs were concerned, women were not denied the opportunity to be performers. Indeed, some of the leading music hall artistes were women, most famously Marie Lloyd. Women also played a prominent role in the more conventional theatre. Nevertheless, men enjoyed far more opportunities.

Mass culture was viewed with dismay by Socialists, who sought to transform the working class into a moral, united and educated force able to transform society. They hoped for self-improvement and 'rational recreation', not the rowdyness and vulgarity of football or music hall, and founded bodies such as the Co-operative Holidays Association and the Clarion Vocal Unions and Cycling Clubs. These, however, made scant impact on the bulk of the working class.

Summary

◆ In judging the period, it is important to consider contemporary as well as modern assessments.

◆ There was a diversity of styles in all aspects of cultural production, from novels and journalism to music, painting and drama..

◆ The eighteenth-century cultural inheritance had to adapt to a world of mass culture.

◆ Industrialisation and its consequences were unwelcome to many artistic circles.

◆ Popularised forms of entertainment developed according to the rich new marketplace of the urban world.

Points to discuss

◆ What is your response to nineteenth-century culture?

◆ How and why were nineteenth-century cultural assessments different to our own?

◆ How do artistic styles develop?

References and further reading

P. Bailey (ed), *Music Hall: The Business of Pleasure* (Milton Keynes, 1986).

M.R. Booth, *Theatre in the Victorian Age* (Cambridge, 1991).

J.W. Childers, *Novel Possibilities: Fiction and the Formation of Early-Victorian Culture* (Philadelphia, Pa., 1993).

T. Hilton, *The Pre-Raphaelites* (1987).

J.S. McLeod, *Art and the Victorian Middle Class: Money and the Making of Cultural Identity* (Cambridge, 1996).

T. Newman and R. Watkinson, *Ford Madox Brown and the Pre-Raphaelite Circle* (New York, 1991).

E. Prettejohn, *Rossetti and his Circle* (1991).

J. Rose, *The Intellectual Life of the British Working Classes* (2001).

D. Russell, *Popular Music in England, 1840–1914: A Social History* (Manchester, 1987).

N. Russell, *The Novelist and Mammon: Literary Responses to the World of Commerce in the Nineteenth Century* (Oxford, 1980).

J.R. Stephens, *The Profession of the Playwright: British Theatre, 1800–1900* (Cambridge, 1992).

D. Samson (ed.), *Man and Music: The Late Romantic Era* (1991).

J. Treuherz, *et al.*, *Hard Times: Social Realism in Victorian Art* (1987).

M. Wheeler (ed.), *Ruskin and Environment* (Manchester, 1995).

J. Wolffe and J. Seed (eds), *The Culture of Capital: Art, Power and the Nineteenth-Century Middle Class* (Manchester, 1988).

Into the Twentieth Century

CHAPTER 18

Contents

Introduction

The concluding discussion in this book is divided into two chapters: Into the Twentieth Century (Chapter 18) and the Conclusion (Chapter 19). They are related, but separate ways of summing up the nineteenth century. One form of conclusion is to look at what came next and how it emerged from the nineteenth century; while another ranges over the period as a whole. Throughout, the emphasis is on an open-ended approach. It is possible to see varied conclusions, and scholars have focused on different points. More specifically, it can be argued that the years from the death of Queen Victoria in 1901 to the outbreak of the First World War in 1914 were a continuation of the late nineteenth century, or, conversely, that they presented its dissolution, a dissolution that had gathered pace before the outset of the First World War.

Key issues

▶ How did Britain change in the period 1900–14?
▶ How far were these changes a continuation of developments in the late Victorian period?

18.1 A new political world?

Some of the change in the pre-1914 period reflected not a new political world, but the gain of power by the Liberals, who had been in opposition in 1886–92 and 1895–1905. The

Conservatives, who had been in power in those years, had not sought to transform the country, although they did wish to strengthen it. They stood for Church, Crown, Empire, property and order, and followed a cautious line on domestic reform, ceding workmen's compensation, but not old-age pensions. However, the relatively benign 1890s gave rise to a more troubling situation in the following decade. There was no Edwardian calm to British politics. Instead, Edward VII's reign (1901–10) was a period of uncertainty and tension. The century opened with Britain at war (the Second Boer War, of 1899–1902, in South Africa), the National Debt rising, and politicians uncertain as how best to respond to growing industrial militancy, as well as concern about national efficiency and pressures for social reform. To pay for the war, the government raised taxes, including income tax from 8d to 1s 3d, and borrowed £135m. War and domestic issues were linked in a concern about Britain's strength relative to other powers, particularly Germany. Far from there being any general complacency, there was a widespread feeling that something had to be done. This was exacerbated by serious defeats in the early stages of the war.

What was to be done was less clear. Salisbury and the Conservatives (then called Unionists because of their support for the existing constitutional arrangements in Ireland) won a 'khaki election' held in October 1900. It was held when the Boer War was arousing patriotic sentiment and going well and the Liberals were publicly divided over its merits. Most of the electorate had no such doubt about the expansion of empire. Only 184 Liberals were elected and no fewer than 163 government supporters were elected unopposed. However, this victory could not, for long, conceal important weaknesses in the Conservative position, including the inability to respond positively to the growing demands of organised labour. The Liberals were also helped by the declining, but still considerable, strength of their Nonconformist constituency. Salisbury failed to take advantage of the 1900 general election in order to reorganise and strengthen the government. Very few middle-class politicians were brought into office.

More generally, in the 1900s, there was a freneticism that reflected a sense that real issues were at stake. There was no consensus over how best to analyze and respond to Britain's relative decline. The first lightning rod was cast by Joseph Chamberlain (1836–1914), Colonial Secretary from 1895 to 1903. Chamberlain, a major Birmingham manufacturer of screws, who employed 2,500 workers by the 1870s, and became Mayor of Birmingham, had sold his holdings in the family firm and become a professional politician. A former Radical, who had broken with the Liberals, Chamberlain was convinced that the British empire had to be strengthened and British society and the economy protected from decline, although his imperial vision was very much a 'white' view and, even so, it is by no means clear that his vision was welcomed in Australia and Canada. Chamberlain sought a new relationship with the outside world, namely a replacement of free trade, the powerful economic creed of nineteenth-century liberalism, by tariffs (import duties) with a system of imperial preference to encourage trade within the empire. The revenues tariffs produced were to be spent on social welfare, thus easing social tension, without increasing taxes, the last a necessary strategy for the Conservatives, because their supporters were increasingly sensitive to rising rates of taxation.

To Chamberlain, this offered populist revival and an opportunity to strengthen the Conservative government, but, in fact, his policy divided and weakened the party. Conservative free traders were put in a difficult position and several joined the Liberals, including Winston Churchill in 1904. The popularity of the tariff policy was compromised, because it was presented as a taxation on food imports that would hit the urban working class by increasing the price of food. Furthermore, the issue united the Liberals and increased their popularity, thus demonstrating the political limitations of tariff reform for the Conservatives. Never underestimating the credulity of their audience, Liberal speakers focused on the price of food and ignored the wider questions posed by the challenges to the British economy represented by free trade, especially the competition for British industry. On the other hand, given the developing New Liberalism, the Liberals were also far better placed than the Conservatives to give voice to popular pressure for social reform and, more generally, for change. In the 1906 general election, the majority of Liberal candidates included pledges for social reform in their election addresses.

Unable to unite the party over tariff reform, or to offer solutions on questions such as social reform, the Conservative Prime Minister, Arthur Balfour, resigned on 4 December 1905. He hoped that the Liberals would divide in office, but, instead, they were better placed to win the general election in January 1906 with a landslide, gaining 401 seats to the Conservatives' 157. The Liberals had recovered well from earlier divisions over Ireland and the Boer War. Since 1903, the Liberals in England and Wales had been secretly allied with the Labour Party, agreeing not to fight each other in certain seats lest they help the Conservatives. This co-operation was helped by common hostility to tariffs and by Labour anger with the government's attitude towards trade union rights. Furthermore, Balfour was unable to unite his party. He was also no populist and a poor campaigner. The Conservatives in government were seen as overly linked to sectional interests – the employers, the agricultural interest, the Church of England and the brewers – and had not acquired any reputation for competence. They were blamed for the mismanagement of the Boer War and suffered from the sour taste the conflict had left. Furthermore, the Conservatives did not seem a credible source for the changes necessary to ensure the 'national efficiency' that was widely called for. Conservative policies were also unwelcome. Tariff reform was rejected in favour of free trade. Workers preferred to think about the cost of food rather than the threat to their jobs. In the election, the Conservatives lost some of their urban working-class support, while the Liberals took the former Conservative strongholds of London and Lancashire, and also made important gains in rural and suburban parts of southern England, the Conservative heartland. Many of the latter gains were lost in the two elections of 1910, but the Liberals then retained Lancashire and London, ensuring that they were the major party in all the leading industrial areas.

Victory gave the Liberals a mandate for action. As President of the Board of Trade in 1905–8, David Lloyd George increased state regulation of the economy. The Trade Disputes Act of 1906 gave trade unions immunity from actions for damages as a result of strike action, and thus legalised strike action, rejecting the attempts of the courts, through the Taff Vale Judgment of 1901, to bring the trade unions within the law, and thus make strike action potentially expensive. That judgment had made the trade unions liable to damages for strike action, and had specifically awarded the Taff Vale Railway Company damages against the Amalgamated Society of Railway Servants arising from the rail strike of 1900. The Salisbury government had rejected trade union pressure to change the law, strengthening union concern about Conservative views and the commitment to intervene in electoral politics. The Workmen's Compensation Act of 1906 met Trades Union Congress (TUC) demands for the enforcement of national standards against local variations. The government intended to prevent a rail strike in 1907. The Mines Regulations Act of 1908 limited the number of hours that miners could spend underground.

The Liberals, however, found themselves thwarted by the conservatism of the House of Lords, especially over attempts to modify the Education Act and the Licensing Act that determined public house licences. The latter issue opposed the Nonconformist lobby to the brewers, most of whom were close to the Conservative Party. The Prime Minister, Sir Henry Campbell-Bannerman, ably held his talented Cabinet together, but, until he resigned in April 1908, there was only limited drive to Liberal government; Campbell-Bannerman was content with a policy of 'filling up the cup'. Rather than producing a coherent blueprint for change, he responded to the Liberal lobbies, and this encouraged a somewhat ad hoc feel to government policies.

Campbell-Bannerman was replaced by the abler and more decisive Herbert Henry Asquith. He managed the rare trick of combining intellectual ability and political skill, leading a Cabinet of much ability. Asquith faced a difficult financial situation. The government wanted both new battleships, to keep a lead over the Germans (see Chapter 13), and old-age pensions in order to fulfil the expectations that New Liberalism could enhance social welfare (see Chapter 2). In 1894, Balfour, had stated that 'the best antidote to Socialism was practical social reform'. It was the Liberals who seemed most determined to implement this policy.

Current taxes could not meet the bill; the deficit rose from £700,000 for 1908–9 to an estimated £15m for 1909–10. The Old Age Pensions Act of 1908 cost £8.5m in its first full year of operation and over £12m by 1913. So, in 1909, Lloyd George, now Chancellor of the Exchequer, introduced what, with a characteristically popular flight of rhetoric, he called the 'People's Budget'. This raised direct taxation, on higher incomes, and prepared the way for taxes on land. He proposed a redistributive budget, designed to maintain free trade and to heal divisions within the Liberal Party at the cost of landlords. The Conservatives, in contrast, argued that revenues should be raised by tariff reform. They were also concerned about the principle and the practice of significant redistribution by taxation. The Liberals had lessened concern about the issue, by planning no tax increases on annual earned income below £2,000, a figure that then excluded the middle class; but the notion of redistributive taxation was indeed a threat to this group, as was to be shown clearly under Labour in the 1970s. The Conservatives were also anxious about the impact of the Budget on the landed interest. The House of Lords, in which this interest was well represented, rejected the Budget on 30 November 1909, claiming that they were doing so in order to refer the measure to the electorate.

The Liberals called an election in January 1910. Public excitement was great, and the turnout rose considerably, in part because there was a new electoral register. The Conservatives increased their percentage of the vote over the 1906 election, and gained 116 seats, especially in rural southern England. Much of the electorate rejected the 'Socialism' that New Liberalism appeared to offer. However, Conservative support for tariffs prevented them from regaining the working-class support in Lancashire and London they had lost in 1906, and, although the Conservatives gained more votes than the Liberals, the latter were able to remain in office, thanks to winning more seats, and to support from Labour and the Irish Nationalists. The Conservatives won 273 seats, the Liberals 275, Labour 40, and the Irish Nationalists 82. Conservative policies helped to keep both of these groups behind the Liberals. Liberal success led the Lords to accept the budget.

Another election that December confirmed the result. Balfour was to be a Prime Minister who never won an election, but, instead, lost three. The Labour Party had advanced rapidly since the formation of the Labour Representation Committee (LRC) in 1900, and the creation of the Labour Party itself in 1906, winning more seats each election, but it was still less powerful than the Liberals as a party of the left. Campbell-Bannerman did not see Labour as a threat, was happy to co-operate with it, and appointed John Burns, the first member of the working class to join the Cabinet. Labour had problems of identity in the face of Liberal welfare reforms and its electoral performance after 1910 was mixed at best. It enjoyed no by-election successes and even the municipal advance involved strengthening support in areas already won over to Labour.

Yet, it was unclear how far the Liberals could adjust to the rising number of working-class voters and the growing importance of class issues by backing social reform, and thus lessen Labour's appeal in class-based politics. In 1907, Philip Snowden urged the Durham miners' gala to reject the Liberals and support only Labour. Many prominent Liberals did not favour a focus on social reform, because, more generally, the Liberals were unhappy with class politics. The Liberals did not adopt working-class candidates to any great extent, were unhappy with using the language of class, unenthusiastic about powerful trade unions, and unwilling to accept working-class power. Furthermore, the Liberal leadership was opposed to votes for women, and this encouraged many female and male activists to switch their support to Labour.

Yet, there was a powerful radical strain to 'New Liberalism'; and the government was definitely out to appeal to working-class support. The National Insurance Act of 1911 sought to provide security against sickness and unemployment, although employee contributions were unpopular with many and led the Conservatives in 1913 to promise repeal. The pace of reform was maintained. In late 1913, Lloyd George proposed state-funded rural housebuilding and a minimum agricultural wage. When war began in 1914, it cut short government initiatives that were being planned for health, housing, education, and a minimum wage.

Although the Lords had passed the budget, their own powers were now a major political issue. The Irish Nationalists insisted that the Lords' veto be reduced in order to pave the way for home rule. The Lords themselves, however, were unlikely to pass such a measure unless the King threatened to create a large number of Liberal peers, the same threat that had been employed in 1832 in order to push through the First Reform Act. Edward VII refused to make such a threat unless a second election produced a clear mandate, and Asquith was able to persuade his successor George V (1910–36) to pledge to do so. This led to the election in December 1910: 270 Liberals, 274 Conservatives, 42 Labour and 84 Irish Nationalists were returned. The threat of a mass creation of peers, led the Conservative leaders to accept the legislation, although a 'diehard' right-wing opposition rejected such concessions. On 10 August 1911, the Parliament Act was pushed through the Lords under the threat of such creations. The Lords lost their veto on legislation, although they retained the power to delay it for up to two years. This was a major blow to traditional constitutional, political and social assumptions, and one inflicted in the full glare of publicity (see Chapter 9).

Irish Nationalist support, and the new limitation in the power of the Lords, led the Liberals to return again to Home Rule, a policy that the Conservatives were pledged to resist. They had established themselves as the defenders of the Union when Gladstone introduced his first Home Rule Bill in 1886 and this helped both to provide the Conservatives with their identity and to divide the Liberals. Indeed, the Liberal Unionists were formally amalgamated with the Conservative Party in 1912. Home Rule moved to the forefront. The Protestant majority in much (but not all) of Ulster had no intention of yielding to rule from a Dublin Parliament, which would be Catholic-dominated, and felt abandoned by the government. The Asquith administration, indeed, paid insufficient attention to the particular character of Ulster society.

Tensions rapidly escalated. Andrew Bonar Law, who became leader of the Conservatives in November 1911, dropped hints about supporting armed opposition in Ulster, in a famous speech at Blenheim Palace on 27 July 1912, an extremist step that suggested that Conservative support for the status quo was putting them in an exposed position. Bonar Law's Presbyterian Ulster-Scottish background made the fate of Ulster particularly urgent to him, but he also saw Ireland as an opportunity to reunite a party divided by tariff reform and to attack the government. Bonar Law also abandoned support for taxes on food imports.

Having lost three successive general elections, the Conservatives were both divided and unable to reach out to new electoral constituencies and other political parties. The party was rescued from this only by the course of the First World War, a reminder of the major role of events in political history. The Home Rule Bill passed the Commons in 1912 and 1913, under the terms of the Parliament Act, but, opposition and the escalating crisis in Europe, ensured that the Act was finally passed in 1914 with the proviso that it was not to be implemented until after the war and that the Ulster situation was to be reconsidered.

18.2 A society under strain?

The political history of the period can be seen in very different lights. It can be argued that the ability to confront major issues without widespread and sustained civil disorder and to see through a major and controversial constitutional change with the peaceful reform of the House of Lords was a reflection of the mature state of the British political system. This can then be related to, indeed seen as a second stage of, the major controversy over franchise reform that was the background of the 'Great' (First) Reform Act of 1832. Again the emphasis can be on a political system that was sufficiently mature to accept, even encourage, bitter debate, without collapsing into violent disorder, as had happened in 1638–42 with the collapse of the Stuart system and the outbreak of the British Civil War.

At the same time, a less benign account can be offered, both of the early twentieth and, more generally, of the nineteenth century. The former would focus in particular on industrial militancy and on Ireland. Within Britain, labour relations deteriorated from 1909, when there were major strikes in the shipyards. Difficult economic circumstances led in 1910 to downward pressures on pay, industrial disputes, sabotage and riots. Disputes in the coal industry arose from pressure on the profitability of pits and on miners' living standards, due, in part, to geological factors which reduced pit productivity. Employers tried to restrict customary rights and payments. Sabotage by striking miners in 1910 against collieries, strike-breakers, and the trains attempting to bring them in, as well as extensive looting, was resisted and led to much violence. At Tonypandy a miner was killed by police, and troops were sent in by the Liberal Home Secretary, Winston

Churchill, although he held them back and was criticised for allowing the rioters to destroy property. The following year, the first general rail strike led to sabotage at Llanelli, and also to the deployment of troops who killed two strikers in Liverpool. Nearly 41 million working days were lost through industrial action in 1912. As with other such disputes, there was a potent mixture of workers dissatisfied with specific conditions and others seeking political transformation.

Yet in Britain as a whole in 1914 the Liberal party, with its desire for the co-operation of capital and labour and its stress on class harmony for all except the aristocracy, still displayed few signs of decline at the hands of Labour, and showed much confidence in its future. Another election was due by 1915, and, although the Conservatives were in a better shape than they had been after the 1905 election, there seemed many reasons to assume that they would face a fourth election defeat, not least because they had fewer allies than the Liberals. On their other political flank, the Liberals were also in a strong position. Lib–Lab, not syndicalism, held sway in the valleys of the Rhhonda. Over 75 per cent of the working population were not members of trade unions and many voted Liberal or Conservative. This was to change dramatically within a decade.

In Ireland, the situation had become more partisan and sectarian in the 1900s, especially with the growing vociferousness of Ulster Unionism. The willingness in the early 1910s by both nationalists and Unionists to talk of conflict and to make (pseudo-) military preparations was disturbing. So also was evidence of dissatisfaction among sections of the army with government policy, specifically signs that they would not suppress Unionist opposition. To some commentators, the situation looked back to the 1790s, which had culminated with the bloody (and unsuccessful) nationalist rising of 1798. On the other hand, in the early 1780s, it had proved possible to settle another Irish crisis, that had focused on demands for enhanced powers for the Dublin Parliament and that had included military-style preparations, without violence and by means of concessions.

Thus, the crises of the early 1910s sent mixed messages about the strength and adaptability of the nineteenth-century system.

This was more generally true about other aspects of the period. The position of women is one that has attracted particular interest in recent decades. In the years before the First World War, there was growing pressure for votes for women from a vociferous, although largely middle-class, suffragette movement. Women ratepayers had had the vote for local government since 1869 and were able to stand for urban and rural district councils from 1895 and for town and county councils from 1907, but they lacked the same role in national politics. The militant tactics of the Women's Social and Political Union (WSPU), founded by Emmeline Pankhurst in 1903, were designed to force public attention, although democratic, non-violent tactics were advocated by other feminist leaders, such as Millicent Fawcett, the leader of the National Union of Women's Suffrage Societies (NUWSS). Labour, which was associated with most of the leaders of the movement, officially endorsed women's suffrage in 1912. Several prominent Liberals, including the Prime Minister Asquith and Churchill, were more hostile, and the progressive character of Liberalism was in part undermined by its position on women's suffrage. The following year, women comprised over 40% of the membership of the influential left-wing Fabian Society. Suffragette activism paralleled, and in some cases was related to, trade union activism.

Less dramatically, but also indicative of pressure from women for a different society, the Women's Labour League, founded in 1906, campaigned for child care, free school meals, improvements in midwifery and nursery care to cut infant mortality, the Poor Law, and the condition of sweated labour, although the last proved very divisive. The League was affiliated to the Labour Party, and came to support women's suffrage. In 1918, it was replaced by the Labour Party Women's Organisation.

The suffragette movement can be seen as a reaction against but also a development from the Victorian period. It is possible to look at the rise of the 'new woman' in the late nineteenth century in two ways. First, the degree to which there was an articulate and public challenge to gender roles cannot be dismissed. For example, the degree to which the journalist and novelist Eliza Linton (1822–98) could write, for women, so extensively against the 'new woman', as in her *The Girl of the Period and Other Essays* (1883), is an indication of the fears that were aroused. On the other hand, the practical impact is easily over-stated, even for middle-class (let alone working-class) women. The 'separate spheres' ideology displayed both resilience and adaptability, and was to continue to do so during the twentieth century.

18.3 A new culture?

The suffragette movement and the broader issue of the role of women was an important instance of the degree to which, although the strains and consequences of the First World War (1914–18) dissolved much of the old order, it was already fast eroding before the pressures of change and the sense of the inexorability of development.

This was the most important continuity between Britain in the late nineteenth and early twentieth centuries. The former is frequently presented today in a distinctly conservative light. Period costume dramas on television and film suggest that it was an elysian (or far less than perfect) world that was to be swept aside by war. This is an image of class, gender, and political stereotypes that dramatically underplays the dynamism of the period. There was extensive change and a conviction that change was necessary and beneficial. Liberals, Labour, and Conservative paternalists all supported measures for social welfare. Material culture was changing rapidly. There was a new world focusing on electricity and the internal combustion engine. By 1907 the Britannia Foundry at Derby included a motor-cylinder foundry making 400–500 items weekly for car manufacturers, such as Jowett Motors of Bradford. The sense of new possibilities was captured in the cinema opened in Harwich in 1911, the Electric Palace. Science fiction was increasingly potent in the imaginative landscape. *The Time Machine* (1895) was the title of the first major novel by H.G. Wells (1866–1946). His scientific futurism seemed increasingly appropriate in the rapidly changing world.

Wells also focused on another important feature of British society, the support for state-imposed reform. In his *The New Machiavelli* (1911), he presented as narrator Richard Remington, a politician who advocated universal education, a 'trained aristocracy', feminism, and a more perfect and thus stronger Britain. Public culture and political ideology in the Victorian age and the early twentieth century depended on the notion of progress and the improvability of mankind. It thus rejected the Christian lapsarian view of mankind. Although they varied in their political, economic, social and cultural analyses and prescriptions, secular ideologies shared a belief that it was possible and necessary to improve the lot of humanity, or at least life in Britain, and that such a goal gave meaning to politics and society. In short, reform was seen as a goal in itself, and progress as being attainable. Evolutionary change was held to be the hallmark of the British political system, as exemplified by the staggered process of franchise and social welfare reform. There was only limited support for continuity and stability, as opposed to reform, as public goals; and for an institution or government to pledge itself to inaction became unthinkable. Commitment to change rested on powerful ideological currents, rather than on prudential considerations, although these were clearly important as well, as in any political system which allows governments to be voted in and out of office at regular intervals. Thus reform, as means *and* goal, had become and remained the foremost secular ideology.

The general thrust, however, was for more government intervention. This linked the late nineteenth to the early twentieth century, more than to the first quarter of the nineteenth century. That is a reminder of the danger of thinking of centuries as distinct and distinctive units. It would be wrong to under-rate signs of change in the first quarter, but the overwhelming impression then was of economic transformation and social change without comparable political shifts. This owed much to the ideological and political hostility to radicalism that stemmed from the French Revolution, and is a reminder of the need to be cautious before assuming any automatic relationship between socio-economic and political–ideological developments. Aside from this methodological point, the situation in the early nineteenth century forms an obvious contrast with that a century later. This is central to the history of the period and a theme that this book has tried to approach from a number of angles, in order to explain why change became normative and reform the slogan of choice. We will return to these themes in the conclusion. This chapter concludes with the observation that the period 1900–14 indicates the extent to which Victorian Britain now saw change as normal. The Conservatives might oppose reform of the House of Lords, but they supported tariff reform. Others might oppose votes for women, but relish the independence brought by the motor car. It was indeed a rapidly changing Britain.

■ Summary

◆ Alongside the benign view of a system that could cope well with division, there were signs over labour relations and Ireland of major difficulties.

◆ A sense of change was very strong and part of a mind-set in which reform appeared normal.

◆ The Liberal government that came to power in 1906 pushed forward the reform process.

■ Point to discuss

◆ How far was the early twentieth-century different to the Victorian world?

References and further reading

H. Emy, Liberals, *Radicals and Social Politics, 1892–1914* (Cambridge, 1973).

S. Koss, *Asquith* (1976).

P. Marsh, *Joseph Chamberlain: Entrepreneur in Politics* (New Haven, Conn., 1994).

D. Powell, *The Edwardian Crisis: Britain, 1910–1914* (1996).

J. Ramsden, *The Age of Balfour and Baldwin* (1978).

P. Rowlands, *The Last Liberal Governments: The Promised Land, 1905–10* (1968).

D. Tanner, *Political Change and the Labour Party, 1900–1918* (Cambridge, 1990).

Conclusions

CHAPTER 19

Contents

Introduction

Nineteenth-century Britain was the leading imperial power in the world, and the first to industrialise and to become an industrialised society. As such, its history is important and instructive, not simply for Britain but also for the world. What emerges? First, that the key processes of *imperialism* and *industrialisation* were problematic. Both they and their consequences were controversial and unwelcome to many. The processes were also not problem-free. Thus, the creation of the most extensive empire that the world had ever seen took place within the context of concern about French and Russian competition. Economic development was also affected by concern about foreign competition, especially from the early 1870s.

Aside from these particular problems, there was also considerable uncertainty about social and religious circumstances and changes. Yet, it would be misleading to present the century simply in terms of challenges and problems. There was also, especially in mid-century, a determination to mould present and future that was until that time unprecedented in British government and society. Previous episodes of major state-centred change, the Protestant Reformation and the Interregnum governments of 1649–60, had not enjoyed such widespread support and encouragement. This belief in improvement in part arose from the problems of industrial society, but it also reflected deep currents in the thought of the period. Furthermore, all great powers have faced severe problems. It is necessary to avoid the tendency to see Britain in isolation and too readily to view her as a weak state and a flawed society.

Key issues

▶ Is the major theme of this period crisis overcome, or the moulding of a new Britain?

▶ Why was Britain the leading state in the nineteenth-century world?

19.1 Local activism and progress

On the evening of 22 November 1880, there was a public meeting in Colchester; indeed there were frequent public meetings throughout Britain on most evenings. In his opening speech, the Chairman of the meeting, John Bawtree, stated that they were 'meeting in a lawful and constitutional manner to consider a law, which in the opinion of, not only a good many people in Colchester but a great many in other parts of the land, [was] … a very bad law … so bad indeed that they did not talk of amendment but of its unconditional repeal. The papers of the National Society showed them how this matter had been taken up all over the country as a serious question affecting the character of the nation … They had now felt that there should be a meeting in Colchester to test the feeling here, so that if possible Colchester might do something to help in getting rid of the Acts.'

Local activism and an emphasis on persuasion and proselytisation through public meetings: such a meeting appears characteristic of Victorian Britain. It suggests a world of consent, part of a spreading politicisation that was appropriate for a state expanding the (male) franchise and literacy. This can for example be seen in the rising calls for accountability seen in the press and in public meetings, which were not only true of major cities nor solely of the central themes of political and ecclesiastical life. There was also a demand for action on more mundane, but still very important, topics. The *Taunton Courier* of 13 February 1828 criticised the Taunton Turnpike Trust for the state of the roads between Taunton and Lonport.

Yet to turn to another publication, a note of general optimism in unalloyed progress was offered on 2 July 1824 in the first issue of the *North Devon Journal*:

> It is this desire for quick and incessant intercourse that has arisen in this kingdom within the last half a century, that has tended so much to increase our powers as a nation … The grand lever in all these astonishing inventions has been the press; for while with our steam engines we smile at the winds and disregard the operations of the tides, with the press we surpass the powers of Archimedes; for we actually lift the universe – not the material world, certainly, but the world of thought – of mind – of conception! And by this power we shall be enabled, eventually, to overcome all the obstacles which prevent the great family of mankind from uniting cordially in the bonds of affection and brotherhood.

19.2 A national political culture

Yet, other accounts can also be offered. Some cast doubt about the process and consequences of reform. For example, in his *Polities and the People. A Study in English Political Culture 1815–1867* (1993), James Vernon emphasized the vitality of pre-reform popular politics, stressed the strength and multi-faceted character of popular libertarian politics, and argued that this popular constitutionalism was adversely affected by the rise of a more democratic constitution, more specifically by being limited by the invention of party structures that disciplined popular politics. This is not therefore a text about improvement. Instead, Vernon emphasised the way in which the themes of pre-reform popular constitutionalism, with its utopian emphasis on a just people struggling to restore a lost golden age, struck a strong and immensely popular (and populist) chord. Vernon problematised working-class politics as well as reform. Instead of presenting a clear-cut working-class radicalism, he argued that there was a plasticity and multi-vocality of political languages, namely an ability to be appropriated from different perspectives and endowed with conflicting meanings. A focus on constitutionalism enabled political groups to make a great mass of diverse and frequently conflicting identities coherent. Vernon also drew attention to the popularity of flag-waving, monarchy-loving patriotic celebrations which provided occasions at which individuals right across the social, gender and political spectrum, non-voters and voters alike, were allowed to demonstrate their attachment to the nation, however variously defined.

Considering a range of constituencies – Boston, Devon, Lewes, Oldham and Tower Hamlets – Vernon concluded that it was their similarities that were most striking. This suggests, at least for England, the existence of a national political culture, albeit with strong local and regional mediations. He showed that radicals used the representative structures of their organizations and their practical political strategies symbolically to define and yet expand the terrain of struggle. However, the formalization of political organizations from the 1830s made them more amenable to oligarchic control, although they preserved a fiction of consultative democracy.

19.3 The ambiguities of reform

Vernon's arguments are controversial, but they serve as a reminder about the need to understand the ambiguities of reform, rather than taking it on its own terms. In particular, it is important to assess the pre-reform situation dispassionately (and not simply through the polemic of the reformers, important as that was) and, also, to consider those who were excluded from or suffered from the reform process. This is pertinent for example in judging religious as well as secular reform. The pre-reform Church of England was far less hedonistic and self-satisfied than the proponents of evangelical reform and later the Oxford Movement might suggest.

Returning to Colchester on the cold November evening of 1880, is to be reminded clearly that an emphasis on contention and casualties is not one dreamt up by faddish modern historians. As Bawtree moved to propose a petition to Parliament for the repeal of the Contagious Diseases Acts, he was greeted by repeated barracking. Succeeding speakers met stronger abuse and control of the proceedings was taken by Henry Laver, a surgeon from the Essex County Hospital, who carried an amendment in favour of the Acts. Jessie Craigen, who had seconded Bawtree, tried to propose a vote of thanks to the Chairman, 'who has done his duty nobly in the face of the opposition of a howling mob who are unworthy of the privileges of Englishmen', but some of the crowd made a rush at the speakers and the meeting broke up in the 'wildest confusion'.

In a subsequent legal case the magistrates refused to find against one of the demonstrators on a charge of assault, a verdict that was received 'with much applause'.

The Acts were suspended in 1883 and subsequently repealed, much to the disquiet of some of their supporters. Indeed, in 1886, the town's Board of Guardians voted to petition the government for their re-enactment.

The Colchester disturbances are a reminder of the folly of assuming too peaceful an account of post-Chartist Britain. Because the actions of government and the process of reform affected so many people and interests, and were capable of different interpretations, they were highly contentious (Box 19.2). Furthermore, there was much social tension even in a period of growing overall prosperity. In 1877, there were serious riots in Selston in Nottinghamshire, involving the destruction of six miles of fences and the destruction or theft of over £1,200 worth of crops, in response to attempts to enclose the commons. Extra police were moved in and 17 men, mostly colliers, were found guilty of riot, but protests continued into 1879. The Pinder, Henry Granger, whose job involved gathering stray animals and who thus was a central figure in the implementation of enclosures, faced intimidation and the forcible release of the animals he had seized. In 1879, he sought police protection and felt it unsafe to leave his house after dark (C. Leivers, 'The Pinder's tale', *Nottinghamshire Historian*, 65 (2000). In 1888, the 3rd Earl of Sheffield, a Sussex landowner, received a letter including the passages:

> my duty to let you know, as I do not think you do, or you would not have the heart to turn out an old tenant like poor Mrs Grover out of her home after such a hard struggle to maintain and bring up her family ... you and your faithful steward want it all ... My knife is nice and sharp.

The letter was signed Jack the Ripper, then at his brutal work among the prostitutes of poverty-stricken Whitechapel. In fact, nothing happened to the Earl, Mrs Grover was staying with her children after a fall, and Edward Grover, a failed butcher, admitted writing the letter.

This was not, however, an isolated episode. Indeed, in 1889, the Earl wrote an open letter to the Secretary of Sussex County Cricket Club, explaining his resignation as President, in which he referred to 2½ years of pestering by anonymous threats. The same

Box 19.2

Calls for reform

The conduct of the Crimean War was bitterly criticised, especially in *The Times*. The *British Mirror* (6 January 1855) referred to the fact that in *The Times* there was:

Advocacy of unbiased opinion of the English people versus flunkeyism, red-tapeism, and every other 'ism' that represents official misrule and love of clique ... God help us it we are left alone to the tender mercies of the government, and of that narrow social circle which thinks it is treason to say a word against a lord, especially if he belongs to a ducal house.

year, Charles Booth represented poverty as a threat to civil society in his *Life and Labour of the People in London ... Poverty I*:

> The lowest class, which consists of some occasional labourers, street sellers, loafers, criminals and semi-criminals ... Their life is the life of savages, with vicissitudes of extreme hardship and occasional excesses ... their only luxury is drink ... From these come the battered figures who slouch through the streets, and play the beggar or the bully.

This unsympathetic view highlighted a sense of menace, to which the frequent crime reports in the press also contributed. It also serves as a reminder of the degree to which large numbers were not integrated into a British society that was steadily more prosperous. Many lacked the energy to wave the flag. The social surveys of Booth in East London and of Seebohm Rowntree in York in 1899 revealed that over a quarter of their population were living below the perceived poverty level. Disquiet about the state of the nation encouraged social analysis, calls for public action, and private missions. A preoccupation with national degeneration dated back to the 1880s. Indeed, social reform had not ended all abuses. In 1907, there were still 560 half-timers under 13 working in Bradford.

A reminder that these were not 'the best of times' is not, however, a sufficient conclusion. Liberty, internal peace, social mobility, and institutional flexibility may all have been limited and constrained, but they were still more extensive than in other major European states. This situation encouraged imperial and economic expansion in specific terms, for example by reducing the risk of investment, but also contributed to a sense of self-confident exceptionalism that was an important asset and a resource-multiplier. The political culture of the dominant majority did not reach all sections of the community, but it was not constrained by religious, regional, class or political factors so as to be limited to only one constituency. Politics incorporated the Establishment, the middle class and skilled workers. This was not a seamless process, and women were excluded, but the incorporating nature of political practices and policies and the national myth inhibited the development of class-based politics and held adversarial tendencies away from violence. Modern Irish nationalists obsessed by the myth-sodden character of Irish history are apt to forget how many Irishmen volunteered for King and Country in the First World War.

Had Britain had a civil conflict over the extension of the franchise in the early 1830s or in 1848, then this would probably have inhibited her economic and imperial development. America managed both a savage civil war (1861–5) and such development, but it is unclear that the situation would have been so fortunate in Britain. Yet, the character of British public culture in the nineteenth century is suggested by the implausibility of such conflict in the early 1830s or 1848. So also with the repression under the Liverpool government. Peterloo might rhyme with Waterloo, but it was no battle. Not only was there no equivalent to the American Civil War, but also none to the Paris Commune which followed the Franco-Prussian War (1870–1).

The domestic protection costs of the British system remained relatively low. Empire was expanded and industry grew without civil war or a massive programme of social welfare to deal with the consequences. Nevertheless, the development of police forces and workhouses were seen as necessary to contain tension. In his pamphlet *The Antipauper System* (1828), the Reverend J.T. Becher (1770–1848) explained his belief in workhouses to offer care for the 'deserving poor' and to deter those who were 'idle and profligate'. Instead of 'outdoor relief' – paying, but not housing, the poor, which was seen as expensive and unable to provide an improving environment – the poor were to be scrutinised and controlled, at a lower cost, in a purpose-built workhouse.

Such remedies were grim, and not only by modern standards. They were different to earlier systems in being state-regulated: Union Workhouses, for example, were created under the 1834 Poor Law Reform Act. Yet, the solutions worked in nineteenth-century terms as far as those incorporated in the benefits of society were concerned. There was state intervention, but not too much. Government increasingly took a proactive role in society and the economy but did so very much in terms that were acceptable to the bulk of the political nation: the 'state' lacked the capacity and resources to drive government in an unacceptable fashion. To use a modern term, the 'democratic deficit' was acceptable. That did not offer much help to the poor, and they were all too many, but paternalism rather than Socialism seemed to answer.

Summary

◆ Reform and progress are ambiguous concepts.
◆ There were many disputes about the details of government policy.
◆ Government did not seek to exceed the bounds of what was acceptable to the political nation.

Points to discuss

◆ What is your response to this period?
◆ In what ways can we see this period as coherent and cohesive?
◆ How stable was nineteenth-century Britain?

References and further reading

J.T. Becher, *The Antipauper System* (1828).

C. Booth, *Life and Labour of the People in London…Poverty I* (1889).

C. Leivers, 'The Pinder's Tale', *Nottinghamshire Historian*, 65 (2000).

J. Vernon, *Politics and the People. A study in English Political Culture 1815–1867* (Cambridge, 1993).

Bibliography

It is all too easy to offer a list of books stretching off towards the horizon, but that serves particularly little point for this subject, for fresh information and insights arrive with great rapidity. It is more useful to encourage readers to turn to sources from the period. Most libraries will hold newspapers, either in hard copy or on microfilm. It is very instructive to read national newspapers, such as *The Times* and *The Observer*, which survive in widely-available microfilm editions. Local newspapers can also offer much insight. They show how national developments, such as the spread of the railway, affected communities and were perceived. Prominent newspapers worthy of attention include the *Leeds Mercury* (founded 1808), the *Manchester Guardian* (founded in 1821(, the *Halifax and Huddersfield Express* (founded 1831), the *Newcastle Journal* (founded 1832), the *Bradford Observer* (founded 1834), the *Northern Star* (founded 1837), *Lloyd's Illustrated London Newspaper* (founded 1842), the *North Shields and South Shields Gazette* (founded 1849), the *Daily Telegraph* (founded 1855), the *Morning Leader* (founded 1892) and the *Daily Mail* (founded 1896). Less prominent newspapers also have much to offer. For example it is possible to read papers such as the *Birmingham Chronicle* and *Birmingham Commercial Herald* in Birmingham Central Library.

For radical voices, the *Political Register* was founded in 1892, and it is also worth looking at *Black Dwarf* (1817–24) and the *Poor Man's Guardian* (1831–5). Conservative periodicals included *White Dwarf* (1817–18). *The Economist* was founded in 1843.

It is also useful to turn to visual images, such as cartoons and caricatures, for example those in *Punch* (founded 1841), or illustrations, as in the *Illustrated London News* (founded 1842). National and local art galleries are valuable, as are museums. The Castle Museum at York is particularly useful for its collections of household items and their display in rooms of particular periods.

Maps are important. Changing editions of the Ordnance Survey show some aspects of how areas have altered. *Mapping the Past: Wolverhampton 1577–1986* (Wolverhampton Libraries and Information Services, 1993) is a fine collection of successive maps.

Historical atlases can hold much of value. Noteworthy ones include *Newcastle's Changing Map* (Newcastle, 1992); *An Historical Atlas of County Durham* (Durham, 1992); Peter Wade-Martins (ed.), *An Historical Atlas of Norfolk* (Norwich, 1993); Stewart and Nicholas Bennett (eds), *An Historical Atlas of East Yorkshire* (Hull, 1996); Joan Dils (ed.), *An Historical Atlas of Berkshire* (Reading, 1998); Roger Kain and William Ravenhill (eds), *The Historical Atlas of the South West* (Exeter, 1999), and Kim Leslie and Brian Short (eds), *An Historical Atlas of Sussex* (Chichester, 1999).

More specialised mapping can be found in J. Langton and R.J. Morris, *The Atlas of Industrialising Britain, 1780–1914* (London, 1986); Rex Pope (ed.), *Atlas of British Social and Economic History since c. 1700* (London, 1989); Hugh Clout (ed.), *The Times London History Atlas* (London, 1991); Andrew Charlesworth *et al.*, *An Atlas of Industrial Protest in Britain 1750–1990* (London, 1996); and Robert Woods and Nicola Shelton, *An Atlas of Victorian Morality* (Liverpool, 1997).

On mapping, Catherine Delano-Smith and Roger Kain, *English Maps. A History* (London, 1999). Historical geography is best approached through the articles in the *Journal of Historical Geography*, for example I.S. Black, 'Money, Information and Space: Banking in Early-Nineteenth Century England and Wales' (1995).

The vital local and regional perspective is overly ignored. The Longman series 'A Regional History of England' includes such valuable works as Norman McCord and Richard Thompson's *The Northern Counties from AD 1000*, C.B. Phillips and J.H. Smith's *Lancashire and Cheshire from AD 1540*, David Hey's *Yorkshire from AD 1000*, Marie Rowland's *The West Midlands from AD 1000*, J.V. Beckett's *The East Midlands from AD 1000*, J.H. Betty's *Wessex from AD 1000* and Peter Brandon and Brian Short's *The South East from AD 1000*.

Local history publications include much of value. Those interested in pursuing this dimension should read works such as the *Transactions of the Birmingham and Warwickshire Archaeological Society*, the *Journal of the Royal Institution of Cornwall*, the *Transactions of the Cumberland and Westmorland Antiquarian and Archaeological Society*, *Derbyshire Miscellany*, the *Devon Historian*, the *Proceedings of the Dorset Natural History and Archaeological Society*, the *Bulletin of the Durham County Local History Society*, the *Essex Journal*, the *Hatcher Review*, the *Transactions of the Historic Society of Lancashire and Cheshire*, the *Transactions of the Leicestershire Archaeological and Historical Society*, the *Leicestershire Historian*, the *Manchester Regional History Review*, the *Journal of the Merioneth Historical and Record Society*, *Northamptonshire Past and Present*, the *Nottinghamshire Historian*, *Notes and Queries for Somerset and Dorset*, *Sussex History*, *Tyne and Tweed*, *Warwickshire History*, the *Transactions of the Worcestershire Archaeological Society*, *Wychwoods History*, the *Yorkshire Archaeological Journal*, and *York Historian*.

Library sources tell us much about society, and interested readers should turn to Collins, Dickens, and other writers. Simon Dentith, *Society and Cultural Forms in Nineteenth-Century England* (Basingstoke, 1999) and David Daiches (ed.), *The New Companion to Scottish Culture* (Edinburgh, 1993) contain valuable introductions. Travel accounts by British and foreign writers offer much. William Cobbett's *Rural Rides* (London, 1830) is particularly valuable. The range of contemporary sources stretches from cookery books to parliamentary debates (*Hansard*). All are useful.

For background, J.M. Black, *The History of the British Isles* (2nd edn., Bassingstoke, 2002). The sights and smells of the period can be approached via two recent illustrated books, John Davis, *The Great Exhibition* (Stroud, 1999) and Steven Halliday, *The Great Stink of London. Sir Joseph Bazalgette and the Cleansing of the Victorian Metropolis* (Stroud, 1999). And for more on this see John Hassan, *A History of Water in Modern England and Wales* (Manchester, 1998).

Wales can be approached through Philip Jenkins, *A History of Modern Wales 1536–1990* (Harlow, 1992), and Scotland through T.C. Smout, *A Century of the Scottish People, 1830–1950* (London, 1986) and T.M. Devine and R. Mitchison (eds.), *People and Society in Scotland* (Edinburgh, 1988).

Recent work of demography can be approached through E.A. Wrigley and others, *English Population History from Family Reconstitution 1580–1837* (Cambridge, 1997). For social history, David Hirst, *Welfare and Society, 1832–1991* (London, 1991); Alan Kidd, *Society and the Poor in Nineteenth-Century England* (London, 1999); Arthur McIvor, *A History of Work in Britain, 1880–1950* (London, 2001); Hugh McLeod, *Religion and Society in England, 1850–1914* (London, 1996); G.E. Mingay, *Land and Society in England 1750–1980* (London, 1994); David Taylor, *Crime, Policing and Punishment in England, 1750–1914* (London, 1998) and John Tosh, *A Man's Place. Masculinity and the Middle-Class Home in Victorian England* (New Haven, 1999).

Other important works include W.H. Fraser, *A History of British Trade Unionism, 1700–1998* (London, 1999) and Peter Kirby and S.A. King, *British Living Standards, 1700–1870* (London, 1999).

The political side can be approached through Rodney Barker, *Politics, People and British Political Thought since the Nineteenth Century* (London, 1994); John Belchem, *Popular Radicalism in Nineteenth-Century Britain* (London, 1995); Eugenio Biagini, *Gladstone* (London, 1999); Lawrence Brockliss and David Eastwood (eds), *A Union of Multiple Identities. The British Isles 1750–1850* (Manchester, 1997); David Eastwood, *Government and Community in the English Provinces, 1700–1870* (1997); Angus Hawkins, *British Party Politics, 1852–1886* (London, 1998); Terry Jenkins, *Disraeli and Victorian Conservatism* (London, 1996); *The Liberal Ascendancy, 1830–1886* (London, 1994) and *Sir Robert Peel* (London, 1999); H.S. Jones, *Victorian Political Thought* (London, 1999); John McCaffrey, *Scotland in the Nineteenth Century* (London, 1998); Rohan McWilliam, *Popular Politics in Nineteenth-Century England* (London, 1998); and Ian Machin, *The Rise of Democracy in Britain, 1830–1918* (London, 2001).

The Further Reading section at the end of each chapter should be consulted.

Index

Royal Albert Dock (1880) 27
Royal College of Music 316
Royal Commissions
  into electoral bribery (est. 1869) 154
  on policing 241
Royal Navy 7
Royal Niger Company 35, 203
RSPCA
  see Society for the Prevention of Cruelty to Animals
Rubinstein, W.D. 33, 34
Rural population 65
Rural unrest 95, 133
  in Ireland 182
Ruskin College, Oxford 196
Ruskin, John 266, 311
Russell, Lord John 142, 144, 151, 152, 286

S

Sainsbury, J., provisions' store owner 33
Saint-Saëns 229
St Helens 143
St James Chronicle 48
'St Monday' 104
St Pancras Station, London (1873) 48
  Midland Hotel at 311
Salisbury, Robert 3rd Marquess, prime minister 159, 160, 161, 162, 232, 236, 320
Saltash 44
Salvation Army 296
Sankey Brook navigation 41
Sarsfield, Arthur (Sax Rohmer) 81
Savery, Thomas, engineer 7
School Boards 153
Scotland 4, 5, 6, 17, 21, 56, 196–204
  Borders 63
  bridges in 47
  growing industrial capacity 27, 201–4
  Highlands of 18, 62, 63, 64, 68, 73, 86, 282
    call for land reform 163
  Irish migration in 72
  religion in 278
  see also Catholicism
Scott, Gilbert, architect 67, 311
Scott, Sir Walter, romanticising Scotland 199, 303
Scott, William Bell, painter 230
Scottish Home Rule campaign 197
Scottish Miners' Federation 164
Scottish Poor Law system 150
Scunthorpe 30, 64
Seaton Sluice, Northumberland 94
Seaside resorts, rise of 92, 118
Sedition 135
Seeley, J.R., historian 232
Sefton Park, Liverpool 93, 150
Self-help 262–4
Sellars, Patrick, factor in Sutherland 197
Seven Years' War 209, 212, 216
Sewers and sanitation 3, 100
Sewing Machine (Singer) 29
Sexuality 270

Shardwell, A, author 33
Shaw, George Bernard 176–8, 242, 308
Shaw, Norman 311
Sheffield 9, 22, 44, 83
  Chartist activity in 142
  newspapers in 155
  urban growth in 84
Sheffield Independent 40
Shelburne, Earl of 11–12
Shelley, Percy Byssche 306
Shetland 200
Shildon 50
Shipbuilding
  Ireland 171
  labour migration and 70, 71
  Scotland 202
Sidmouth, Viscount 132
Silas Marner (1861), George Eliot novel 304
Simeon, Charles 281
Sinn Fein 179
Sloane, Sir John 310
Smallpox 225
Smiles, Samuel 262–4
Smirke, Sir Robert, architect 310
Smith, Adam 2, 3, 211, 262
  Wealth of Nations 2, 10
Smith, W.H. 157
Smith O'Brien, Willian 176
Social class
  see class
Social Democratic Foundation 162
Socialism 162, 196, 242, 254
  attacks on leader in novels 304
Society for the Liberation the Church from State Patronage and Control (1853) 284
Society for the Prevention of Cruelty to Animals 117
South Africa 31, 225, 320
  emigration to 69, 70
Southend 52, 118, 154
Southey, Robert 214
South Sea Bubble 4
South Shields 78, 84
South Wales Miners' Federation 196
Spain
  war with 216
Speenhamland system 3
Spencer, 3rd earl, John Althorp 136
Spinning Mule 20
Staffordshire 19, 32, 42
Staffordshire Advertiser 48
Standard of living, debate 109–13
Stanford, Charles Villiers 316
Stanley, Henry Morton 194
Statute for Mending Highways 40
Stephenson, George 45
Stevenson, R.L. 305
Stewart, Charles Edward, 'Bonnie Prince Charlie' 5
Steam power 7, 18–19, 155, 240
  transport before 43–4
Steam ships 47